Family Firms and Merchant Capitalism in Early Modern Europe

This fascinating study follows the fortunes of the Höchstetter family, merchant-manufacturers and financiers of Augsburg, Germany, in the late-fifteenth and early-sixteenth centuries, and sheds light on the economic and social history of failure and resilience in early modern Europe. Carefully tracing the chronology of the family's rise, fall and transformation, it moves from the micro- to the macro-level, making comparisons with other mercantile families of the time to draw conclusions and suggest insights into such issues as social mobility, capitalist organization, business techniques, market practices and economic institutions. The result is a microhistory that offers macro-conclusions about the lived experience of early capitalism and capitalistic practices.

This book will be valuable reading for advanced students and researchers of economic, financial and business history, legal history and early modern European history.

Thomas Max Safley is Professor of Early Modern European History at the University of Pennsylvania, USA.

Routledge Explorations in Economic History

Edited by Lars Magnusson, *Uppsala University, Sweden*

European Banks and the Rise of International Finance
The Post-Bretton Woods era
Carlo Edoardo Altamura

The Second Bank of the United States
"Central" banker in an era of nation-building, 1816–1836
Jane Ellen Knodell

War, Power and the Economy
Mercantilism and state formation in 18th-century Europe
A. González Enciso

The Western Allies and Soviet Potential in World War II
Economy, Society and Military Power
Martin Kahn

Money, Currency and Crisis
In search of Trust, 2000 BC to AD 2000
Edited by R.J. van der Spek and Bas van Leeuwen

The Development of Modern Industries in Bengal
Re-Industrialisation, 1858–1914
Indrajit Ray

The Economic Development of Europe's Regions
A Quantitative History Since 1900
Edited by Nikolaus Wolf and Joan Ramón Rosés

Family Firms and Merchant Capitalism in Early Modern Europe
The Business, Bankruptcy and Resilience of the Höchstetters of Augsburg
Thomas Max Safley

For more information about this series, please visit www.routledge.com/series/SE0347

Family Firms and Merchant Capitalism in Early Modern Europe

The Business, Bankruptcy and Resilience of the Höchstetters of Augsburg

Thomas Max Safley

Routledge
Taylor & Francis Group
LONDON AND NEW YORK

First published 2020
by Routledge
2 Park Square, Milton Park, Abingdon, Oxon OX14 4RN

and by Routledge
52 Vanderbilt Avenue, New York, NY 10017

Routledge is an imprint of the Taylor & Francis Group, an informa business

British Library Cataloguing-in-Publication Data
A catalogue record for this book is available from the British Library

Library of Congress Cataloging-in-Publication Data
A catalog record for this book has been requested

ISBN: 978-0-367-13710-6 (hbk)
ISBN: 978-0-429-02820-5 (ebk)

Typeset in Bembo
by Apex CoVantage, LLC

Contents

Figures

Maps

Note on money

In most important commercial and financial centers of Europe, many kinds of money circulated regularly. In Augsburg, for example, traders frequently encountered the Imperial *Taler*, the Bohemian *Groschen* and the Munich *Schilling*, among many others. During the late-fifteenth and early-sixteenth centuries, according to Elsas, the city minted and used the *Pfund, Schilling, Pfennig* and *Heller*, in which 1 *Pfund* = 20 *Schilling* = 60 *Pfennigen* = 120 *Heller*.[1] Only in 1539 did the *Pfund* disappear from accounts, though it remained a common coin in circulation, to be replaced by the *Gulden*, abbreviated "fl", *Kreutzer*, abbreviated "kr", and *Pfennig*. Not until 1546 did the *Heller*, abbreviated "hl", reappear in place of the *Pfennig*.

The matter of money is not so straightforward, however. In nearly all accounts rendered by the Höchstetters, their creditors or the authorities, sums owed or paid appear as *Gulden, Kreutzer* and *Heller*, all coinage reforms notwithstanding. Moreover, parties to the bankruptcy recorded even more varieties of money, all of which had to be specifically recorded in the proceedings. The following equivalencies apply as a general rule:

1 *Gulden* (fl) = 60 *Kreutzer* (kr) = 420 *Heller* (hl); 1 *Kreutzer* = 7 *Heller*.
1 *Gulden* = 15 *Batzen* = 60 *Kreutzer*; 1 *Batzen* = 4 *Kreutzer*.
1 *Gulden* = 60 *Kreutzer* = 210 *Pfennigen* (pf); 1 *Kreutzer* = 3.5 *Pfennigen*.
1 *Gulden* = 30 *Schilling* (β) = 360 *Heller*; 1 *Schilling* = 12 *Heller*.

Unless noted, all money values have been rendered in *Gulden* and *Kreutzer*, just as the historical accounts of the Höchstetter firm and its bankruptcy were kept. For the reader's ease, these are usually rounded to the nearest *Gulden* in the text.

Note on translations

It is a common practice among scholars to provide the original texts from which they have made translations. This enables the attentive reader who is familiar with the languages to reach independent conclusions about the accuracy of the author's interpretations. In the present volume, historical sources are quoted at considerable length. To achieve a degree of economy and relieve the text of many, long, possibly intrusive notes, I decided to include the original language only when translating unpublished archival sources, that is, sources that did not make the original text and language available in an easily accessible form. Should questions of translations arise, I beg the reader's indulgence and encourage her or him to make use of the original texts as they appear in the cited, published editions.

Acknowledgements

My fascination with the topic of bankruptcy and my conviction that it provides an under-appreciated and under-utilized point of entry to economic practices in the past began nearly 40 years ago. The Alexander von Humboldt Foundation enabled me to spend two years in Augsburg, at which point began an apparently permanent fascination with the city and its history. During my stay there, I worked daily in the City Archive and was permitted at one point to go unaccompanied into the stacks, a thing unimaginable to most historians and horrifying to all archivists. As I wandered from room to room, each filled with double-tiered shelving that held the collections of what is today one of the largest civic archives in Germany and by most accounts by far the richest for the early modern period, I stumbled quite literally upon the collection entitled "*Schuld-, Klag- und Appellationssakten*", roughly "Debt, Complaint and Appeal Acts". It contains hundreds, perhaps thousands of bound and boxed documents having to do with default, insolvency and bankruptcy.

For an economic historian looking for evidence of early economic life, it was like discovering Ali Baba's cave. With other projects in hand and in mind, I made a swift note at the time and promised myself that one day I would explore this room and its contents with more attention. Nearly 30 years after that initial encounter, I returned to the topic of bankruptcy and settled among the many riches of the City Archive on the Höchstetter family and the failure of its family firm, "Ambrosius and Hans, the Brothers Höchstetter and Associates". I was by no means the first to do so; the Höchstetters have attracted historians' attention since the sixteenth century. I felt there was more to say, however. Slowly, over the ensuing ten years, amidst many distractions and other commitments, the present volume took shape.

In the process, I have accumulated many debts. The directors and staffs of several archives, foremost the *Bayrisches Hauptstaatsarchiv München*, the *Österreichisches Staatsarchiv Wien*, the *Stadtarchiv Nürnberg*, the *Stadtarchiv Ulm* and the *Tiroler Landesarchiv*, made their superb collections available for study and aided my efforts to make sense of them. I wish in particular to thank Herr Dr. Michael Cramer-Fürtig, Frau Kerstin Lengger and their staff at the *Stadtarchiv Augsburg*, and Herr Prof. Dr. Dietmar Schiersner and Herr Franz Karg, M.A. at the *Fürstlich und Gräflich Fuggersches Familien- und Stiftungsarchiv Dillingen*, where

I have spent weeks and months exploring their truly singular and fascinating collections. Frau Sarah Klein of the *Städtische Kunstsammlung der Stadt Augsburg* provided invaluable and efficient assistance in locating images of the Höchstetters and their hometown. Tanya Buckingham, Emily Petit and Meghan Kelly of the Cartography Laboratory of the Department of Geography and the University of Wisconsin – Madison created the maps that appear throughout the text. Without the guidance and support of all these colleagues, this book would truly not have been possible.

Extended archival research in Europe requires the generous support of those institutions that still believe in the value of scholarship and give that belief tangible form. Research for this volume received funding from the Alexander-von-Humboldt Stiftung, the American Council of Learned Societies, the National Endowment for the Humanities, the University of Pennsylvania and the Institute for Research in the Humanities at the University of Wisconsin. Colleagues and friends at Duke University, Grinnell College, the Free University of Berlin, the Humboldt University of Berlin, the University of Antwerp, the University of Augsburg, the University of Cambridge, the University of Chicago, the University of Leipzig, the University of Manchester, the University of New York at Binghamton, the University of Oxford, the University of Pennsylvania, the University of Rotterdam, the University of Utrecht, the University of Wisconsin and Yale University provided opportunities for me to present fragments of my research on bankruptcy Their invaluable criticism, encouragement and perspective made my thinking clearer and certainly contributed much to this project. Particular thanks, once again, go to Professors Bert De Munck, Jeroen Puttevils and Peter Stabel of Antwerp, Professor Christoph Becker of Augsburg, Professor emerita Claudia Ulbrich of Berlin, the late Professor Philip Kintner of Grinnell, Professor Markus Denzel of Leipzig, Professor D'Maris Coffman, then of the University of Cambridge, now of the University of London, Professor Philipp Roessner of Manchester, Professor Lyndal Roper of Oxford, Professor Oscar Gelderblom of Utrecht, Professor Timothy Guinnane of Yale and Professor Francesca Trivellato, then of Yale, now of the Institute for Advanced Study, all of whom have done so much, each in their own way, to improve my scholarship with their own. These institutions and individuals, these friends and colleagues, are for me a true republic of letters.

Thanks to my family and to the friends who read all or part of this book as it took shape. They know, I hope, what they have contributed, whether it be the careful reading of a draft, assistance in compiling a bibliography or guidance through the arcane world of digital technology. I hope they know as well how profoundly grateful I am.

I wish, however, to acknowledge separately three who have accompanied this project most intimately from beginning to end. They have each in their own way contributed so much to my work over decades that I cannot begin adequately to express my gratitude. Of this and most things I have written, they have each discussed nascent ideas, read multiple drafts, offered unflinching criticism and, more important still, unfailing encouragement.

It is my hope that every word of this book reflects my enduring conversation with Professor-emeritus Leonard N. Rosenband of Utah State University. Colleague, critic and companion from the very beginnings of our careers, most valued of friends, he enriched me with his incredible command of scholarship, both as theory and practice. Our on-going discussion of labor and capital has kept me mindful of history as the "lived experience" of the past and encouraged me to strive always for the meta-level of meaning.

More than any other single individual, Professor emeritus Rolf Kießling of Augsburg taught me the importance of place in history. With extraordinary generosity, he introduced me to his hometown, my home-away-from-home, and in countless excursions through the Swabian countryside and conversations late into the night revealed to me its fascination and beauty. His truly peerless command of the histories of Augsburg and Swabia saved me from countless errors and added depth to my thinking and writing.

Professor Lee Palmer Wandel of the University of Wisconsin kept me mindful of the irreducible importance of the individual. She has proven through good times and bad quick to laugh, alert to wonder and unfailing in support. Her careful attention to meaning in history and its writing and her profound skepticism of generalizations have complicated – and, so, improved – my thinking about such axiomatic economic notions as "value", "rationality" or "networks". Her influence on this book cannot be over-stated.

Each of these superb scholars and steadfast companions, each in his or her own way, made this book possible, when it seemed to me impossible. To them goes much of whatever credit it is due. I retain only the responsibility.

Note

1 M. I. Elsas, *Umriß einer Geschichte der Preise und Löhne in Deutschland vom ausgehenden Mittelalter bis zu Beginn des neunzehnten Jahrhunderts*, vol. I, 2 vols. (Leiden 1949), 118.

Introduction

Ambrosius Höchstetter enjoyed both fame and infamy in his day, a reputation that has endured to the present. Few among his contemporaries could lay claim to such ambiguous standing, a quality that stemmed from his rise and helps to explain his fall. It gave him a degree of importance that cannot be measured solely in terms of wealth or status. And it has made him an object of study, especially among economic historians, out of proportion with the scope of his business.

The Augsburg chronicler and Benedictine monk, Clemens Sender, provides the earliest history of the man, his family and their fortunes:

> Ambrosius Höchstetter, burgher of Augsburg, with his company, was a renowned merchant in all of Europe, who took as his wife the daughter of Jacob Rehlinger, who brought to him as dowry and inheritance 60,000 fl. Ambrosi Höchstetter was a fine, lordly, tall, large and strong man, of princely appearance, considered of great trust and faith, who did business with kings and emperors, princes and lords and all others likewise with great trust and faith, until the very year [of his bankruptcy, 1529, tms]. Princes, counts, noblemen, burghers, peasants, servants and maids deposited such money as they had with him and took 5 fl on the 100. Many peasants and those who had not more than 10 fl, deposited it with him in his company and thought it very well secured and had as well an annual income. This Höchstetter had at one point ten hundred thousand fl at interest in his company (it was commonly rumored, [though] rumors lie readily). No person knew, that he paid so much in interest.[1]

Höchstetter's commanding appearance and successful business created a reputation of great trust and faith (*groß trauens und glaubens*)[2] that attracted customers, borrowers and depositors from every level of society, aristocratic and common, urban and rural, rich and poor.

Richard Ehrenberg might refer to the century as "The Age of the Fugger", but he had to admit that "in the first decades [. . .] the Höchstetters in Augsburg were in addition to the Fugger and the Welser the most important Upper German commercial house".[3] Jacob Strieder took it a step further: "As Augsburg merchants, such as the Gossembrot, the Rehlinger, the Baumgartner, the Fugger and a dozen other names began around 1500 to take their place in the foreground of German firms and in the leadership of global trade, the Höchstetters also drew control of wholesale trade and high finance into their hands".[4] More recently, Hermann Kellenbenz set the Höchstetter in third place among the leading merchants of the premodern German economy, behind only the Fugger and the Welser.[5] Ambrosius was clearly one of the great capitalists of his age, deeply engaged in state finance, worldwide commerce and industrial manufacturing. With his colleagues and competitors, he helped the European economy to encircle the globe.

Yet, he also violated some of the fundamental social and moral principles of his day. Sender did not mince words:

> And he was a good Christian, completely opposed to Lutheranism, but he often oppressed the common good and the poor man with his commercial wealth, not only with valuable, noteworthy goods and merchandise, but also with cheap and mundane wares. He bought up ash wood in a good way [i.e., at a low price, tms] and took it to market when the way was better, the same with wine, grain and lute strings. And he often completely bought up a commodity at a price higher than it was worth, so he could pressure as he pleased other merchants, who lacked the means. Accordingly, he would raise the price of the commodity in all lands and sell it as he wished. No merchant with 50,000 or 100,000 fl could transact business in competition with him, because he gained whatever he wanted.[6]

Ambrosius conducted his business like a classic monopolist, whose ruthless efforts to corner markets and rig prices affected everyone, rich and poor, producers and consumers.

Ambrosius entered business as his father's factor in the 1480s and took control of the family firm in 1486. Sharp practice and spectacular success marked the decades that followed. By 1527, however, a series of business reverses placed him and his partners, brother Hans, sons Ambrosius II and Joachim, son-in-law Hans Franz Paumgartner and nephew Joseph, in financial difficulty. Though they took ever more desperate measures to maintain liquidity, to keep the family firm afloat, their insolvency quickly became common knowledge, and a formal declaration of bankruptcy followed in 1529. The catastrophic collapse that followed cast him from merchant's palace to debtors' prison and proved as economically ruinous as it was historically memorable. Creditors and authorities called upon Ambrosius to account:

> as he the elder Höchstetter has always increased his advantage through great understanding and brilliance, what has he done to himself, an honorable Council, the common citizenry and the outstanding trade and traders of the highly profitable merchant association in this famous imperial

> commercial city of Augsburg, giving them such an evil status and reputation that will work to their disadvantage in the future beyond his actual ruin?[7]

At first, he replied defiantly:

> He said that he knew not otherwise than that his affairs stood as well as they had 30, 20, 10, 6, 5 and 4 years earlier, that he understood and found his credibility, creditworthiness and business to be not otherwise than in all the days of that time, and had he understood that he was in difficulties and that his business would not succeed or the like, he would have ceased and quit much earlier.[8]

Formal, legal proceedings extended over two years. At the conclusion of his final interrogation, after increasingly severe imprisonment, the last few months in chains, he abandoned all pretense of innocence or confidence:

> The old Höchstetter pleads earnestly that the honorable Council will, for the love of God, have mercy in consideration of his extreme illness, such that four men must carry and lay him in his cell and [. . .] let him come to a room in his house and receive care for which he will renounce or do everything the honorable Council requires.[9]

To this plea a note was appended, whether by a jailer or interrogator, that Ambrosius was so badly injured on his lower leg that it might have to be amputated, about which a barber-surgeon should be consulted.[10] Sixty-eight years of age at the time, he would spend another three years chained to a wall before dying of the effects of his imprisonment.

From the first rumors of insolvency to the final consequences of bankruptcy, the Höchstetters left a huge documentary trail scattered in archives across Europe. Sifted and fitted together, it tells a remarkable tale about the rise and fall of a great merchant-banking house. That tale offers insights into economic life in early modern Europe that do not sit easily with what we think we know about family firms and early capitalism. By shedding light on the workings of economic institutions, the strategies of economic agents and the nature of economic organizations in the past, it reflects as well on the economic concerns of the present.

★ ★ ★

This book is about a bankruptcy. In late medieval and early modern Europe, bankruptcies were read as signs of ethical decay and economic decline. The shrill accusation of the creditors makes this clear. Before anything else, they wanted him to admit the magnitude of his crime. Moralists of the eighteenth century concurred when they decried bankruptcy as "theft in the form of honesty [. . .] extravagance with other people's money [. . .] [deserving of] the gallows".[11] They understood that business failures affected much more than the merchants who could no longer pay their debts. Bankruptcy had a ripple effect, ruining not only the bankrupts but many of those who had dealings with them. Residents of the Free Imperial City of Augsburg had cause to know.

Close studies of the economies of Europe and Augsburg in the second half of the sixteenth century generally reflect a rapidly growing economy.[12] Drawing wealth from textile, spice and metal trading, Augsburg merchants extended credit to princes and, by so doing, helped lay the foundation for globalization, underwriting overseas exploration, trade, conquest and empires. The amount of taxable property and the number of wealthy families in the city increased steadily. These were not the worst of times.

Yet, they may not have been the best of times in the minds of Augsburg merchant-bankers. Though they dominated markets across the continent and bankrolled enterprises around the world, their position did not endure unchallenged or unchanged. Bankruptcies were by no means unusual. The Höchstetter failure was the first, but by no means the last, in a long series. As early as 1560, Paul Hektor Mair chronicled no fewer than 26 Augsburg merchants who "became bankrupt and, because of debts, sought sanctuary, fled the city, or suffered arrest until they settled and were released".[13] Had he been able to extend his count to 1580, as Jacob Strieder did in 1938, the total would have risen to 70 "great and famous commercial houses".[14] Many may have been related to the inconsistencies of state finance, the defaults of Spain, Holland, France, Portugal and, again, Spain that marked the century.[15] Commercial reverses finished the rest. The decline of European copper mining and the "rise of the Atlantic economies" placed Augsburg merchants at a competitive disadvantage.[16]

Until very recently, historians held that the bankruptcies of the 1500s marked a turning point: The end of "The Age of the Fugger"; "The Catastrophe of the Early Capitalist Age"; or "The Collapse of Southern- and Middle-European Early Capitalism".[17] Contemporaries agreed. In the eyes of Hans Fugger, who had witnessed two insolvencies in his own family, Augsburg had become "a small village where once was a great city [. . .] all is in decline and all matters give evidence of worsening rather than bettering".[18]

The City Archive of Augsburg preserves legal proceedings of hundreds, if not thousands, of prosecutions for nonpayment of debts that involved high and low in Augsburg society.[19] Yet economic history has paid scant attention to bankruptcy.[20] Apart from Joseph Schumpeter's notion of "creative destruction", which saw failure as a precursor to innovation and, thus, intrinsic to modern capitalism, it has figured merely as a by-product of business mismanagement or economic crisis.[21] Economists usually see bankruptcy as an outlier to economic development; economic historians, by contrast, seize it as an opportunity to examine social relations. It has not yet been fully integrated into scholarship on early economic life, though the study of even one of these bankruptcies can shed light on economic change, business practices and what happened when things went wrong.

The legal resolution of bankruptcy was a highly complex matter, involving varying degrees of private and public action – negotiation and litigation, execution and evasion – that could extend over many decades and leave voluminous documentation. In general, it opened with a declaration of insolvency either by the bankrupt or his creditors. The creditors registered their claims with the civil authorities, who assumed responsibility for assessing the legitimacy of the claims, liquidating the capital of the bankrupt and paying at least a portion of the outstanding debts. Its further course depended on the bankrupt's ability to offer satisfaction.

Yet, bankruptcy remained a fluid affair, given to extraordinary variation based on the personalities and circumstances involved. The actions and tactics of debtors and creditors alike were predicated in part upon their perceptions of the situation. They were shaped also by bankruptcy laws and legal practices that became increasingly normalized over time. Some debtors settled, but others still occasionally took to their heels. After all, an early Augsburg statute treated bankruptcy as a criminal offense.[22] The magistrates understood default to be dishonorable as well as potentially criminal, a derogation of status that struck at the heart the city's commerce and prosperity, a violation of common trust and faith (*gemeinen treuen und glauben*). Accordingly, defaulters were to be banished or arrested, stripped of their right to membership in the merchants' corporation (*Kaufleutestubengesellschaft*), required to remove their stands from the privileged positions of honest merchants in the arcade at the foot of the city's watch tower, prohibited from bearing arms in public, and compelled to take their place with the women at the tail end of public processions. Should a bankrupt abscond, his creditors might seize his goods or person by whatever means necessary, acts of private execution that could result in ruthless competition to recover their capital. Many took the law into their own hands, risking legal penalties, rather than accepting partial or nonpayment.

Some were satisfied, but more were ruined. To prevent such damage and loss, the City Council of Augsburg attempted to promote an orderly settlement of all claims by forbidding the removal of property or accounts belonging to the bankrupt, proscribing the collection of debt by private execution and requiring all creditors to pursue payment through the offices of a council-appointed commission of representatives. These regulations and procedures were pragmatic as well as systematic: They were applied according to the circumstances and necessities of each case; the state did not stipulate specific solutions.[23] Rather, it provided a framework that minimized the disruption: It encouraged debtors to negotiate with their creditors; it encouraged settlements that were orderly and, occasionally, compassionate. As a result, bankruptcy became a transition, in which creditors might be satisfied and debtors rehabilitated, in which capital might be redistributed and enterprises restructured.

The Höchstetter bankruptcy occurred early in this process, however, at a point in time when individual default procedures were just beginning to be collected and revised into general bankruptcy ordinances. The financial and legal maneuverings that comprised it reveal the traction of these emergent civil ordinances: The degree to which the parties observed them, the degree to which the authorities enforced them and the degree to which they functioned as intended. A single bankruptcy case, studied in the context of business practices and bankruptcy procedures, becomes thus a metric for the function of economic organizations and institutions.

Douglass C. North famously defined "institutions" as the "formal rules, informal rules, and their enforcement characteristics" that define "the way the game is played", any socially imposed constraints on human behavior that permit certain expectations of what others will do in a given circumstance.[24] They are particularly important in economic life, according to North, because they facilitate human interaction and exchange by reducing uncertainty and its associated cost.

His observation seems to have little relevance to Augsburg. The city government steadfastly refused to modify its economic institutions in ways that might have sustained an already burgeoning economy. It expelled Jews and harassed many sorts of Christians and, thus, made it difficult for various groups to do business within its jurisdiction. It never introduced laws to govern the organization of the firm.[25] It never, to the lasting regret of historians, publicized market information. And it was tardy at best in establishing legal procedures to resolve bankruptcy.[26] Yet, throughout the fifteenth and sixteenth centuries, Augsburg remained one of the most important commercial and financial centers of the Empire. What mattered more than public-order institutions were traditional mercantile practices that might be encouraged but could not be consistently enforced by merchants or magistrates.

Moreover, as the Höchstetter bankruptcy makes clear, their function was neither always predictable nor always desirable. To recall North's often neglected caveat, institutions "may be incorrect and produce unexpected consequences".[27]

By implication, therefore, institutions could be reactive. They might determine "the way the game is played", but they also were determined by self-conscious changes in the game. The emergence of new forms of conflict resolution, capital redistribution and debt settlement can be viewed as attempts to regulate alterations to the established principles and practices of economic life. Institutional change reflected new ways of organizing and conducting business in the early modern period that rose from the bottom up and contributed to the so-called great transformation to our time.[28] Bankruptcy proceedings raise questions about the connections between institutions and practices.

* * *

This book is also about a family and a family firm. The bankruptcy of Ambrosius Höchstetter and his partners exposes the social relations, cultural values and business techniques of economic agents in pursuit of their trade. The earliest chroniclers and contemporaries understood this clearly. Sender's *obiter dicta* about "the daughter of Jacob Rehlinger, who brought brought to him as dowry and inheritance 60,000 fl" signaled his awareness that the fate of a great merchant related intrinsically to that merchant's social milieu, beginning with his family.

Studies of families and fortunes in past times commonly assume that the family was a unit, bound together by a common purpose, and that the household and its enterprise, whether it was a farm, workshop or *comptoir*, were essentially identical and usually stable.[29] Husbands and wives, fathers and mothers, had their appointed tasks, but the division of their labors was not necessarily the prescribed public and private, or business and household, spheres of ancient philosophy, medieval theology or even modern historiography.[30] Women could enter the counting house, where they might conduct business in their own or their husbands' names.[31] The young could be present, too, undertaking simpler tasks and learning by doing. Economic cooperation could also exist at the level of capital. Husbands retained the dowries of their wives and fathers the inheritances of their children, all of which they invested in the family business, even though they had to preserve the principal as their dependants' property. In the broadest sense, family and company capital flowed in and out of each other.[32]

More recent work on the family firm has built upon these suppositions and findings. David Landes, writing with romantic fervor about great capitalist dynasties, portrayed the family as "a nursery of knowledge and skill, an embodiment of trust, and a store of capital, in house or among relatives".[33] Harold James turned from Landes's microhistorical consideration of success to a macrohistorical reflection on development, in which he celebrated the solidarity of "the family" and its business. "[T]he family can be understood as providing a link across generations, and with this a perspective on time".[34] Without this long-term outlook, institutions and markets are, according to James, impossible. Though aware of the historical force of "misfortune", their discussions of "family" and "firm" remain ideal-typical in ways that make failure a deviation from the norm.

Bankruptcy proceedings reveal immediately, however, that families and family firms did not always exist in splendid isolation or generational solidarity. Rather, they lived and worked within specific communities and markets that influenced their activities, helped determine how they invested their capital and performed their labors. And, they changed over time as succeeding generations introduced their own talents, personalities, interests and engagements to the family enterprise.

The Höchstetters neither created nor commissioned annals of glorious ancestors (*Familien-*, *Ehren-* or *Ahnenbuch*), such as were fashionable among elite families in late medieval and early modern Augsburg, to strengthen their claim to high status and its material advantages.[35] A recent genealogy reverses this pattern and attempts to argue that the family "represents a Christian, Swabian-Augsburg lineage that is identifiable in the area around Donauwörth from the twelfth century and in Augsburg from the thirteenth century", the "not unimportant lineage of knights of Höchstädt on the Danube", who occupied the castle there as *ministeriales* of the Hohenstaufen dynasty and later played significant roles in the city of Donauwörth and in the court of the Counts of Dillingen.[36] This account tends to gloss over the humbler, late-fifteenth-century foundation "in the at that time rapidly expanding textile industry, first as bleachers, later as clothe-cutters (retailers in small and large quantities)".[37]

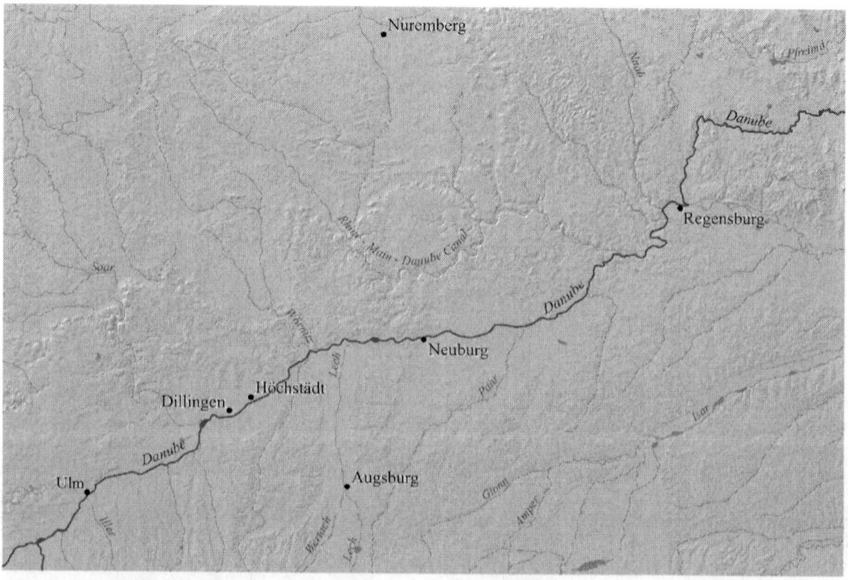

Map 0.1 Danube Basin with Höchstädt

The antecedents of the Höchstetters in Augsburg remain opaque until three generations before Ambrosius, however. The first clearly documented forefather, "Seyfried von Hoechstettern, became a burgher of Augsburg in 1367, found employment as a bleacher (*Bleicher*) of textiles and paid a tax of 1 fl 30 kr".[38] By 1418, Seyfried's/Sigfrid's tax assessment had risen to 4 fl.[39] This signals an increase in wealth over 15 years from as little as 300 to as much as 1,600 fl, or anywhere from 166 to 433 percent, depending on Augsburg tax rates.[40] Though his means appear to have increased only modestly, when compared to the wealth amassed by his descendants, his occupation may help to explain their rising fortunes.

Bleachers were often itinerant, independent craftsmen in the fifteenth century, moving from one weaving community to the next and offering their services on a contract basis.[41] Before the discovery of chemical reagents in the eighteenth century, those services did not constitute an exact science. Bleachers were masters of an arcane craft; their techniques were closely guarded secrets that varied from one to the next. They managed the operation of large physical plants. They oversaw the work of the many hands required to complete the bleaching process, which could take anywhere from three weeks to four months, depending upon weather conditions and cloth types. Proprietary techniques that were labor-intensive and time-consuming may have made bleachers among the earliest industrial capitalists. Their arcane knowledge gave them absolute control over the entire operation. They invested their own resources, exercised a free hand, bore all the risks and pursued unlimited profits. They

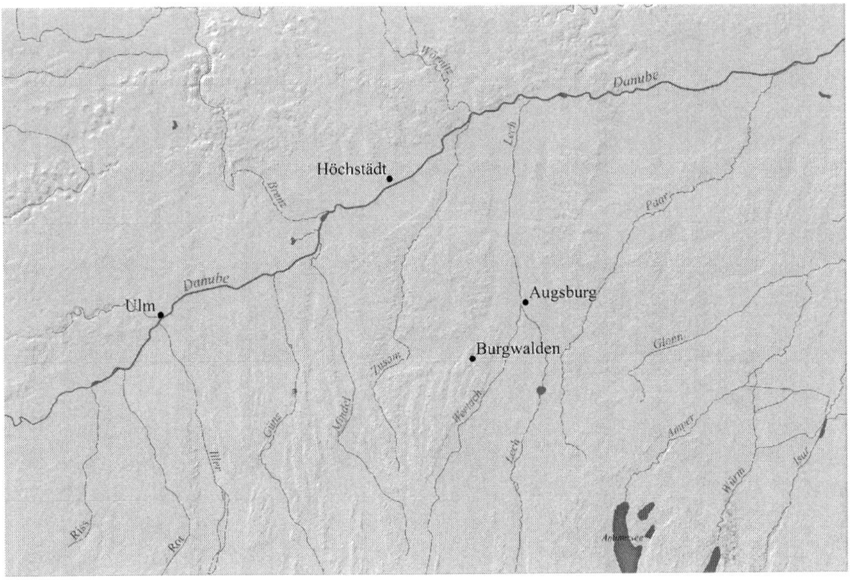

Map 0.2 Swabia with Augsburg

solely and entirely controlled the flow of money.[42] The potential margin of profit could be increased by informal exchanges that might occur on the side. An unscrupulous bleacher might cut corners and costs or accept some form of *douceur* at the expense of his clients. Given the business receipts and tax revenues on hand, he might offer short-term credit to cash-strapped weavers, even seize the product of those who defaulted, setting himself up as a textile merchant in his own right.

Based on his tax liabilities, Seyfried/Sigfrid Höchstetter could not have underwritten a radical change in fortunes for succeeding generations. Yet his occupation may have provided opportunities to develop knowledge and skills in a variety of financial operations and manipulations. It might explain the appearance in the 1408, 1413, 1418 and 1422 tax registers of the next, named Höchstetter, Ulrich I, supposedly Seyfried's son, as a "cloth-cutter" (*Sartor* or *Gewandschneider*), that is, a retailer who cut and sold cloth from the bolt.[43] Scholars have marked the earning potential of cloth-cutting and the role it could play in the commercial and financial strategies of mercantile families, how the selling of fabric from the bolt could lead these tradesmen to consider the possibility of importing textiles and could move them hence into the ranks of long-distance wholesale traders.[44] Strieder argues:

> Our Höchstetters belonged to those bolder cloth-cutters, of whom Keutgen speaks, who were not satisfied to stand behind the shop counter year out and year in and to sell to the burghers of Augsburg the materials

> they required for their various garments. It also did not satisfy them to round out supplies for themselves and others at local markets. They made for the lands of origin of their textiles, for Bruges and for Antwerp; doubled profits rewarded greater effort and risk.[45]

Ulrich I left bleaching and entered the profitable world of textiles, and his tax declaration rose from 2 fl in 1408 to 17 fl in 1441, an increase in taxable worth from 400 to as much as 6,800 fl, 100 to 1,600 percent, over the course of an adult life.[46] (See Appendix 1, "Rising Höchstetter Fortunes".)

The fortunes of his sole surviving son, Ulrich II (1422–1497), improved steadily, if unspectacularly, until the second half of the fifteenth century. Initially, he practiced the trade of cloth-cutter, or maintained membership in their corporation, like his father, but he presumably moved from small-scale, retail trade in textiles to large-scale, wholesale commerce. It is one of the few ways to explain his rapid rise in wealth: In 1467, his declared tax liability of 40 fl made him the eighteenth wealthiest man in Augsburg;[47] by 1489, it reached 145 fl 24 kr.[48]

The Höchstetters appear to have drawn both experience and capital from occupations that were less regulated and that may have been more entrepreneurial. An argument could be made on the basis of their general characteristics that bleaching and retailing were more exposed to market forces, that they relied to a greater extent on the bleacher's or retailer's capacity to contend and compete successfully. It might also be argued that bleachers and retailers experienced more continuous and immediate contact with producers and sellers of textiles, which put them in a position to understand the economics of manufacturing and commerce and rendered these two trades thus well suited to be vehicles of mobility within urban society. Some precapitalistic trades may have fostered capitalistic practices.

Three of his sons would follow Ulrich II into wholesale commerce and propel the family's rising fortunes higher before ruining them in bankruptcy. Georg I (1453–1514)[49] and Ambrosius I (1463–1534) partnered with their father, then assumed control of the family firm. A year after their father's death, in 1498, they joined as partners in an eponymous firm and declared tax liabilities that place them at the eleventh and twenty-ninth positions, respectively, among Augsburg's wealthiest men.[50] Their youngest brother, Hans I (1471–1527), became a partner in the family firm in 1515, having served in it as a factor since the 1490s. He never achieved the level of affluence enjoyed by his elder brothers.

Ulrich II's four other sons would pursue independent careers. Two entered the Roman Church.[51] Two started separate family firms. The third-born brother, Jacob I (1460–1525), continued to practice their father's first trade as a retail seller of cloth from the bolt.[52] Fourth-born Hieronymus I (1465–1508), established his own mercantile company in Augsburg and his own short-lived, cadet branch of the family. These two brothers achieved a substantial, albeit more modest, level of prosperity. Despite their separate paths, they would reappear – almost literally rise from their graves – to play a part in the bankruptcy of 1529.

Figure 1 Portrait of Ambrosius I Höchstetter

Moreover, Jacob's son, Sebastien, would lead his family into new enterprises, resurrect its fortunes and raise them to new heights during the late sixteenth and seventeenth centuries.

The Höchstetters moved from bleacher to wholesaler over three generations, but they made their dramatic leap in wealth over the course of a single lifetime. Ulrich II may have increased his gross worth by as much as 2,670 percent through trading in textiles, he may have been "not satisfied to stand behind the shop counter year out and year", but neither accumulated capital nor psychological states, alone or together, explain how he managed entry into the ranks of Augsburg's merchant association, much less how he engaged in mercantile activity. Wholesale trade in raw materials and finished products requires information and planning. This is an essential key to economic and occupational mobility in the Middle Ages or in any age. It requires an analysis of potential competitors and possible customers. It requires knowledge of trade barriers, market practices, current prices and local culture, among other things. It requires access, connection, experience and a host of other resources. It must involve accumulating and learning within one's given occupation as well as

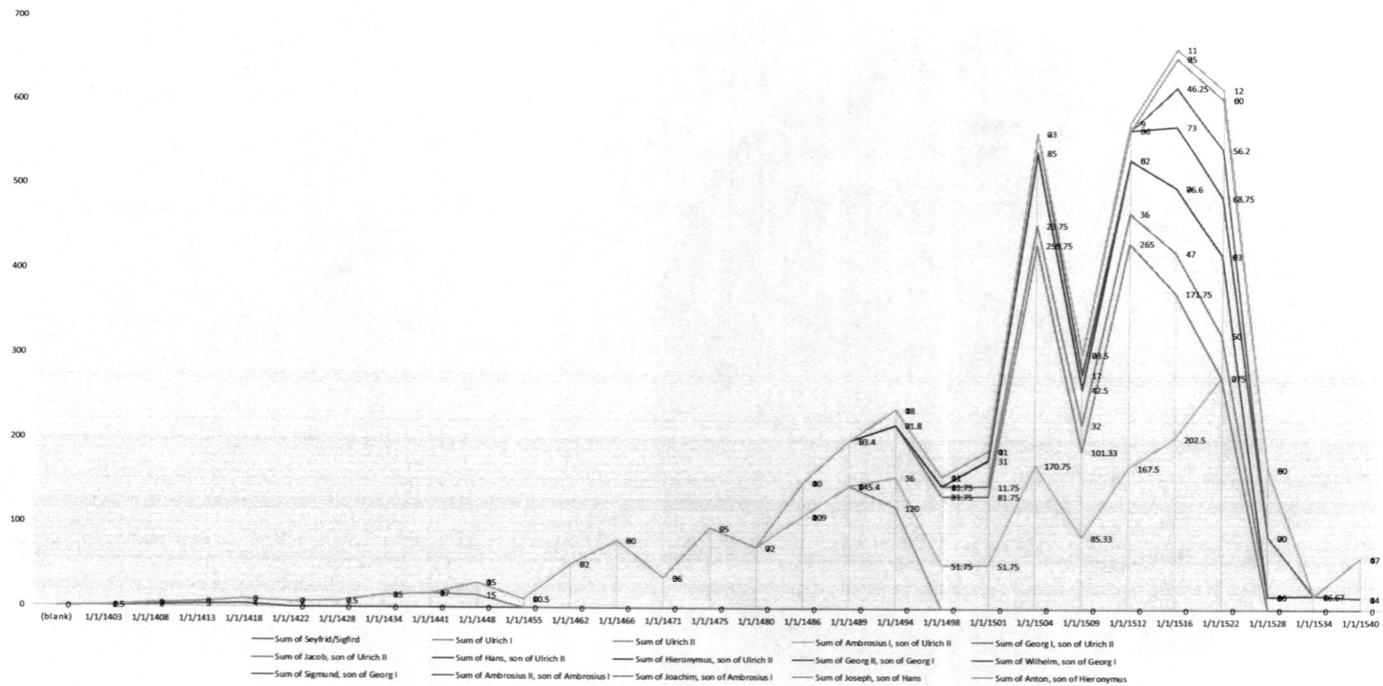

Figure 2 Rising Höchstetter fortunes

exposure to the practices of trades other than one's own. In addition to financial capital, it must include social capital: Acquaintance, status, patronage and protection. Ulrich II must somehow have achieved all of this and passed it to his sons. It may be that their marriages connected them with families that could help in all these regards.

Ulrich I married Barbara Köhler in or around 1420.[53] Little is known about her family; no record survives of her marriage settlement, but Ulrich's tax liability rose from 7 fl 30 kr in 1428, the year after his marriage, to 15 fl in 1434, suggesting that Barbara's dowry might have provided an infusion of capital.[54] The meteoric rise of his son in wealth and stature may have had something to do with his marriage in 1447 to Barbara Peutinger, the daughter of Johann Peutinger, a well-established merchant and councilor of Augsburg. Again, no contract survives to reveal the amount of Barbara's dowry, but there is nonetheless little reason to doubt that Barbara brought her parvenu husband advantages. Not only did Ulrich II join the *Kaufleutestubengesellschaft* of Augsburg, while maintaining his position as member and master of the *Gewandschneider*, but he repeatedly held the civic office of *Baumeister*, one of the highest officials of Augsburg, charged with the city's financial administration.[55] Ambrosius's marriage to Anna Rehlinger brought his family and firm wealth and provided a link to one of the oldest, most important patrician families of Augsburg.[56] Though father-in-law Jacob represented a cadet branch of the family, this was arguably the most potent social connection the Höchstetters achieved.[57] Ambrosius's brothers and sons – indeed, also his sisters and daughters – all found spouses among aristocratic and patrician families with mercantile interests, social station and political power, demonstrating continued social ambition.

Despite the emphasis placed by Keutgen, Strieder and others on resources accumulated through artisanal crafts, historians have long noted the role of marriage in enabling manufacturers to become traders, providing labor power, investment capital and social connection.[58] More recently, they have taken up the notion of networks in social and economic life, greatly advancing both the history of the family and the history of business.[59] Economic historians have sought to demonstrate the degree to which families were "embedded" not just in marriages but in patterns of relationship and interaction that connected them to other families and broader communities and the ways that influenced their business activities.[60] It has become axiomatic that networks are an essential feature of economic life and that so-called multiplex relationships – relationships that reinforced economic interaction through ties of kinship, marriage, association or other forms of community – solved the problems of impersonal trade by increasing trust and reducing costs.[61]

Close studies of individual bankruptcies can raise questions about the function of networks, like the questions they raise about institutions. Familial relationships are fluid, and network theory does not capture their dynamics or predict their outcomes. As we shall see, ties of kinship and marriage created patterns of interest that did not always result in solidarity or cooperation. The mere fact of connection reveals little about the nature of a relationship and nothing about its capacity to change over time. Families have a certain mythos: Their structure symbolizes unity and solidarity; their engagements display stability and singularity. The Höchstetter bankruptcy demonstrates, however, that families are not monolithic, not orderly. They can have multiple branches that prospered differently. They can have complicated relations, engage in multiple markets, often with conflicting interests. Such observations do not disprove or discount the importance of social networks; rather, they add complexity and contingency to abstract notions of their function.

Bankruptcy reveals the business organizations and techniques of family firms in similar ways: It problematizes the abstract and prescriptive by exposing conflict, negotiation and adaptation. Sender made immediately clear what his contemporaries likely believed or guessed, that Ambrosius Höchstetter's failure was due to unscrupulous or imprudent management. He supposedly fell victim to the structural weaknesses that characterize all family firms. In addition to monopolistic methods, in which he cornered the supply of goods to set the market price and "pressure other merchants at his pleasure",[62] he accepted huge numbers of deposits at 5 percent interest – in essence, borrowed massive short-term credit. He placed much of his business in the hands of his descendants, a procedure consistent with family firms past and present, then suffered losses when they proved improvident, incompetent or just plain unlucky. His success and failure had to do with family firms as well as social networks

Studies of merchant capitalists in the medieval and early modern periods have long attended closely to their business organization and technique.[63] One issue that bedevils this scholarship is the lack of direct, archival sources. The resort to indirect and prescriptive evidence is not unusual, given the lack of business records that survive from late medieval and early modern companies. These documents were secret, as a rule, and often vanished with the firm that generated them. Noteworthy exceptions exist, such as the extensive and valuable archives of the Medici and Fugger enterprises, but they remain exceptions. Bankruptcy records can provide a useful replacement for or extension of business documents. Creditors demanded – and frequently received – access to the bankrupt's accounts, correspondence and records. These documents were not only copied fair in many instances, but were subjected to close, expert analysis to determine questions of management and probity. In consequence, bankruptcy not only exposes the proprietary procedures of a merchant-financier but provides a benchmark for their analysis in business- and economic-historical terms.

One example is capitalization: How family firms financed their operations. The degree to which firms relied on family resources as opposed to foreign investment is often taken as a metric for modernity.[64] Reliance on foreign as well as familial capital, an "exceedingly high willingness to entertain risk among Augsburg merchants", was a benchmark of Upper German finance.[65] The bankruptcies that swept through Augsburg's merchant community in the sixteenth century seem to typify – and to justify – Max Weber's characterization of the premodern, traditional capitalist as a swashbuckler, who "would sail through hell for profit, even if his sails were singed".[66] Constantly hungry for capital, these early businessmen readily compiled short-term debts, which might be redeemed at a day's notice, against their long-term investments, which was remunerative but insecure.[67] Bankruptcy records confirm the Höchstetters as early pioneers in the resort to outside investment, as Sender made clear, in their own day, but qualify their depiction as risk-seeking. Their bankruptcy captures, therefore, the interconnections between financial practice, merchant culture and economic environment.

Traditionally, economic history employs grand narratives, but economic agents do not respond in a linear, mechanical manner to economic theories or social forces. States do not simply create order; individuals do not predictably employ best practice. Rather, they identify interests, assess risks and make choices according to criteria that are not always clear. The study of bankruptcies underscores the empirical nature of economic life.[68] It reveals how bankrupts and creditors shaped routines and appropriated institutions for their own individual ends. As such, bankruptcy becomes a sort of seminar in the workings of early capitalism.

* * *

Ultimately, this book is about capital, capitalists and capitalistic practices in early modern Europe. Sender chronicled the Höchstetter bankruptcy in detail as an indictment of the economic system of his day. Ambrosius Höchstetter, who "traded with trust and faith" and was a "good Christian, completely opposed to Lutheranism", nonetheless "oppressed the common good and common man with his commercial fortune".[69] Taking a notorious monopolist as representative, Sender decried the state-supported rigging of markets by wealthy merchant-bankers for individual advantage at the expense of the common good.

The chronicler presents thus the conundrum of rationality versus opportunism. On the one hand, Ambrosius's business success, born of a kind of instrumental rationality, whereby agents adopt actions best suited to achieve their goals, lured "[p]rinces, counts, noblemen, burghers, peasants, servants and maids [to deposit] such money as they had with him". On the other hand, Ambrosius's actions, whatever their logical consistency, were amorally opportunistic, taking self-interested advantage of circumstances with little regard for the violation of principles or the consequences for others, such that "he gained whatever he wanted".

The tension between rationality and opportunism reflects a more profound friction, one between capitalistic practices and capitalistic society. Ambrosius was an entrepreneur in the broadest sense, an individual who "devotes their own independent efforts to the acquisition of wealth, power, and prestige",[70] who lived in a world that, with some exceptions, largely experienced "entrepreneurship without entrepreneurs".[71] He was not a non-conformist, as Sender makes clear, but his actions sat uneasily with the norms of his society. By controlling the supply of commodities, such that he precluded market competition and set unjust prices, Ambrosius allegedly benefited himself at the expense of what was shared and beneficial for all or most members of the community. This would seem to suggest that capitalistic practices can exist without a more systematic capitalism. That tension between rationality and opportunism, between capitalistic practices and noncapitalistic society would result in great wealth and end in a dramatic fall.

Of course, Sender never employed the term "capital" or an any of its variations. Unknown in his day, its usage is essentially modern. The authoritative source for German usage offers nothing on capital or capitalism before the nineteenth century.[72] "Capitalism" entered the English language in the work of William Makepeace Thackeray as meaning no more than "having ownership of capital."[73] The modern sense of an economic system, based on capital as a factor of production and markets for the allocation of resources, emerged thereafter in the works of Louis Blanc and Pierre-Joseph Proudhon.[74] One might reasonably conclude, therefore, that capitalism applied to any other, earlier economy would run the risk of anachronism.

Yet the elements of capitalism have always existed, as noted, and the roots of the term are far older. In the late twelfth and thirteenth centuries, the Italian "capitale" described a variety of funds, from stocks of merchandise to sums of money and interest-bearing instruments.[75] "At least as early as the mid-seventeenth century, the *Hollandische Merkur* used "*Kapitalist*" to describe the owner of capital.[76] Arthur Young and David Ricardo are credited with the first English usage in its modern sense.[77] Capital and capitalists have been around for a long time, even if "capitalism" has not.

While a consensus exists as to the characteristics of a capitalistic system, as well as the practices that would contribute to or derive from it, no precise definition of capitalism finds universal approval. Likewise, considerable controversy surrounds the use of capitalism as a historical category. Scholars generally accept the notion that capitalism involves private ownership of the means of production, creation of goods and services for profit in a market and, to a varying degree, governmental support for private property in the form of appropriate legal institutions. Having existed to varying degrees since the beginning of human history, these characteristics do not justify the distinction of an economy at a particular point in time as "capitalistic". As Werner Sombart wrote in 1930, "It cannot be said that a clear-cut definition has ever been attempted".[78] And, as Joseph Schumpeter ironically pointed out, "The term capitalism was, throughout the nineteenth century, hardly used except by Marxists and writers directly influenced by Marxism".[79] That is to say, "capitalism" was a dirty word favored most by those who rejected it.

Indeed, from the earliest reflections on economic life, capitalism, whether mentioned explicitly or described implicitly, has provoked misunderstanding and misgiving. Aristotle held that "the art of producing wealth, not in every way, but by exchange [. . .] is justly to be censured, for it is unnatural and a mode by which men gain from one another".[80] Throughout the Middle Ages, moralists expressed their unease with capitalistic practices by condemning usury. By the sixteenth century, the real costs and potential benefits of capitalistic practices had entered the public discussion of economic behavior, as the so-called

Monopoly Debate (*Monopoldebatte*) and a growing body of didactic literature make clear.[81] Outrage reached such a pitch that the Imperial Diet (*Reichstag*) seriously considered outlawing the practice of monopoly and limiting the size of merchant-banking firms, an intention frustrated only by the Imperial veto of Charles V.[82] The critical reflections of a Thorsten Veblen, Richard Tawney, Karl Polanyi and E. P. Thompson – to say nothing of Karl Marx and his followers – demonstrate that, for many scholars, capitalism and capitalistic practices remained associated with economic predation, material waste and social conflict and that capitalists remained shadowy figures.[83]

This enduring discontent has influenced the latest surge of scholarship, the so-called new capitalism. The term may first have been coined by Richard Sennett, who used it to capture the negative impacts of globalization: "This new economy does not 'grow' personal skills and durable purposes, nor social trust, loyalty, and commitment".[84] Thomas Piketty's conclusion that inequality, considered in terms of disparities of wealth, is an intrinsic characteristic of capitalisms old and new, because rates of capital return consistently outstrip those of economic growth in developed countries, seemed to give empirical substantiation to such concern and criticism.[85] The "new capitalism" has not gone unchallenged, however. Kevin Doogan's study of labor relations mines empirical data to argue that work regimes have not changed radically under the influence of globalization.[86] Developed economies still rely, per his analysis, on stable, full-time employment. And, indeed, his argument appears to support recent overviews that insist modern capitalism has created greater prosperity for a greater proportion of the world's population, especially marginal groups, than any socioeconomic system of which we have historical knowledge and that it needs only appropriate regulation to perfect it.[87] Such sanguine assessments have not satisfied scholars of the "new capitalism" who have taken up the history of coerced labor and capitalism's historical reliance on it. Edward Baptist, Sven Beckert, Seth Rockman and others have returned to Eric Williams' old argument that the Industrial Revolution would not have occurred without the capital accumulation made possible by the trade in and labor of African slaves.[88] In their telling, slavery drove the expansion of capitalism, propelling the development of long-distance trade, the commoditization of workers into hands, the emergence of the modern state and the industrialization – indeed, the globalization – of the economy. In all of these works, the "new" in capitalism refers to new discontents and renewed attention to old tropes.

Old and new capitalisms leave unexplained the prehistory and causes of that which they purport to analyze. They treat capitalism as an essential system rather than a historical construct. They also tend to focus on its impact on labor rather than the development of capital. Little historical research has yet emerged on so-called corporate welfare, that is, money subsidies, tax breaks or other such favorable treatments given by states to select corporations. A microhistory of bankruptcy redresses this imbalance by setting aside abstractions and models to examine capital, capitalists and capitalistic practices in context.

Terminological discontents and scholarly debates notwithstanding, something clearly happened to the European economy of the eighteenth and nineteenth centuries that differentiated it from earlier periods. Terms were taken up and debates occurred as people grappled with what seemed to be unprecedented change. Economic history emerged at the same time for the same reason. It drew inspiration from two simultaneous developments: The attempts of English classical economists, such as Adam Smith and John Stuart Mill to explain the wealth, progress and development of contemporary society;[89] and the debates between the Austrian School, which represented the classical economic view, and the German Historical School about the function of theory in the social sciences and the use of history in explaining human behavior.[90] Economists insisted upon an ideal form of capitalism to answer questions about the production, distribution and consumption of goods at all times. Against this ideal type, historians argued that economic theory must be drawn from historical evidence and that this evidence demonstrates the division of human history into at least three distinct stages – feudalism, mercantilism and industrialization – with their own distinct economic systems, their own distinct capitalisms. This led, in turn, to the consideration of particular socioeconomic systems to determine how a variety of factors, including but not limited to the ownership of resources and the function of markets, determined the structures of economic, social and political organizations. Historians came thus to debate the origins and causes of capitalism, at what point it came into existence or how and when one form changed into another.

Marx and his followers found the answer in the so-called primitive accumulation, of the feudal economy. The expropriation of small landowners and the consequent concentration of landownership and conglomeration of rents in the Middle Ages constituted the beginnings of a long, ineluctable, historical process.[91] Henri Pirenne and Henri Sée, on the other hand, emphasized medieval commerce rather than in agriculture.[92] Foreign trade, especially as practiced in Italian city-states as early as the twelfth century, demonstrated many of what are held to be essential features of early capitalism: Industrial enterprise, commercial profits, financial innovation and rational laws. A vast historiography maintains that declining productivity, demographic crisis and labor scarcity caused a collapse of the feudal economy and a caesura of economic organization between the mid-fourteenth and late-fifteenth centuries.[93] There followed an age often described in terms of mercantilism or commercial capitalism, during which the merchant emerged as the owner of capital, who penetrated international and global markets to organize and coordinate the production, distribution and consumption of goods and whose activities were supported by increasingly strong governmental institutions and rational ideologies.[94] These activities, at last, generated the capital that would fund the building of great factories and the development of machine technologies.

More recently, attention has shifted from capital accumulation to market – or, more broadly, institutional – development and cultural transformation as the keys to the historical emergence or existence of capitalism. The debate persists, therefore, when "true capitalism" came properly into existence. This approach relies, not only on more recent institutional and game theories, but also directly or indirectly on Weber's "Protestant Ethic". The essence of modern capitalism has to be located, above all, in the economic values and behaviors of mercantile elites, especially their emancipation from "traditionalism", an attitude to life and an approach to management comprised of a resistance to incentives and a preference for leisure:

> By nature, humans do not wish to earn more and more money. They wish to live as they are accustomed to live and to earn only so much as is necessary to that end.[95]

To develop, capitalists and capitalism had to overcome this resistance. Many historians still emphasize the traditionalism of early modern merchants, who remained noncapitalistic capitalists in that they failed to understand the true nature and multiple forms of capital.[96]

These studies provide benchmarks for comparisons between theory and practice over time and space. The important questions are to what extent and with what effects the traditionally accepted elements of capitalism – private ownership, market allocation, government support – existed in any time or place and how the economic agents of that time or place appropriated them for their own purposes. This book uses the bankruptcy of a single family and firm to explore these issues. The fates of Ambrosius Höchstetter, his firm and his family help move the discussion to the everyday lives and lived experiences of historical individuals, the constraints, contingencies and choices confronted by women and men engaged in economic life in the past.

* * *

This book is not about models or theories of economic change. It seeks to move beyond ideal types that can obscure contingency, complexity and change. The study of bankruptcy provides a uniquely appropriate point of entry.

Until very recently, economists and historians paid scant attention to failure, except because of crisis. That fact notwithstanding, it remains widely accepted as an element of capitalistic development. And it generates the kind of documentation that makes possible the close study of the development of capitalistic practices.

Joseph Schumpeter, whose work in many ways defines the modern discussion of the topic, wrote:

> A society is called capitalist if it entrusts its economic process to the guidance of the private businessman. This may be said to imply, first, private ownership of nonpersonal means of production [. . .] second, production for private account, i.e., production by private initiative for private profit.[97]

He thus called attention to the individual entrepreneur as the agent, to private enterprise as the modality, and to personal profit as the motive of change under capitalism. As he explained in *The Theory of Economic Development* and in *Business Cycles*, entrepreneurs are "New Men", whose enterprises are "New Firms" that pursue innovation by creating new commodities, forming new organizations or opening new markets.[98] Innovation is the essence of "creative destruction", as he defined it in *Capitalism, Socialism and Democracy*, which "incessantly revolutionizes the economic structure from within, incessantly destroying the old one, incessantly creating a new one".[99] For Schumpeter, who held that capitalism undermines social relations and moral values, the benefits of increased prosperity nonetheless outweigh the costs in human suffering. Capitalism is essential to progress, and failure is essential to capitalism.

When it occurs, it exposes the interactions of economic life, cultural values, social relations and human agency, and it shows how the entrepreneur made sense and use of capital and capitalistic practices in a specific institutional setting. When failure took the form of bankruptcy, the legal proceedings compelled exposure. Entrepreneurs, whether investment bankers or merchant-financiers, would never otherwise countenance the detailed disclosure of matters most secret: The value of their enterprise and the forms of their capital; the people who owed them money and the people to whom they owed it; the strategies they pursued and the forms that pursuit took. Bankruptcy captures a moment in which risks were revealed, organizations were altered and capital was reorganized. It permits answers to questions of what various agents knew and how that knowledge shaped their actions in the market. It reveals the *praxis* of counting-houses and marketplaces, where persons made decisions and faced consequences. It makes of capitalistic practices flesh-and-blood experiences and of capitalism a contingent system.

The following chapters examine the nature of capitalists, capital and capitalistic practices in the early modern period through the lens of a single family and firm. Their organization is both chronological and thematic.

Chapter 1 turns to the companies that the Höchstetters organized to pursue long-distance, wholesale trade. Comparing their founding charters to one another and to those of contemporaneous family firms, it examines the structural strengths and weaknesses of late medieval and early modern mercantile companies. It asks particularly in what ways the family firms of that era were susceptible or resistant to collapse and promoted or hindered economic development.

Chapter 2 details the Höchstetters' major engagements and interests to capture how they conducted their businesses, especially their methods of market entry and exit. Relying particularly upon the documentation from their bronze manufactory in Pflach, Tyrol, it traces the ways in which early capitalist enterprise evaluated and entered commercial and financial markets, mobilized factors of production from raw materials to labor forces and, finally, relied on sympathetic regulation, political patronage and even brute force to protect their interests.

Chapter 3 opens with market manipulation through monopolies, another business practice, of which the Höchstetters were understood to be past masters. Their failed attempt in the 1520s to control the European supply of mercury and cinnabar ultimately contributed to their ruin. The ensuing insolvency and their efforts to escape it reveal much about business practice in the sixteenth century, the role of trust in economic life, the function (and dysfunction) of social networks and the tension between opportuneness and opportunism.

Chapter 4 examines the initial phase of the Höchstetter bankruptcy to explore the function of economic organizations and institutions. The first stage of the proceeding occurred on the local level, in the city of Augsburg, before its magistrates and subject to its procedures and laws. It shows that institutions, far from being *a priori* "rules of the game", are created and manipulated, in this case, by the economic agents involved in credit-debt relations. They are historical constructs and, therefore, incomprehensible apart from their historical context.

Chapter 5 follows the Höchstetter bankruptcy from a local and civil to a regional and imperial level to analyze credit-debt relations. The identities of the creditors and their relationships among one another and to the Höchstetters reveal the influence of social networks and the workings of financial markets. It finds that networks, though important in economic relations generally, neither explain the borrowing and lending of capital, nor predict the behaviors of debtors and creditors. They remain constructs that arise from relations but do not determine them.

Chapter 6 opens with the dissolution of the Höchstetters' family firm and the death of its senior partner to take up the question of resilience. In an age when opportunism was little restricted and business turned on trust, bankruptcy signaled economic and social death. Yet, the Höchstetters recovered. How they did so speaks to the vitality and flexibility of the family and the family firm in early modern Europe and prompts questions about the historical interpretation of both.

Finally, a conclusion returns to issues of early capitalism and the role of the family firm in it. The study of bankruptcy offers something genuinely and importantly new to each of those bodies of scholarship, but it has yet to be fully integrated into the study of economic life. Summarizing findings based on the Höchstetters, the study of their failure suggests new avenues of inquiry into business organization and economic development in the late medieval and early modern periods.

A microhistory cannot overturn theories or models. Instead, it seeks to juxtapose those theories and models with the experiences and practices of a single family of early capitalists. This requires close examination of qualitative and quantitative sources and yields an analytical narrative that reveals human agency and opens theoretical dimensions. The Höchstetters' did not merely respond to the constraints and opportunities offered by early modern society; they negotiated, seized and manipulated them for their own purposes. Subject to them, they also made intrinsic, idiosyncratic sense of them. Their experience seems to upend much of what we think we know about family firms and early capitalism.

Notes

1 Clemens Sender, *Die Chronik von Clemens Sender von den ältesten Zeiten der Stadt bis zum Jahre 1536. Die Chroniken der schwäbischen Städte. Augsburg*, vol. IV (Leipzig 1894), 219.

2 The phrase "trauen und glauben" appears frequently in the records of early modern, South German, family firms. Though literally translated as "trust and faith", it is not to

be confused with modern notions of "trust" in business life and history, a firm belief in the reliability, truth or ability of someone or something, usually a credible commitment to honor an obligation. Its sense might be translated as "credit-worthiness and credibility", indicating a wider range of qualities, including a well-established position in the mercantile community, a hard-eyed capacity to assess business opportunities and, not least, a long-term reputation for success. A person, whether merchant-financier or company servant, established his credit-worthiness and credibility over time, demonstrated it through performance and recognized it on the basis of experience.

3 Richard Ehrenberg, *Das Zeitalter der Fugger: Geldkapital und Kreditverkehr im 16. Jahrhundert* ([Jena 1896] New York 1990), 212.

4 Heinz Friedrich Deininger (ed.), *Das Reiche Augsburg: Ausgewählte Aufsätze Jacob Streiders zur Augsburger und süddeutschen Wirtschaftsgeschichte des 15.und 16. Jahrhunderts* (Munich 1938), 95.

5 Hermann Kellenbenz, *Deutsche Wirtschaftsgeschichte*, vol. I, 2 vols. (Munich 1977), 282.

6 Ibid., 219–20.

7 "*Erstlich zufragen, dieweyl er alter Hochstetter doch je und allwegen seinem vromen nach hoches verstanndts unnd prachts sich angemast, was er sich dann selbst unnd ain erbern Rath gemaine Burgershafft und den treffennlichen Hanndel und Handler vom hochgewerbigen kauffmannsleuten in diser beraumbten Kay. Kauffstatt Augspurg besigen, jnen ain soliche bosen Geruff und Laimbdt zu Nachtail kunfftiglich raichend und enntspringennde uber sien wars Verderben gemacht hab*". Stadtarchiv Augsburg (hereinafter StAA), Literaliensammlung, Höchstetter-Selekt I, Dok. 24, Erste Hochstetters Fragstuck.

8 "*Uff den ersten Articul sagt, er hab nit anderst bewisst dann sein sach stand so wol alls vor 30, 20, 10, 6, 4 unnd 4 jare, auch sein trawen glauben und handlung jn allen Tagen gehabt die Zeit wie vorgemelt anderst nicht gewesst verstanden noch befundenn, wie er auch verstanden, das er sich ubel beignden het und das er der Handlung nit mogen erstrecken oder der gleichen, wellt er von langst alls von 4 jaren auf gestossen und aufgehert haben*". StAA, Literaliensammlung, Höchstetter-Selekt I, Urgicht, Actum auf 26 Tag Septembris Anno 31, Jn praesentibus Herrn Hofmann, Sighart, Paler, Schollenberger, Ambrosi Hochstetter der Elter sagt an gutlichen Frag wie hernachfolgt.

9 "*Alt Hochstetter bit auch lauter umb Gots Willen zum aller hoechsten ein ersam Rat welle jme so genedig seie jne jnn Ansehenung seiner mercklichen Krankheit so jn die an Kerke mussen jne 4 menschenn tragen unnd legenn und sich gar nicht verwissen jnn sein Behausung jnn ein Stuben komen und Fursehung thon lassen, welt er verbergen vershreiben und alles das thon das jm ein erbar Rat zu [] desshalb auf legen muss*". StAA, Literaliensammlung, Höchstetter-Selekt 1, Dok. 27, Actum den 5 Tag Octobris Anno 31. Ambrosi Hochstetter der Elter sagt uf die gestreckten Articul wie hernachfolgt.

10 "*Zu dem so seie er hochlich an seiner Shencklen verletzt das zu besorgenn er mecht sich zu tragen, das man jme ein abnemenn mocht, wie dan der Barbier mag anzaigen unnd gefragt werd bit wie vor*". Ibid.

11 "*Sie stehlen unter dem Schein eines ehrlichen Mannes. Sie machen Figur mit anderer Leute Geld. Sie erwerben sich Freunde mit dem ungerechten Mammon. Sie sind die besten Männer; denn die schenken alles ihren Weibern. Wenn sie hernach nicht weiter können, so geben sie ihren ehrlichen Namen mit samt der Handlung auf. Sie zahlen niemand. Es heisst, sie wären unglüklich gewesen. Sie wären um allen kommen und leben hernach von dem Vermögen ihrer Frauen ebenso gemächlich als zuvor*". StAA, "Von dem bürgerlichen Stande," *Augsburger Intelligenzzettel*, 1752/37.

12 Ingomar Bog, "Wachstumsprobleme der oberdeutschen Wirtschaft, 1540–1618," *Jahrbücher für Nationalökonomie und Statistik* 179 (1966): 493–537; Hermann Kellenbenz, "Gewerbe und Handel, 1500–1648," in: Hermann Aubin and Wolfgang Zorn (eds.), *Handbuch der deutschen Wirtschafts- und Sozialgeschichte*, vol. I (Stuttgart 1971), 414–64; Hermann Kellenbenz, "Augsburger Wirtschaft, 1530 bis 1620," in: *Welt im Umbruch: Augsburg zwischen Renaissance und Barock*, vol. I (Augsburg 1980), 51–71; Friedrich Lütge, "Die wirtschaftliche Lage Deutschlands vor Ausbruch des Dreißigjährigen Krieges," in: Hermann Kellenbenz (ed.), *Studien zur Sozial- und Wirtschaftsgeschichte* (Stuttgart 1963), 336–95; Bernd Roeck, *Eine Stadt in Krieg und Frieden: Studien zur Geschichte der*

Reichsstadt Augsburg zwischen Kalenderstreit und Parität, 2 vols. (Göttingen 1989); Eckart Schremmer, "Die Wirtschaftsmetropole Augsburg," in Max Spindler (ed.), *Handbuch der bayrischen Geschichte*, vol. III (Munich 1971), 1080–96.

13 Bayerische Akademie der Wissenschaft (ed.), *Die Chroniken der deutschen Städten vom 14. bis ins 16. Jahrhundert*, vol. 33, 2nd ed. (Göttingen, 1965–67), 78–81.

14 Jacob Strieder, "Der Zusammenbruch des süd- und mitteleuropäischen Frühkapitalismus," in: Heinz Friedrich Deininger (ed.), *Das Reiche Augsburg*, 46. Cf. Wolfgang Zorn, *Augsburg: Geschichte einer europäischen Stadt*, 3rd ed. (Augsburg 1994), 236. More reccently, Mark Häberlein set the total at 63. See Mark Häberlein, *Brüder, Freunde und Betrüger: Soziale Beziehungen, Normen und Konflikte in der Augsburger Kaufmannschaft um die Mitte des 16. Jahrhunderts* (Berlin 1998), 397–9.

15 Häberlein, *Brüder, Freunde und Betrüger*, 38–9. See also Ramón Carande, *Carlos V. y sus banqueros*, 3 vols. (Madrid 1942/47); Reinhard Hildebrandt, "The Effects of Empire: Changes in the European Economy after Charles V," in: Ian Blanchard, Anthony Goodman and Jennifer Newman (eds.), *Industry and Finance in Early Modern History: Essays Presented to George Hammersley on the Occasion of His 74th Birthday* (Stuttgart 1972), 58–76; Hermann Kellenbenz, "Die frühen Bankgeschaäfte der Fuggerschen Faktorei in Sevilla," *Revue internationale d'Histoire de la Banque* 8 (1974): 200–15; Hermann Kellenbenz, *Die Fugger in Spanien und Portugal bis 1560*, 2 vols. (Munich 1990).

16 This argument was first made by Ralph Davis in his eponymous book, *The Rise of the Atlantic Economies* (Ithaca, NY 1973).

17 Ehrenberg, *Das Zeitalter der Fugger*, II, 174–78; Josef Kulischer, *Allgemeine Wirtschaftsgeschichte des Mittelalters un der Neuzeit* (Munich 1958); Jacob Strieder, "Der Zusammenbruch des süd- und mitteleuropäischer Frühkapitalismus," in: Deininger (ed.), *Das Reiche Augsburg*, 45–9.

18 Letter dated 23 July 1582 to Graf von Salm as cited in Leonhard Lenk, *Augsburger Bürgertum im Späthumanismus und Frühbarock (1580–1700)* (Augburg 1968), 15.

19 Hildebrandt, "The Effects of Empire," 62–4.

20 For references, see the bibliography in Thomas Max Safley (ed.), *The History of Bankruptcy: Economic, Social and Cultural Implications in Early Modern Europe* (London 2013).

21 Joseph A. Schumpeter, *Capitalism, Socialism and Democracy* (New York 1942), c. 7. Cf. Franklin Allen and Douglas Gale, *Understanding Financial Crises* (Oxford 2007); Walter Bagehot, *Lombard Street: A Description of the Money Market* (London 1873); Charles W. Calomiris and Stephen H. Haber, *Fragile by Design: The Political Origins of Banking Crises and Scarce Credit* (Princeton 2014); Douglas Diamond and Philip Dybvig, "Bank Runs, Deposit Insurance, and Liquidity," *Journal of Political Economy* 91 (1983); Charles P. Kindleberger and Robert Aliber, *Manias, Panics, and Crashes: A History of Financial Crises* (Basingstoke 2005); Gernot Kohler and Emilio José Chaves (eds.), *Globalization: Critical Perspectives* (New York); Hyman P. Minsky, *Stabilizing an Unstable Economy* (1986, 2008); Charles Mackay, *Extraordinary Popular Delusions and the Madness of Crowds* (1841); Didier Sornette, *Why Stock Markets Crash* (Princeton 2003); Joachim Vogt, "Fear, Folly, and Financial Crises – Some Policy Lessons from History," UBS Center Public Papers, Issue 2 (Zurich 2014).

22 StAA, Evangelisches Wesensarchiv, Lit. 155, Vol. I, Augsburger Zucht- und Polizeiordnung, 1537. Ainu Erbern Rats der Stat Augspurg Zucht und Pollicey Ordnung, 1537. See also Reichspolizeiordnung von 1548; Matthias Weber, *Die Reichspolizeiordnungen von 1530, 1548 und 1577: Historische Einführung und Edition* (Frankfurt Main 2002).

23 Axel Flessner, "Philosophies of Business Bankruptcy Law: An International Overview," in: Jacob S. Ziegel (ed.), *Current Developments in International and Corporate Insolvency Law* (Oxford 1994), 19–28.

24 Douglass C. North, *Understanding the Process of Economic Change* (Princeton 2005), 48. See also Lance E. Davis and Douglass C. North, *Institutional Change and American Economic Growth* (Cambridge, UK 1971); Douglass C. North and Robert P. Thomas, *The Rise of the Western World* (Cambridge, UK 1973); Douglass C. North, *Institutions, Institutional Change and Economic Performance* (Cambridge, UK 1990).

25 Katharina von Ciriachy-Wantrup, *Familien- und erbrechtiche Gestaltungen von Unternehmen der Renaissance: Eine Untersuchung der Augsburger Handelsgesellschaften zur frühen Neuzeit* (Berlin 2007).

26 Thomas Max Safley, "Business Failure and Civil Scandal in Early Modern Europe," *Business History Review* 83 (2009): 35–60.

27 North, *Understanding the Process of Economic Change*, 50.

28 Karl Polanyi, *The Great Transformation: The Political and Economic Origins of Our Time* (Boston 1944).

29 The most influential early histories of the family include the following: Otto Brunner, "Das 'ganze Haus' und alteuropäische 'Oekonomik'," in: Otto Brunner (ed.), *Neue Wege der Verfassungs- und Sozialgeschichte*, 2nd ed. (Göttingen 1968); Peter Laslett, *The World We Have Lost: England Before the Industrial Revolution*, 2nd ed. (New York 1971), 2; Frédéric Le Play, *Les ouvriers européens. Études sur les travaux, la vie domestique et la condition morale des populations ouvrières de l'Europe*, 6 vols. (Paris 1855–78); Wilhelm Riehl, *Die Naturgeschichte des Volkes als Grundlage einer deutschen Sozial-Politik*, 3rd ed., 3 vols. (Stuttgart 1855); Lawrence Stone, *The Family, Sex and Marriage in England, 1500–1800* (New York 1977). Their work has also proven to be an ideal type. See Thomas W. Robisheaux, *Rural Society and the Search for Order in Early Modern Germany* (Cambridge, UK 1989); David Warren Sabean, *Property, Production and Family in Neckarhausen, 1700–1870* (Cambridge, UK 1990).

30 Myriam Carlier and Tim Soens (eds.), *The Household in Late Medieval Cities: Italy and Northwestern Europe Compared* (Leuven 2001); Mary Carpenter Erler and Maryanne Kowaleski (eds.), *Women and Power in the Middle Ages* (Athens, GA 1988); Tine de Moor and Jan Luiten van Zanden (eds.), *Vrouwen en de geboorte van het kapitalisme in West-Europa* (Amsterdam 2006); Barbara Hanawalt, "Women and the Household Economy in the Preindustrial Period: An Assessment of Women, Work, and Family," *Journal of Women's History* 11 (1999): 10–16; Barbara Hanawalt, *The Wealth of Wives: Women, Law and Economy in Late Medieval London* (Oxford 2007); Martha C. Howell, *Women, Production and Patriarchy* (Chicago 1986); Martha C. Howell, *The Marriage Exchange: Property. Social Place, and Gender in Cities of the Low Countries, 1300–1550* (Chicago 1998); Martha C. Howell, *Commerce Before Capitalism in Europe, 1300–1600* (Cambridge, UK 2010); Alan Macfarlane, *Marriage and Love in England: Modes of Reproduction, 1300–1840* (Oxford 1986); Margret Wensky, *Die Stellung der Frau in der stadtkölnischen Wirtschaft im Spätmittelalter* (Cologne 1980); Heidi Wunder, *He Is the Sun, She Is the Moon: Women in Early Modern Germany* (Cambridge, MA 1998).

31 See, for example, Raimund Eirich, *Memmingens Wirtschaft und Patriziat von 1347 bis 1551: Eine wirtschafts- und sozialgeschichtliche Untersuchung über das Memminger Patriziat während der Zunftverfassung* (Weißenhorn 1971), passim.

32 Demographic studies have revealed that households and families changed size and shape in accordance with economic imperatives. See: David Herlihy and Christiane Klapisch-Zuber, *Tuscans and Their Families: A Study of the Florentine Catasto of 1427* (New Haven 1985); David Levine and Keith Wrightson, *The Making of an Industrial Society: Whickham, 1560–1765* (Oxford 1991); E. A. Wrigley and R. S. Schofield, *The Population History of England, 1541–1871: A Reconstruction* (London 1981); J. DuPaquier, et al. (eds.), *Marriage and Remarriage in Populations of the Past* (New York 1981); W. R. Lee, "Past Legacies and Future Prospects: Recent Research on the History of the Family in Germany," *Journal of Family History* 6 (1981): 156–76; Michael Mitterauer, "Zur Familienstruktur in ländlichen Gebieten Österreichs im 17. Jahrhundert," in: Heimo Helczmanovski (ed.), *Beiträge zur Bevölkerungs- und Sozialgeschichte* (Vienna 1973), 167–222; Michael Mitterauer and Reinhard Sauer, *The European Family: Patriarchy to Partnership from the Middle Ages to the Present* (Chicago 1982); Sabean, *Property, Production and Family in Neckarhausen, 1700–1870.* Material conditions also influenced the emotional life of families. See: Michael Anderson, *Approaches to the History of the Western Family, 1500–1914* (London 1980); Lutz Berkner, "The Stem Family and Developmental Cycle of the Household: An

Eighteenth-Century Austrian Example," *American Historical Review* 76 (1972): 398–418; Pierre Goubert, "Family and Province: A Contribution to the Knowledge of Family Structure in Early Modern France," *Journal of Family History* 2 (1977): 179–95. The particular role and status of women and children has likewise been subject to revision. See Susan Amussen, *An Ordered Society: Gender and Class in Early Modern England* (London 1988); Sarah Hanley, "Engendering the State: Family Formation and State Building in Early Modern France," *French Historical Studies* 16 (1989): 4–27; Christiane Klapisch-Zuber, *Women, Family and Ritual in Renaissance Italy* (Chicago 1985); Lyndal Roper, *The Holy Household: Women and Morals in Reformation Augsburg* (Oxford 1989); Thomas Kuehn, *Law, Family and Women: Toward a Legal Anthropology of Renaissance Italy* (Chicago 1991); Thomas Max Safley, *Let No Man Put Asunder: The Control of Marriage in the German Southwest, A Comparative Study, 1550–1610* (Kirksville, MO 1984).

33 David Landes, *Dynasties: Fortunes and Misfortunes of the World's Great Family Businesses* (New York 2006), 291.

34 Harold James, *Family Capitalism: Wendels, Haniels, Falcks, and the Continental European Model* (Cambridge, MA 2006), 2.

35 A recent museum exhibition displayed the riches of this genre produced by elite Augsburg families alone in the early modern period. The Bimmel, Fugger, Gossembrot, Herwart, Langenmantel, Linck, Peutinger, Pfister, Rehlinger, Sulzer, Von Stetten and Welser all immortalized and aggrandized themselves in this manner. See Christoph Emmendörffer and Helmut Zäh, *Bürgermacht und Bücherpracht: Augsburger Ehren- und Familienbücher der Renaissance* (Lucerne 2011).

36 Ibid, iv. Over the course of time, according to this genealogy, members of this lineage allegedly became cathedral canons and other ecclesiastical officials. During the thirteenth and fourteenth centuries, again allegedly, the family made the transition from the feudal countryside to a bourgeois urban setting, during which time and process "aristocratic and common Höchstetters lived side-by-side in Augsburg" ("*lebten [. . .] adelige und bürgerliche Hoechstetter in Augsburg nebeneinander*").

37 Ibid.

38 StAA, Steuerregister, 1403. Cited in Jacob Strieder, *Zur Genesis des modernen Kapitalismus: Forschungen zur Entstehung der großen bürgerlichen Kapitalvermögen am Ausgange des Mittelalter und zu Beginn der Neuzeit, zunächst in Augsburg*, 2nd ed. ([Munich 1935] New York 1968), 158–63, here 158. With reference to an unpublished, manuscript genealogy, he identifies this anonymous Höchstetter with "Sigfrid Höchstetter", that is, with the "Seyfried von Hoechstettern" of the genealogy. Strieder cites Möhner, *Genealogia Familiarum Patriciarum Augustanarum a Reginbaldo Moehnero conscripta*, located in the *Stadtarchiv Augsburg* at the time of his research. Ibid., 158, fn 1. See also Hoechstetter, *Stammtafel der Hoechstetter*, 2.

39 Strieder, *Zur Genesis des modernen Kapitalismus*, Table 46, 160–1. Reproduced in Klinkert, "Die Augsburger Handelsgesellschaft der Höchstetter," 18.

40 The city of Augsburg assessed taxes on the total of real and moveable property, the value of which can be calculated as the product of tax assessment and tax rate. Burgher provided self-assessments of their property. Tax officials applied two rates – 0.25 percent (0.0025) for real property and 0.50 percent (0.0050) for moveable property – but listed only a single, undifferentiated figure as the liability of a given taxpayer. In consequence, the result is a range rather than a specific value. See Claus-Peter Clasen, *Die Augsburger Steuerbücher um 1600* (Augsburg 1976), 77–9; Anton Mayr, *Die großen Augsburger Vermögen in der Zeit von 1618 bis 1717* (Augsburg 1931), 5–9.

41 For a discussion of preindustrial bleaching, see Thomas Max Safley, "Production, Transaction and Proletarianization: The Textile Industry of Upper Swabia, 1580–1660," in: Thomas Max Safley and Leonard N. Rosenband (eds.), *The Workplace Before the Factory: Artisans and Proletarians, 1500–1800* (Ithaca 1993), 118–45. See also Archibald Clow and Nan L. Clow, *The Chemical Revolution: A Contribution to Social Technology* (London 1952).

42 Cities assessed a tax (*Ungeld*) on every piece of textile destined for sale. The owner of the raw cloth, be he weaver or merchant, paid this tax directly to the bleacher, who collected and held these revenues until he submitted them to the city on one given day of the year. The owner of the cloth also paid a piece-rate to the bleacher as a fee for bleaching services. Claus-Peter Clasen, *Die Augsburger Weber: Leistungen und Krisen des Textilgewerbes um 1600* (Augsburg 1981), 409.

43 "Vom Kunolt. Item Heinr Perchinger – Hoechstetter sartor – ain pfleg Hz Hoechstetter." Stadtarchiv Augsburg, Steuerregister, 1407, fol. 11c; "Item: Hoechstetter sartor dat iii gulden x sh." StAA, Steuerregister, 1409, fol. 12d. Cited in Klinkert, Die Augsburger Handelsgesellschaft der Höchstetter; Strieder, *Zur Genesis des modernen Kapitalismus*, 159, n. 2. The family genealogy names him Ulrich IV, assuming common descent from earlier Hoechstetters of that name and ignoring the fact that neither that lineage nor Seyfried's paternity can be established clearly. See Höchstetter, *Stammtafel der Höchstetter*, 2.

44 See, among others, Friedrich Keutgen, "Der Großhandel im Mittelalter," *Hansische Geschichtsblätter* 34 (1901): 67–138, esp. 94ff.

45 Strieder, *Zur Genesis des modernen Kapitalismus*, 159.

46 StAA, Steuerregister, 1408, 1441. Cited in Strieder, *Zur Genesis des modernen Kapitalismus*, 161.

47 Strieder calculates his wealth as of 1467 in the range of 4,800–9,600 fl. See Strieder, *Zur Genesis des modernen Kapitalismus*, 15. Also cited in Kern, *Studien zur Geschichte des Augsburger Kaufmannshauses der Höchstetter*, 4.

48 Strieder, *Zur Genesis des modernen Kapitalismus*, 160–1.

49 The family genealogy refers to him as Georg III, following Georg I, ostensibly a brother of the aforementioned Seyfried, and Georg II, a brother of Ulrich II who died in infancy. See Hoechstetter, *Stammtafel der Hoechstetter*, 2.

50 Strieder calculates their wealth in the range of 16,365–32,730 fl and 10,365–20,730 fl respectively. See Strieder, *Zur Genesis des modernen Kapitalismus*, 17.

51 The eldest, Ulrich III (1450–1527), pursued an ecclesiastical career, earning a doctorate in Roman law, becoming the prior of the Collegiate Church of St. Johann in Freising and a canon of the Cathedral of Sts. Mary and Corbinian of Freising, where he lies buried. His younger brother, also named Ulrich, Ulrich IV (1462–1527), followed him as a member of the Cathedral Chapter in Freising. There is also a reference to an Ulrich V, who died in infancy around 1466. The repeated use of the father's name is interesting and unusual. Could it be that the choice of religious careers raised the need to preserve a traditional name in the secular engagements of the family? Cf. Hoechstetter, *Stammtafel der Hoechstetter*, 2–4.

52 Strieder, *Zur Genesis des modernen Kapitalismus*, 159.

53 Hoechstetter, *Stammtafel der Hoechstetter*, 2.

54 Strieder, *Zur Genesis des modernen Kapitalismus*, 161.

55 Hoechstetter, *Stammtafel der Hoechstetter*, 2.

56 Geffcken, "Soziale Schichtung in Augsburg 1396–1521," 140, 198, 205, Anh. 6–214, 231–3; Mayr, *Die großen Augsburger Vermögen*, 28–31; Reinhard Hildebrand, *Quellen und Regesten zu den Augsburger Handelshäusern Pahler und Rehlinger 1539–1642* (1996); Reinhard, *Augsburger Eliten des 16. Jahrhunderts*, 652–72; Franz Josef Schöningh, *Die Rehlinger von Augsburg* (Paderborn 1927); Jacob Strieder, *Zur Genesis des modernen Kapitalismus*, 53 ff.

57 Cf. Klinkert, *Die Augsburger Handelsgesellschaft der Höchstetter.*

58 Here, too, the literature is vast. See, among many possible examples: Anna Bellavitis, *Identité, marriage, mobilité sociale: Citoyennes et citoyes à Venisa au XVIe siècle* (Rome 2001); Lilly Braun, *Die Frauenfrage: ihre geschichtliche Entwicklung und wirtschaftliche Seite* (Leipzig 1901); Karl Bücher, *Die Frauenfrage im Mittelalter*, 2nd ed. (Tubingen 1910); Alice Clark, *The Working Life of Women in the Seventeenth Century* (London 1919); Edith Ennen, "Die Frau in der mittelalterlichen Stadtgesellschaft Mitteleuropas," *Hansische Geschichtsblätter*

98 (1980); Edith Ennen, *Frauen im Mittelalter* (Munich 1984); Jean-Louis Flandrin, *Families in Former Times: Kinship, Household and Sexuality* (Cambridge, UK 1979); Richard Goldthwaite, *Private Wealth in Renaissance Florence* (Princeton 1968); Jacques Heers, *Family Clans in the Middle Ages* (Amsterdam 1977); David Herlihy and Christiane Klapisch-Zuber, *Les Toscans et leurs Familles: une étude du "catasto" florentin de 1427* (Paris 1978); Howell, *The Marriage Exchange*; Julius Kirschner and Anthony Molho, "The Dowry Fund and the Marriage Market in Early *Quattrocento* Florence," *Journal of Modern History* 50 (1978); Bruno Kuske, "Die Frau im mittelalterlichen Wirtschaftsleben," *Zeitschrift für handelwissenschaftliche Forschung* 11 (1959); Peter Laslett and Richard Wall (eds.), *Household and Family in Past Time* (Cambridge, UK 1972); Claude Meillassoux, *Femmes, greniers et capitaux* (Paris 1975); Michael Mitterauer and Reinhard Sieder, *The European Family: Patriarchy to Partnership from the Middle Ages to the Present* (Oxford 1982); David Nicholas, *The Domestic Life of a Medieval City: Women, Children and the Family in Fourteenth-Century Ghent* (Lincoln, NE 1985); Eileen Power, *Medieval Women* (Cambridge, UK 1975); Gertrud Schmidt, *Die Berufstätigkeit der Frau in der Reichsstadt Nürnberg bis zum Ende des 16. Jahrhunderts* (Erlangen 1950); Stone, *The Family, Sex and Marriage in England, 1500–1800*; Louise Tilly and Joan Scott, *Women, Work and Family* (New York 1978); Richard Vann, "Women in Preindustrial Capitalism," in: Renate Bridenthal and Claudia Koonz (eds.), *Becoming Visible: Women in European History* (Boston 1977); Thilo Vogelsang, *Die Frau als Herrscherin im hohen Mittelalter* (Göttingen 1954); Helmut Wachendorf, *Die wirtschaftliche Stellung der Frau in den deutschen Städten des späteren Mittelalters* (Quakenbrück 1934); Wensky, *Die Stellung der Frau in der stadtkölnischen Wirtschaft im Spätmittelalter*.

59 See, for example, Franco Angiolini and Daniel Roche (eds.), *Cultures et formations négociantes dans l'Europe moderne* (Paris 1995); Natacha Coquery, et al., (eds.), *Ecrire, compter, mesurer. Vers une histoire des rationalités pratiques* (Paris 2006); Gunnar Dahl, *Trade, Trust, and Networks: Commercial Culture in Late Medieval Italy* (Lund 1998); Martin Fiedler, "Vertrauen ist gut, Kontrolle ist teuer: Vertrauen als Schlüsselkategorie wirtschaftlichen Handelns," *Geschichte und Gesellschaft* 27 (2001): 576–92; Ute Frevert (ed.), *Vertrauen: Historische Annäherungen* (Göttingen 2003); Häberlein, *Brüder, Freunde und Betrüger*; Wolfgang Kaiser and Biagio Salvemini (eds.), "Informazione e scelte economiche," *Quaderni storici* 42 (2007); Paola Lanaro (ed.), *La pratica dello scambio. Sistemi di fiere, mercanti e città* (Venice 2003); Craig Muldrew, *The Economy of Obligation: The Culture of Credit and Social Relations in Early Modern England* (New York 1998); James Murray, "Of Nodes and Networks: Bruges and the Infrastructure of Trade in the Fourteenth Century," in: Peter Stabel, Bruno Blondé and Anke Greve (eds.), *International Trade in the Low Countries (14th-16th Centuries)* (Leuven 2000); Katia Occhi, *Boschi e mercanti. Traffici di legname tra la contea di Tirolo e la Repubblica di Venezia (secoli XVI-XVII)* (Bologna 2006); Walter W. Powell, "Neither Market nor Hierarchy: Network Forms of Organization," *Research in Organizational Behavior* 12 (1990); Margrit Schulte Beerbühl, et al. (eds.), *Spinning the Commercial Web. International Trade, Merchants, and Commercial Cities, c. 1640–1939* (Frankfurt Main 2004); Francesca Trivellato, *The Familiarity of Strangers: The Sephardic Diaspora, Livorno, and Cross-Cultural Trade in the Early Modern Period* (New Haven 2009).

60 The term itself is by no means new. "Embeddedness" was first coined by Karl Polanyi to describe the inseparability of economic from political and religious life in a precapitalistic age. See: Polanyi, *The Great Transformation*, passim. Economic life is "embedded" in social relations, although Richard Swedburg and Mark Granovetter, among others, have argued the notion elegantly and compellingly over the last 25 years, and a host of empirical studies of a variety of socioeconomic issues have substantiated it. See: Mark Granovetter and Richard Swedburg (eds.), *The Sociology of Economic Life*, 2nd ed. (Boulder, CO 2001); Neil Smelser and Richard Swedburg (eds.), *The Handbook of Economic Sociology* (New York 1994); Arthur Stinchcombe, *Economic Sociology* (New York 1983); Richard Swedburg, "Economic Sociology: Past and Present," *Current Sociology* 35 (1987): 1–22; Richard Swedburg, "Major Traditions in Economic Sociology,"

Annual Review of Sociology 17 (1991): 251–76; Richard Swedburg, "New Economic Sociology: What Has Been Accomplished? What Is Ahead?" *Acta Sociologica* 40 (1997): 161–82; Harrison White, "Where do Markets Come from," *American Journal of Sociology* 87 (1981): 517–47; Harrison White, *Identity and Control: A Structural Theory of Action* (Princeton 1992).

61 The insights of these works are certainly valuable, although the realization that economic relations are also social relations – that social connections provide a basis for and fundamentally influence economic interactions – is actually an axiom of economic theory that can be traced back to Adam Smith, if not earlier, even if modern econometrics seems but recently to have rediscovered the fact. See Adam Smith, *An Inquiry into the Nature and Causes of the Wealth of Nations,* edited with an introduction and notes by Edward Cannan ([London 1776] New York 1994), passim..

62 Sender, *Die Chronik*, 220.

63 The bibliography on this topic is truly vast, stretching from early business manuals that began to circulate in manuscript and print form in the fifteenth century to modern works of scholarship, including the present volume. For specific references, see n. 32–35 on pp 95–96 in Chapter 2 as well as the bibliography.

64 Ehrenberg, *Das Zeitalter der Fugger*, passim.

65 Reinhard Hildebrandt, "Augsburger und Nürnberger Kupferhandel, 1570–1580: Produktion, Marktanteile und Finanzierung im Vergleich zweier Sädte und ihrer wirtschaftlichen Führungsschicht," in: Hermann Kellenbenz (ed.), *Schwerpunkte der Kupferproduktion und des Kupferhandels in Europa, 1500–1650* (Cologne 1977), 190–224, here 216. See also Gerhard Seibold, *Die Manlich: Geschichte einer Augsburger Kaufmannsfamilie* (Sigmaringen 1995).

66 Max Weber, *Die protestantische Ethik und der "Geist" des Kapitalismus*, reprint 1904/05 ed. (Weinheim 1996), 19.

67 David Landes, *The Unbound Prometheus: Technological Change and Industrial Development in Western Europe from 1750 to the Present* (Cambridge, UK 1969), esp. 124–92.

68 Cf. Thomas Max Safley, *Charity and Economy in the Orphanages of Early Modern Augsburg* (Leiden 1996), 12 and passim.

69 Sender, *Die Chronik*, 219–20.

70 William J. Baumol, "Preface," in: David S. Landes, Joel Mokyr and William J. Baumol (eds.), *The Invention of Enterprise: Entrepreneurship from Ancient Mesopotamia to Modern Times* (Princeton 2010), IX–XIV, here X.

71 James M. Murray, "Entrepreneurs and Entrepreneurship in Medieval Europe," in: Landes, Mokyr and Baumol (eds.), *The Invention of Enterprise*, 88–106, here 104; James Munro, "Tawney's Century, 1540–1640: The Roots of Modern Capitalist Entrepreneurship," in: Landes, Mokyr and Baumol (eds.), *The Invention of Enterprise*, 107–55, here 110.

72 Grimm lists only "capitalist", equating it with a rentier and crediting Gotthold Ephraim Lessing with its first use in the eighteenth century. See "Capital," *Deutsches Wörterbuch von Jacob und Wilhelm Grimm*, 16 Bde. in 32 Teilbänden (Leipzig 1854–1961, Quellenverzeichnis Leipzig 1971), Bd. 2, Sp. 605–6. Online-Version vom 18 November 2018. Available at: www.woerterbuchnetz.de/DWB?lemma=capitalist.

73 "capitalism, n.2." OED Online, July 2018. Oxford University Press. Available at: http://proxy.library.upenn.edu:2817/view/Entry/27454?rskey=6u4i6B&result=7 (accessed 27 November 2018). William Makepeace Thackeray, *The Newcomes: Memoirs of a Most Respectable Family* (London 1854).

74 Louis Blanc, *Organisation du Travail* (Paris 1850); Pierre-Joseph Proudhon, *Système des contradictions économiques ou Philosophie de la misère* (Paris 1846). See also R. M. Hartwell and Stanley L. Engerman, "Capitalism," in: *The Oxford Encyclopedia of Economic History* (Oxford 2003). Available at: http://proxy.library.upenn.edu:2400/view/10.1093/acref/9780195105070.001.0001/acref-9780195105070-e-0104.

75 "capital, adj. and n.2." OED Online, July 2018. Oxford University Press. Available at: http://proxy.library.upenn.edu:2817/view/Entry/27450?rskey=fwAtBq&result=2 (accessed 27 November 2018).

76 "capitalist, n. and adj." OED Online, July 2018. Oxford University Press. Available at: http://proxy.library.upenn.edu:2817/view/Entry/27455?redirectedFrom=capitalist (accessed 27 November 2018).
77 Arthur Young, *Travels, During the Years 1787, 1788, and 1789. Undertaken More Particularly with a View of Ascertaining the Cultivation, Wealth, Resources, and National Prosperity, of the Kingdom of France* (London 1792); David Ricardo, *On the Principles of Political Economy, and Taxation* (London 1816).
78 Werner Sombart, "Capitalism," in: *Encyclopedia of the Social Sciences*, vol. 3 (New York 1930), 195–208, here 195. Cited by R. M. Hartwell and Stanley L. Engerman, "Capitalism," in: *The Oxford Encyclopedia of Economic History*.
79 Joseph A. Schumpeter, *History of Economic Analysis* (New York 1954), 552, fn 15.
80 Aristotle, *Politics*, Bk 1, chapter 9.
81 See Josef Höffner, *Wirtschaftsethik und Monopole im 15. und 16. Jahrhundert* (Darmstadt 1969); Bernd Mertens, *Im Kampf gegen die Monopole: Reichstagsverhandlungen und Monopolprozesse im frühen 16. Jahrhundert* (Tubingen 1996).
82 See also Jacques Le Goff, *La bourse et la vie: économie et religion au Moyen Age* (Hachette 1986); Abert O. Hirschman, *The Passions and the Interests: Political Arguments for Capitalism Before Its Triumph* (Princeton 1977); Istvan Hunt and Michael Ignatieff (eds.), *Wealth and Virtue: The Shaping of Political Economy in the Scottish Enlightenment* (Cambridge, MA 1983); J. G. A. Pocock, *Virtue, Commerce, and History: Essays on Political Thought and History, Chiefly in the Eighteenth Century* (Cambridge, MA 1985).
83 Cf. Polanyi, *The Great Transformation*, passim; Richard Tawney, *Religion and the Rise of Capitalism* ([London 1926] London 2006); Edward P. Thompson, *The Making of the English Working Class* (New York 1966); Thorsten Veblen, *The Theory of the Leisure Class* (New York 1899).
84 Richard Sennett, "The New Capitalism," *Social Research* 64 (1997): 161–80, here 179. See also Richard Sennett, *The Culture of the New Capitalism* (New Haven 2006).
85 Thomas Piketty, *Capital in the Twenty-First Century*, translated by Arthur Goldhammer (Cambridge, MA 2017).
86 Kevin Doogan, *New Capitalism? The Transformation of Work* (Cambridge, UK 2009).
87 Laurence Fontaine, *Le Marché. Histoire et usages d'une conquête sociale* (Paris 2014); Jürgen Kocka, *Geschichte des Kapitalismus* (Munich 2013).
88 Edward E. Baptist, *The Half Has Never Been Told: Slavery and the Making of American Capitalism* (New York 2014); Sven Beckert, *Empire of Cotton: A Global History* (New York 2014); Seth Rockman, *Scraping by: Wage Labor, Slavery and Survival in Early Baltimore* (Baltimore 2009). Cf. Eric Williams, *Capitalism and Slavery* (Chapel Hill, NC 1944). Respectively, see also, Gene Dattel, *Cotton and Race in the Making of America: The Human Costs of Economic Power* (Chicago 2009); Giorgio Riello, *Cotton: The Fabric That Made the Modern World* (Cambridge, UK 2013).
89 Smith, *The Wealth of Nations*; John Stuart Mill, *The Principles of Political Economy: With Some of Their Applications to Social Philosophy* (London 1848).
90 The "methods controversy" (*Methodenstreit*) began with exchanges between Carl Menger, who represented the Austrian School, and Gustav von Schmoller, who formulated the German School's initial response. See Carl Menger, *Grundsätze der Volkswirtschaftslehre* ([Vienna 1871] Aalen 1968); Carl Menger, *Untersuchungen über die Methode der Sozialwissenschaften und der politischen Ökonomie insbesondere*, edited by Friedrich August von Hayek ([Vienna 1883] Tubingen 1969); Gustav von Schmoller, *Grundriss der allgemeinen Volkswirtschaftslehre* (Leipzig 1900–1904).
91 Karl Marx, *Capital: A Critique of Political Economy*, vol. I, 3 vols. (New York 1992/1993), esp. chapters 26, 32–3. This is far from a settled notion, as demonstrated by the so-called Brenner Debates of the 1970s and 1980s that swirled around the question whether rural class development or demographic change in late medieval England transformed land tenures and created rural capitalism. See Robert Brenner, "Agrarian Class Structure and Economic Development in Pre-Industrial Europe," *Past & Present* 70 (1976): 30–75;

Trevor Aston and C. H. E. Philpin, *The Brenner Debate: Agrarian Class Structure and Economic Development in Pre-Industrial Europe* (Cambridge, UK 1985).

92 Henri Pirenne, *Medieval Cities* (Princeton 1952); Henri Sée, *Modern Capitalism: Its Origins and Evolution* (New York 1968).

93 Among the most recent studies, see Robert Duplessis, *Transitions to Capitalism in Early Modern Europe* (Cambridge, UK 1997); Fontaine, *Le marché*; Kocka, *Geschichte des Kapitalismus*. Each echoes in its own way, Duplessis's notion of the nonlinear development of multiple capitalisms, each dependent upon local specificities of land tenure, commercial development and state policy, but all return to the basic state-theory of capitalist development.

94 Some scholars see mercantilism as a special type, the earliest stage, of capitalism. Most of the elements existed, if to a limited degree, and the sum of their interactions tended in the right direction. Others reject that position. Ironically, they draw support for their arguments from the abstract theories of economists, on the one hand, and upon the work of various Marxist-inspired historians, on the other. The former group includes neoclassical economists who insist upon the dominance of, indeed the exclusive reliance upon, an *a priori* set of characteristics – again, private ownership, market allocation and, in some instances, legal and/or ideological institutions – before the term can be correctly applied. Duplessis stands as an example. The latter group may be fairly represented by Karl Polanyi's *The Great Transformation*, which argued that "mercantilism, with all its tendencies toward commercialization, never attacked the safeguards which protected [the] two basic elements of production – labor and land – from becoming the elements of commerce". In other words, it never developed the signal characteristics of capitalism, markets for the "fictitious commodities" of land, labor and money.

95 Ibid., 20.

96 For Howell, early merchants failed to grasp or treat status-laden resources, such as land or titles, as "fungible." See Howell, *Commerce Before Capitalism in Europe, 1300–1600*. Her argument is, in fact, nothing more than the newest recrudescence of an old debate concerning the substantial differences between premodern and modern merchants and entrepreneurs, the assumption being that the earlier version had, somehow, to be different. Cf. Ashton and Philpin (eds.), *The Brenner Debate*; Fernand Braudel, *The Wheels of Commerce, Vol. II, Civilization and Capitalism* (London 1982); Richard H. Britnell, *The Commercialization of English Society, 1000–1500* (Cambridge, UK 1993); Carlo Cipolla, *Before the Industrial Revolution* (New York 1976); Maurice Dobb, *Studies in the Development of Capitalism* (New York 1946); Duplessis, *Transitions to Capitalism in Early Modern Europe*; Jean Favier, *Gold and Spices: The Rise of Commerce in the Middle Ages* (New York 1998); Peter Kreidte, *Peasants, Landlords and Merchant Capitalists* (Cambridge, MA 1983); Harry Miskimin, *The Economy of Early Renaissance Europe, 1300–1460* (Cambridge, MA 1975); Harry Miskimin, *The Economy of Late Renaissance Europe, 1400–1600* (Cambridge, MA 1977); Henri Pirenne, *Mohammed and Charlemagne* (London 1939); Henri Pirenne, *Histoire économique de l'occident medieval*, edited by Emile Coornaert (Bruges 1951); M. M. Postan, et al. (eds.), *The Cambridge Economic History of Europe, Vol. II, Trade and Industry in the Middle Ages* (Cambridge, UK 1987); M. M. Postan, et al., *The Cambridge Economic History of Europe, Vol. III, Economic Organization and Policies in the Middle Ages* (Cambridge, UK 1965); Marten Roy Prak (ed.), *Early Modern Capitalism: Economic and Social Change in Europe, 1400–1800* (London 2000); Paul Sweezy, et al., *The Transition from Feudalism to Capitalism* (London 1978); Richard W. Unger, "Thresholds for Market Integration in the Low Countries and England in the Fifteenth Century," in: Lawrin Amstrong, et al. (eds.), *Money, Markets and Trade* (Boston 2007); Hermann Van der Wee, *The Growth of the Antwerp Market and the European Economy* (The Hague 1963).

97 Joseph A. Schumpeter, *Essays on Entrepreneurship, Innovation, Business Cycles, and the Evolution of Capitalism* (London 2000), 189.

98 Joseph A. Schumpeter, *The Theory of Economic Development* (Cambridge, MA 1934), passim; Joseph A. Schumpeter, *Business Cycles: A Theoretical, Historical and Statistical Analysis of the Capitalist Process*, 2 vols. (New York 1939), passim.
99 Schumpeter, *Capitalism, Socialism and Democracy*, 83.

1 Family firms considered

"Ambrosius and Hans, the Brothers Höchstetter and Associates"

On 1 January 1524, various relatives and friends of the Höchstetter family gathered in Augsburg to found a mercantile company. It was a matter of some consequence: They were successful merchant-financiers; they were members of an elite corporation, the Patrons of Society (*Mehrer der Gesellschaft*);[1] they had substantial financial interests at stake. Accordingly, they formalized the event and their intentions in a charter.

> We, the following named Ambrosius and Hans Höchstetter, brothers, burghers of Augsburg, Hans Ungelter the Younger, Hans Frannz Bongarttner, Ambrosi Höchstetter the Younger, Joseph Höchstetter, Joachim Höchstetter, our son, son-in-law and brother-in-law, who have been by and with one another in company since the first day of January of the year [15]20 until the first day of January of the year [15]24 according to the form and content of the same agreement, which was created according to that same agreement. And having performed and closed our entire general accounting on the first day of January of the year [15]24, we the aforementioned persons have been well satisfied and content. [. . .] And in so far as we, in friendly, brotherly and fatherly affection have decided and planned to keep a brotherhood and business with one another [. . .], so have we the hereafter named persons and above all our dear Lord God for us, all our heirs and descendants together and jointly united and agreed as follows.[2]

The partners had been in business together since 1520. Having settled accounts, they now emphasized their kinship to one another, their affection for one another and their satisfaction with one another. Accordingly, they wished to renew their joint efforts in the form of "a brotherhood and business" (*ein gepruederschafft unnd handtierung*) for eight more years, until 1532.[3] Thus was founded the family firm, "Ambrosius and Hans, the Brothers Höchstetter and Associates".

But, why a "brotherhood"? The term appears seldom in the extant business charters of the age. The Höchstetter charter of 1515 makes no reference to it at all.[4] The partners at that time claimed nothing more than satisfaction with one another. The term's distinctiveness should not be over-emphasized, however: In

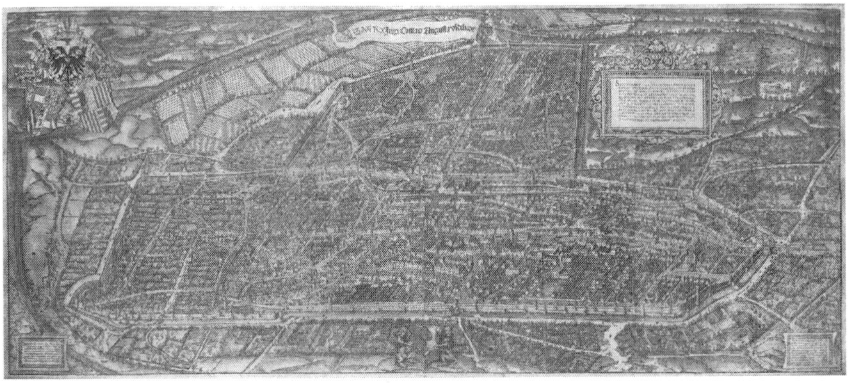

Figure 3 Seld Plan of Augsburg, 1521

medieval Venice, a common form of business organization for long-distance, overland trade was known as a *fraternal compagnia*.[5] "Brotherhood" evokes that common, medieval sense of a community of "equally entitled and equally responsible" partners, a *Genossenschaft*, as Clemens Bauer once described it.[6]

The resort to "brotherhood" in 1524 seems nonetheless an unusual departure. Applied to a family firm, it raises fundamental questions about organization, capitalization and administration. Generally speaking, family ownership and control characterize the family firm, suggesting a vertical rather than horizontal organization, with family employees privileged above outsiders. Its management is usually described as personal, even autocratic. Cooperative relations are based on identity rather than reciprocity; human and material resources are closely held and controlled. "Brotherhood" not only contradicts basic theoretical assumptions, but also obscures the real, historical structure and function of family firms.

The Höchstetters' charters offer an opportunity to reconsider the theory and its limits. They reveal some of the structures and mechanisms by which the family and its firm rose and fell. They help to map the terrain between opportuneness and opportunism in family life. They reveal, finally, that "familial" relations, whether limited to the firm members, extended to an entire family group or broadened to include outsiders, might offer intimacy and proximity, but they did not guarantee stability or certainty. For the Höchstetters, "brotherhood" was a rhetorical device. They understood that families and their firms were not necessarily brotherly.

* * *

The emphasis on partnership as a form of "brotherhood" reaches back to the early history of the merchant house of Höchstetter. When the founder, Ulrich II, died in 1497, his sons Georg I and Ambrosius I assumed control of the family firm. On 1 April 1514, "Georg and Ambrosius, the Brothers Höchstetter" ceased operations.[7] Though this firm's charter no longer exists, the common business practices of that age permit a reconstruction of what probably transpired at that point. Having concluded business together, the partners completed a final accounting and distributed profits or losses according to the proportion of their investments.[8] This permitted them to establish the degree to which their partnership had succeeded. It also permitted them to recruit new partners – and new capital – without a complicated redistribution of shares. It required, however, that the agreement among all parties that the accounting was correct.

In this case, however, Bartholomäus III Rem, who was both stakeholder and bookkeeper in the firm, challenged the final account, the claims made in the 1515 charter to being "completely and fully satisfied" notwithstanding. The legal difficulties that followed exposed the firm's business practices and drained its operating capital. They forced the named partners to reconsider their relations among themselves and the structure of their firm.

The contemporary Augsburg chronicler and Benedictine monk, Clemens Sender, again provides a lively account.[9] According to his 1520 entry, Rem had invested 900 fl "at profit and loss" (*zu gewinn und verlust*) in the company. Separate documents allege that the Höchstetters owed Rem not only invested capital of 500 fl and earned profits of 130 fl, but also a share of 149,770 marks (roughly 150 tons) of silver, "*schwarzer Brand*", and 52,915 hundredweight (roughly 120 tons) of copper.[10] According to Rem himself, as reported by Sender, this amounted to an extraordinary 33,000 fl. Ambrosius responded that Rem's capital had earned no more than 26,000 fl and offered him a payment of 2,000 fl for living expenses.

Rem refused this settlement and lodged a legal complaint against his former employer with the Imperial authorities. He found considerable support among the nobility, because he "showed them what extraordinary profits the merchants earned in so short a time, whereupon they rejoiced and said the merchants' profits exceed the Jews' usury sevenfold".[11] Rem also sued Höchstetter before the bailiff (*Stadtvogt*) of Augsburg, winning judgments that Sender attributed to "a clever, silver-tongued lawyer from Leipzig, who pled his case ably".[12] Meanwhile, the City Council appointed mediators, by whose judgment all parties agreed to abide. They decided that Höchstetter must pay Rem 28,000 fl in addition to 2,000 fl for the expense of his housekeeping, a total judgment of 30,000 fl. Höchstetter accepted the settlement, but Rem refused it. To prevent the City Council imprisoning him for violation of his oath, he sought and received sanctuary in the Benedictine Abbey of Sts. Ulrich and Afra, where he remained for 12 days. Sender admits: "There I often heard from him how it had gone, how the Höchstetters became so rich in such a short time".[13]

Rather than risk prison in Augsburg, Rem fled to Spain and took refuge at the court of Emperor Charles V, whom he accompanied to his coronation in Aachen and further to the *Reichstag* at Worms in 1521. While there, Rem organized an armed attack on the Höchstetters, attempting to seize two wagon-loads of their commercial wares. Because Rem had violated his oath in Augsburg and acted lawlessly while under Imperial protection, the Imperial fiscal ordered his arrest. Rem was imprisoned for more than a year in Worms and later transferred to Augsburg, where he died in 1525, still insisting on payment of 33,000 fl instead of 30,000 fl.[14]

The conflict was finally settled while Rem lay in prison.[15] An Imperial commission, headed by Jacob II ("the Rich") Fugger, one of the Höchstetters' chief business competitors, reached a decision on 21 March 1522 that the Höchstetters would pay Rem 24,500 *Goldgulden*. Ambrosius I and Hans Rem signed and sealed the agreement, but that was by no means the end. The conflict and settlement had an enduring impact on the Höchstetters' companies, if not their fortunes. They suffered a massive loss of capital, and their reputation was likewise damaged. Sender's chronicle demonstrates that the details of the settlement quickly became common knowledge. His narrative of the conflict, using information about their business practices probably divulged by Rem, combined with his discussion of the bankruptcy set them among the most notorious monopolists of their day and blackened their name over centuries. Their charters of 1515 and 1524 can be read as attempts to limit such conflicts in the future.

Rem's vehement contention that he had been cheated of his fair share may well have put before the other partners the potential advantages of family firms. He may have been a distant relation by marriage to Georg I and Ambrosius, whose sister Ursula was the wife of one Gilg Rem,[16] but his clash with Ambrosius demonstrated the real costs that could arise when familial solidarity did not exist. Family firms could, as Lutz recognized, expand human and financial capital by combining the resources of the members, reduce principal-agent problems by resort to patriarchal authority and familial loyalty and lower transaction costs by combining or over-layering kinship and business relations.[17] By appealing to the notion of a brotherhood, the Höchstetter partners not only set an ideal for their business relations, a moral constaint to open conflict, but they also underwrote it with an explicit reference to family relationships.

* * *

Historical studies overwhelmingly express the conviction that the family was a unit, bound together by a common purpose, and that the household and its enterprise, whether a farm, a workshop or a firm, were substantially identical and usually stable.[18] By extension, the family firm is assumed to draw advantage from this solidarity. In his study of the organization of South German mercantile companies, for example, Elmar Lutz noted, "[t]he three principal considerations in founding a company were [. . .] the unification or concentration on the basis of work, the merger of capital and the solidarity of the family".[19] As these companies were founded to overcome the barriers to impersonal exchange, that is, trade in distant markets with unknown parties, they required trustworthy employees, large amounts of start-up capital and loyalty or obedience to the partners.[20] In these uncertain matters – personnel, capital, constancy – trust is thought to have provided the essential basis of any cooperation. And, as Lutz romantically concluded, "It is almost unnecessary to mention that this basis in trust was most easily achieved from within the family circle".[21] A spatial, personal, financial, legal and moral identity supposedly existed between household and business that was seldom exposed to change before the modern age.[22]

Among the economic conditions thought to have transformed the monolith of family and firm, historians point to the resort to wage labor outside the household as having had the greatest impact, opening possibilities for gainful employment that worked a sea-change on familial relationships and household structures.[23] Supposedly, it signaled for many families the beginning of the end of their existence as cohesive economic units, because members were able to earn independent livings. Supposedly, it signaled also the gradual displacement of the family firm, in which a single family provides the majority of working capital and family members control governance and management, by the managerial firm, which draws capital from a broader base and places management in the hands of outside professionals, because the increasing complexity of business in a rapidly expanding and intensifying economic environment made professional management essential.[24] Until that point in time, however, the family remained a unit, led by a single authority and joined in a shared enterprise.

Such stage theories do not apply universally, however. The close identification of family and firm, household and enterprise demands rethinking. Certainly, family members could work together in a common enterprise, contributing their capital and labor as well as submitting to direction. But that work was not always cooperative. Leaving the historical evidence aside, a broader familiarity with classic literary treatments of family life would lead to the conclusion that families are as much susceptible to conflict as to cooperation.[25]

The 1515 dispute that rent and nearly wrecked the Höchstetter firm suggests as much. In fact, conflicts among family members or among members and stakeholders are a commonplace of family firms.[26] Modern studies have taken up this susceptibility to discord, which appears to arise from a structural characteristic: Despite the nomenclature, "family firm", the family may not overlap perfectly with the ownership or the management of the firm.[27] Family businesses can be particularly prone to conflict, therefore, when the interests of one or more members of a family do not align with those of its firm's ownership or management, for example, when an unqualified family member wishes to manage the firm, when a member of a family needs its firm to distribute capital for lifecycle events, when a family member wishes to withdraw her or his capital from the firm, or when managers of the firm make impossible demands upon members of the family, such as demanding inordinately high compensation or engaging in unusually risky ventures. The emotional ties among relatives may also lead to sharp divisions among family members and firm stakeholders. The affection and solidarity that sometimes exists among family members may strengthen trust and cooperation,[28] but it may also give firm managers a positive reason to engage in opportunism or free-riding. It may decrease their propensity to discipline and control their relatives in the firm or increase their willingness to reward them inappropriately, behaviors that scholars describe in terms of "altruism".[29] The affection and solidarity that can exist among relatives by blood or marriage may also underwrite "dynastic motives" that many scholars believe to be central to family firms, a means of explaining their other, supposedly common characteristics, such as an autocratic, personal style of management, a tendency toward longevity and conservatism and a high instance of failure through some form of liquidation.[30] Family firms, saddled with altruistic practices and motivated by dynastic considerations, emerge from all these studies as both fragile and irrational. They seldom escape "the Buddenbrooks syndrome", that is, survive beyond the third generation.[31] Or so it is supposed.

Certainly, the Höchstetters and their peers appear to fit the model. Through their charters they created family firms in the formal sense of ownership and management dominated by family members. Yet, these charters also indicate that family firms altered their leadership and expanded their capitalization in response to changing circumstances, recruited external resources as necessity – and opportunity – dictated and demonstrated a variety of trajectories. The Höchstetters remind us that families and firms are not monolithic unities, but complex, mutable entities, artefacts far removed from ideal types.

★ ★ ★

Early charters that established family firms in South German cities reflect a continued reliance on familial ideologies and structures in an age when the changing circumstances of economic life supposedly encouraged merchant-financiers to experiment with the organization of the firm.[32] The risks and costs of long-distance and overseas trade in a globalizing economy resulted not in the abandonment of the family firm but in the creation of larger, some would argue more suitable, business forms that could command greater human and capital resources. As larger companies became more common in the course of the fifteenth century, that is, as the number of partners grew to include persons from outside the most immediate family circle, the necessary degree of trust and cooperation could no longer be assumed.[33]

Certain commercial centers, such as Nuremberg[34] and Frankfurt[35] during the fifteenth and sixteenth centuries, began slowly to develop statutory laws to govern company charters, a legal process that reflected the gradual economic and structural loosening of the firm from its strict connection to the family. In Augsburg, by contrast, the essential connection between firm and family remained in place.[36] The city lacked specific legal parameters for the creation of mercantile companies, relying instead on its *Stadtbuch* of 1276, which remained the often amended and extended fundament of the city's legal practice throughout the early modern period.[37] The city's merchants depended on the existing *ius commune* as it applied to contract, supported and supplemented by familial instruments, such as testamentary codicils and marriage contracts.

Over the course of the Middle Ages, a common law had emerged that adopted from canon law the principle, *pacta sunt servanda*, which essentially made any contractual agreement binding, regardless of its specific form. This freedom of form permitted such a degree of flexibility that partners could reasonably expect their interests to be incorporated into any agreement. As a result, a more or less standard form of company charter emerged in practice as early as the thirteenth century and remained unchanged until the incorporation of the city into the Kingdom of Bavaria in 1806.

When the Höchstetters established their firms in the sixteenth century, the signatories mobilized such legal institutions and practices as Augsburg possessed. They relied on a series of charters, formal contracts of association that defined their responsibilities and rights to the company and to one another.[38] Apart from the conduct of business, they offered no indication of the company as its own legal personality.[39] They addressed the capitalization of their firm and the distribution of profits, a common engagement of capital and labor that scholars take to distinguish early modern capitalistic enterprises.[40] They also allowed sufficient flexibility to respond to changing familial and business circumstances. In all these respects, the partners followed the *ad hoc* established standard for creating family firms in Augsburg.

The Höchstetter firm of 1515 included a broad range of partners, not only sons- and brothers-in-law, but also associates with no other identifiable ties to the family. In addition to the named partners, Ambrosius I and Hans I, seven others participated: Georg II, Sigmund I and Wilhelm I, the sons of the deceased elder brother and partner, Georg I Höchstetter; Hans Ungelter, the brother-in-law of Georg II, Sigmund I and Wilhelm I by virtue of his marriage to their sister, Sibilla; Lukas II Rem, Stephan Gabler and Philipp I Gassner, who were not otherwise related to the Höchstetters. They all had participated – whether or not as partners cannot be determined – in the preceding company, "Georg and Ambrosius, the Brothers Höchstetter", that had ceased operation on 1 April 1514.[41] They all would function henceforth as equal named partners – would "be held in all matters and undertakings the same as we aforementioned" – with one exception: Hans II Ungelter would receive no *Fürlage*.[42] The charter revealed thus that his participation would be limited.[43]

That three of the nine partners were not members of the family raises immediate questions about the Höchstetters' control of governance and management and about their reasons for diluting both. Though the 1515 charter makes no specific mention of any dispute, indeed insists on the partners' satisfaction and solidarity, it names Rem at several points, hinting that the problem was already known to the partners, even if it had not yet seized the attention of the authorities. Anticipating the conflict's potential damage, they may have wished to increase working capital, broaden social connections and establish strategic alliances. Perhaps because of the real costs of Rem's lawsuit, the 1515 partnership proved on the whole to be less successful in terms of persistence. Of the seven new partners, only Wilhelm I Ungelter would reinvest his capital, time and effort in the next Höchstetter firm.

In 1520, now long embroiled in their conflict with Rem, the Höchstetters limited partnership to close relatives. Though the charter no longer exists, a change in the relationship of family to firm is nonetheless visible. The 1524 charter indicates that the signatories had "been by and with one another in company since the first day of January of the year [15]20 until the first day of January of the year [15]24 according to the form and content of the same agreement". The partners in 1524 were thus the same as those of 1520. Georg I Höchstetter's sons, Georg II, Wilhelm I and Sigmund I, as well as the unrelated partners, Philipp Gassner, Stefan Gabler and Lukas II Rem, left the firm in 1519. Only Hans II Ungelter, the husband of Sibilla Höchstetter, the daughter of the late Georg I, remained with the named partners, Ambrosius and Hans. New partners in 1524 were as follows: Hans Franz Paumgartner, the husband of Ottilie Höchstetter, the daughter of Ambrosius I; Ambrosius II, the eldest son and presumptive successor of Ambrosius I; Joachim I, the youngest son of Ambrosius I; and Joseph, the son of Hans I and nephew of Ambrosius I.[44] The Höchstetters exercised thus a degree of flexibility in partnerships, including or excluding nonmembers of the family at need. In 1520, with the Rem dispute still hanging in the balance, Ambrosius I seems to have concentrated authority in the hands of his more immediate kin. In 1524, two years after settlement, they emphasized their solidarity with an insistence on "brotherhood".

* * *

Though the term "brotherhood" appears nowhere in the text, the 1515 charter of "Ambrosius and Hans the Brothers Höchstetter and Associates" expressed an analogous intention: To be a level company, operated by a set of equal partners, who managed the business as each saw fit and represented the company in the wider world.[45] No one of them received explicitly the absolute authority of a director (*Regierer*).[46]

That is not to say that no hierarchy existed. The *Geheimbuch*, the central record of any early modern company, in which the most important contracts and accounts were recorded, would be kept in the house of Ambrosius and secured in a common chest. "This same chest should have four locks and four keys, one to be used by me, Ambrosius Höchstetter, the other by me, Hans Höchstetter, the third for me, Georg Höchstetter [. . .] and the fourth by me Philipp Gassner, Steffan Gabler and Lukas Rem".[47] The location of the chest and distribution of the keys suggests the internal hierarchy of the company: Ambrosius and Hans would head the new firm with the elder and first-named Ambrosius as *primus inter pares*. He alone would have the power to decide weighty matters, such as the guaranteeing of loans or the lending of money, in which the other partners could not or would not rule.[48] This left them a still very wide range of independent discretion in business affairs.

Perhaps for this reason the 1515 charter specified a number of expectations. It demanded of all partners that they make good use of their freedom, exerting their very best efforts in the conduct of business for the firm:

> We, all nine partners, want also, according to the oath that we will swear to the following document, together with one another and each as individuals

> to deal in the most industrious, truest and best manner possible, in buying and selling [goods], paying and collecting debts, giving and taking [letters of] exchange and everything else that touches upon this our company and its business, as may be most profitable and fruitful for this our company.[49]

Nor were they expected to serve any other business, but "to pursue our common company, enterprise, trade and business with all possible industry to the extent that each one's life and energy permits".[50] The 1515 charter included one small, but enlightening, exception. Were a partner to have capital on hand, whether due to inheritance or marriage, beyond that which he invested in the company, he might conduct a narrow range of business on his own: exclusively in fustian thread or in bills of exchange for ducats.[51] In all other respects, they were to give their entire energy and attention to the firm. The freedom granted the partners brought with it the possibility that non-family interests might be served. Such competition had to be explicitly proscribed.

Other restrictions followed as well. Were a partner to make or guarantee loans on behalf of the firm, presumably without the consent of Ambrosius, he alone would bear all risks and costs; the company would assume no responsibility or liability.[52] The charter included a list of dangerous behaviors, such as gambling or waste, that were specifically to be avoided, because they posed a threat to the firm's capital and reputation. Those partners who caused damage through neglect, inattention or laziness would be required to bear the costs, either by paying those losses back to the firm or by having them deducted from their share. Likewise, the charter enjoined all partners to behave in a manner that reflected honor on the company: "No one among us [should] undertake or engage in risky games; also all loose women, wives and persons, from whom shame or scandal might stem, should be avoided".[53] They might gamble in honorable company, but losses in excess of 20 fl would be penalized by paying twice that amount, half to the company and half "to the honor of God". The gambler, like the businessman, would be judged by the success he enjoyed. The Höchstetters went a step further, not only forbidding certain behaviors, but also naming specific sanctions. Were one of the partners to violate the clauses of the charter or "behave or show himself to be improper, dishonorable or shameful", Ambrosius would have the authority, as he alone saw fit, to conduct an immediate, final reckoning with the guilty partner "to expel and remove from the company and to pay capital and whatever else is owed according to the accounts within four or five Frankfurt fairs, as indicated above".[54] The clause even hinted at the possibility of further sanctions "according to the nature of the matter and his behavior". There would be no appeal by the former partner, no immediate release of capital and no threat to the firm.

No less striking than Bartholomäus III Rem's demand for compensation was his willingness to act, a fact that might have influenced the content of the 1515 charter. He refused Ambrosius's settlement and appealed his case to civil and imperial authorities, which violated a requirement to keep all disputes within the company:

> The lords [i.e., partners, tms] and associates, as many as are present, upon hearing the arguments of both parties, should resolve such tension, disagreement or turmoil and thereupon resolve and set aside all disputation, by which resolution both parties should abide without refusal or appeal to anyone, either inside or outside our company's oath and charter.[55]

When his appeals yielded decisions that proved unacceptable, Rem risked prison by seizing upon extralegal solutions: He fled to the sanctuary of a church, he told his story to a third party and he attacked a Höchstetter caravan. In devulging not only his complaint but also company practices to Clemens Sender, Rem violated yet another clause of the 1515 charter, one that was standard in most surviving business charters of the age: The requirement of secrecy. Just as the partners could engage in no other business than that of the company, had to give all their honor, energy and ability to it alone and resolve all disputes internally, so they were expected to protect the company's interests absolutely, not sharing any business information with any outsider: No partner "would reveal anything great or small to strangers or friends, but rather keep it secret to himself or among us".[56] The Höchstetters clearly laid great emphasis upon the closed, secret nature of their company, a hard lesson learned at the hands of Bartholomäus III Rem, even as they strove to keep fields of action open among themselves.

The missing charter of 1520 apparently contained terms the same as or similar to that of 1524, as repeated references in the latter to "the form and content of the same agreement" seems to indicate. Hence, the return to governance limited more exclusively to members of the family brought with it representative equality among the partners, as befits a "brotherhood". Whether it hedged that brotherhood with behavioral prescriptions and prohibitions or assumed greater consensus and constancy among its members is another question.

The 1524 charter granted each named partner "in this brotherhood power and authority" to consult all records and conduct all business as he saw fit, as long as he acted in the clear interest of the company, consulting the others only in matters of greatest importance.[57] The charter left that interest and those matters undefined with wording strikingly similar to that of 1515. It continued, then: "And in so far as we commit ourselves in a brotherly manner, each of us should attend and serve our businss to the best of his ability and understanding, as is proper and need dictates". Whereas all might be expected to do their best, a sense of "brotherhood" bound them more strictly – and explicitly – to this end.

Whoever possessed authority "to conduct all business" was *ipso facto* an unlimited representative of the firm, empowered to commit its resources to a given enterprise and thus make all liable for its obligations.[58] Though no specific clause elevated Ambrosius I to a position of singular leadership, a position from which to determine what business their firm would or would not conduct, various considerations and arrangements indicated that he would again be the senior partner. His named appeared first in the company title; his dwelling housed the company books. Of particular interest is a clause, which appears for the first time in the 1524 charter, regulating amounts to be paid, "should one of us in the service of our firm be held captive and ransomed, which God forefend":

> [I]t should be handled thus that Ambrosius Höchstetter the Elder should be released with up to 4,000 *Gulden*, after which all the others with no more than 2,000 *Gulden* each. Should one be ransomed for more than that, he should pay that himself, unless it should be that he is seized by Bartholomäus Rem and concerning that affair, in which case one will have to see according to the nature of the situation. And, as we among ourselves and with the old company have not yet settled the Rem affair, we can have no clarity how it comes to rest.[59]

Clearly, the Rem dispute – in this case, specifically, the monetary settlement imposed by the imperial commission and accepted by the Höchstetter and the Rem families – continued to affect the Höchstetter family firm, years after Bartholomäus III himself was dead and a mediated resolution signed and sealed.

In all other respects, the charter treated Ambrosius as the equal of his "brothers". Because their labors had to be in the company's interest, the charter also explicitly required all partners "to practice trading with complete industry, to promote gain and prevent damage for us all".[60] This extended to a noncompete clause, similar to the one that forbade the partners of 1515 from undertaking any other trade than that which concerned their common business alone, a not unusual feature of early modern charters: "And each of us should truly serve our company and otherwise neither submit to nor undertake any other business than alone that which concerns our common business".[61] All partners were to avoid any opportunism or misbehavior that might damage company resources or reputation, such as "games" (*Spill*), by which was presumably meant gambling.[62] So serious had this prohibition become that all gambling was proscribed and violaters placed on leave from the company with immediate effect.[63] Separation served both to penalize the behavior and shield the firm. Other dangerous activities were lending money or offering surety to third parties, which could render the firm liable in cases of default. Addressed in 1515, these eventualities were taken up again in 1524. No partners could extend credit or guarantee loans, "unless he could determine that it occur to the good and profit of the firm".[64] If any partner so wished, he was free to lend his own capital, provided that he did so in such a proper manner that it did not damage the firm. Like its predecessors, the 1524 charter set forth measures to resolve any eventual conflict among the partners, prescribing internal mediation and a prohibiting external involvement.[65] In this case, however, it placed decisive authority not in the hands of Ambrosius alone, but in the hands of all the partners together: "so should we among ourselves, as many as may safely be gathered together, after having heard both parties, amicably resolve such tension, disagreement and uproar". Once that decision had been reached, all appeal was forbidden: "[A]nd both parties must willingly abide by this [decision] and each on his behalf appeal to no one outside our agreement and contract by the loyalty we have sworn by oath". The admonition to keep company matters within the company extended, finally, to the secrets and interests of the firm. Both Höchstetter charters required partners to protect absolutely and eternally the secrets and interests of the firm, but that of 1524 excluded even immediate family and friends from such knowledge and information, "be it wives, sisters, brothers or other relations without exception".[66] In so doing, the "brotherhood" raised a barricade between the firm and the family that squares poorly with assumptions about the community of interests that supposedly connected and strengthened both.

Between 1515 and 1524, the business interests of the Höchstetters expanded. They continued to trade in a variety of commodities, and they moved more deeply into metals and finance. Whether the costs and profits of these new enterprises required a reorganization of their partnership cannot be determined for lack of business records. They also confronted a major suit and scandal caused by their conflict with Bartholomäus III Rem. Its implications for the family firm seem far clearer. The growing dispute, its outcome presaged by no less than three decisions against the Höchstetters, may well have made other, even related, merchant-financiers leery of joint ventures or exchanges with them. The Höchstetters responded by granting partners greater discretion in seeking and closing transactions and expanding the ranks of partners who were also relatives. They tightened in every way possible the bonds within their firm, emphasizing cohesion and limiting externalities.

* * *

At the time of his failure, Ambrosius I would boast of himself that "he had with God's help earned great wealth and made all his friends, even the servants, who were employed by him, rich".[67] The chronicler's narrative and the bankrupt's justification portray him as a man, self-made and self-unmade. This was not entirely the case. As the charters of the Höchstetter family firms make clear, the named principals were joined by their partners, who transacted the firm's business and contributed to the family's rise and fall. Moreover, the partners drew upon the expertise and efforts of a range of employees, whose responsibilities varied from strictly limited to nearly unlimited. Family firms are not strictly limited to a single family.

During the course of his business life, with a few noteworthy exceptions, Ambrosius partnered with brothers, sons and sons-in-law, which anchored the firms' governance and management ever more firmly within the family, but he and his partners also recruited leadership and capital from the merchant community of Augsburg and its neighbors. Through their marriage strategies, the Höchstetters established a broader connection to the merchant community.

Their father, Ulrich II, had approved unions consistent with their station as members of the merchant community and association. This applied most immediately to his eligible sons, but the marriages of his daughters followed a similar pattern: Ursula married Gilg Rem in 1470; Apollonia married Peter Loy of Ulm in 1472; daughter Felizitas married Hans Heinrich von Sandizell of Munich in 1494[68] (see the Introduction for more information). The Loy marriage represents connection to the Ulm elite. Von Sandizell was a descendant of an ancient Bavarian ministerial family that would include among its prominent members a Prince-Bishop of Freising, Moritz von Sandizell (1559–1567).

As the father, so the sons. Ambrosius I chose his children's spouses from among his peers, most of them Augsburg merchants: Daughter Ottilie married Hans Franz Paumgartner, a nephew of Hans I and cousin of Hans II Baumgartner, in 1519; son Joachim I married Anna Langenmantel in 1522; son Ambrosius II married Katharina Neumann of Villach in 1527; daughter Brigitta married Ambrosius Hagk in 1533.[69] The Langenmantels were Augsburger patricians, as the Paumgartners would be after 1538. The Hagks were merchants, who would become members of the Patrons of Society (*Mehrer der Gesellschaft*) in 1548.[70] The Neumanns were important, established mine operators (*Gewerke*) in Idria, located in the Archduchy of Austria, present-day Slovenia; the union of Ambrosius II to this family signaled his father's serious commitment mercury as an increasingly valuable commodity. Ambrosius's brother and partner Hans I had four children, only one of whom is known to have married. His son, Joseph, who joined his father and uncle as business partner in 1524, married Benigna Adler, in 1528, just as the firm's bankruptcy broke.[71] Benigna was the daughter of Philipp Adler, a member of the Salt Handler Guild (*Salzfertigerzunft*), who rose to become one of the ten richest citizens of Augsburg, a civil official, a financier to the Habsburgs and an Imperial councilor.[72]

While marriage should not be reduced to a mere function of strategic thinking, the Höchstetters appear to have consistently and self-consciously sought domestic partners from families that would foster their fortunes. Sons- and daughters-in-law brought portions and dowries that could underwrite the capitalization of the firm, either in the form of at-risk investments or interest-bearing deposits. They brought social status that could by association strengthen the reputation and standing of the family. They also brought business experience and information, acquired from exposure to the firms of their own families, that could expand the competency of the Höchstetter firm's governance and management. Finally, they brought their own personal bearing, appearance, value and behavior that are seldom discussed in the scholarship on early modern society, but that doubtless influenced the family's fortunes.

Yet, even as relatives by marriage could expand financial, social, instructional and human capital, they could endanger it by introducing new challenges and potential conflicts. The solidarity of social networks is notoriously fluid, unpredictable and ephemeral, subject not only to changing circumstances but also to individual aspirations, a fact too seldom reflected in the scholarly literature. Adding new members to the family and new leaders to the firm increased the likelihood that the interests of family and firm might not align perfectly. Less competent or reliable family members might demand management positions in the firm. So too, the interests of individual members might not align perfectly, leading to conflict over business engagements or capital expenditures. Such conflicts could jeopardize the solidarity that marriages within one's social or professional group are thought to foster. In the course of the Höchtetter bankruptcy, all of the families with which they intermarried would take active roles, some as supporters, more as creditors.

The Höchstetter charters attempted to foresee and forestall such eventualities. They defined the relationships of partners to the firm and of partners among themselves. They established mechanisms for conflict resolution. They set limits to capitalization, as will become clear. But they left partners free to conduct business, drawing only subjective boundaries in terms of their individual interpretations of the firm's interest or their self-professed "brotherhood". This freedom opened the door to moral hazard. Whatever their feelings for the family firm, the Höchstetter partners were all self-interested. They had entered business not only to promote the prosperity and power of their family, but also to profit individually. Being partners, they were free to conduct any business they saw fit, including business independent of the firm. Being unequal partners, however, they undertook tasks, made decisions and suffered risks, delegated to them by the named principals, for which they were not equally compensated. The partners were, after all, only free and equal "brothers" in the sense of their commitment to the company and the capacity to conduct its business. This simultaneous exercise of two potentially conflicting roles could create incentives to shirk or free-ride. It also could create information asymmetries that enabled the partners to engage in activities that were contrary to the interests of their firm. Checking moral hazard required monitoring business behavior. The charters created no mechanisms for this purpose.

Partners alone could not and did not conduct all business in the premodern family firm, however. The Höchstetters extended rights of limited representation to factors and agents through individual agreements of employment.[73] The most important Höchstetter employees, the factors who represented the firm at distant commercial sites, cannot all be indentified. Those whose names are known appear often to have been recruited them from among younger members of the family, junior partners of the firm. Ambrosius I's extended presence in the Low Countries suggests that he worked as his firm's factor there during the late-fifteenth century. Hans I served as factor in Antwerp from 1495, probably until his elevation to partner in 1515. Some of their sons likewise became agents of the family firm in their turns. Ambrosius II was active in Antwerp during the 1520. Joseph represented the firm in Venice. And Joachim I represented it in Antwerp and elsewhere from 1524 until its bankruptcy in 1529. The Höchstetters also drew factors from the ranks of associates, members of families to which they were related by marriage or with which they had close business connections.[74] Hans II Rem was their agent in Antwerp in 1509,[75] and Konrad II Rehlinger was their factor there in 1510.[76] Ulrich Ehinger represented their interests in Lisbon from 1511 until 1518.[77] After extended periods of employment by them, Wolfgang Vittel became the Höchstetters' factor in Hall, Tyrol,[78] and Hans Gutrater their factor in Nuremberg from 1503 to 1520.[79] Generally speaking, these choices suggest a reliance on long-term and highly trusted elite associates and families, as well as long-term, highly trusted employees and servants, when ties of blood or marriage would not serve.[80]

Early modern commercial firms employed specialists and laborers in a variety of capacities, some of which involved considerable responsibility. In addition to a bookkeeper, secretaries, teamsters and servants might appear on the company rolls. Though family owned and directed, the Höchstetter firm included 25 identifiable employees, only eight of whom appear to have been distantly related to the Höchstetters.[81] The remaining 17 had no identifiable relationship of the Höchstetters beyond employment. These lower ranks within the firm's hierarchy appear never to have enjoyed immediate connection to the family.

Yet, the sense of an immediate connection could arise from multiple causes, of which marriage was but one. Long-term employment could foster identification and loyalty, too.[82] For the majority of persons known to have found employment with the Höchstetters at one point or another, the nature of their work and the length of their engagement cannot be determined at all. They remain little more than names, *obiter dicta* in sources committed to other purposes. In the course of the 1529 bankruptcy proceedings, however, the prosecuting creditors identified eight employees as "confidential servants" (*Geheimdiener*), the nature of whose service to the Höchstetters made them persons of particular interest: Hans Doll, secretary for more than a decade; Georg Hagen, employed in a variety of capacities, managing the Höchstetters' brass foundry in Pflach (see Chapter 2), collecting their debts in Austria, Moravia and Hungary and serving as factor to their mining interests in Reutte, Tyrol; Thomas Konig, bookkeeper after Rem with nearly 30 years of service; Simon Noll, a "woollen-worker" (*Wollknecht*) engaged in the buying and selling of wool, a substantial part of the Höchstetters' business; Wolf Preischuh, for more than a decade factor in Spain; Mathäus Rem, factor in Lyon, France for nearly 20 years; Leonhard Riederer, a jack-of-all-trades (*er hab mussen zu allen Sachenn gerecht sein*);[83] and Wolf Vittel, for over 20 years their factor in Hall, Tyrol, where he "was used in all their affairs" (*jn allen jrn Sachen gepraucht worden*).[84] Clearly, these men enjoyed positions of some importance, which enabled them to know their employers' business and to help them evade their creditors.

Of particular interest in the context of the organization and composition of late-medieval and early-modern family firms is the testimony of Mathäus Rem. As he explained his employment:

> From the beginning of [his] service until the conclusion of the Bartolomäus Rem affair, he earned by investing his capital at profit and loss.

> Thereafter, he [earned] 200 fl engaged in his own business on foot and horseback.[85]

In other words, Rem began his employment as an investor and stakeholder, perhaps even a partner, in 1511–12. Around 1517–18, when Augsburg authorities settled (but did not end) the dispute between Bartolomäus III Rem and Ambrosius Höchstetter, he worked without contract as their commission agent – a mixed employment in Lyon on behalf both of the Höchstetters and of himself – for a retainer of 200 fl. This corresponds roughly to the involvement of Lucas II Rem with the Höchstetters: He was a partner from 1515–20, after leaving the employment as the factor in Lisbon of "Anton Vöhlin, Konrad Welser and Company" and before becoming the partner to his brother in "Andreas Rem and Siblings", as recorded in his autobiography. Lucas and Andreas Rem joined other creditors of the Höchstetters for an amount in excess of 7,000 fl.

This inner circle of long-term employees reveals elements of structure and function in late-medieval and early-modern family firms that founding charters do not elaborate. Those charters bound the signatories – partners in the firm – to certain standards and activities. It did not apply to or reflect upon employees. The pattern that emerges from the information provided by these Höchstetter *Geheimdiener* is one of employment by revolving, long-term, contracts and of stability with increasing levels of compensation and specialization.[86] Individual contracts established terms of employment that varied according to type and length of service. The sparse detail about compensation indicates that earnings increased with length and type of employment. Remuneration, including wages, expenses and bonuses, was not standardized: Some received a fixed annual salary; some had their salary augmented by housing allowances or performance bonuses; some received only a commission for specific tasks or transactions. There was no such thing as a wage regime. There is some limited indication that the Höchstetters hired the sons of their most trusted employees, a second generation of Riedlers and Dolls appearing in the surviving records, but the majority of their employees came from common, Augsburg families that had no apparent connection to the family. Nor did the confidential employees demonstrate any unusual sense of relationship to the firm.[87] Though they had been employed for decades, serving the Höchstetter firm through several different charters, they did not identify it as their employer, but spoke of one or the other partner as the master to whom they bound themselves in service.[88] Most importantly, they reveal a surprising degree of independence. The confidential employees worked for the Höchstetter family firm, but simultaneously conducted their own business on the side; Hagen, Preischuch, Riederer and Rem made specific reference to their own affairs; Vittel and Noll were similarly engaged.

Taken together with the independence granted partners in the conduct of business, such arrangements raise questions about the unity and solidarity of family firms, especially that of the Höchstetters. They pursued what appears to be a quite different strategy of partnership from that of many of their peers.

Their horizontal, business collective – their "brotherhood" – permitted a lack of central oversight and leadership that would have fatal consequences. A more "dynastic" approach to partnership and an autocratic approach to management might have provided greater control and, consequently, avoided certain problems.

Family firms confronted the difficulties posed by the limited experience and expertise of family members. The Höchstetters responded by hiring outside employees and retaining them over extended periods of time. Such tactics enabled their family firm and others to extend the reserve of talent upon which they could draw and, possibly, to ameliorate some of the principle-agent problems and transaction costs that accompany the hiring of outsiders. In all of these ways, the Höchstetters demonstrated an adaptability at odds with theoretical assumptions about family firms. By rewarding loyal service and maintaining long-term associations, they demonstrated that "trust" could be established in a variety of ways, despite Lutz's flat statement that it "was most easily achieved from within the family circle".[89]

* * *

The charters of premodern family firms also address issues of capitalization. As a rule, they identify the signatories as investors, listing the specific amounts only in the first charter.[90] Subsequent contracts that extend the business activities of a family firm, albeit with different partners according to different terms, reveal nothing of the exact values. They restrict the withdrawal of capital during the life of the firm in order to prevent a sudden loss of capital, whether through departure of a partner or demands from the family. They also balance the division of capital and labor among partners through the convention of the *Fürlegung*. Yet, this initial, start-up capital constitutes by no means the entirety of a firm's financial resources. For the Höchstetters and other South German family firms alike, the complete reconstruction of business funding requires attention to a broader range of engagements and interest. Capitalization, like participation, could extend substantially beyond the single family, whose name the firm bore.

The Höchstetter partners of 1515 and 1524 were the owners of the firm. Their charters signaled as much by indicating that each had invested a certain amount without specifying how much.[91] Each wrote the exact value of his share in the chief financial record, the *Geheimbuch*, which has since been lost.[92] Fortunately, an extract created during the bankruptcy proceedings preserves the amounts invested as start-up capital in 1524.[93] It begins with a sum, referred to only as "our Lords capital" (*unnser herrgotts hauptgut*) of 4,026 fl, an indistinct designation. Thereafter follows the investments of each partner:

Ambrosius I Höchstetter 38,334 fl;
Ambrosius I Höchstetter's inheritance
from Lucas I Rem 429 fl;

Hans I Höchstetter 16,022 fl;
Hans II Ungelter 7,900 fl;
Hans Franz Paumgartner 10,000 fl;
Ambrosius II Höchstetter 5,000 fl;
Ambrosius II Höchstetter's marriage
portion, invested in the company by his father 4,000 fl;
Joseph Höchstetter 5,330 fl;
Joachim I Höchstetter 7,902 fl.

It is interesting to note that the majority shares of Ambrosius and Hans indicate clearly the brothers' interest and weight in the company. These initial investments were made in cash, rather than some other form of capital, and could not be leveraged in any way for fear of third-party interference.[94] The same appears to have been true in 1515. They signified thus the real value and interest of the partners, but not necessarily their entire worth. The fact that initial investments did not constitute the totality of the partners' private capital suggests that the Höchstetter firms of 1515 and 1524 adopted the common form of a limited, trading company, a *societas certae pecuniae*.[95] This aspect of their family firm would matter tremendously, when it came time to rebuild their fortunes.

As regards the matter of business finance, the charters of 1515 and 1524 made similar arrangements. The initial capitalization of the firm, which totaled 89,843 fl in 1524, could not be withdrawn under any circumstances before the firm's eight-year life had run its course.[96] In the event of disability or even death, the invested capital would remain at risk with the firm until the contracted business period had ended and the final accounting had been completed. This measure appeared commonly in the charters of South German family firms.[97] Nor could that start-up capital be augmented.[98] The 1515 charter included a similar provision: "No one may be permitted or allowed, should not have the power, to invest or to keep more or other money in our company, during the contracted period of time, than alone that which he had previously registered as his capital".[99] It also allowed what it called "friendship-money" (*freuntschaftgelt)* to be deposited, but not invested. A partner in 1524 could invest dowries or legacies up to 3,000 fl at risk, "*zuo gewin und verlust*"; greater values could only be deposited at 5 percent interest. The Höchstetters thus increasingly restricted the possibility that supplementary investments might alter the distribution of interest in the firm.[100]

Should a partner find himself in need of funds, the 1515 charter allowed him to withdraw 300 fl at a time, up to an absolute maximum of one-third his invested capital.[101] The withdrawn capital remained on the company's books "*zuo gewin und verlust*", and the partner was expected to repay the full principle plus 5 percent annual interest before the final accounting. The 1524 partners were given somewhat freer rein. Each could withdraw from his invested capital such money as he required for "his physical needs and nourishment" (*seiner leybs notturfft unnd narung bedarff*).[102] The charter set no formal limits on such withdrawals, apart from an admonition that they be "honest and appropriate sums" (*ungefarliche unnd unvermessen suma*), but it treated these amounts as loans from the firm to the partner. It called for payment of 5 percent per annum interest. The partners were required to repay principle and interest before the final accounting; any unpaid obligations would be deducted from their earnings. As a limited trading company, the Höchstetter family firm did not establish regular compensation for its partners, because their invested capital did not necessarily represent the totality of their assets.[103] They might draw living expenses from other sorts of income, if they so wished, and contracted accordingly to let their investments serve the firm until its dissolution.

Only at the conclusion of the charter and the dissolution of the firm would a final allocation of profits and losses occur. Should one or more partners wish to leave the brotherhood before that point in time, the firm would gradually distribute their capital appropriately adjusted for accumulated profits or losses: Amounts less than 10,000 fl would be distributed in equal portions over three consecutive years at the Frankfurt fair: Amounts from 10,000 fl to 20,000 fl over four years; amounts above 20,000 fl over five years.[104] The former partner would remain responsible for paying any of his outstanding expenses and collecting his share of any outstanding debts. The 1524 charter declared the results of all accountings to be final and binding on all partners and their relatives and heirs.[105] Such provisions protected the firm, not only from the kind of conflict that had arisen with Bartolomäus III Rem but, more importantly, from a sudden loss of capital, such as might arise at any time from changed circumstance or interest on the part of the family.

Indeed, the financial arrangements of the 1515 charter breath an unease about conflict and loss that received far less emphasis in the context of "brotherhood" that informed its 1524 successor. Though the conflict with Rem had not yet run its course, the continuing partners understood its destructive potential. Their charter's repeated mention of his name leaves no doubt that his claims weighed upon their calculations. Their several provisions to limit and resolve conflict within the company reflect the same general concern. The 1515 charter included as well an extraordinary clause about the winding-down of their business: The partners "agree to discuss and negotiate with one another, so that each and every one of us knows how to judge according to his necessity and condition before the conclusion of our company whether or not we wish to continue in business at the end of the nineteenth year", that is, by the end of 1519.[106] The charters for family firms ordinarily contained no such provision for discussion in advance of the close of business, because there was no way to know its financial status before the final accounting. If the partners were unable to come to terms, then the company dissolved, and each one was "obliged and committed, in discount of his debts, expenses and whatever else he may have received in payment from our company, to accept and in no way to reject or refuse the accurate accounting and appropriate division of our company's assets, cash and debts".[107] For an entire year following the conclusion of business in 1519, the partners agreed to enter into no other partnership or business, but to engage exclusively in collecting the company's debts and monetizing its assets.[108] This, too, is a singular restriction, requiring each partner to accept extraordinary opportunity costs for the sake of the Höchstetter family firm. In essence, the 1515 charter bound the partners to decide in advance of any reckoning whether they would continue in business together, to accept that last reckoning as accurate and binding and to labor without compensation for one year to dispose of all company capital. There followed a further and final provision.[109] Were any partner to reject the results of the company's final accounting as "too little or too meager", he had "the power and authority" to assume those disputed assets and debts in their current condition and location as his capital, or to redeem them to the successor company (that is, the Höchstetters' new family firm) for payment at the next Frankfurt fair. In short, the objecting partner assumed the entire risk of getting his money's worth. Under these circumstances, Rem would have had little success in court. Under these circumstances, Ambrosius Höchstetter hoped, futilely, to avoid another catastrophic court case. Supposedly, the 1524 "brotherhood" had no need of such measures.

In 1524, the Höchstetters created a limited trading company that granted maximum freedom to the partners and engaged only a portion of the family's capital. Beyond this start-up capital, the charter set forth the parameters for broader "investment" in the firm. It would accept deposits at a fixed, annual interest rate of 5 percent. It also described a second category, the so-called good friends, silent investors who placed capital at risk in the firm, but who did not participate actively in its business affairs.[110]

Jacob Strieder argued that all signatories to charters were fully and personally liable (*Solidarhaftung*) for all the obligations of their company.[111] Though this assertion has been debated by later scholars and remains open to dissent, bankruptcy proceedings clearly indicate that in practice creditors and courts held all company stakeholders – not only active but also silent partners – fully and equally liable for all company debts and, accordingly, pursued them with an astonishing, single-minded determination. Bankruptcy gave investors very good reason to remain silent and anonymous therefore. Limited liability had not yet come fully into existence in South Germany with the result that any investor – whether active or silent, whether "*Bruder*", "*Gesellschafter*" or "*Freund*" – might be held responsible for payment of the entire debt of a bankrupt firm, risking much more than the loss of her or his own investment. By contrast, depositors and other nonparticipating stakeholders were liable only for the value of their investments.[112]

The degree to which the Höchstetters relied on foreign capital, that is capital acquired from outside the family, and the role that depositors played in the firm's bankruptcy and the family's fortunes will be treated in a later chapter. Insolvency, bankruptcy and liquidation would have the effect of shaping interpretations of business representation and investor liability over time. It was one point at which business conduct and outcome would directly impact company theory and function.

* * *

The Höchstetter family firm suffered bankruptcy in 1529. It resulted from Ambrosius's unsuccessful attempt to monopolize the world market in mercury, but was aided by the opportunism of his sons and nephews, as well as by simple business misfortune. To what extent was this failure predicated upon the organization and finance of the family firm?

Premodern business charters did not establish the structure and function of firms. Rather, they regulated relations among the partners. They did not address the nature of future business and, so, did not anticipate the risks that business might involve. Rather, by permitting the partners to pursue whatever business opportunities they saw fit, an allowance extended also to the trusted employees, the charters freed them to engage in the dynamic pursuit of profits entirely consistent with capitalism. And, by prescribing the partners' rights and responsibilities to one another and to their firm, the charters bound them and attempted to prevent the kinds of opportunism that might arise from the moral hazard born of information asymmetries or control failures.

The Höchstetter charters created dynastic family firms, albeit of very different type from those of their peers: They formed a *societas certae pecuniae* that prescribed a horizontal organization with limited investment; others adopted a *societas omnium bonorum* that depended on a vertical, authoritarian organization with total investment. Both types relied upon non-familial, foreign capital to expand their funding, but they did so in potentially distinct ways. Because it utilized only a portion of the family's capital, that is, domestic capital, the Höchstetter firm required foreign capital and turned to foreign capital markets much more extensively than others might have done.

It can be argued that the Höchstetters suffered the limitations of their own organization and finance. Their "brotherhood" granted too much initiative and independence to the partners; it failed to include sufficient controls and sanctions to limit misjudgment or misbehavior on their parts. Ambrosius could over-commit the firm's resources to the pursuit of a mercury monopoly without any consensus among the other partners. When this venture failed, the losses proved catastrophic. Further losses arose from the extravagant lifestyles of Ambrosius II and Joseph Höchstetter and, especially, the gambling debts of Joachim I Höchstetter and Hans Franz Baumgartner. These direct violations of the firm's own guidelines also went unaddressed and unredressed. When their insolvency became known in 1528, the large number of small depositors proved implacable in their demands for payment in full.[113] The partners reacted by pursuing their own individual interests, which helped to seal their fates. Claims about the fragility of family firms must be qualified by careful inquiry into which family and which firm.

All family firms are not alike. Though characterized by family ownership and control, they make use of these characteristics in a variety of ways. They are not *ipso facto* guarantors of trust. They can display marked differences in management and finance. They fall victim differently to their assumed weaknesses: Conflicts among owners, managers and stakeholders; divergences between family and firm interests; problems with weak or incompetent management.

Scholarship has assigned such characteristics and problems to premodern, irrational economic life. They are assumed not to be capitalistic in the full sense. Concomitantly, scholars have associated the practices of a logically coherent discipline, whether by resort to production-related incentives, double-entry bookkeeping or professionally qualified management, with the priorities of a modern, capitalistic mentality, since Werner Sombart claimed that it must be linked to profit-orientation and abstract calculation.[114] From these perspectives, family firms such as those that were characteristic of late medieval and early modern enterprise can seem uninterestingly antiquarian. Alfred Chandler embraced this opinion and its corollary, when he contrasted the premodern family firm with the modern, managerial corporation, in which ownership and management are strictly separated.[115] The former belonged to an inefficient past of limited growth; the latter marked the way to a future of unlimited accumulation.[116] Yet, the family firm for all its ancient heritage belongs very much to the present and future.[117] Its structural shortcomings have not consigned it to the past of business organization and finance.

Family firms are not fixed, static structures. As the Höchstetter charters make clear, they respond to crisis. Such organizations can reach well beyond the family to recruit foreign leadership, foreign expertise and foreign capital. They can alter internal relationships, allowing greater or lesser freedom of action, greater or lesser oversight of behavior, greater or lesser access to capital. They can loosen the ties of identity and fortune that might otherwise too closely bind family to firm. And they can make money through the initiative granted their owners and employees. Finally, family firms are not always coterminous with a single family. Nor as we shall see, does a single family always support only one eponymous family firm.

Such flexibility offers no guarantee against failure, as the further history of "Ambrosius and Hans the Brothers Höchstetter and Company" makes clear. Its exercise speaks, however, to the capitalistic nature of family firms, to their capacity to pursue logically coherent, rationally calculated strategies in an age when such things were supposed to have been impossible.

Notes

1 The *Mehrer* of Augsburg are generally understood to represent a social stratum between the urban aristocracy, the *Patrizier*, and the various guilds, including the merchant association. Membership required some form of relationship to the patricians, usually marriage, and permitted access to the patrician assembly hall (*Herrentrinkstube am Weinmarkt*), but it also allowed membership in one or the other of the city's 17 guilds. These guilds formed the basis of representation and participation in the city government until the constitutional changes of Emperor Charles V in 1548. Thereafter, the *Mehrer* formed one of the city's recognized, political corporations, along with the merchant association (*Kaufleutestubengesellschaft*) and the guilds, organized as the commons (*Gemeinde*). See, Pius Dirr, "Kaufleutezunft und Kaufleutestube in Augsburg zur Zeit des Zunftregiments (1368–1548)," *Zeitschrift des historischen Vereins für Schwaben* 35 (1909): 137; Olaf Mörke and Katharina Sieh, "Gesellschaftliche Führungsgruppen," in: Günther Gottlieb, et al. (eds.), *Geschichte der Stadt Augsburg von der Römerzeit bis zur Gegenwart* (Stuttgart 1984), 301; Katherina Sieh-Burens, *Oligarchie, Konfession und Politik im 16. Jahrhundert: Zur sozialen Verflechtung der Augsburger Bürgermeister und Stadtpfleger* (Munich 1986), 26. Against these standard discussions, Andreas Rogge dissents, raising doubts that the *Mehrer*

ever existed as a discrete body separate from the *Patrizier*. See Andreas Rogge, *Für den gemeinen Nutzen: Politisches Handels und Politikverständnis von Rat und Bürgerschaft im Spätmittelalter* (Tubingen 1996), 187 ff.

2 "*Wir, die nachbenannten Ambrosius unnd Hanns die Höchstetter, geprueder, burger zu Augsburg, Hanns Ungelter, der jung, Hanns Frannz Bongarttner, Ambrosi Höchstetter, der jung, Joseph Höchstetter, Joachim Höchstetter, unnser sun, dochterman unnd schwäger, die bey- und miteinannder inn gesellschafft gewesen sendt von dem ersten tag des monatz Jenner anno 20 bis auf den ersten des monatz Jener anno 24 nach laut und inhalt derselben verschreybung, so uber dieselb verschreybung gemacht worden. Und mir alsdann unnser ganntz generalrechnunng mitainannder gethon unnd beschlossen haben dergestalt auf den ersten tag des monatz Jenner anno 24 derselben rechnung mir all obgenannt personen ein gut benuegen unnd zufriden gewesen senndt [. . .] Unnd nachdem mir unns aus freuntlicher unnd bruderlicher, auch vatterlicher liebe darzu bewegen ferrer ein zeyt lanng miteinannder ein gepruederschafft unnd handtierung zu halten furgesetzt unnd furgenomen haben [. . .] so haben mir unns dise nachbenannten personen zu dem ersten unnser lieber herrgott [. . .] fur unns, all unnser erben unnd nachkomen samentliche unnd unverschaydenliche veraint unnd verpunden wie nach*". StAA, Literaliensammlung, Höchstetter-Selekt I, Höchstetter'scher Gesellschaftsbrief 1524. Also transcribed in Elmar Lutz, *Die rechtliche Struktur süddeutscher Handelsgesellschaften in der Zeit der Fugger*, vol. II (Tübingen 1976), 39–48, here 39–40.

3 Lutz, *Die rechtliche Struktur*, 40.

4 "*Wir dyss nachbenantten ambrosius und hanss die hoechstetter gebrueder, jerg der juenger, wylhelm und siegmund die hoechstetter auch gebrueder, waylland unsserss lieben bruder und vatterss jergen hoechstetters seligen verlassen sün, fylip gassner als buerger zu augspurg und steffan gabler buerger zu nurnberg bekennen fuer unns selbs unsser geselschaft nachkomen und Erben unsser nachfolgenden auch forygen geselschaft, so wyr mitt vor ernentten jerg hoechstetter dem Eltern sellygen in zeytt seines lebens und darnach auf sein absterben, dessgleichen bartelme rem mitt etlichen vergeitten gehaptt haben und thond kundt aller meniklych mitt dyssem brief, allss wyr [. . .]wider einander ein follyges und ganz genyegen gehapt [. . .] Und nachdem wir unns auss ursachen unss darzu bewegt, ferer ain zeitt lang mitt ain ander geselschaft zu haltten fuergesetzt und fuergenomen, darum so habend wir unns ob bemeltten syben person mitt samptt andern noch zwen nach bemeltten personnen fur unss und all unsser Erben und nachkomen samblich und unverschaideklych von neuem, nemlich von ob bemeltten ersten tag des monaz abrill des fuenffzechenhundersten und fiertzechenden jar an zu fachen biss auf den Ersten tag des monaz jenner der in fuenftzechenhundersten und zwaintzigesten Jar sein wurtt, geselschaftweyss zusamen gedon und verpflicht und veraintt*". StAA, Höchstetter-Sammlung, Handelshaus, Nr. 1, Ambrosius und Hans Gebrueder die Hoechstetter und Gesellschaft. Gesellschaftsvertrag vom 19. Dez. 1515.

5 Jacques Le Goff, *Marchands et Banquiers du Moyen Age* (Paris 1956), 23.

6 Clemens Bauer, *Unternehmung und Unternehmungsformen im Spätmittelalter und in der beginnenden Neuzeit* (Aalen 1982), 69. See also David T. Beito, *From Mutual Aid to the Welfare State: Fraternal Societies and Social Services, 1890–1967* (Chapel Hill 2000).

7 Georg's death in 1514, and the reorganization of the family firm as "Ambrosius and Hans, the Brothers Höchstetter and Associates" point to 1514 as the end of the previous firm's operation and a general accounting of its assets and liabilities.

8 Lutz, *Die rechtliche Struktur*, 239–40, 388–96.

9 Clemens Sender, *Die Chronik von Clemens Sender von den ältesten Zeiten der Stadt bis zum Jahre 1536. Die Chroniken der schwäbischen Städte. Augsburg*, vol. IV (Leipzig 1894), 146–9. Also mentioned in B. Greiff, *Tagebuch des Lucas Rem*, 18, 92–4. See StAA, Literaliensammlung, 7 September 1518, 25 November 1518, 2–11 December 1518; Literaliensammlung, 31 May 1519; Literaliensammlung 23 February 1521, 26 February 1521, 11 March 1521, 8 April 1521, 16 May 1521, 20–29 May 1521; Literaliensammlung 25 January 1523; Schuld-, Klag- und Appellationssachen II, 158.

10 Greiff refers to a *Rem'schen Urkundenbuch* in the Bibliotheque nationale in Paris. See Greiff, *Tagebuch des Lucas Rem*, 94. Reinhard also sets Rem's investment at 500 fl. See Wolfgang

Reinhard, *Augsburg Eliten des 16. Jahrhundert. Prosopographie wirtschaftlicher und politischer Führungsgruppen 1500–1620* (Berlin 1996), 680. With regard to the term "schwarzer Brand," Grimm identifies it as a form of silver with a high copper content. *Deutsches Wörterbuch von Jacob und Wilhelm Grimm*, 16 vols. (Leipzig 1854–1961. Quellenverzeichnis Leipzig 1971). Available at: www.woerterbuchnetz.de/DWB?lemma=schwarz (accessed 3 December 2018).

11 Sender, *Die Chronik*, 147; Greiff, *Tagebuch des Lucas Rem*, 92.

12 Sender, *Die Chronik*, 148.

13 Ibid.

14 Ibid., 149.

15 Greiff, *Tagebuch des Lucas Rem*, 94. See also Oesterreichisches Staatsarchiv-Wien (hereinafter OeStA) / HHStA, RHR, Judicialia, APA 140–5. Remen, Bartholomäus 1523.

16 Gilg remains an otherwise unidentifiable merchant and member of the extended Rem family. Reinhard, *Augsburg Eliten des 16. Jahrhunderts*, 682.

17 Lutz, *Die rechtliche Struktur*, 59.

18 The most influential early histories of the family include the following: Otto Brunner, "Das 'ganze Haus' und alteuropäische 'Oekonomik'," in: Otto Brunner (ed.), *Neue Wege der Verfassungs- und Sozialgeschichte*, 2nd ed. (Göttingen 1968); Peter Laslett, *The World We Have Lost: England Before the Industrial Revolution*, 2nd ed. (New York 1971), 2; Frédéric Le Play, *Les ouvriers européens. Études sur les travaux, la vie domestique et la condition morale des populations ouvrières de l'Europe*, 6 vols. (Paris 1855–78); Wilhelm Riehl, *Die Naturgeschichte des Volkes als Grundlage einer deutschen Sozial-Politik*, 3rd ed., 3 vols. (Stuttgart 1855); Lawrence Stone, *The Family, Sex and Marriage in England, 1500–1800* (New York 1977). See also Thomas W. Robisheaux, *Rural Society and the Search for Order in Early Modern Germany* (Cambridge, UK 1989); David Warren Sabean, *Property, Production and Family in Neckarhausen, 1700–1870* (Cambridge, UK 1990).

19 Lutz, *Die rechtliche Struktur*, 59.

20 Ibid., 38. See also Clemens Bauer, *Unternehumung und Unternehmungsformen im Spätmittelalter und in der beginnenden Neuzeit* (Jena 1936), 5.

21 Lutz, *Die rechtliche Struktur*, 59.

22 Demographic studies have revealed that households and families changed size and shape in accordance with economic imperatives. See: David Herlihy and Christiane Klapisch-Zuber, *Tuscans and Their Families: A Study of the Florentine Catasto of 1427* (New Haven 1985); David Levine and Keith Wrightson, *The Making of an Industrial Society: Whickham, 1560–1765* (Oxford 1991); E. A. Wrigley and R. S. Schofield, *The Population History of England, 1541–1871: A Reconstruction* (London 1981); J. DuPaquier, et al. (eds.), *Marriage and Remarriage in Populations of the Past* (New York 1981); W. R. Lee, "Past Legacies and Future Prospects: Recent Research on the History of the Family in Germany," *Journal of Family History* 6 (1981): 156–76; Michael Mitterauer, "Zur Familienstruktur in ländlichen Gebieten Österreichs im 17. Jahrhundert," in: Heimo Helczmanovski (ed.), *Beiträge zur Bevölkerungs- und Sozialgeschichte* (Vienna 1973), 167–222; Michael Mitterauer and Reinhard Sauer, *The European Family: Patriarcy to Partnership from the Middle Ages to the Present* (Chicago 1982); Sabean, *Property, Production and Family in Neckarhausen*. Material conditions also influenced the emotional life of families. See: Michael Anderson, *Approaches to the History of the Western Family, 1500–1914* (London 1980); Lutz Berkner, "The Stem Family and Developmental Cycle of the Household: An Eighteenth-Century Austrian Example," *American Historical Review* 76 (1972): 398–418; Pierre Goubert, "Family and Province: A Contribution to the Knowledge of Family Structure in Early Modern France," *Journal of Family History* 2 (1977): 179–95. The particular role and status of women and children has likewise been subject to revision. See Susan Amussen, *An Ordered Society: Gender and Class in Early Modern England* (London 1988); Sarah Hanley, "Engendering the State: Family Formation and State Building in Early Modern France,"

French Historical Studies 16 (1989): 4–27; Christiane Klapisch-Zuber, *Women, Family and Ritual in Renaissance Italy* (Chicago 1985); Lyndal Roper, *The Holy Household: Women and Morals in Reformation Augsburg* (Oxford 1989); Thomas Kuehn, *Law, Family and Women: Toward a Legal Anthropology of Renaissance Italy* (Chicago 1991); Thomas Max Safley, *Let No Man Put Asunder: The Control of Marriage in the German Southwest, a Comparative Study, 1550–1610* (Kirksville, MO 1984).

23 Alice Clark, *Working Life of Women in the Seventeenth Century* (London 1919). See also, by way of example: Roberta Hamilton, *The Liberation of Women: A Study of Patriarchy and Capitalism* (1978); Heide Hartmann, "The Family as the Locus of Gender, Class and Political Struggle: The Example of Housework," *Signs* 6 (1981): 366–94; Merry Wiesner, *Working Women in Renaissance Germany* (New Brunswick, NJ 1986); Louise A. Tilly and Joan Scott, *Women, Work and Family* (New York 1978); Christina Vanja, "Frauen im Dorf. Ihre Stellung unter besonderer Berücksichtigung landgräflich-hessischer Quellen des späten Mittelalters," *Zeitschrift für Agrargeschichte und Agrarsoziologie* 34 (1987): 147–51; Sara Mathews Grieco, "Breastfeeding, Wet Nursing and Infant Mortality in Europe (1400–1800)," in: *Historical Perspectives on Breastfeeding* (Florence 1991), 15–62; David Levine, *Family Formation in an Age of Nascent Capitalism* (London 1977); Hans Medick, "The Proto-Industrial Family Economy: The Structural Function of the Household and Family During the Transition from Peasant Society to Industrial Capitalism," *Social History* 1 (1976): 291–315.

24 See, among others, see works by Carlo Cipolla, Richard A. Goldthwaite, Henry Kamen, David Landes, Robert Lopez, Peter Payne and others. This list goes on and on. Andrea Colli recently attempted a revision of this teleological orthodoxy by arguing that, far from disappearing as the relic of a simpler past, the family firm survives in many regions of the world today because it offers the most efficient organizational structure at certain stages of development and in certain sectors of the economy. See Andrea Colli, *The History of Family Business, 1850–2000* (Cambridge, UK 2003).

25 One need consider only Alberti's *On the Family*, to say nothing of works by Homer, Aeschylus and scores of others. See Leon Batista Alberti, *The Family in Renaissance Florence*, translated and edited by Renée Neu Watkins (Prospect Park, IL 1994).

26 An internal dispute in the Fugger family had analogous effects in 1563.

27 On the family firm, among many others, see Gary Becker, *A Treatise on the Family* (Cambridge, MA 1981); Ralph Chami, "What Is Different About Family Businesses?" (May 2001), IMF Working Paper, 01/70. SSRN. Available at: https://ssrn.com/abstract=879571; Kelin E. Gersick, et al., *Generation to Generation: Lifecycles of the Family Business* (Cambridge, MA 1997); Michael C. Jensen, "Self-Interest, Altruism, Incentives and Agency," in: *Foundations of Organizational Strategy* (Cambridge, MA 1998); Harry Levinson, "Conflicts that Plague Family Business," *Harvard Business Review* 49 (1971): 90–8; Ian Molho, *The Economics of Information: Lying and Cheating in Markets and Organizations* (Oxford 1997); Pramodita Sharma, James J. Chrisman and Jesse H. Chua (eds.), *A Review and Annotated Bibliography of Family Business Studies* (Boston 1996); Oliver Williamson, *The Economic Institutions of Capitalism* (Boston 1985).

28 Theodore C. Bergstrom, "On the Evolution of Altruistic Ethical Rules for Siblings," *American Economic Review* 85 (1995): 58–81; Stefano Zamagni (ed.), *The Economics of Altruism* (Aldershot: E. Elgar 1995). Cf. Becker, *A Treatise on the Family*; Michael C. Jensen and William H. Meckling, "Theory of the Firm: Managerial Behavior, Agency Costs and Ownership Structure," *Journal of Financial Economics* 3 (1976): 305–60; Jensen, "Self-Interest, Altruism, Incentives and Agency"; Schulze, et al., "Agency Relationships in Family Firms"; Richard H. Thaler and Hersh M. Shefrin, "An Economic Theory of Self-Control," *Journal of Political Economy* 89 (1981): 392–406.

29 On altruism in economic life, see Becker, *A Treatise on the Family*; Howard Margolis, *Selfishness, Altruism and Rationality* (Cambridge, UK 1982); Edmund S. Phelps (ed.), *Altruism, Morality and Economic Theory* (New York 1975); William S. Schulze, Michael H. Lubatkin,

Richard N. Dino, and Ann K. Buchholtz, "Agency Relationships in Family Firms: Theory and Evidence," *Organizational Science* 12 (2001): 99–116; Oded Stark, "Altruism and the Quality of Life," *American Economic Review* 79 (1982): 86–90.

30 Mark Casson has most vigorously advocated this approach to the family firm. See Mark Casson, "The Economics of the Family Firm: An Analysis of the Dynastic Motive," University of Reading Discussion Papers in Economics and Management, 1998; Mark Casson, "The Economics of the Family Firm," *Scandinavian Economic History Review* 47 (1999): 10–23. Early discussions of the concept focused on "intergenerational altruism" as an explanation for saving assets to finance an inheritance rather than consuming them for short-term purposes. See Robert Barro, "Are Government Bonds Net Wealth?" *Journal of Political Economy* 82 (1974): 1095–117; John J. Seater, "Ricardian Equivalence," *Journal of Economic Literature* 31 (1993): 142–90.

31 Thomas Mann's great classic, *Buddenbrooks*, chronicles the decline of a wealthy, North German merchant family over the course of four generations. Set in the nineteenth century against a backdrop of economic industrialization and national unification, it is a tale of life and mores, but also of economic misfortune, commercial incompetence and personal dishonesty. It has become a catchphrase for the fate of family firms, a tag for their supposed tendency to evolve "shirtsleeves to shirtsleeves" in three generation. See Cinzia Lorandini, "Looking Beyond the Buddenbrooks Syndrome: The Salvadori Firm of Trento, 1660s-1880s," *Business History* 57 (2015): 1005–19; Thomas Mann, *Buddenbrooks. Verfall einer Familie* (Berlin 1901).

32 Katharina von Ciriachy-Wantrup, *Familien- und erbrechtiche Gestaltungen von Unternehmen der Renaissance: Eine Untersuchung der Augsburger Handelsgesellschaften zur frühen Neuzeit* (Munster 2007), passim.

33 Ibid., 222.

34 See among others Clemens Bauer, *Unternehmung und Unternehmensformen im Spätmittelalter und in der beginnenden Neuzeit* (Munich 1982); Eduard Neuschütz, *Die Nürnberger Reformation und das Recht der Reichsstädte Dinkelsbühl und Rothenburg ob der Tauber* (Borna-Leipzig 1936).

35 See among others Helmut Coing, *Die Frankfurter Reformation von 1578 und das gemeines Recht ihrer Zeit* (Weimar 1935); Wolfgang Kunkel, Hans Thieme and Franz Beyerle (eds)., *Quellen zur neueren Privatrechtsgeschichte Deutschlands* (Weimar 1936); Markus Söhnchen, *Die historische Entwicklung der rechtlichen Gründungsvoraussetzungen von Handels- und Aktiengesellschaften* (Berlin 2005).

36 Katharina von Ciriacy-Wantrup has examined a number of company charters in some detail and argues that the lack of specific laws governing the firm in Augsburg had to do with two facts: Most importantly, capitalistic firms were anchored in families and, accordingly, governed by the laws of marriage and inheritance; equally interesting, the efforts of early capitalists to keep their business arrangements and dealings secret prevented the development of any body of legislation. Ciriacy-Wantrup, *Familien- und erbrechtiche Gestaltung*, 214. See also Klaus Kammerer, *Das Unternehmensrecht süddeutscher Handelsgesellschaften in der Montanindustrie des 15, und 16. Jahrhunderts* (Stuttgart 1977), 142; Lutz, *Die rechtliche Struktur*, 140.

37 Leiser describes the *Stadtbuch*, especially as it applied to commercial practice, as "*sehr dürftig*". W. Leiser, *Die Bedeutung des Augsburger Stadtrechts: Festvortrag anlässlich der Ausstellung des Stadtarchivs Augsburg "700 Jahre Augsburger Stadtrecht 1276–1976* (Augsburg 1976), 14. See also F. Schmidt, *Geschichte Augsburgs* (Handelsgesellschaften in den deutschen Stadtrechtsquellen des Mittelalters: Untersuchungen zur deutschen Staats- und Rechtsgeschichte, 15) (Breslau 1883), 143.

38 The Fuggers, in comparison, used a combination of business charters, final testaments and special codicils. Ciriacy-Wantrup, *Familien- und erbrechtliche Gestaltungen*, passim; Lutz, *Die rechtliche Struktur*, passim, esp. II: 84–225; Georg Simnacher, *Die Fuggertestamente des 16. Jahrhunderts*, 2 vols. ([Tubingen 1960] Weissenhorn 1992); Jacob Strieder,

Jakob Fugger the Rich: Merchant and Banker of Augsburg, 1459–1525, translated by Mildred L. Hartsough (Whitefish, MT 2010).

39 Wilhelm Endemann, *Studien in der romansich-kanonistischen Wirtschafts- und Rechtslehre bis gegen Ende des 17. Jahrhunderts*, vol. I (Berlin 1874), 398 ff.

40 Bauer, *Unternehmung und Unternehmensformen*, 58; Lutz, *Die rechtliche Struktur*, 280.

41 Reinhard, *Augsburg Eliten des 16. Jahrhunderts*, 680.

42 "*dass der genant Lucass Rem mitt allen sachen und massen gehalten sol werden, wie unsser ainer ob genantten gehalten wird, mit dem dritten und fierden pfennig fyrlegung und sunst mit allen sachen nach laut des kheim buchss, und hanss ungelter auch der massen gehalten werden, aus-sgenomen doch dass er weder den dritten noch fierden Pfennig fyrlegung kein teyll haben soll, sunst weitter ferer mit sein hab gehalten werden nach laut dess kheim buchss*". StAA, Höchstetter-Sammlung, Handelshaus, Nr. 1, Ambrosius und Hans Gebrueder die Hoechstetter und Gesellschaft. Gesellschaftsvertrag vom 19. Dez. 1515.

43 A common practice in medieval and early modern business, *Fürlegung* involved the payment of a sum of money by the company itself to one of its partners as compensation or incentive, either to reward particularly demanding work or to encourage greater productivity or efficiency. It increased the dividend paid to a partner without increasing his share in the firm and often distinguished between active and silent partners. Jacob Strieder, "Die sogenannte Fürlegung, eine Institution des deutschen Gesellschaftsrechts im Zeitalter des Frühkapitalismus," *Vierteljahrschrift für Sozial- und Wirtschaftsgeschichte* 10 (1912): 521–7.

44 Wolfram Baer, et al. (eds.), *Augsburger Stadtlexikon. Geschichte, Gesellschaft, Kultur, Recht, Wirtschaft* (Augsburg 1985), 168; Klinkert, "Die Augsburger Handelsgesellschaft der Höchstetter," 32; Joachim Riebartsch, *Augsburger Handelsgeschichte des 15. und 16. Jahrhunderts* (Bergisch Gladbach 1987), 230.

45 "*Es soll auch ein jetlicher unnter uns obgemelte newn geselschaffter macht und gewaldt haben in und ausserhalben der stat augspurg unser geselschaft puecher/register/und briff zuo ersuchen und zuo vjssentjeren/schulden scultbrieff und quittungen was unser geselschaft handlungen und gewerb antreffen mag/zuo machen zuo geben zuo nemn und zuo empfachen auch sunst in andern wegen zuo handlen zuo kauffen und zuo verkauffen/darzuo wechsell zuo geben zuo nemen und zuo empfachen, wie das der geselschaft gelegenhajt und notturft zuo jeder zejt erfodert truellich und ungeferlich*". StAA, Höchstetter-Sammlung, Handelshaus, Nr. 1, Ambrosius und Hans Gebrueder die Hoechstetter und Gesellschaft. Gesellschaftsvertrag vom 19. Dez. 1515.

46 It was otherwise with the Fugger, whose family firm serves as an apt counterexample. Partnership in their firm was limited strictly to male members of the family, a pattern established in 1502 in a contract, through which Jacob II ("the Rich") assumed leadership with the advice and consent of his brothers and stipulated that the company would be governed henceforth by a few, select, male members of the family. In 1512, Jacob II declared the 1502 agreement terminated and named his nephew Anton as his successor and the principal of what he called "this, my business". He confirmed this arrangement in his final testament shortly before his death in 1525. In this way, he set the Fugger firm apart from other South German merchant houses of the day. He swept aside any notion of fraternal equality, reciprocity or even cooperation in favor of a specific principal as "director" (*Regierer*). Fuerstlich und Graeflich Fuggersches Familien– und Stiftungsarchiv Dillingen (hereinafter FA), 31.7, Gesellschaftsvertrag 14 September 1532, 31.7, Gesellschaftsvertrag 14 September 1532. See also Lutz, *Die rechtliche Struktur*, I: 247–8, 267–72, 282; I: 91–2; Strieder, *Jakob Fugger the Rich*, 69–70.

47 "*Die selb truch soll auch halten fier schloesser und fier schluessel und ainer von mir ambrosius hoechstetter der ander von mir hans hoechstetter, der dritt von mir jerg hoechstetter fuer mich und mein zwey bruder und schwager, der viert von mir fillip gassner steffan gabler und lucas rem die obgemelt zeit aus darzuo gepraucht werden*". StAA, Höchstetter-Sammlung, Handelshaus, Nr. 1, Ambrosius und Hans Gebrueder die Hoechstetter und Gesellschaft. Gesellschaftsvertrag vom 19. Dez. 1515.

48 "*es wer dan sach, das solch mit unser gemainen geselschafter, wo wjr anderst pej ein ander in der stat augspurg werrent, oder aber allein aus ambrosius hoechstetters gutt beduncken, rat, fuerwjssen und wjllen beschach*". Ibid.

49 "*Wir all newn mit geselschafter wollen auch also pei den eiden, die wir auf dise verschreibung, wie hernach volgt, geschworen haben, samentlich mit einander und ein jetlicher in sunderhait mit kauffen verkauffen schulden machen und ein zuo pringen wechsell geben und nemen und auch sunst allen andern, was dise unsere geselschaft und derselben hanttierung berueren mag, das fleissigst truellichst und pest handlen, wie das unser geselschaft zum nutzlichsten und fruchtparsten sein kann und mag*". Ibid.

50 "*allein unser gemaine geselschaft kauffmanshandlung gewerb und hanttierung mit allen mueglichem fleiss, so fill eines jetlichen zeitlichem leib und leben raicht, auswartten und solches alles mit allen guten trewen wie gemelt fueren, der geselschaft nuts, frucht und fordern schaffen auch schaden und nachteill wenden treullich und ungeferlich*". Ibid.

51 "*so fer aber unser ainer oder mer solch sein uberig forgestanden gelt so er erbs- oder hejratsweis uberkommen hett in die geselschaft legen, sundern sunst domit handlen wolt/ als dan soll er solches nit anderst noch keener andern gestalt thon den allein mit parchatt/faedlen oder gebuerenden wechslen der duchatten, aber suns taller ander gewerb hanttierung und kauffmanshandlung ausserhalben derer, die er im und unser gemainer geselschaft uebt, wie die erdacht werden muegen, allerdings frej und gentzlich obbemelte zejt aus muessig steen*". Ibid.

52 "*Wir haben auch von merer und unser geselschaft nutz handhabung und ainigkajt wegen untter uns angesehen, auch uns des gegen einander verdingklich verbunden, das keiner untter uns gantz kein puergschaft thon noch jement gelt leichen soll, wo aber solches beschah/so soll doch solch puergschaft und anlehen der geselschaft gantz on alle entgeltnus unnachtajllig und unschedlich sein, auch derselb so solchen thet oder thon wuerde, deshalben die wagknus und den schaden, so im daraus entstuendt, selbs gedulgen und tragen*". Ibid.

53 "*keener aus uns ainich geferlich spill thon fuernemen noch treiben, auch eingerllei leichtfertig frawen oder weiber und personen, daraus schandt oder laster erwachsen moecht, muessig sein soll*". Ibid.

54 "*aus der geselschaft zuo setzen und zuo urlauben und im sein hauptgutt und anders, was im nach vermoegen solcher rechnung gepueren wuerdt, in diesen fiern oder fuenff franckfurtter messen, in massen wie dan oben gemelt ist, zuo bezallen*". Ibid.

55 "*solche spen wider willen und auffruer sollent die hern und geselschafter, so fill man der ungeferlich dapei haben mag, nach paiden taillen genugsamen beschaidt vergonen und darauff guetlich entschaiden und irren wider willen entlich ablainen und hinlegen, darpei auch baid taill ungewaigert beleiben sollen und innerhalb noch ausserhalb unser geselschaft spruch und vertrag kain taill noch iemant von irent wegen weitter nit angfacht werden*". Ibid.

56 "*Wir sollen auch all obgenannt inn disser pruderschafft macht unnd gewalt haben alle püecher, register, prieff zu ersechen unnd fysytiern, schulden, schuldbrfieffen unnd quittungen, was unnser hanndlung unnd gewerb antreffen mag, zu machen, zu geben unnd nemen unnd zu empfachen oder sonnst inn annder weg zu hanndlen, zu kauffen unnd verkauffen, darzu wexl zu nemen unnd geben unnd zu empfachen wie dann zu der hanndlunng gelegenhaytt, notturft erayscht, nix hindan gesetzt trewlichen unnd ungefarliche. Unnd die weyll mir unns also bruederliche darzu begeben, soll ein jettlicher seinem pösten vermugen unnd verstandt nach dem hanndel auswartten unnd nach denncken wie pillich unnd die notturfft erayscht*". StAA, Literaliensammlung, Höchstetter-Selekt I, Höchstetter'scher Gesellschaftsbrief 1524. Also transcribed in Lutz, *Die rechtliche Struktur*, II: 44. See also Bauer, *Unternehmung und Unternehmensformen*, 67; Riebartsch, *Augsburger Handelsgeschichte*, 231.

57 "*in diser pruderschafft macht und gewalt*". StAA, Literaliensammlung, Höchstetter-Selekt I, Höchstetter'scher Gesellschaftsbrief 1524. Also transcribed in Lutz, *Die rechtliche Struktur*, II: 44. See also Bauer, *Unternehmung und Unternehmensformen*, 67; Riebartsch, *Augsburger Handelsgeschichte*, 231.

58 See also Ciriacy-Wantrup, *Familien- und erbrechtliche Gestaltungen*, 239–41; Max Jansen, *Jakob Fugger der Reiche: Studien und Quellen*, vol. I (Leipzig 1910), 263–4; Lutz, *Die rechtliche Struktur*, II: 123; Riebartsch, *Augsburger Handelsgeschichte*, 241–4, fn 7; Söhnchen, *Die historische Entwicklung*, 42.

59 "*Unnd, da gott vor sey, ob unnser einer inn der gesellschafft diennst gefanngen unnd geschetzt wurde, soll es also gehalten werden, das Ambrosius Höchstetter der elter soll mit unnd pis inn vier taussennt gulden gelest werden; darnach die annder all jettlicher nit mer als mit zwaytausent guldin. Was sich ainer daruber laßt schetzen, das soll er selbs bezalen, es wer dann, das er durch Bartleme Remen gefanngen unnd denselben hanndl betreffe, da soll man einsechen nach gestalt der sachen unnd nachdem das wir unnder unns unnd der alten gesellschafft desselben Remen hanndels halben noch nit erlediget sendt, darumb kinden wir unns deshalben kain clarhayt machen darbey bestatts*". StAA, Literaliensammlung, Höchstetter-Selekt I, Höchstetter'scher Gesellschaftsbrief 1524. Also transcribed in Lutz, *Die rechtliche Struktur*, II: 43–4.

60 "*Wir sollen auch all unnd ein yettlicher inn sunderhaytt mit ganntzem fleyß hanndlen, prattiziern, allen unnsern nutz zu furdern unnd schaden zu wennden so weytt unnser vermuglichayt strecht*". StAA, Literaliensammlung, Höchstetter-Selekt I, Höchstetter'scher Gesellschaftsbrief 1524. Also transcribed in Lutz, *Die rechtliche Struktur*, II: 44–5.

61 "*unnd soll ein jettlicher der hanndlung trewlichen auswartten unnd sonnst sich kains anndern hanndl unnderston noch treyben, dann alen was unnser gemainen hanndl betreffen ist*". StAA, Literaliensammlung, Höchstetter-Selekt I, Höchstetter'scher Gesellschaftsbrief 1524. Also transcribed in Lutz, *Die rechtliche Struktur*, II: 45. See also Mayer, *Die Fürlegung*, 120.

62 "*Zu bedenncken der spill halben, ist die mainung, das ein jettlicher allen gefarliche spill lassen soll unnd kainswegs nit treyben noch thon. Wa aber einer unnder uns solliche gefarliche spill wurde thon, so haben wir macht demselben von stundt an urlaub zu geben unnd soll auch bey seiner glip unnd trewen, so er auf dise geschrifft gethan hatt, das alles meyden nocht nit yeben kains wegs, alles trewlich unnd ungevarlich*". StAA, Literaliensammlung, Höchstetter-Selekt I, Höchstetter'scher Gesellschaftsbrief 1524. Also transcribed in Lutz, *Die rechtliche Struktur*, II: 46.

63 That charters specified such matters in detail reflects the as yet under-developed distinction between public and private resources, the capital of the firm and the capital of the family, in early modern private law. See Ciriacy-Wantrup, *Familien- und erbrechtliche Gestaltungen*, 128.

64 "*Es soll auch unnder unns kainer kain purgschafft fur niemandt thon, noch gelt aus gemainem hanndl leychen er kindt dann ermassen, das der hanndlung zu gutt unnd nutz bescheh. Wölt aber ainer im selb zu gutt gelt ausleychen, das mag er thon von seinem aigen gelt unnd gutt doch zimblicher weyß der gesellschafft on schaden*". StAA, Literaliensammlung, Höchstetter-Selekt I, Höchstetter'scher Gesellschaftsbrief 1524. Also transcribed in Lutz, *Die rechtliche Struktur*, II: 46.

65 "*Begebe sich auch, da gott vor sey, das einer oder mer unnder unns vorgenannten personen umb was sachen das were, dissen hanndl berurenndt mit unnd gegen einannder widerwillig oder aufrurig wyrrden und sallichs sich mit worten oder wercken zutruege, sollichen spann widerwillen unnd aufrur sollen mir under unns, sovill man dann ungefarlichen darbey gehaben mag, nach bayden taylen genugsam verhörr unnd darauf guetigclichen entschayden unnd iren widerwillen entliche ablonen unnd hinlegen, darbey auch bayden tayll ungewegert bleyben unnd jener nach außerhalben unnser spruch unnd vertreg kain tayll noch yemanndt von iretwegen weytter nit angefachten worden bey gutten trewen so mir darumb gethon haben an aidt statt*". StAA, Literaliensammlung, Höchstetter-Selekt I, Höchstetter'scher Gesellschaftsbrief 1524. Also transcribed in Lutz, *Die rechtliche Struktur*, II: 45–6.

66 "*Es soll auch ein yettlicher allen gehaim hanndtierung unnd was zu der gesellschafft kont gehört im ganntz still unnd gutten kont halten alzeyt inn der unnd nach der zeyt der acht jaren unnd hinfuro weig niemant nix unnser rechnung, gewin oder verlust oder annder hanndlung zu offenbaren die in disem hanndl nit verwanndt senndt, es seyen weyber, schwestern, prueder oder annder freunden nix ausgenommen in allweg trewlich unnd on alls gefärde*". FA, 31.7, Gesellschaftsvertrag 14 September 1532. Quoted in Lutz, *Die rechtliche Struktur*, II, 47.

67 "*er hab mit der Gotzhilff groß gut gewunnen vnd all freundt, desgleichen all Diener, die bisher bei Jme gewesen sein hab er auch all reich gemacht*". StAA. Literaliensammlung. Hoechstetter-Selekt I, fol. 217.

68 Höchstetter, *Stammtafel der Höchstetter*, 2f.

69 Ibid., 4f. Reinhard identifies the husband of Brigitta Höchstetter as Ambrosius Hagk and set the date of their marriage as 1533, a clear departure from – and possible correction

of – the *Höchstetter Stammtafel*, which they cite as their source. See Reinhard, *Die Augsburger Eliten des 16. Jahrhunderts*, 298. Cf. *Die Augsburger Eliten*, 211.

70 Ambrosius Hagk was executed for *Veruntreuung* in 1567. *Chroniken des Augsburger Ratsdieners Paul Hektor Mair* in: Bayerische Akademie der Wissenschaft (ed.), *Die Chroniken der deutschen Städte vom 14. bis ins 16. Jahrhundert*, vol. XXXII, vols. 23, 25, 29, 32–4 (Gottingen 1965–7), 445.

71 Höchstetter, *Stammtafel der Höchstetter*, 4.

72 The *Salzfertigerzunft* was the corporation of Augsburger merchants and associates who traded in salt, the most important preservatives of the Middle Ages and early modern period. Because of high, inelastic demand for the commodity, its trade formed one of the most important branches of long-distance commerce in all of Europe. The city's salt staple, which was first recorded in 1275, forced foreign merchants, most of whom came from Munich or Salzburg, to store and sell their salt in Augsburg and placed its further trade in the hands of local merchants. Augsburg merchants resold the Bavarian and Salzburg salt in Swabia and Switzerland. In 1368, the salt traders came together with the various occupations and crafts that assisted them to form a common guild, the *Salzfertigerzunft*. By 1443, the *Salzfertiger* operated the city's salt warehouse (*Salzstadel*) as a common corporation, known as the Salt Handler Company (*Salzfertigergesellschaft*). It was one of the most lucrative of the city's wholesale commodities, as a result of which membership in the *Salzfertigerzunft* became an economic springboard to higher station, membership in the *Kaufleuteschaft*, the *Mehrer der Gesellschaft* or the *Herrenstube*, that is, the patriciate. Adler's career testifies to this upward mobility

73 Lutz, *Die rechtliche Struktur*, I: 336; Riebartsch, *Augsburger Handelsgeschichte*, 243.

74 By contrast, the Fugger recruited their factors, those crucially important and strategically placed employees who represented the firm abroad, from families that were related, but not too closely, by blood or marriage. Jacob II made a habit of drawing factors from a distant branch of the family, Fugger "vom Reh", whose financial fortunes had not kept pace with his own Fugger "von der Lilie". He also drew upon male members of the Meuting, Rem and Reihing families, all of which were connected to the Fugger by marriage. Georg Hörmann, whose descendants frequently served as Fugger factors, was one of Anton Fugger's closest associates and husband to Anton's cousin, Barbara Reihing. See Jansen, *Jakob Fugger*, 50, 67–8; Kellenbenz, *Die Fugger in Spanien*, I: 168–9; Götz Freiherr von Pölnitz, *Anton Fugger*, vol. I (Tubingen 1958–1986), 343; Götz Freiherr von Pölnitz, *Jakob Fugger*, II:14, 18, 29–31, 35, 48, 50, 111; Thomas Max Safley, "Die Fuggerfaktoren Hörmann von und zu Gutenberg: Werte und Normen einer kaufmännischen Familie im Übergang zum Landadel," in: Johannes Burkhardt (ed.), *Augsburger Handelshäuser im Wandel des historischen Urteils* (Tübingen 1996), 244–5.

75 Renée Doehaerd, *Etudes anversoises. Documents sur le commerce international à Anvers, 1488–1514*, vol. II, 3 vols. (Paris 1962–3), 293–4.

76 Ibid., III: 205–6.

77 Ekkehard Westermann, "The Brass-Works of the Höchstetter at Pflach near Reute in the Tirol, 1509–1529," in: Ian Blanchard, et al. (eds.), *Industry and Finance in Early Modern History: Essays Presented to George Hammersley on the Occasion of His 74th Birthday* (Stuttgart 1992), 168; W. Großhaupt, "Commercial Relations Between Portugal and the Merchants of Augsburg and Nuremberg," in: Jean Aubin (ed.), *La Découverte, le Portugal et l'Europe. Actes du Colloque Paris, les 26, 27 et 28 mai 1988* (Paris 1990), 382.

78 Blendinger, "Zur Geschichte der Messinghütte," 60; Heinrich Heimer, "Die Glasshutte zu Hall in Tirol und die Augsburger Kaufmannsfamilie der Höchstetter" (Ph.D. dissertation, University of Munich 1959), 11; Mutschlechner and Palme, *Die Messingwerk in Pflach bei Reutte*, 37; Pölnitz, *Anton Fugger*, I: 499, fn 158; Westermann, "The Brass-Works of the Höchstetter," 163.

79 Blendinger, "Zur Geschichte der Messinghütte," 56.

80 Again, by way of contrast, the reliance of the Fuggers on factors drawn from elite merchant families declined and was supplanted by the sons of long-term employees and artisanal craftsmen. See Reinhard Hildebrandt, "Diener und Herren: Zur Anatomie

großer Unternehmen im Zeitalter der Fugger," in: Johannes Burkhardt (ed.), *Augsburger Handelshäuser im Wandel des historischen Urteils* (Berlin 1996), 161–3.

81 Jacob II Fugger and his successor did likewise. Extant documents identify no fewer than 104 employees, ranging from factors to secretaries, accountants to miners, cashiers to teamsters, the majority of whom were not related to the Fugger family. See Reinhard, *Augsburger Eliten*, 142–4.

82 The claim has been made that the Fuggers also displayed a marked tendency to maintain loyal, skilled employees over long periods of time and to hire their sons, thus creating lineages of employees, analogous to those of some of the factors. While the hypothesis makes some sense, it is borrowed from the secondary literature, not based on an analysis of primary records for all the company's employees. See Mark Häberlein, *The Fuggers of Augsburg: Pursuing Wealth and Honor in Renaissance Germany* (Charlottesville 2012), 130.

83 Ibid.

84 StAA, Literanliensammlung, Höchstetter-Selekt I, Dok. 15, Urgichten 1531/32, 23 Oktober 1531.

85 "*Von Anfang sein Dienst biss zu Austrag Bartolome Remen Handlung hab er zu Gwinn und Verlust seines Hauptguts gedient, volgend jarlich zwei hundert Gulden, darauf er alhie jn aigner Liferung mit Person und Pferd gelegen*". Ibid.

86 Whether this reflects increasing professionalization, as has been argued elsewhere, cannot be determined on the basis of such limited data. See Markus Denzel, "Professionalisierung und sozialer Aufstieg bei oberdeutschen Kaufleuten und Faktoren im 16. Jahrhundert," in: Günther Schulz (ed.), *Sozialer Aufstieg: Funktionseliten im Spätmittelalter und in der frühen Neuzeit* (Munich 2002), 413–42; Hildebrandt, "Diener und Herren," 149–74.

87 The creditors wished to have him questioned with particular care, not because his long service made him particularly knowledgeable, but "due to the fact that he did not wish to give a statement" ("*Auss was Ursachen der Riederer ein Anzaigung [. . .] nit hat geben wollen*"). StAA, Literaliensammlung, Hoechstetter-Selekt I, Dok. 15, Urgichten 1531/32, 23 Oktober 1531.

88 "*Jnnsonnderhait alle Diener zufragen wer jre Herrn unnd Geselschaffter gewesen wem sy gelopt unnd geschworn haben und von wolher aller wegen der Aide von jnen begert unnd uffgenomen worden sei unndershidlich anzuzaigen*". Ibid.

89 Lutz, *Die rechtliche Struktur*, I: 59.

90 Ibid., 246–8.

91 Like the Höchstetters, Fugger partners did not record their initial investments in their company charters. In fact, the first charter, signed in 1494, specified that the initial investments would be recorded only at the final accounting in 1500. In consequence, no extant Fugger charter records the start-up capital; business correspondence and accounts reveal this sensitive information. Surviving account books permit a reconstruction, however. Rising from an initial capitalization of 54,385 fl, "Ulrich Fugger and Brothers" increased in value to 198,915 fl in 1510. By 1525, the year of Jacob II's death and Anton's succession, it was worth 2,021,201 fl. See Jansen, *Jakob Fugger*, 77; Lutz, *Die rechtliche Struktur*, I: 252, fn 35, 253–4.

92 The *Geheimbuch* was a business record, be it accounts or correspondence, kept by the merchant himself and open, in principle, to no one but himself and his partners.

93 StAA, Literaliensammlung, Höchstetter-Selekt II, fol. 56–64.

94 Lutz, *Die rechtliche Struktur*, I: 261.

95 Unlike the Höchstetters and their limited trading company, the Fugger family firm took the form of a *societas omnium bonorum*, an unlimited company that involved the entire wealth of the partners. In the 1494 charter, the brothers Ulrich, Georg and Jacob bound themselves to invest all their capital and all the company's profits. The 1502 reorganization, which set aside the Hungarian business as whole, indivisible and inalienable, expanded this policy: All participants swore to leave their whole business capital, all property and profits, in the family firm. Moreover, certain properties and their contents in Augsburg – real and moveable capital – were dedicated inalienably to the company, thus increasing its capitalization and providing representative dwellings for the partners. The 1512 charter that created "Jakob Fugger and Nephews" added still more real

property to the financial base of the firm now under Jacob's sole direction. See Lutz, *Die rechtliche Struktur*, I: 255; Strieder, *Jakob the Rich*, 62, 72–3.

96 StAA, Literaliensammlung, Höchstetter-Selekt I, Höchstetter'scher Gesellschaftsbrief 1524. Also transcribed in Lutz, *Die rechtliche Struktur*, II, 40–1.

97 Lutz, *Die rechtliche Struktur*, I: 253–4.

98 StAA, Literaliensammlung, Höchstetter-Selekt I, Höchstetter'scher Gesellschaftsbrief 1524. Also transcribed in Lutz, *Die rechtliche Struktur*, II: 43.

99 "*keiner gestat noch zuo gelassen werden moechte, das nit macht haben soll, ainich ander oder mer gelt in gesatzter zeit in unser geselschaft zuo legen oder zuo halten den allein so fill eines jeden forbemelt eingeschriben fuer hauptgutt und fuerlegung anzaigt*". StAA, Höchstetter-Sammlung, Handelshaus, Nr. 1, Ambrosius und Hans Gebrueder die Hoechstetter und Gesellschaft. Gesellschaftsvertrag vom 19. Dez. 1515.

100 According to Riebartsch, this was a common feature of South German business organization. See Riebartsch, *Augsburger Handelsgeschichte*, 253. By contrast, Bauer seems to find it unusual, calling it an "idiosyncracy for which no reason is apparent" ("*eine Eigentümlichkeit, für die ein besonderer Grund nicht ersichtlich ist*"). Bauer, *Unternehmung und Unternehmungsformen*, 120.

101 "*Wir obgenantte newn mitgeselschafter haben uns auch fuer uns und unser erben mit einander veraint und einander verwilligt verguendt und forbehalten ob einer oder sein erben in obgenanter zejt etwas seins eingeschriben hauptguts aus der geselschaft zuo kuenftig ligende guetter underhaltung seins haus oder sunst aus anderer seiner notturft nemen wolt dass ein solcher doch nit mer noch wajtter den ein dritten tajll und dennocht fon solchem dritten tajll auf ein mall nit mer denn drejhundert gld. zuo thon macht haben soll*". StAA, Höchstetter-Sammlung, Handelshaus, Nr. 1, Ambrosius und Hans Gebrueder die Hoechstetter und Gesellschaft. Gesellschaftsvertrag vom 19. Dez. 1515.

102 "*Doch was unnser einer zu seiner notturft zu prauchen ungefarliche unnd unvermessen summa seiner leybs notturfft unnd narung bedarff oder heraus nimpt, soll man im dieselben suma unnd einem jettlichen was er also dermaßen nimpt funff vom hundert des jars der auf rechnung unnd bezalen unnd wann also dann ganntzen rechnung geschicht, so soll ein jettlicher was er praucht hatt abziehen und den rest wider ligen lassen*". StAA, Literaliensammlung, Höchstetter-Selekt I, Höchstetter'scher Gesellschaftsbrief 1524. Also transcribed in Lutz, *Die rechtliche Struktur*, II: 43.

103 As a *societatis omnium bonorum*, by contrast, the Fugger family firm had to arrange finances differently. The 1532 charter of "Raymund, Anton and Hieronimus, the Brothers Fugger and Nephews" allowed that any and all expenses incurred by the partners on behalf of the firm would be paid from its available funds. The charter made further allowance for those expenses that arose for each partner "on account of himself, for his sustenance, his housekeeping and his need" ("*allain von sein selbs wegen fur sich, zu seiner narung, auch haushaltung und anderer seiner notturfft*"). For these, each partner was permitted to withdraw up to 4,000 fl per year in quarterly installments of 1,000 fl, which would be debited from his own invested capital. Extraordinary expenses, such as arose with the purchase of more costly items, such as real estate, were permitted to a maximum of 6,000 fl, but only once during the lifetime of the company and only with the approval of the other partners. FA, 31.7, Gesellschaftsvertrag 14 September 1532. See Lutz, *Die rechtliche Struktur*, II: 84–103, here esp. 93.

104 StAA, Literaliensammlung, Höchstetter-Selekt I, Höchstetter'scher Gesellschaftsbrief 1524. Also transcribed in Lutz, *Die rechtliche Struktur*, II: 42. The 1515 charter made similar arrangements: "*den andern einen oder mer irer kraft des hauptguts was sich in gepuerender Rechnung erfunden hatt/ nach folgender form und gestalt hinausgeben und bezallen/nemlich wuerde solches untter zehentaussend gld. sein in disen franckfurter messen/wuerd es aber sich in zwainsigktaussend gld. in fuenff franckfurtter messen, alles den nesten kuenftigen nach solcher zejt in der stat franckfurtt ein jetlichen gepuerenden tajll*". See StAA, Höchstetter-Sammlung, Handelshaus, Nr. 1, Ambrosius und Hans Gebrueder die Hoechstetter und Gesellschaft. Gesellschaftsvertrag vom 19. Dez. 1515.

105 StAA, Literaliensammlung, Höchstetter-Selekt I, Höchstetter'scher Gesellschaftsbrief 1524. Also transcribed in Lutz, *Die rechtliche Struktur*, II: 41.

106 "*Domit sich auch ein jetlicher untter uns zuo und for ausgang der obbestimpten zejt unser geselschaft darnach sein notturft und gelegenhajt erfoerdrt zuo richten wajss/so haben wjr uns, des jetzt mit ein ander veraint und vergliecht das wjr auff das bemelt nest kunftig newnzehendt jar vor ausgang des selben von ferren vertragen und ob wjr uns in wajtter geselschaft zuo endt des newnzehenden jars mit ein ander einlassen und begeben wollen oder nit/mit ein ander redden und handlen muegen/und sollen, wo wjr uns dan wejtter mit ein ander vergleichen, so hatt es sein bescheidt/ob ander aber uns mit ein ander ferer ainhelligklichen mit verainen noch vertragen mochten als dan so soll wan dasselb nest kuenftig newnzehendt jar foellencklich verschinen ist, dise geselschaft ir endt auch haben*". StAA, Höchstetter-Sammlung, Handelshaus, Nr. 1, Ambrosius und Hans Gebrueder die Hoechstetter und Gesellschaft. Gesellschaftsvertrag vom 19. Dez. 1515.

107 "*ob ander aber uns mit ein ander ferer ainhelligklichen nit verainen noch vertragen mochten als dan so soll wan dasselb nest kuenftig newnzehendt jar foellencklich verschinen ist, dise geselschaft ir endt auch haben und ein jetlicher under uns schuldig und verpflicht sein, in abschlag seiner schulden und kosten und anders so er dan in unser geselschaft zuo gutter rechnung so zuo mall haben wjrdt, nach anzall und auff gebuerender thajllung gedachter unser geselschaft pfenberten parschaften und schulden anzuo nemen und sich des keinswegs zuo wajgern noch zuo sperren*". Ibid.

108 "*Es soll auch alsdan ein jetlicher untter uns nach foellendung des newnzehenden jars ein gantz jar und also pis zuo gantzem ausgang des zwainsigisten jars darnach fulgent mit gantz keinem andern kauffmanshandell und gewerb zuo thon haben, sunder deshalben aller ding gentzlich still halten und allein verhelfen der geselschaft schulden ein zuo pringen und die pfenbert gepuerender weiss zuo geld zuo machen*". Ibid.

109 "*So auch einer oder mer nach ausgang der obbestimten zejt aus der geselschaft komen und sich ob der achtung messigung oder schatzung der pfenbert oder schulden so also in der gantzen hauptrechnung untter uns beschach/beschwerren und verjahnen wuerdt, als ob das zuo wenig oder zuo gering oder anders zuo geschatzt und angeschlagen sein solt/alsdan hatt derselb macht und gewalt aindtweder die selben pfenbert und schulden in der achtung wie sie gesetzt und an den oertten do si glegen sind, an seinem gepuerenden tajll und hauptgutt anzuo nemen/oder aber die selben gutten pfenberten und schulden in solchen anschlag der newen nachfolgenden geselschaft zuo loessen, doch soll er alsdan so er solches der geselschaft in der gemachten anschlag last/sein gelt dagegen zuo empfachen pflichtig und schuldig sein in den franckfurtter messen wie forgemeldt*". Ibid.

110 StAA, Literaliensammlung, Höchstetter-Selekt I, Höchstetter'scher Gesellschaftsbrief 1524. Also transcribed in Lutz, *Die rechtliche Struktur*, II: 42–3.

111 Jacob Strieder, *Zwei Handelsverträge aus dem 15. und 16. Jahrhundert: Ihre Geschichte und ihr Recht* (Leipzig 1908), 56 ff. See also, Lutz, Die rechtliche Struktur, I:267–75.

112 Ciriacy-Wantrup, *Familien- und erbrechtliche Gestaltungen*, 245.

113 This is exactly the danger that Jacob II Fugger had foreseen and one of his reasons for establishing the Fugger family firm on the basis of a *societas omnium bonorum*.

114 Werner Sombart, *Der moderne Kapitalismus* (Munich 1924), II: 110 ff. See also Raymond de Roover, "Aux d'une technique intellectuelle: la formation et l'expansion de la comptabilité à partie double," *Annales d'histoire économique et sociale* 9 (1937): 171–93, 270–97, esp. 270 ff.

115 Alfred D. Chandler, Jr. *The Visible Hand: The Managerial Revolution in American Business* (Cambridge, MA 1977); Alfred D. Chandler, Jr., *Scale and Scope* (Cambridge, MA 1990).

116 See, among others, works by Carlo Cipolla, Richard A. Goldthwaite, Henry Kamen, David Landes, Robert Lopez, Peter Payne and others. This list goes on and on. Andrea Colli recently attempted a revision of this teleological orthodoxy by arguing that, far from disappearing as the relic of a simpler past, the family firm survives in many regions of the world today because it offers the most efficient organizational structure at certain stages of development and in certain sectors of the economy. See Colli, *The History of Family Business, 1850–2000.*

117 The *Family Business Review* reported in 1996 that 80 to 90 percent of all business enterprises in North America were family owned. These businesses accounted for 60 percent of total employment, 78 percent of all new jobs and 65 percent of wages paid in the United States. Nor do these figures refer to small- or medium-scale enterprises alone, as is so often assumed by economists and economic historians. Among those companies listed on the Standard & Poor's 500 Index, 34 percent are family businesses. See Melissa Carey Shanker and Joseph H. Astrachan, "Myths and Realities: Family Businesses' Contribution to the US Economy – A Framework for Assessing Family Business Statistics," *Family Business Review* (1996): 107–23. For similar remarks and characteristics, see David Landes, *Dynasties: Fortunes and Misfortunes of the World's Great Family Businesses* (New York 2006), XI–XII.

2 Capitalistic practices

The Höchstetter brassworks at Pflach

On 13 December 1509, Emperor Maximilian I granted to the brothers Georg I, Ambrosius I and Hans I Höchstetter the right to establish a brass foundry in Pflach, a small locality at the meeting of the Ach and Lech rivers near the town of Reute in Tyrol.[1] He acknowledged that

> the beloved and loyal Georg, Ambrosius and Hans, the Höchstetter brothers, burghers of Augsburg, wish to erect a foundry and smithy for copper and brass in our territory, the County of Tyrol, and have petitioned and asked of us that we graciously grant and give them an appropriate space and place for the foundry and smithy with buildings, stalls, charcoal and wood storage, as well as sawmills and waterfalls.[2]

Noting the benefits that would follow – "in light of the modesty and propriety of this petition, also that such may promote our mines in Schwaz and bring benefit and good to our subjects" – and passing in silence over his own potential profit, he agreed to an advantageous location, "where once the ironworks stood, which is now decayed and broken". On this spot, iron had been mined and worked since the eighth century, if not earlier.[3] The language of the contract makes clear that the Höchstetters had chosen the location with care, already aware of its many advantages: It lay in a region that had a rich tradition of mining and metallurgy; it lay at the confluence of two rivers that could provide power and transportation; it lay near forests that could provide lumber and fuel; it lay near mines that could supply raw ores and reagents; it lay on a major shipping route that crossed the Alps and connected the mining centers of Tyrol with the commercial cities of Swabia, Franconia and points north. In short, it possessed all the qualities that might recommend it to merchants interested in the metal trade.

Maximilian's authority played an essential role in this endeavor. Only he, as Archduke of Austria, could underwrite the Höchstetters' venture with legal privileges. The 1509 grant contained several. In addition to the right to erect the foundry on property that measured roughly 2.14 acres,[4] the brothers and their heirs received the right

> to create, build and make a waterfall and pond and to possess, use, exploit, enjoy, alienate and sell, also to found and manufacture copper and to make

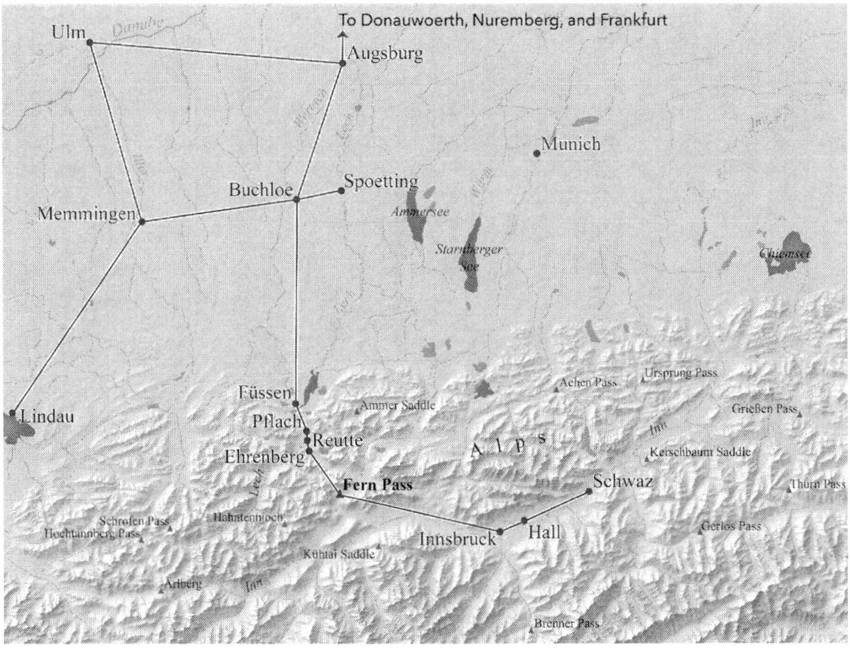

Map 2.1 Tyrol

> brass as their own unencumbered property, and in every other way to produce, trade, make or leave according to their profit, advantage and necessity also to chop, cut, burn and transport as much charcoal and wood as they may need for their founding, copper-smithing and brass-making from the aforementioned wood on both sides of the Zwiselbach and the Ach.[5]

Maximilian retained his right as prince, but the Höchstetters enjoyed full power under his authority to dispose of the land as they wished. The use of this small parcel extended beyond its proper boundaries to include forestry rights on both sides of the Zwiselbach from it to the Ach and water rights to both of the streams, rights that were limited only by the needs of the foundry.[6] Finally, Maximilian expressly prohibited the construction or creation of anything that might in anyway hinder or damage the foundry.[7] Although in private hands, the new manufactory clearly would enjoy the status of a princely enterprise.

Maximilian expressed concern for his subjects as well as his entrepreneurs. The Höchstetters' right to establish a foundry would involve certain responsibilities to the locality. They could construct a foundry and use the forests, but only to the extent that production required it. They were not permitted to sell the timber outside the locality.[8] Local residents retained the right to harvest wood from those forests to meet the needs of their households, but they could not readily cut more.[9] Any surplus had to be offered for sale to the Höchstetters;

if their foundry master did not need it, residents had to "cease wood-cutting and charcoal-burning". The Höchstetters received permission to construct a dam and pond to supply their foundry with waterpower. These structures could not hinder traffic on the rivers and streams, however; the foundry master had to assure safe passage for all barges and rafts on them.[10] Raftsmen who "wished passage had to give the foundry master notice the evening before, and the master would name a time the next day that was most convenient and least damaging to production". The Höchstetters exercised exclusive control over the banks of the Ach, but they could not interfere with droving and pasturing rights (*Allmendrechte*) on common lands adjacent to it. Specifically, they had to allow unhindered passage to and from the water for local herds and herdsmen.[11] The Höchstetters could hire foreigners "so that their necessity is discharged and not neglected", but they had to give preference to local laborers who were able and willing to do the required work, hiring them for "the customary and appropriate wage".[12] Intended to foster the utility and benefit (*Nutzung und Geniessen*) of the prince's subjects and realm, the grant left control in the hands and at the discretion of his capitalists. The new foundry should bring wealth and work to Tyrol – and to its regent. Nothing would be allowed to hinder those ends.

The 1509 agreement was not the first time that Habsburg and Höchstetter worked hand-in-glove. Their increasingly close, reciprocal relationship may have begun two decades earlier. In 1488, according to Clemens Sender, "Ambrosi Hostetter" gave a helping hand to Maximilian von Habsburg, husband of Duchess Mary of Burgundy and King of the Romans, who would in time also become Archduke of Austria and Holy Roman Emperor Maximilian I. At that point, however, the king was a prisoner of the burghers of Bruges.[13] As Sender put it:

> It came to pass at about this time that Ambrosius Höchstetter, a merchant of Augsburg, was in the city of Bruges. He had free access to the king and kept him company, raised his spirits and loaned him a great deal of money, which the pious king used to quiet the evil youths, charged with guarding and serving him, and still their impetuous, riotous, wicked and malicious uproar and life.[14]

Only when Emperor Friedrich III, appeared before the city with an army of 40,000, according to Sender, were the burghers of Bruges compelled to release Maximilian and make amends for the offense. The revolt in Bruges and Flanders ultimately collapsed; Höchstetter fortunes rapidly improved. Habsburg patronage had much to do with it.

As this incident suggests, it was not the wholesale trade in textiles – or any other commodity – alone that fueled the family's rise. Such things do not figure, however, in the received histories either of the Höchstetter family specifically or mercantile elites generally, both of which have been shaped by two broad streams of scholarship. The one emphasizes sharp-eyed and rough-shouldered practices, such as those that helped place Ambrosius among "the most hated

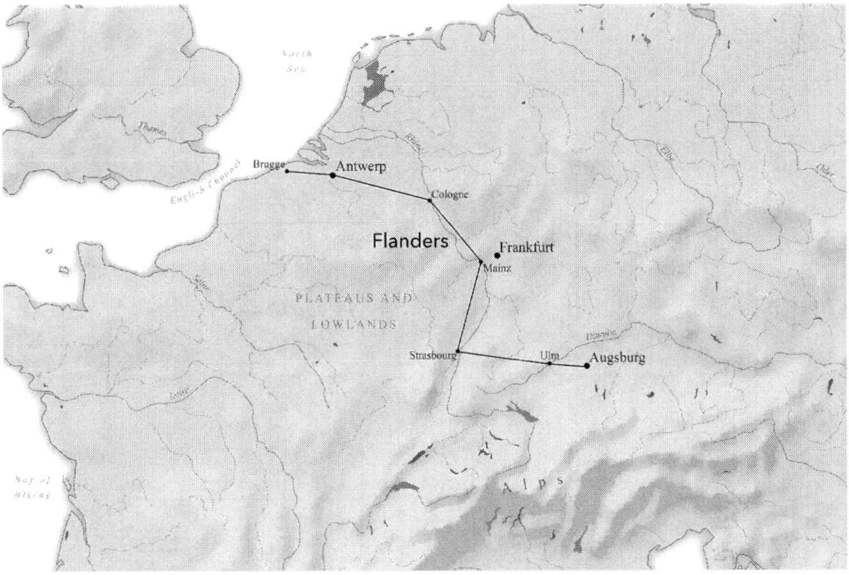

Map 2.2 Flanders

monopolists" of his day.[15] The other offers a kind of stage theory that privileges modern rationality: Premodern mercantile elites rise from production to sales, undertaking new enterprises by means of capital and experience gained in old ones;[16] they underwrite acquired wealth and personal ambition through instrumental networks of marriage alliances with established elites.[17] Evidence supports both of these accounts, but they remain incomplete. Rationality is notoriously hard to define, its meaning being embedded in specific contexts and perspectives. Ambrosius's ruthlessly consequent pursuit of wealth followed a logic of its own but violated the communal mores of his day. Social connections and political patronage possess a dynamism and fluidity of their own that deprive them of much explanatory or predictive value. The fact that Ambrosius married well does not prove that his wife's dowry or family necessarily improved or even altered the course of his career.

A third possibility, less frequently discussed by scholars, deserves greater attention: Ambrosius's actions in Bruges, risking direct contact with the Habsburg ruler in the midst of an increasingly hostile situation, were followed by decades of service and patronage that would raise the family's fortunes. Again, no evidence speaks explicitly to a connection, but his actions suggest unusual business foresight – to say nothing of sheer physical courage. Rising families may show an early capacity for accurate risk assessment and successful, opportune behavior. The Höchstetters were "always among the first" to enter new markets. They were less bound by established or traditional business practices.

Opportunism encompasses the practice or policy of exploiting circumstances or opportunities to gain immediate advantage, rather than following a predetermined plan; it describes the ability or tendency to seize advantage in a way that puts self-interest before other interests, with the implication of cynicism or disregard for moral or ethical principles or the interests of others.[18] It implies, but must be distinguished from, opportuneness, a more benign recognizing and grasping opportunities when they are timely.[19] The question is whether rising entrepreneurs, like the Höchstetters, are more inclined to be more successful practitioners of opportunism and opportuneness than are established or stable members of the business community.[20] Schumpeter's notion of entrepreneurs as "new men", less bound by traditional values and practices, suggests that some might think it so.[21]

That combination of opportuneness and opportunism, that capacity both to seize an opportunity and to act ruthlessly served Ambrosius and his family firm well. In 1490, when Maximilian succeeded to the Archduchy of Austria, which included the County of Tyrol and its wealth in mineral resources, he turned to the merchant-financiers of Augsburg for money with which to govern and defend his widespread realm and, possibly, recalled the assistance given him in Bruges only a few years earlier.[22] Profitable trading companies attracted the attention of credit-hungry princes and their financial agents.[23] As compensation and security for loans, they tendered access to princely resources, whether these were income streams from fiscal revenues, such as specific rents or taxes, or natural resources that could be exploited from princely estates. Certain German dynasties, especially the Habsburgs, whose lands were rich in mineral deposits, could offer the right to mine, refine and sell those ores. These were considered regalia of the crown, that is, the rights, prerogatives and privileges enjoyed exclusively by the sovereign. The state as such possessed no legal personality and could not engage directly in credit relations. The sovereign, therefore, had personally to guarantee payment and offer surety. Regalian rights proved particularly useful for this purpose; in exchange for the right to mine and refine minerals, the trade in which there was highly profitability, merchants advanced vast sums in credit to princes.

Exactly when the Höchstetters became involved in these exchanges is difficult to determine. By the first decade of the sixteenth century, the Höchstetter family and firm had established themselves among the social and commercial elite of South Germany. Their wealth had placed them among the urban plutocracy. They had contracted social and economic relations with powerful mercantile and patrician families. By 1501, they appear as recipients of a living and storage space (*Kammer samt Gewolbe*) that had belonged to "Heinrich Stamler and Brothers" in the *Fondaco dei Tedeschi* in Venice and thus expanded their commercial presence from the Low Countries to the Mediterranean basin. In 1505, they joined a consortium of German merchants, including the Welser and Vöhlin, Fugger, Gossenbrot, Imhof and Hirschvogel to outfit ships for the Indian spice trade under license from the Portuguese crown.[24] At about the same time, they began contracting with mine operators in Hall, Tyrol, to purchase copper and silver on a regular basis, paying at fixed rates over time.[25] "Georg and Ambrosius, the Brothers Höchstetter" had expanded beyond long-distance, wholesale trade in textiles to become leading participants in an emergent global economy. In little more than 50 years they had risen from obscure artisans and retailers to famous – and increasingly infamous – merchant-financiers. Their business expanded steadily, as did their relationship with and reliance upon the Habsburg dynasty.

Late medieval and early modern merchant-financiers cultivated political patronage and influence. In this, the Höchstetters brothers, Georg I, Ambrosius I and Hans I, were not exceptional. The practice was commonplace, especially among long-distance, wholesale merchants, whose trade crossed political borders. It seems to have belonged to the accepted techniques of trade, but it deserves closer analysis. This chapter takes up the business techniques of the Höchstetters and their family firm, not only their practices, but also their *praxes*, especially the political.

* * *

In the English language, "practice" has several familiar meanings. It is commonly and, in the case of a historical study of family firms and capitalist enterprise, properly understood as "the actual application or use of an idea, belief, or method, as opposed to the theory or principles of it" or as "the habitual doing or carrying on of something".[26] Simple as this seems, the definition masks multiple ambiguities.

The use of the term may imply moral as well as immoral actions. Though negative connotations, such as the "action of scheming or planning, especially in an underhand way or malevolently", are not unknown, they have become antiquated and uncommon in modern English usage. The same applies to the German cognate, "*Praktik*", which is commonly taken to mean a "particular manner of performance, operation; procedure", but also a "(perceived as dubious) method; not always perfect or permissible action".[27] Early German references to commercial practice likewise brought forward the potentially negative implications of "practice".[28] Lorenz Meder's *Handel Buch*, published in Nuremberg in 1558, took up practices (*practica*), and that sense of obscure – and, therefore, potentially unfair – methods remains unmistakable.[29] Nearly two centuries later, Johann Heinrich Zedler, a bookseller and publisher whose signal achievement was the creation of the most comprehensive German-language encyclopedia of the eighteenth century, the *Grosses Universal-Lexicon*, similarly saw immorality in obscurity.[30]

"Practice" also conflates two distinct, but related notions of action. It can refer to a procedure or technique, such as the daily recording of transactions in account books or the daily study of market conditions through price currents. It can also denote a *praxis*, meaning a "conscious, willed action [. . .] through which theory or philosophy is transformed into practical social activity",[31] of which examples might be the utilization of double-entry bookkeeping for the purpose of market analysis or the creation of relationships to other merchants to gather or distribute business information.

The fascination with commercial techniques – business practice in the narrow, traditional sense – may be as old as economic and business history itself. Historians have always attended to how late medieval and early modern merchants conducted their trade.[32] Where did they travel? What did they buy and sell? How did they transfer funds? What kinds of organizations and institutions did they create? Such questions have persisted over decades of research, even as the focus of that research has shifted from great merchants in the late-nineteenth and early-twentieth centuries,[33] to economic modernization in the mid-twentieth century,[34] to economic differentiation and specialization in the early-twenty-first century.[35] This scholarship shares what might be called a macrohistorical perspective on technique. Even those studies that address individual merchants or companies tend to sketch the larger traffic in various commodities and the consequences of this trade for economic development.

The Höchstetters chose their spot with care. Pflach was in every respect, as the grant stated, "an appropriate space and place for the foundry and smithy". The grant of 1509 reveals the choice but begs the following question: How did the Höchstetters learn about Pflach? They would have needed an experienced eye for the manufacturing and marketing requirements of metallurgy, but the mercantile elite of South Germany possessed such experience in full measure. How did they reach a decision to enter the market for brass? Certainly, the enterprise promised a profit, but that realization alone could not suffice. Long experience in wholesale enterprise and long association with other merchant-entrepreneurs might have inclined them to take a chance, but the care with which they conducted so much of their business – the charters that structured their firms, the grants that gave them access, the contracts that regulated transactions – suggests that they would have needed something more than a profit-seeking, risk-taking disposition. The Höchstetter brothers needed a clear understanding of the strengths and weaknesses of their family firm as an entrant in a new market, as a producer and seller of brass. They needed to know exactly what kinds of capital they possessed to underwrite the building, supplying and operating of a foundry. The 1509 grant mobilized social capital, the institutions that would help maintain and develop the enterprise, above all the approval and protection of the prince. It suggests further that the Höchstetters had a fair notion of the natural and human capital the location might provide; events would prove that these alone were not adequate. The grant also suggests that they estimated what manufactured capital – fixed assets such as building, machinery, tools, etc. – would be required. They needed also a precise notion of the financial and cultural capital they would need: What it all might cost in money, skill and labor.[36] The practices that provided this information are all but invisible.

Lack of adequate source materials too often precludes an engagement with techniques on a more detailed, process-oriented, microhistorical level. At their most technical, these can include such arcane things as market analysis, information management, negotiation routines, risk assessment and financial evaluation. The internal records that preserve this analysis survive only in a few, exceptional cases for late medieval or early modern, family firms.[37] Public archives often hold contracts that record the conclusion of negotiations, but historians rarely capture the actual thrust and parry of discussions that lead up to the final agreement, the offers and counters that grow out of both the detail of a given transaction and the culture of business conduct. How firms determined the qualitative or quantitative estimate of risk as related to a well-defined situation and a recognized threat before the discovery of mathematical probability in the mid-seventeenth century remains a mystery. Yet premodern merchant-financiers clearly understood – and calculated – acceptable risk on the basis of the expectation of loss, that expectation being most likely based on shared experience, weighed against the cost of implementing effective counter-measures. Financial analysis – the examination of historical data to gain information about past financial performance and the current and future financial health of a company – would make such a calculation conceivable in theory. Detailed financial accounts would provide a record of past commercial and financial performance and, accordingly, a rough metric of the likelihood of gain or loss in specific situations. Whether or not business functioned in this manner in fact, apart from theory, is another question. Historians simply know too little about practice at this level.

Keeping an accurate, useful record of a firm's current, running transactions requires not only careful attention, but also adequate techniques. In the sixteenth century, the technical standard in accounting was double-entry bookkeeping, a mechanism that historically has fulfilled a variety of functions: By listing witnesses and guarantors to a firm's commercial transactions, it increased legal security; by recording all a firm's business activity, it provided judicial evidence; by recording the flow in and out of a firm's cash, it controlled employee malfeasance; by precisely balancing a firm's debits and credits, it offered a running account of business success or failure.[38] Such information would have provided the Höchstetter brothers a means to analyze the costs and benefits of a brass manufactory at Pflach, to say nothing of an early warning of their later insolvency. The method was certainly available to them. Double-entry bookkeeping appears to have reached Italian merchant-banking companies from the Muslim world by the thirteenth century and to have reached the counting houses of southern Germany by the late-fifteenth or early-sixteenth century. Yet, there is no evidence that the Höchstetter firm made use of it; that only *vidimus* copies of the Höchstetter accounts survive makes the reconstruction of their bookkeeping methods impossible. Surviving accounts from many South German firms offer inconclusive evidence of it through the early-seventeenth century.[39]

Double-entry bookkeeping is a demanding and rigorous system, the costs of which might have weighed against its apparent benefits in the eyes of many premodern merchants. It requires, for example, more than the simple recording of debits and credits in a ledger. In relatively simple terms, it calls for the keeping of at least three separate books: journal or *ricordanze*; a ledger or *memorial*; and, finally, that account, *libro secreto* or *Geheimbuch*, which in the case of early modern firms might also include fair copies of other important documents, such as business charters, exchange contracts or management agreements. This last, most complete record preserves the most valuable information on premodern business techniques.

Because of the complexity of the system, double-entry bookkeeping requires not only multiple ledgers but also skilled accountants who are trained in the technique and assigned to its daily implementation. Even the requisite knowledge and personnel did not guarantee that the system would be correctly or completely applied, however. Experienced merchants, who often possess tacit knowledge of the markets in which they are active – the forces at work in them, the idiosyncrasies of suppliers and consumers, the concerns of borrowers and lenders – might use or rely irregularly on double-entry bookkeeping. B. S. Yamey has pointed to the careless manner with which medieval Italian merchants, despite being masters of accounting methods and schoolmasters of European commerce, actually applied double-entry, making it a less than accurate tool for the measurement of profit and loss.[40]

Its lack should not be taken as an indication of carelessness or of backwardness, but of the structural and organizational constraints of the day. For double-entry bookkeeping to function properly, merchants had to keep immediate, exact records of all transactions. This required, in turn, a steady flow of accurate, up-to-date information about all business activities. Late medieval and early modern business life permitted neither to function consistently.[41] All efforts notwithstanding, news of important deals could take days or weeks to move from the marketplaces of Europe to the Höchstetter *comptoir* in Augsburg.[42] And there was no guarantee either that information was recorded accurately or that it was subject to daily or even regular review. The Höchstetter partners acted as free agents, per their 1515 and 1524 charters, able to contract whatever business and commit whatever resources they wished, bound only by their oath to act on the firm's behalf. Their notions of the firm's interest remained largely uncoordinated, not only by the lack of constraint, but also by the venues of exchange. They moved frequently from marketplace to marketplace, representing the firm and transacting business at its various far-flung factories. Between the slowness of communication and the freedom of the partners, accurate and current accounts of any sort likely proved the exception rather than the rule and could not serve as a guide for quotidian, much less long-term decision-making. One gets the impression not of a delinquent disorder, but of an accommodation to the workaday messiness of business life. Accordingly, accounting techniques, like other business practices, should be considered not in the abstract but within a specific social context.

Attention to the sociological work of Pierre Bourdieu has helped economic and business historians to expand attention from techniques as such to the social settings in which they occur. At the center of Bourdieu's theory is a "logic of practice" that emphasizes physical proficiency and competent ability in a social situation or field.[43] In other words, Bourdieu understood practice as *praxis*. People do not, according to Bourdieu, continuously calculate in line with explicitly articulated, rational criteria, but act on an implicit practical sense or feel for what is appropriate in a given setting or situation that Bourdieu equates roughly with *habitus*, defined as patterns of feeling, thought and action, acquired in response to the real social conditions individuals have encountered, which guide actions within similar social situations. Bourdieu's theory of action seeks to show that social agents develop unconscious and conscious strategies that are adapted to the needs of their social settings and lives. *Habitus* operates within these settings to yield *praxis*. Historians have taken up Bourdieu's emphasis on the importance of *habitus* in a social setting, looking at the ways various structures and relations can shape practice and, *mutatis mutandis*, be subtly altered by it.

The Höchstetters and many of their peers understood and anticipated this messiness. The independence accorded partners and agents was a necessary response to it. The slowness of communication required the presence of representatives, whether partners or employees, company factors or commission agents, to gather local information and to transact company business in the great marketplaces and entrepôts of Europe. The European market of the sixteenth century resembled a series of spot markets, in which bills or commodities are traded immediately – on the spot – at a price agreed between buyer and seller and with settlement within a fixed, usually brief, if not immediate, period of time. Agents, whether partners or employees, needed a degree of freedom to buy and sell for their principals, because the principals were seldom as well informed about local conditions as their agents, and because opportunities might otherwise be lost in the time required for communication and approval. Hence the asymmetry of information, the fear of opportunism and the need for trust.

Lorenz Meder confirms unmistakably the fragmented nature of the European market, when his *Handel Buch* rehearses the different units of measure and specie and the varying customs of exchange, to say nothing of the different commodity and transaction costs, that existed simultaneously in the great marketplaces of Europe.[44] He has nothing to say about double-entry bookkeeping, though as a *Rechenmeister* active in a manufacturing and commercial environment, he must have been familiar with it.[45] That was not his point or purpose.

The "practices" he wished to teach were matters of local knowledge, insider information that made business success possible. To take a single case in point, his book opens with a chapter on "The Venetian Trade", the largest chapter of the entire volume, a reflection on the importance of Venice for German commerce and manufacturing. It begins with the warning: "Whoever wishes to engage in buying and selling in Venice must necessarily pay good attention and ask himself about the following items":[46] The arrival seasons of the great convoys and their cargoes; the condition of various perishable commodities and market information about commodities of interest, "so that he knows how to create his advantage". For all his emphasis on "*practica*", Meder's introduction testifies to the supreme importance of accurate, up-to-date information. The *Handel Buch* serves as a guide to local mercantile usage and custom. As Kellenbenz noted in his 1974 critical edition of the *Handel Buch*,

> It was not Meder's main concern to give his reader an overview of the extent of Nuremberg or Upper German trade in his day, but his focus was much more to offer instruction to fellow Nurembergers and other South German landsmen from a rich treasury of experience about what was important to note in individual trading centers, which would be helpful in questions of business technique.[47]

He assumed that his readers, even young merchants, already knew business practices but needed local information, everything from local weights and measures to customary fees and *douceurs*, commodity inspection procedures, customary payment methods and frequently encountered coinage.

Meder understood "*practica*" as *praxes*, purposeful actions undertaken in social settings. Techniques were commonplace, could be learned anywhere; local usages and customs constituted essential, arcane – and, therefore, potentially unethical, because they allowed one to take advantage at another's expense – knowledge. Kellenbenz makes the point that Meder quite deliberately exposed what merchants had long held secret: "He was the first in the German-speaking world to renounce secrecy, and it would require a number of generations finally to overcome this taboo".[48] Even Jacques Savary, as he notes, who wrote his business handbook a century later, still had to defend himself against the accusation of revealing secret knowledge.[49] "Here Meder trod in fact on uncharted territory, as his introduction suggested".[50] In his treatment of practices, he resolved both their conceptual and their moral ambiguities.

The imperial grant of 1509 offers an example of business practices in all their ambiguity and business *praxes* in all their complexity. Though itself a perfectly legal and routine document, its terms indicate, without exposing, the practices employed by the Höchstetter brothers: Market analysis, financial planning, information management, risk assessment. The document makes clear the importance of the social fields in which these techniques were applied: Their political relationship with the territorial prince and their economic relationship to the neighboring community. It also suggests the moral ambivalence of the transaction. Though Maximilian takes pains to protect the local economy, he enables the Höchstetters to exploit it for their own ends. Scholars insist that preindustrial economic agents commonly underwrote their activities in precisely this manner, by embedding – the word itself frequently employed – them in a variety of social relationships, including not only clientage, but also kinship, partnership and confession, among others.[51] Yet, the same scholars also note that these systems of relationships could malfunction, even rupture. At Pflach and elsewhere, business *praxis* did not translate smoothly into business success.

* * *

The Höchstetters did not explicate their reasons for deciding to construct their foundry and manufacture brass at Pflach. The 1509 grant suggests broadly the factors under consideration and the terms of negotiation that would influence the venture's success. And successful it ultimately was. Though no financial records exist, the foundry appears to have increased capacity in the first decades of its existence.[52] The physical plant grew to include housing for workers, stalls for livestock, storage for wood and clamps or kilns for charcoal production, all in addition to the basic forges, smithies and smelteries that brass manufacturing required. It even included an elegant chapel. That success relied on the Höchstetters' business *praxes*.

The decision to produce brass may seem unusual at first glance. Histories of early modern mining and metallurgy concentrate on the extraction of such raw materials as lead, copper and silver, all of which were strategic, commercial commodities of the age.[53] Even Georg Agricola, the great Renaissance expert on mining and metals, gave it only passing mention under the rubric of smelting. His reserve was substantial, as he noted:

> Whether brass, however, is found as a native metal or not, cannot be ascertained with any surety. We only know of artificial brass, which consists of copper tinted with the colour of the mineral calamine. And yet if any should be dug up, it would be a proper metal.[54]

Confusion existed whether brass was a true metal, in nature like copper or silver. It is, in fact, a metallic alloy of copper and zinc, in which variations in the proportion of its components result in varieties of brass with different characteristics. Increasing the zinc content resulted in greater fusibility, brittleness and hardness of the brass. In general, brass is more malleable than bronze, an alloy of copper and tin, and has a relatively low melting point, which makes it easier to work than many "true" metals and possesses flow characteristics that make it relatively easy to cast. The comparative efficiency of production, combined with the variability of product, explains its historical popularity after iron and copper, which are the most frequently forged of all metals.

Evidence of brass-making exists from prehistory. Commonplace from Western Europe to South Asia and Africa during the first millennium BCE, its secrets appear to have been lost after the fall of the Roman Empire and not rediscovered until the tenth century CE. Brass manufacturing reemerged in areas close to accessible deposits of zinc – usually in the form of the mineral calamine (*Galmei*) – including England, the Low Countries and Germany.[55] In general, two manufacturing methods existed in the Middle Ages and persisted into the Renaissance: An open-crucible, liquid process[56] and the cementation process.[57] The cementation process was more efficient than the open-crucible method because it required less heat and resulted in less waste. It is unclear which method the Höchstetters employed, though inventories taken at Pflach in the late-sixteenth century indicate that the foundry at some point adopted cementation.[58] In either case, making brass required skilled and experienced workers, a fact that haunted the Höchstetters throughout their tenancy.

For all that scholars past wondered about its true nature and scholars present consign it to a modest place among metals, brass played a central role in early modern metallurgy and metal-working. Lead, copper and silver were more important, served a multitude of purposes, were mined in greater quantities and generated greater wealth. Copper and silver, for example, served as monetary metals and their supply, accordingly, affected the rate of economic expansion in the period. Copper and lead were also used extensively in construction and manufacturing. Because of its efficiency, variability and appearance – the addition of zinc made copper look like bright gold – brass found use in all sorts of quotidian and decorative objects. It could be made into buttons or housewares. It figured importantly in the trade with Africa. It was used extensively in musical instruments and decorative objects because of its combination of high workability and durability. For the same reasons, brass found growing military application, being cast into firearms and artillery. It comes as no surprise, therefore, that an impecunious, marshal prince like Maximilian would wish to promote domestic industry by encouraging copper and calamine mining and brass manufacturing in his realm. It comes as no surprise, likewise, that merchant-entrepreneurs like the Höchstetters would seize the opportunity such a wish provided.

They were not the first to forge brass in Tyrol.[59] In 1492, a Peter Rumel from Lichtenau sold a brass foundry to Maximilian I. Earlier still, in 1476, the Augsburger Hans Mayenstetter received permission to extract calamine, which he could sell or use to produce brass. In this case, it remains unclear whether, in fact, the mining of calamine led to the making of brass. Whether or not the first, the Höchstetters' foundry *am Steinenberg* by Pflach quickly became the most important, becoming capable of altering commercial and social relations in Tyrol.

The production of brass required supplies of copper, calamine, wood, charcoal and crucibles. All of these were locally available, except for the special, fire-resistant clay for the crucibles, which had to be imported from locations in Lower Bavaria.[60] The Höchstetters knew this, and one of their first tasks, apart from constructing the foundry itself, would have been to secure their supply. The charter of 1509 and subsequent contract arrangements granted them monopoly rights to raw materials and encouraged vertical integration of production.

The earliest references to Höchstetter copper purchases precede the foundry at Pflach. Beginning in 1507 and occurring regularly between 1515 and 1519, they purchased copper from Schwaz, Tyrol, northeast of Innsbruck and Pflach.[61] Thereafter, such purchases become more isolated, raising the possibility that

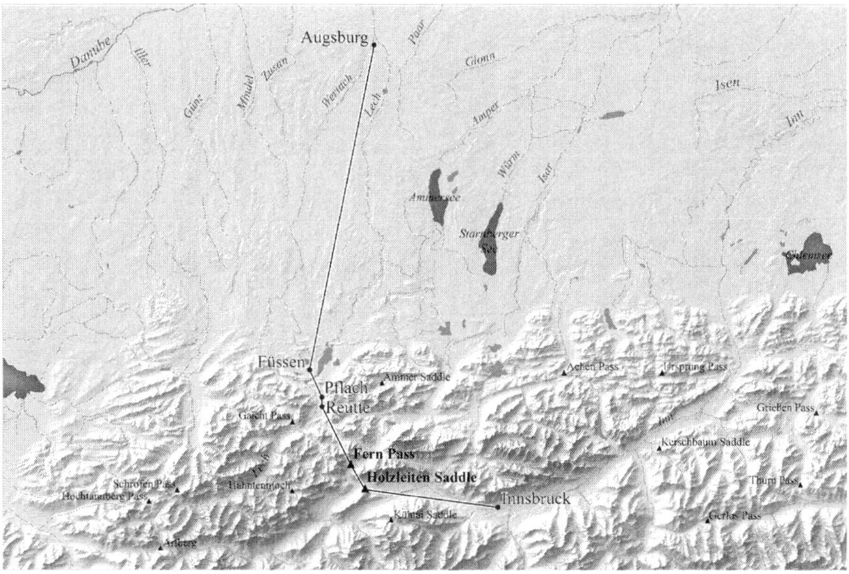

Map 2.3 Detail of Tyrol, showing Steinenberg, Tauffers and vicinity

they acquired ore in some other manner. Whether the brothers acquired their own copper mines to supply their brass foundry cannot be reconstructed with certainty. Bankruptcy records in 1529 indicate that they possessed shares of one or more copper mines near Schwaz. Kern's reasoning that the Höchstetters acquired at least some of their interest in copper mines via the bankruptcy of the Nuremberg Paumgartners in 1522 may have merit.[62] The same records also mention mines in St. Joachimstal, in Bohemia, but the exact dates of their acquisitions, the extent of their holdings and the nature of their activities remain unclear. They seem to have relied chiefly on purchases from producers; record of such activity becomes frequent from the year 1511. This suggests the possibility that the brassworks at Pflach began operation in that year after a two-year construction period.

With or without copper mines of their own, the Höchstetter trafficked heavily in the metal. Paul von Liechtenstein, the Lord of Ehrenberg, the region around Pflach, reported in 1510, "Once the Höchstetters have assumed the contract to purchase complete inventories of copper, they may export it without hindrance".[63] Tariff records confirm that they shipped 1,311 hundredweight of copper between June and December of that year.[64] And the volume grew over the following 15 years. Höchstetter copper probably made its way to all the major trading centers of Europe, traveling south to Venice and north to Antwerp, where it was resold to other merchants and moved to other manufacturing centers. Records from the city of Nuremberg, for example, indicate wide-ranging sales of copper to local artisans from the 1510s forward. Contz Distler, for example, became deeply indebted to the Höchstetters, using his house as security to pay for copper.[65] The Höchstetter factor Stephan Gabler advanced copper in large and small amounts to Nuremberg coppersmiths (*Keßler*), wire-makers (*Drahtzieher*) and others against repayment in cash and kind.[66] By so doing, the firm drew them into credit relations that resulted in durable dependency on the part of the artisans.

Of particular interest is the practice of acquisition. Regardless of the metal, mining and metallurgy formed a concentrated, heavy industry.[67] It was extremely capital-intensive, not only by virtue of the technology, which required large investments, but also by virtue of the regents, who required financial advances. Under Ambrosius I's leadership, the Höchstetters focused in tried and true ways on the Habsburg territories of Tyrol; they offered credit to the dynasts in exchange for the industrial and commercial rights to produce and sell metals created from ore deposits in their lands.[68] In 1511, the Höchstetters extended 5,000 fl in credit to Emperor Maximilian I to support his armies in their war against the Republic of Venice. Maximilian guaranteed repayment on 27 June 1511 by promising the Höchstetters a supply of "*Tauferer Kupfer*", that is, copper from Taufers in Munstertal, far to the south of Pflach, for a three-year period.[69] For the following three years, until 1514, they received exclusive rights to purchase 1,000 to 1,500 Viennese hundredweight (*Zentner Wiener Gewichts* = 56 kilograms) at 5 fl 45 kr per hundredweight, which they could dispose as they pleased.[70] Presumably, some of this copper found its way to the foundry at Pflach. It also made its way to the armory in Innsbruck, where the Höchstetters sold it.[71] Excess copper could be sold to no one other than the Höchstetters, but had to be left lying until they claimed it. In 1514, Maximilian extended for five years the previous three-year agreement to include all copper produced at Taufers at a fixed price of 5 fl 45 kr per hundredweight, effectively giving the Höchstetters monopoly control.[72] As before, the guarantee set aside 200 hundredweight, which the Höchstetters had to supply at need to the armory at Innsbruck and for the casting (*Grabguß*) of the brass figures that would eventually adorn Maximilian's tomb in the *Hofkirche* at Innsbruck.[73] It also required a further 300 be sold to Ulrich Kissinger for his foundry in Mühlau.[74] At about the same point in time, on 10 November 1514, Maximilian reached a similar agreement with Jacob Fugger and company regarding copper from the mines at Schwaz.[75] The Fuggers received exclusive rights to sell this copper with the proviso that 2,500 hundredweight "*Schwazer Kupfer*" be sold to the Höchstetters at 5 fl per hundredweight, that is, for a unit price above that of Taufers.[76] Copper brought the Höchstetters into ever more intense competition with other South German merchant families, especially the Fuggers. In 1517, Maximilian I compelled them to join the Fuggers in a cartel that sought to regulate the production and sale of Tyrolean copper.[77] A loan of more than 5,000 fl may have prompted an extension of the 1514 agreement that gave the Höchstetters control of the sale of Taufers copper. On 25 February 1518, Maximilian I negotiated another five-year term.[78] Until 1524, they would continue to enjoy the right to purchase all copper produced at Taufers for the fixed price of 5 fl 45 kr per hundredweight. This agreement would extend then indefinitely until Ulrich Kissinger and other creditors, to whom the Höchstetters would continue to sell their copper, were repaid in full. Without production records from Pflach, it seems clear that producing brass consumed a great deal of Tyrolean copper. Initial supplies from Taufers proved insufficient, requiring supplementation from the mines around Schwaz. The Höchstetters secured raw materials, not by purchasing them openly at the mines or foundries that produced them, but by extending credit repeatedly to the regent, who guaranteed in return fixed supplies at fixed prices for a fixed period.

Thus secured by political arrangement against market volatility, the Höchstetters could begin to reckon their own costs of production and to project the price for finished brass. From 1511 until 1524, they paid no more than 5 fl 45 kr per hundredweight of copper, regardless of any changes in supply of or demand for the metal, and purchased only so much as they pleased. Nor did they cease with guarantees of fixed supplies and fixed prices. They regularly sought to reduce transaction costs, especially the fees and tolls associated with transportation. These may have been high, given that both Schwaz and Taufers lie at considerable distances through mountain valleys and passes from Pflach, between 122 and 142 kilometers and 140 and 145 kilometers, respectively, depending on the route taken. In this they enjoyed mixed success. On 5 June 1514, the government at Innsbruck ordered two of its toll officers, Gilg Fronheimer in Rattenberg and Adam Ganndtner in Zirl to permit the toll-free passage of 2,000 and 3,000 hundredweight of copper respectively.[79] On 25 February 1518, it sent another order to Ganndtner to permit the Höchstetters to ship 3,000 hundredweight of copper through Zirl without hindrance, in accordance with their contracts, but this time to assess the usual duties for it.[80] Similar orders were sent on 6 February 1522 to Hildebrandt von Speyer and Leonhard Assch, keepers of the toll station, Sigmundsegg, at Nauders in the Reschen Pass in Tyrol: Brass was to pass unhindered and untaxed.[81] And, again, on 22 June 1523, the government ordered its customs officials, Michel Hesse at the Mühlbacher Klause in Mühlbach at the entrance to the Pustertal, Hanns Kugler at Kuttersweg and Sigmund Brandisser in Bozen, to permit passage of 600 hundredweight of Tauferer copper without hindrance or tariff.[82] This last order, it would seem, intended to promote the shipment of Höchstetter copper beyond the boundaries of Tyrol. Central to their business *praxes* was the Höchstetters' political relationship to the regent and his family. They used their long association as reliable providers of credit to negotiate not only access to markets, but also favorable terms of trade.

This applied to calamine, no less than copper. Seeking to acquire this essential raw material for brass manufacturing, the Höchstetters enjoyed a significant advantage, particularly in comparison to their access to copper: It was more immediately available. Calamine proved abundant in the mountains surrounding the Fern Pass, which lies less than 30 kilometers from Pflach.[83] Surviving government records suggest, however, that it caused the Höchstetters disproportionate difficulties. No records of calamine purchases survive from the first years of operation at Pflach. In 1517, eight years after the initial grant of rights to manufacture brass and at least six years after smelting began, the brothers protested to the government at Innsbruck that they were being cheated. Three years earlier, in 1514, the government had appointed Hans Tiefenbrunn, a forester from Reutte, to measure calamine and assess the *Fron* on it.[84] For every "*Tonne*", which could contain at most six "*Ster*" [sic], measured immediately at the mine, he was to collect 12 kr, keeping half as his wage and forwarding to Innsbruck the balance as revenue.[85] The Höchstetters accused him of giving false measure for the calamine they purchased for their foundry, and, because the measure both affected its revenue and offended its creditor, the government considered the matter sufficiently important to take action.[86] It ordered the responsible *Bergrichter*, Heinrich Siegler at Imst, to see to it that the Höchstetters and all others received proper measure as was customary usage in mining and metallurgy.[87] Several months later, on 30 October 1517, the government wrote to Siegler again, noting its previous mandate that the measure for calamine be calibrated to assure accuracy and prevent complaint.[88] Apparently, the problem persisted. It therefore ordered Siegler to repeat the process and to provide the Höchstetters with a *Ster* of their own, should they wish it. That they could obtain a measure of their own may suggest the influence they enjoyed in Innsbruck, an influence they exercised readily.

A second issue, related to payment of the government's *Fron* on calamine, emerged in 1524. The Höchstetters' factor in Pflach, Georg Hagen, had taken untaxed calamine from the mine to his foundry, where he then measured it and paid the *Fron*, despite the dictate of custom and law that it be assessed and paid immediately at the point of extraction. The government charged him with a violation of its tax regulation.[89] It ordered its local *Bergrichter* to forbid anyone from transporting untaxed calamine away from the mine, and it warned Hagen that he faced prosecution should he violate the ordinance again. As the Höchstetters were important producers of brass and consumers of calamine in Tyrol, this sharp note concerned them directly, even though it never mentioned their name. The next day, 8 April 1524, a similar order, issued over the signature of Archduke Ferdinand I to all mining officials along the length of the Inn River, emphasized the importance of enforcing the *Fron* on calamine.[90] For all their financial influence, the Höchstetters were not completely above the law, even in the eyes of their patrons, especially when it concerned revenue.

The difficulties with the *Fron* on calamine involved the market for the mineral. In the same year that the government warned Georg Hagen about paying the tax, Hagen submitted a petition to the government in which he complained about the assessment.[91] He requested that the government allow him and others to pay the *Fron* not in cash, but in kind, or not at all. He reasoned that calamine had lost value and was less often traded. For this reason, a tax of 12 kr per *Ster* had become a financial burden. The government responded by creating a commission to examine the condition of the mine and determine whether Hagen's request was justified.[92] They were to inspect the mine itself, question earlier officials and other nonpartisan experts and report whether it would be better for the archduke and his government to tax calamine in cash or kind and whether doing so would ruin the mining operation. A government edict of 28 July 1525 makes the results clear. The trade in calamine had declined over the past few years, reducing the value of the mineral on the open market. To prevent the mine and its miners from suffering further loss, the *Fron* would be reduced from 12 to 8 kr per *Tonne*. Reducing the tax would reduce the cost of calamine for the merchants who traded in it, so the government's reasoning, allowing them to lower the price, which would increase demand. This would, in turn, spur production at the mine, enabling the miners to earn a living, the operators to make a profit and, not least, the government to collect its taxes. Behind this careful, market-oriented logic, however, stood the influence of the Höchstetter firm, represented by its factor, Georg Hagen. As the principal consumer of calamine, concern for its profit set the entire revision in motion. The necessity of supporting local industry and local workers weighed in the balance as well, but the government's edict focused on the interests of capital.

The Höchstetters utilized their political relations to promote their brass manufactory. The 1509 land grant at Pflach put them in a geographically advantageous position to utilize natural resources, acquire production factors and transport finished products. Their credit transactions correlate closely with the purchase of raw materials, especially copper, at guaranteed prices. Over time, they obtained monopsony control of copper extracted by the mines at Taufers and enjoyed guaranteed rights of purchase at Schwaz. This suggests that the Höchstetters strove for a degree of vertical integration in their brass manufacturing, combining control of supplies with exclusive rights to produce and sell. Their reliance on political influence to secure rational practices did not preclude a degree of opportunism, as their factor's readiness to violate customs ordinances makes clear. Without a willingness to practice in the field of politics, however, the brass foundry at Pflach could hardly have succeeded.

* * *

Despite all signs of growth, even with state-guaranteed supplies of raw materials, operations at Pflach were not flawless, far from it. Indeed, the problems and conflicts that occasionally marked the two decades of business activity, between the founding in 1509 and the bankruptcy in 1529, hint at many of the firm's business *praxes*. Just how steadily the government supported the interests of capital becomes clear in the records of a series of conflicts between the foundry at Pflach and the community of Breitenwang as well as a long-term dispute between the foundry and the city of Nuremberg. These began soon after the brass foundry became established and persisted till the collapse of the family firm in bankruptcy.

In 1513, the government appointed mediators to settle a dispute between the Höchstetters and Breitenwang about the size and placement of the industrial complex.[93] The community complained that buildings had been constructed outside the boundaries of the land grant, but the commission did not find-that to be the case. The buildings could remain as constructed. The community complained about a canal the Höchstetters had ordered dug. It, too, stood within the land grant and, thus, within the entrepreneurs' right, but the commissioners added the condition that it be refilled when no longer needed, so as not to cause damage or loss to local inhabitants. The community objected to the construction of a grill-work (*Rechen*) where the Plansee, a lake to the east of Pflach, flows into the Ach River. The commission noted that the Ach was part of the 1509 grant to the Höchstetters, so the *Rechen* could remain. Likewise, the construction of a clay pit (*Lehmgrube*) stood on land granted to the Höchstetters and could not be hindered. The community complained that the foundry violated their rights of pasturage (*Allmendrechte*), especially the passage of their livestock to customary water and grazing. Again, the commission found this not to be the case, but noted that the foundry manager should permit the herds to pass, provided that the herders asked permission, as the 1509 grant specified. Disputes regarding transportation, whether on road or river, were settled in accordance with the 1509 grant, that is, the Höchstetters were guaranteed free passage, but were required to use local raftsmen and teamster whenever possible. The community also opposed the sale of wine to workers at the foundry, probably fearing the loss of trade for local shop- and tavern-keepers. The commission found that the Höchstetters themselves sold the wine, rather than hiring or permitting an outside vendor. As such, it constituted part of the common practice of *Pfennwert*, in which employers compensated their workers in foodstuffs and other necessities, as well as in wages. The Höchstetters could determine of all such matters.

At nearly every point, the commission found for the Höchstetters, and against Breitenwang. On one level, it merely acted in accordance with the terms of the archduke's grant. At another level, it steadfastly compromised the traditional rights and usages of the local community. The decision handed down in 1513 implies quite clearly that the community did not see many benefits arising from the new industry, contrary to the archduke's frequently stated intention to promote local prosperity. Rather, the brass foundry limited the use of the few natural resources that the community could draw from a region fundamentally lacking in them. The manufactory did little to alleviate local poverty; the commission did nothing to change that.

So fundamental was the opposition between industry and locality that the conflict renewed almost immediately after the commission released its findings. On 18 May 1517, a second commission concluded its attempt to mediate another dispute between the Höchstetters and communities of Reute and Breitenwang.[94] Access to waterways remained an issue. The foundry had continued to expand its complex and intensify its production, adding a second grill-work on the Ach to catch debris as it was floated downstream. The commission found that the structure violated no right or custom and could remain, but that it had to be removed when not in use. Neither could its function be allowed to damage a local oil mill that stood on the bank. The Höchstetters also constructed two new hammer smithies (*Hammerlege*) for working the brass. Apparently, these were water driven, as they required the construction of a new mill pond. The community had complained that the dam obstructed traffic on the stream. The commission responded that it must be so constructed as to create no hindrance, but the Höchstetters need dismantle neither it nor the new works that depended on it. Indeed, the commission expressly permitted continued building within the bounds of the land grant. The Höchstetters had constructed additional charcoal clamps or kilns (*Kohlenmeiler*), and these the commission also permitted, provided they did no harm to neighboring residents. Access to grazing, too, continued to pose a problem. Grill-works and dams not only obstructed traffic on rivers, but also blocked the passage of herds to pastures. In response to the communities' repeated claims that the foundry disrupted the local, agricultural economy, the commission ordered the Höchstetters to construct at their own cost a roadway that would permit the people of Breitenwang to drive their herds and wagons through the foundry grounds to and from the rivers. Further, they had to pay the community compensation of 40 fl annually for these unavoidable inconveniences. The question of foodstuffs arose again as well. This time, the sale not only of wine but also of meat was at issue. The trades of Breitenwang continued to view the foundry as a source of competition, its sales taking desirable custom away from them. The commission of 1517 repeated the decision of its predecessor: The open sale of foodstuffs to workers at the foundry was forbidden, but the provision of foodstuffs to workers by their employers was not.

Foundry and community competed in many respects; the fact that the foundry belonged to foreigners, people from outside the community and the region, heightened competition. The foundry also employed outsiders, and this proved another point of conflict in 1517. The commission ordered the community to permit foundry workers and their families to rent or purchase dwellings, if they paid the *Einkaufsgeld*, a customary fee charged by most Tyrolean communities to outsiders who wished to settle in them. Evidently, the authorities of Reutte and Breitenwang had refused to accept payment from foundry workers and thus made harder both the workers' search for suitable quarters and the Höchstetters' recruitment of skilled labor. The strained economic relationship between foundry and community had reached such a pitch that the commission announced the government's intention to appoint a *Bergrichter* who would henceforth act as judge in such matters.

Occasional concessions to local residents notwithstanding, the government in Innsbruck shielded the foundry and its operators from interference. This was at no point clearer than in 1525, when Emperor Charles V declared the Höchstetters' operation at Pflach to be a sanctuary (*Freiung*).[95] The status of sanctuary meant nothing less than liberation from local jurisdiction. Any person who in any way injured another on the grounds of the foundry as defined in 1509 would answer not to the local authorities in Breitenwang or Reutte, but directly to the justice and jurisdiction of the regent or his representative, the *Bergrichter*. Only in the instance of serious crimes (*Blutvergehen*) would the malefactor be delivered to the local court. This placed another level of legal protection between the foundry and its local critics, assuring the Höchstetters at the very least an impartial hearing, and more likely a sympathetic one.

In 1528, the government in Innsbruck had to intervene again between foundry and community. The conflicts appear to have intensified. An edict from Archduke Ferdinand, dated 20 June 1528, ordered yet another commission to investigate a complaint by Breitenwang.[96] The Höchstetter factor, Georg Hagen, had constructed a grain storage facility (*Speicher*) on foundry grounds and had hired a foreign baker. Consistent with his earlier practices, so the community, he had continued to hire foreign butchers and teamsters, violating not only the local control of food sales but also the requirement to hire local laborers. Hagen, acting as legal representative of his principals, replied that the 1509 grant sanctioned these activities. His firm could build whatever it needed on the land reserved for its use. It could hire butchers or bakers and supply its workers with food and drink in whatever way it decided, without constraint from anyone. Likewise, the decision to hire teamsters lay with it. Though the commission's decision does not survive, it seems unlikely that it would depart radically from the consistent policy of its predecessors. The activities of the foundry should not work to the disadvantage of the community, but the community could not interfere in the legitimate function of the foundry. The Höchstetters could continue to manufacture brass as they saw fit.

At the center of these conflicts lay resources. Foundry and community viewed one another as competitors. Not only the use of local waterways and pasturage, but also the harvesting of trees in local forests and the employing of local laborers figured prominently in all these disputes. The commission of 1513, 1517 and 1528 warned Breitenwang that its residents could not impede the Höchstetters' operations. Only in 1529 did the government find against the Höchstetters. Having taken trees from community forests, they were required to pay a fine of nearly 31 fl, a considerable sum for local foresters, but small change for princely financiers.[97]

What do these disputes and their resolutions reveal about the Höchstetters' business *praxes*? They indicate that foreign capital, in this case, sought its own utility by taking advantage of power and distance to circumvent the customs or needs of local communities. It is true that the Höchstetters upheld the formal letter of their grant, building and operating within its prescribed, geographic and social limits. Yet, they appear to have made no effort to engage Breitenwang and Reute, disarm their concerns or construct positive relations. These communities were impoverished and impotent. What shaped relations were not vaguely defined, socially determined institutional constraints, such as trust, mutuality or reciprocity, but clear-cut articulations of opportunity and power. When conflict arose, the Höchstetters turned to the archduke as judge, confident, one suspects, that their relationship, their capacity to offer him money and materials, would protect their interests. Nor were these expectations disappointed. The archducal commissions steadfastly defended the interests of capital. The contention of local historians that "as authorities one remained interested in the pasturage rights of the populace and upheld them steadfastly" appears to have applied only in the breach.[98] The imposition of compensatory payments did nothing to restore the customary rights or usages that the new industry violated. Moreover, the quotidian resolution of these conflicts lay unreservedly in the hands of the Höchstetters, who granted access as they pleased, took what they needed and remained otherwise masters within their own bounds.

Foundry and community fought over human as well as natural resources. The 1509 land grant specified that the Höchstetters employ local labor to the extent that skill and supply permitted. It expressed the expectation as well that the foundry's local purchases would promote local labor not immediately employed by it and thus stimulate the local economy. Few of these specifications and expectations were met. While its purchases of copper and calamine helped support Tyrolean mining, the foundry stole bread out of the mouths of families, as well as the communities, by refusing to buy local products and by importing foreign suppliers. And it did not increase local employment.

Workers at the foundry were foreigners, a group with which the local populations wanted little or no contact, as demonstrated by the dispute involving payment of the local *Einkaufsgeld*. The foreigners shared that antipathy, an attitude that not only excluded local inhabitants from employment by the Höchstetters but complicated the search for skilled labor. In a 1524 petition to the government in Innsbruck, the Höchstetters complained that their master craftsmen refused to train or employ any Tyroler.[99] If they could not operate the foundry at the appropriate level of craftsmanship, they argued, they would lose money. If the foundry closed, the archduchy would lose revenues from customs and tolls, and its copper and calamine mines would lose sales. Given the potential damage, the Höchstetters requested that the archduke command the master craftsmen at Pflach to teach their craft to local residents who were suited to the work. Those masters who refused to comply should be threatened with severe punishment. The outcome of this petition is not known. It seems unlikely, however, that a governmental order would break the masters' control of skill.

The Höchstetters' foundry required skilled hands to operate it. These they found in Nuremberg. By the mid-fifteenth century, that city was a center for brass-working, a status it sought to preserve by restricting the emigration of its skilled artisans. As their foundry at Pflach began manufacturing brass, the Höchstetters systematically violated these regulations, offering premiums to entice Nuremberg master and journeymen brass-workers and wire-makers away.[100] When their factor, Stefan Gabler, was not selling copper to craftsmen and ensnaring them in credit-debt relations, he was recruiting them for a distant enterprise. The Nuremberg guild of brass-workers reacted swiftly, arguing that the dissemination of brass-working knowledge and skill beyond the boundaries of the city and its manufacturing would "bring deterioration and irreversible destruction to the entire craft, by which more than two hundred people have their livelihoods, and deprive them [sic] of a trade that for many long years has been in and come to this city alone".[101] Nuremberg had enjoyed a commanding position in brass-working and other metal trades; it was in everyone's interest to keep it that way. In 1511, the City Council agreed: Any emigration from Nuremberg for purposes of practicing the skills of brass-making would henceforth result in banishment. It would mean permanent separation from extended family and craft community; it would mean the loss of all the rights and protections of membership in the guild or citizenship in the city.[102]

Yet, the international traffic in labor proved far less easy to steer than the council's edict suggests. Records do not clearly indicate what the Höchstetters offered these workers to encourage them to leave the safety of an established manufacturing center for the risks of joining an emerging commercial enterprise. In 1512, the council responded to a further petition, this time from Paul von Liechtenstein, who was immediate lord of the territory upon which the Höchstetter foundry was located. It noted that unskilled workers – they used the word, *Knecht*, rather than the usual terms of masters or journeymen, *Meister* or *Gesell* – had left Nuremberg with the consent of their craft masters and ordered the proper officials "to consider that, when one or more of these workers, who have moved to the Höchstetter foundries, or would have gone there without permission, returned to Nuremberg and requested rights of citizenship, they should not be accepted".[103] By 1515 at the latest, master and journeymen brass-workers and wire-makers who had left Nuremberg to take employment with the Höchstetters – their firm apparently expanded its enterprise beyond brass-making to the manufacture of wire and, quite probably, other metal goods, for which they continued to seek skilled workers from Nuremberg – began to press for permission to reenter the city.[104] This may have been a consequence of the tensions between foreigners and locals at Pflach. The council responded that it "did not wish to hinder them, they may come in without risk, where they find work or in other ways produce their advantage, the council will allow it". The fact that these petitioners were skilled craftsmen (*Meister* and *Gesellen*), as opposed to the unskilled laborers (*Knechte*) for whom von Liechtenstein interceded, may have influenced policy. Such hands were worth more to the city's manufacturing. Imperial interest and intercession might also explain it; Maximilian I supported the Höchstetters' interests. And capital could find ways to subvert any attempt at regulation. One Nuremberg court record states that, on 28 May 1519, "Steffan Gabler and Ambros Hochstetter paid 5 fl to [the brass-worker Fritz Guntz]".[105] If this was a premium paid for moving to Pflach, the international traffic in labor continued unabated.

Another, greater conflict over the recruitment of brass-workers arose at this point. The Höchstetters' poaching of metal-workers had reached such a level by 1520 that Nuremberg authorities imprisoned and fined the company's representatives, Steffan Gabler and Hanns Gutrat, who, supported by their firm's principals, appealed to the emperor for their release. They also petitioned that those workers who wished to return to Nuremberg from the foundries in Tyrol, but still owed time or money there, be denied entry, just as those workers who wished to go to Tyrol, but still owed time or money in Nuremberg, were to be denied exit.[106] Their foundry was expanding, and they needed hands. Hence their continued activity in Nuremberg. Hence their determination that their masters in Pflach recruit and teach local talent. Hence their concern to retain those they recruited. Turning as usual to their imperial patron, they sought measures to interdict labor loss.

In response to this petition, civic authorities rehearsed the entire history of this traffic in labor. For years, the Höchstetters had lured brass-workers away from the city to the detriment of local industry. The city had instituted penalties to halt this movement, excluding migrants from the practice of their craft, abrogating their rights of citizenship, extending the ban to entire families. The Höchstetters had appealed to the emperor to have these prohibitions set aside, and the result had been further hardship for the city. Many migrating workers violated the terms of their employment or left behind unpaid debts and taxes. If they discharged their obligations, as far as the city was concerned, the workers were free to go and work where they wished. But they could not return to the city. Even this loosening of the strictures on movement had not satisfied the Höchstetters, who "considered their own profit and advantage, unconcerned whether it damaged our own".[107]

The Höchstetters sought to intervene once again, appealing to imperial officials that the Nuremberg authorities had acted hastily, imprisoning, questioning and fining their agent without due cause and process. Civic authorities rejected this argument, repeating that the inquiry had been proper and the punishment lenient. Indeed, according to the authorities, Gutrat had acted on his own as a citizen of Nuremberg, thus excluding his employers from any involvement.[108] Gutrat accepted and paid his fine as a citizen of the city; the Höchstetters as foreigners had no voice in the matter.

Despite the costs, Ambrosius and his partners continued to recruit workers. The need for skilled hands did not cease, especially when their Tyrolean hands started to abandon the foundry and migrate back to Nuremberg. Their system of foreign agents not only kept them supplied, but shielded them from the risk of direct prosecution, as the case of Gutrat makes clear. And they were prepared to act aggressively, engaging their Habsburg patrons to put pressure on local authorities and ease entry into local markets, whether for labor or other resources. Nothing would be allowed to interfere unchallenged with their business interests. This was not the last time that the Habsburgs would come to their aid.

Through these disputes at Pflach and Nuremberg, certain of the Höchstetters' business *praxes* emerge from the shadows. Given the nature of surviving sources, these emphasize the importance of political relations, of patronage and influence. To assure the profitability of their new brass foundry, the Höchstetters relied on political guarantees: Guaranteed access to essential resources, guaranteed freedom from certain transaction costs, guaranteed control of certain commodities and guaranteed immunity from interference. These were in the regent's gift; these he gave to his merchant-financiers. Political relations lowered market barriers, assured market share, stabilized factor prices and reduced transaction costs. This enabled the Höchstetters to project operating expenses over a longer period, effectively easing market analysis and risk management.

Moral ambiguity remained. On the one hand, they enabled the Höchstetters to operate their foundry rationally and efficiently to the advantage of themselves, the region and its regent. On the other hand, they enabled the Höchstetters to pursue their interests opportunistically without regard for, and at the cost of, their neighbors.

★ ★ ★

Throughout their careers as merchant-financiers, the Höchstetters displayed most of the benchmarks of capitalist enterpreneurs: Investment of private capital on a large scale; reliance on a mobile, international labor force; separation of capital and labor and long-distance transport of raw materials and finished products. This was certainly the case at Pflach, where they acquired rights to natural resources, constructed the mills, shops, forges and furnaces and trafficked in production factors and finished products.

Yet, many of their practices – the techniques and *praxes* that characterize capitalistic behavior and distinguish different ages of capitalism – remain obscure. Insufficient documentation complicates and often prohibits closer examination of market analysis, information management and risk assessment. The questions surrounding the regular use of double-entry bookkeeping are a case in point.[109] Without the information double-entry could provide, it is difficult to know what premodern capitalists actually utilized to examine the strengths and weaknesses of their firms in particular markets, to grasp the threats and opportunities that confronted them and, also, to assess risk and formulate market behavior.

As the discussion shifts from techniques to *praxes* with attention to social setting and social interaction, the problems that accompany inadequate sources fall away and new ones emerge. There is still much that cannot be known. The reliance on social networks, while not open to doubt, poses as many questions as it provides answers. Creating a structure based on social connection and exchange yields little insight into the intensity or fluidity of those connections and exchanges. Though it is a structure that arises out of the actions and transactions of commercial agents, it explains little about those actions and transactions, little about business practice.[110] It explains neither why the actions and transactions were undertaken, nor what their consequences were. It cannot reveal what information the agents possessed, how they considered it, what factors influenced their decision and what effects that decision caused.

To take but a single example from the Höchstetters' business at Pflach, they hired Georg Hagen as their factor. According to testimony he offered to the firm's creditors in 1531, the Höchstetters hired him in 1509, the year they received permission to manufacture brass in Tyrol. He spent the following 21 years in their service, performing a variety of tasks, including the collection of outstanding debts in Austria, Hungary and Moravia, until being assigned in 1520 at the latest to the foundry at Pflach, where he served as their administrator, manager, representative and advocate, a position of complete trust. He could or would not reveal the lengths or values of his various contracts of service, though he did say that he had served the Höchstetters for varying lengths of time and at various rates of pay. His service ended with the expiration of his contract around Pentecost in 1530, after their bankruptcy. About Hagen nothing else is known. No records exist of his birth or death. His parents remain anonymous; whether he was related to the prominent Augsburg family, Hag or Hagk, cannot be determined. One fact seems clear: He appears to have enjoyed no other connection to the Höchstetters prior to his hiring in 1509. Yet he served them as factor, a position of trust usually reserved for members of the immediate family or long-term – and, therefore, trusted – associates. The reconstruction of networks as a form of business practice cannot solve the puzzle.

The turn to *praxis* brings forward their moral quality and ambiguity. These are actions adapted to the needs of the agent's social settings and lives. They are *ipso facto* instrumental in that they seek the appropriate outcome as formulated by the agent. The appropriateness of that action, of course, does not exist in a vacuum. It is a matter of position and perspective. Whose good should a capitalist pursue? Whose interests should a prince protect? The answers to these and related questions rely very much on the specific social context of the person being asked. The foundry at Pflach provides such a context and makes some of the Höchstetters' practices and their moral quality quite clear.

This chapter has taken up political practices of early modern merchant-financiers, not because they are the only or most important ones, but because they come to the fore in the firm's interactions with the state and with the community. It remains unclear, for example, how the Höchstetters' family firm decided to found its manufactory at Pflach. It did not have a handbook of the sort that Meder wrote to provide local intelligence; it left no record of information-gathering, although something of the sort must have occurred. The grants and contracts at Pflach, by contrast, suggest that it relied on the state to provide monopsony control of supplies, guaranteed access to markets and operational independence in production. It relied on the state to stabilize prices and reduce costs. This resembles rent-seeking behavior, a thing often set in contrast to supposedly modern, capitalistic practice of profit-seeking. Yet, in the context of an economy that lacked rapid communication and market integration, it constitutes profit-seeking by virtue of the need to project and control costs in order to produce efficiently. Even in the context of an open, market economy, firms still look to the state to reduce the barriers associated with customs charges and the costs of corporate taxes. They expect the state to permit easy access to natural and human resources and not to hinder their use of both.

The Höchstetters also relied on the government at Innsbruck to shield them from outside interference. The 1509 grant set parameters for the exploitation of natural and human resources. The state not only upheld these limits, but deferred regularly to the firm's interpretation and disposition of them. What local communities regularly decried as opportunism, the state upheld as opportune. In permitting and supporting the manufacture of brass, the state sought to foster the common good of community and region. This the grant of 1509 and its renewal in 1523 stated in near-explicit terms. In allowing the Höchstetters to operate their foundry, which disrupted traditional agriculture and forestry, introduced a competitive enterprise and encouraged foreign immigration, the state served its own ends and those of capital. Here is the complaint lodged again and again by the leaders and people of Breitenwang and Reutte, to which the regent and council in Innsbruck proved largely deaf.

Practice stands in all of its ambivalence at the very center of research on pre-modern economic life and activity. It has come to define the discussion of economic development and to distinguish the supposed stages of capitalism. When considered as *praxis*, however, a different image of the family firm emerges. It was a part of the business *habitus* of that age, but it was by no means unequal to the demands of modernity, as Chandler has argued. Its linear development from familial to managerial is ahistorical, regardless of appeals to this or that business technique or technology. The Höchstetters' firm expanded capital and expertise as its engagements required. It trafficked internationally in every conceivable commodity, be it commercial, industrial or, finally, human. It recruited the state to serve its needs and protect its interests at the expense of local needs and the common good. The brass foundry at Pflach, like its parent company, was a fully realized capitalist enterprise in an early capitalist age.

Notes

1 The foundry and its history have been studied some detail. See the careful, detailed treatment in Georg Mutschlechner and Rudolf Palme, *Das Messingwerk in Pflach bei Reutte: Ein bedeutsames Industrieunternahmen zu Begin der Neuzeit* (Innsbruck 1976). On the initial agreement between prince and company, see pp. 15–21. See also: P. Justinian Ladurner, "Veste und Herrschaft Ernberg," *Neue Zeitschrift des Ferdinandeums für Tyrol und Vorarlberg* 15 (1870): 15ff. Cited in Ernst Kern, *Studien zur Geschichte des Augsburger Kaufmannshauses der Höchstetter* (Berlin 1935), 10.

2 "*Wir Maximilian usw. bekennen fur unns unnser Erben und Nachkommen und thun kundt offennlich mit disem brief, als unns unnd des Reichs liebn getreuen Jorg Ambrosy unnd Hanns die Höchstetter Gebrueder Burger zu Augspurg willens sein, in unnserm Lannd der Graffschafft Tirol ain Schmelzhutten unnd Schmitten zu Kupfer unnd Messing zumachen aufzurichten unnd zupauen unnd unns darauf demuetigclich ersuecht unnd gepeten, daz wir jnen zu solher Schmeltzhutten unnd Schmitten ain gelegen Ennde unnd Platz zu Behausung Hoffsteten Kolsteten und Holzlegen unnd darzue Waldholtzwerck und Wasserfall genediglich auszuzaigen unnd zuverleyhen gesuechten, also haben wir angesehen solchn gedemuetig unnd zimlich pete auch das solchs unnserm Percknecht zu Swatz zu Furderung auch Nutz und Gueten unnser Underthanen komen mag, unnd jnen darmit unnd aus besonnderm Gnaden in unnserm Gericht Ernemberg zu Pflach an und bey dem Wasser genant die Ach zu solcher Schmeltzhutten Schmitten Behausungen Hofsteten Kolsteten und Holzlegen den Platz unnd Hofstat da vormalen die Plahutten oder Eysenschmitten gestannden, so erganngen und abgeprochen ist, nemlich von oben herabnach der Ach, die Eben unden am Stainperg am Rain ringsweis hinumb bis widerumb an die Ach mitsambt dem Wasserfall und Wuestat von ainem Gestad zu dem anndern zweech durch das jetzgenannt Wasser wie das die Gelegehait unnd notdurfft jetzbemelter Schmeltzhutten unnd Schmitten erhaischt, zumachen und zugerichten*". Tiroler Landesarchiv Innsbruck (hereinafter TLA), Bekennen 1509, fol. 111r–112v. Bewilligung von 13.12.1509 durch Kaiser Maximilian zur Errichtung einer Kupfer- und Messinghütte bei Pflach.

3 Mutschlechner and Palme note early *florilegia* that refer to ironworks on this spot. See Mutschlechner and Palme, *Das Messingwerk in Pflach bei Reutte*, 14–15.

4 Ibid., 16. See also TLA, Urkunde, I: 9121.

5 "*daz vorgenannt Gebrueder die Hoechsteter auf vorangezaigten Platz ain Behausung, Schmeltzhutten unnd Schmitten und darzue den Wasserfall unnd Wuestat wie vorstet aufrichten pawen und machen, unnd sy und all jr Erben das alles und jedes als jr fray aigen Gueter jnnehaben, gebrauchen, nutzen, nyessen versetzen unnd verkauffen, auch darjne schmelzen, kupferschmiden unnd messingmachen unnd in all annder Weg jrem Nutz Fromen unnd Notdurfft nach damit schaffen, hanndlen, thun unnd lassen, auch das Kohl unnd annder Holtz, was und sovil sy das zu solchem vorangezaigten Schmeltzen Kupferschmiden unnd Messingmachen notdurfftig werden, unnd aus beruetem Wald zu bayden seyten auf den Zwitzlpach und die Ach bringen, kachen, clausen risen treiben unnd flossen moegen, alles unverhindert unns unnser Erben unnd menigkliches*". TLA, Bekennen 1509, fol. 111r–112v. Bewilligung von 13.12.1509 durch Kaiser Maximilian zur Errichtung einer Kupfer- und Messinghütte bei Pflach, 11v.

6 "*unnd darzue den Holzhaw aus dem Wald in Zwizlspach sovil zy der zu paiden Seytten mit Claus Ryswerch oder in annder Weg auf jetzgemelte Pach unnd die Alpen heraus zu obbemelter Schmeltzhutten und Schmitten zu Kol und anndern Holz notdurfftig werden unnd bringen moegen, zuhawen zutreiben unnd zu flossen*". Ibid., 111r–111v.

7 "*Wir mainen unnd wollen auch, das vom Lech hinauf bis zu der Praitenwannger Mull nyemands nichts entzwischen machen unnd pawen soll, das vorgenannter Schmeltzhutten unnd Schmitten nachtailig oder schedlich seye*". Ibid., 112v.

8 "*Doch sollen sy des angezaigten Holz ausserhalb unnsers Gerichts Ereenberg weyter khains verkauffen noch verfueren*". Ibid., 111v.

9 "*Es sol auch demselben jetzgedachten unnsn Underthannen der Holzhau in beruetem Walde unnd Zwitzlspach zu jrer Heus Notdurft frey unnd unverpoten sein*". Ibid., 112r.

10 "*Doch so sollen die Hoechstetter unnd jr Erben den Wasserfall unnd Wuer dermassen machen, richten und halten, dass die Floss so auf der Alpen herab kommen, wann genuegsamlich Wasser ist, ueber und durchfarn moegen*". Ibid., 111v.

11 "*auch sollen die Hoechsteter bey dem Rain auf der Eben am Stainperg zu notdurfft des Viehs so unnsn Unnderthannen in Praitenwanngpfarr zugehoert alzeit ain Trib hin und nider ungeverich zu und in das Wasser on Jrrung sein und belieben lassen*". Ibid., 112r.

12 "*Wann und so offt der jetzgenannten Hochstetter Verweser oder Hutmaister etwas Fuer auf Landt oder Wasser mit Kupfer Holtz Kohl oder anndern Zeug desgleichen Kohler- Holtzknecht oder annder Arbaitter, so darzue kundig truglich unnd verhannden sein, notdurfftig werden, unnd die solln Fuer und Arbait thun wollen, die sollen unnd mogen sich obgedachtem Verweser oder Huttmaister ansagen unnd umb den gewonlichen zimlichen Lon zu solchen Fuer und Arbait so lanng jm der Verwesern oder Hutmaister notdurfftig ist, lassen bestellen und brauchen. Wo aber Verweser oder Hutmaister solcher Arbaitter aus berueten unnsern Underthanen also nit bekommen und gehaben, so moegen sy alsdann annder Arbaitter damit sy zu jr Notdurfft versehen unnd nit gesawmbt werden, bestellen unnd geprauchen*". Ibid., 112r–112v.

13 In 1482, the cities of Flanders had risen against Maximilian and Mary and their ambition to secure Burgundy as the inheritance of their son, Philip, known as "the Handsome". At stake was the civic autonomy, granted to the cities by Mary in the so-called Great Privilege of 1477. Signed on 11 February 1477, the Great Privilege reversed the efforts of the former Dukes of Burgundy to create a centralized state in the Netherlands. Under this agreement, the provinces and towns of Flanders, Brabant, Hainaut and Holland recovered all their local and communal rights. It turned the Burgundian state in the Netherlands into a confederation of provinces and granted to Flanders the privilege that any constitutional change would require their consent. The first stage of the revolt had collapsed in 1486, but hostilities renewed in 1487, when Maximilian's father, Emperor Friedrich III, raised taxes on Flanders to support military operations in the neighboring territories of France. The economic hardships that accompanied this increased fiscal burden prompted the burghers of Bruges to trap Maximilian, who was there to negotiate a settlement, by closing the gates of the city. They demanded that he redress the plundering his troops had inflicted on the Netherlands and that he grant them a voice

in the political process. In February 1488, they increased pressure on him by placing him in prison. At this point in time, Ambrosius somehow gained access to Maximilian and provided him company, entertainment and money, with which he bribed his jailers and eased his confinement.

14 Sender, *Die Chronik*, 47. Also cited in Ehrenberg, *Das Zeitalter der Fugger*, I: 212.

15 It is an accusation that applies no less to many of the other leading capitalists of the age; after all, the monopoly prosecution of 1523 named Ambrosius I Höchstetter in company with Jakob II Fugger, Andreas Grander, Bartholomeus Welser and others, all merchant-financiers who neither considered the common good nor spared the poor man in pursuit of rich profit. See Ehrenberg, *Das Zeitalter der Fugger*, 212. Cf. Heinz Friedrich Deininger (ed.), *Das Reiche Augsburg. Ausgewählte Aufsätze Jacob Strieders zur Augsburger und süddeutschen Wirtschaftsgeschichte des 15. Und 16. Jahrhunderts* (Munich 1938), 100.

16 Leaning on Friedrich Keutgen's conviction that the resources necessary to move into wholesale commerce, capitalized manufacturing and high finance originated in the artisanal crafts that formed the backbone of the medieval, urban economy, Strieder argued that textiles were the springboard to wealth and diversification for the Höchstetters and their Augsburger peers, ultimately setting the stage for early capitalism. Cf. Keutgen, "Der Großhandel im Mittelalter"; Jacob Strieder, *Studien zur Geschichte kapitalistischer Organisationsformen. Monopole, Kartelle und Aktiengesellschaften im Mittelalter und zu Beginn der Neuzeit* (Munich 1925); Jacob Strieder, *Zur Genesis des modernen Kapitalismus*, esp. 159; Deininger (ed.), *Das Reiche Augsburg*. Cf. Sombart, *Der moderne Kapitalismus*; Tawney, *Religion and the Rise of Capitalism*; Mitterauer, "Probleme der Stratifikation im mittelalterlichen Gesellschaftssystem".

17 See, among others, Herlihy, "Three Patterns of Social Mobility in Medieval Society"; Francis R. H. Du Boulay, *An Age of Ambition: English Society in the Late Middle Ages* (London 1970); Christopher Dyer, *An Age of Transition? Economy and Society in England in the Later Middle Ages* (Oxford 2005); Philippa C. Maddern, "Social Mobility," in: Rosemary Horrox and W. Mark Ormrod (eds.), *A Social History of England, 1200–1500* (Cambridge, UK 2006); Simon J. Payling, "Social Mobility, Demographic Change, and Landed Society in Late Medieval England," *Economic History Review* 45 (1992); Oliver Volckart, "Social Mobility, Institutional Choice and Economic Performance: Germany from the Fourteenth to the Eighteenth Centuries,"VIII Annual Conference (2004), International Society for New Institutional Economics. Available at: www.isnie.org/ISNIE04/Papers/volckart.pdf.

18 "opportunism, n.," *OED Online*, June 2017. Oxford University Press. Available at: http://proxy.library.upenn.edu:2946/view/Entry/131970?redirectedFrom=opportunism (accessed 23 August 2017).

19 "opportuneness, n.," OED Online, December 2018. Oxford University Press. Availabe at: http://proxy.library.upenn.edu:2817/view/Entry/131969?redirectedFrom=opportuneness& (accessed 7 December 2018).

20 Cf. Biran F. Shraga, *Opportunism: How to Change the World–One Idea at a Time* (New York 2011).

21 See Introduction. Cf. Joseph A. Schumpeter, *The Theory of Economic Development* (Cambridge, MA 1934), passim; Joseph A. Schumpeter, *Business Cycles: A Theoretical, Historical and Statistical Analysis of the Capitalist Process*, 2 vols. (New York 1939), passim.

22 Cf. Kern, *Studien zur Geschichte des Augsburger Kaufmannshauses der Höchstetter*, 10.

23 Deininger (ed.), *Das Reiche Augsburg*, 5.

24 Wilhelm Rehm, "Chronica newer geschichte," in: Bayerische Akademie der Wissenschaft (ed.), *Die Chroniken der deutschen Städte vom 14. bis ins 16. Jahrhundert*, vol. XXV, vols. 23 (Gottingen 1965–7), 277–9. See also B. Greiff, *Tagebuch des Lucas Rem aus den Jahren 1494–1541. Ein Beitrag zur Handelsgeschichte der Stadt Augsburg* (Augsburg 1861), 85, fn 52, 54, 55; Konrad Häbler, *Die Geschichte der Fugger'schen Handlung in Spanien* (Weimar 1897), 31.

25 Max Jansen, *Jakob Fugger der Reiche* (Leipzig 1910), 147.

26 "practice, n.," OED Online, June 2017. Oxford University Press. Available at: http://proxy.library.upenn.edu:2946/view/Entry/149226?rskey=BxjCwQandresult=1andisAdvanced=false (accessed 4 October 2017).

27 Duden defines the noun as "*bestimmte Art der Ausübung, Handhabung; Verfahrensweise*". Immediately thereafter, however, follows the reservation: "*(als bedenklich empfundene) Methode; nicht immer einwandfreies und erlaubtes Vorgehen*". See www.duden.de/node/707266/revisions/1384619/view. See also the *Deutsches Worterbuch* of Jacob and Wilhelm Grimm. Available at: www.woerterbuchnetz.de/DWB?lemma=practik; www.woerterbuchnetz.de/DWB?bookref=13,2052,42.

28 This fact has not been lost on scholarship. See the introduction in Mark Häberlein and Christoph Jeggle (eds.), *Praktiken des Handels: Geschäfte und soziale Beziehungen europäischer Kaufleute im Mittelalter und früher Neuzeit* (Constance 2010), 15–35, esp. 15.

29 Lorenz Meder, *Handel Buch*. "*Darin angezeigt wird/wlecher gestalt inn den fürnmbsten Hendelstetten Europe/allerley Wahren anfencklich kaufft/diselbig wider mit nutz verkaufft/Wie die Wechsel gemacht/Pfund/Ellen/unnd Müntz uberal verglichen/und zu welcher zeit die Merckten gewönlich gehalten werden. Sampt anderen mehr nutzungen darzu gehörig. Allen Hanchieren/und Jungen Kauffleuten/gantz nützlich und dienstlich*" (Nuremberg 1558). It is one of the earliest German-language handbooks of commercial "practices". Hermann Kellenbenz points out that few handbooks of business technique existed in the sixteenth century, but that a tradition of such writings had existed since the Middle Ages, established by Italian scholars and practitioners. Nuremberg became a leading center for the publication of such works in Germany well before Meder's *Handel Buch* appeared in print. See Hermann Kellenbenz, *Handelsbräuche des 16. Jahrhunderts. Das Meder'sche Handelsbuch und die Welser'schen Nachträge* (Wiesbaden 1974), 6–8. Cf. Richard C. A. Brown, *A History of Accounting and Accountants* (Edinburgh 1905); Eugen Leitherer, *Geschiche der handels- und absatzwirtschaftlichen Literatur* (Cologne Verlag 1961); Raymond de Roover, "The Development of Accounting Prior to Luca Pacioli According to the Account Books of Medieval Merchants," in: Ananais C. Littleton and B. S. Yamey (eds.), *Studies in the History of Accounting* (Homewood, IL 1956), 114–74; Wolfgang von Stromer, "Das Schriftwesen der Nürnberger Wirtschaft vom 14. bis 16. Jahrhundert," *Beiträge zur Wirtschaftsgeschichte Nürnbergs* 2 (1967): 751–99.

30 Johann Heinrich Zedler, *Grosses vollständiges Universal-Lexicon aller Wissenschafften und Künste*, 64 vols. (Leipzig Verlag, 1731–54), 29: 7–8; 54: 1608–9.

31 "praxis, n.," OED Online, June 2017. Oxford University Press. Available at: http://proxy.library.upenn.edu:2946/view/Entry/149425 (accessed 4 October 2017).

32 Among many possible examples, see Violet Barbour, *Capitalism in Amsterdam in the Seventeenth Century* (Ann Arbor 1950); Fernand Braudel, *La Méditerranée et le Monde Méditerranéen a l'époque de Philippe II*, 2 vols. (Paris 1966); Fernand Braudel, *Civilisation matérielle, économie et capitalisme, XVe-XVIIIe siècle*, 3 vols. (Paris 1979/1993); Pierre Chaunu, *Séville et l'Atlantique (1504–1650)*, 12 vols. (Paris 1955–1960); Carlo Cipolla, *Before the Industrial Revolution: European Society and Economy, 1000–1700* (New York 1976); Jan de Vries, *The Economy of Europe in an Age of Crisis, 1600–1750* (Cambridge, UK 1976); Richard Ehrenberg, *Das Zeitalter der Fugger: Geldkapital und Creditverkehr im 16. Jahrhundert*, 2 vols. (Jena 1896); Hermann Kellenbenz, *The Rise of the European Economy: An Economic History of Continental Europe from the Fifteenth to the Eighteenth Century* (New York 1976); Hermann Kellenbenz, *Deutsche Wirtschaftsgeschichte* (Munich 1977); Hermann Kellenbenz, "Europäische Wirtschafts- und Sozialgeschichte vom ausgehenden Mittelalter bis zur Mitte des 17. Jahrhunderts, Bd. 3," in: *Handbuch der europäischen Wirtschafts- und Sozialgeschichte* (Stuttgart 1986); Sylvia Thrupp, *A Short History of the Worshipful Company of Bakers* (London 1933); Sylvia Thrupp, *The Merchant Class of Medieval London, 1300–1500* (Chicago 1948).

33 Again, the examples are too numerous to mention. A few examples are Raymond de Roover, *The Rise and Decline of the Medici Bank, 1397–1494* (Cambridge, MA 1963);

Ehrenberg, *Das Zeitalter der Fugger*; Jakob Strieder, *Jacob Fugger the Rich, Merchant and Banker of Augsburg, 1459–1525* (New York 1931); Götz Freiherr von Pölnitz, *Anton Fugger*, 5 vols. (Tubingen 1958–86); Michel Mollat, *Jacques Cœur, ou, l'esprit d'entreprise au XVe siècle* (Paris 1988); Iris Origo, *The Merchant of Prato: Francesco di Marco Datini, 1335–1410* (New York 1957).

34 Pierre Chaunu, *Séville et l'Amérique aux XVIe et XVIIe siècles* (Paris 1977); Maria Fusaro, *Political Economies of Empire in the Early Modern Mediterranean: The Decline of Venice and the Rise of England 1450–1700* (Cambridge, UK 2015); Maria Fusaro, *Reti commerciali e traffic globali in età moderna* (Rome 2008); Clé Lesger, *The Rise of the Amsterdam Market and Information Exchange: Merchants, Commercial Expansion and Change in the Spatial Economy of the Low Countries, c. 1550–1630* (Aldershot 2006); David Ormrod, *The Rise of Commercial Empires: England and the Netherlands in the Age of Mercantilism, 1650–1770* (Cambridge, UK 2003); James D. Tracy, *The Rise of Merchant Empires: Long Distance Trade in the Early Modern World 1350–1750* (Cambridge, UK 1990); James D. Tracy, *The Political Economy of Merchant Empires* (Cambridge, UK 1991); Immanuel Wallerstein, *The Modern World System*, 3 vols. (New York 1974); Hermann van der Wee, *The Growth of the Antwerp Market and the European Economy*, 3 vols. (The Hague 1963). See also a variety of essays in Häberlein and Jeggle (eds.), *Praktiken des Handels*.

35 The early modern Atlantic world has received feverish attention from economic historians in the past few decades, perhaps more and closer attention than other no less interesting or important regions of the emergent global economy. Noteworthy, recent contributions include. John F. Bosher, *The Canada Merchants, 1713–1763* (Oxford 1987); David Hancock, *Citizens of the World: London Merchants and the Integration of the British Atlantic Community, 1735–1785* (Cambridge, UK 1995); John J. McCusker, *The Economy of British America, 1607–1789* (Chapel Hill 1991); John J. McCusker, *Essays in the Economic History of the Atlantic World* (London 2005); Jacob M. Price, *Perry of London: A Family and a Firm on the Seaborne Frontier, 1615–1753* (Cambridge, MA 1992); Claudia Schnurmann, *Atlantische Welten. Engländer und Niederländer im amerikanischen-atlantischen Raum, 1648–1713* (Cologne 1998). In this context, scholars have rediscovered the controversial and pioneering work of Eric Williams and devoted renewed attention to the connection between the slave trade and the Industrial Revolution. See David Eltis, *The Rise of African Slavery in the Americas* (Cambridge, UK 2000); David Eltis, *Slavery in the Development of the Americas* (Cambridge, UK 2004); J. E. Inikori and Stanley L. Engerman, *The Atlantic Slave Trade: Effects on Economies, Societies, and Peoples in Africa, the Americas, and Europe* (Durham 1992); Herbert S. Klein, *The Atlantic Slave Trade* (Cambridge, UK 1999); Hugh Thomas, *The Slave Trade: The Story of the Atlantic Slave Trade: 1440–1870* (New York 1999). In comparison, the Mediterranean and Indian basins have received less close attention, their crucial roles in early modern economic life notwithstanding. Among more recent works on the Mediterranean, see David Abulafia, *Commerce and Conquest in the Mediterranean, 1100–1500* (Aldershot 1993); Franscisco Apellániz, "Venetian Trading Networks in the Medieval Mediterranean," *Journal of Interdisciplinary History* 44 (2013): 157–79; Benjamin Arbel, *Trading Nations: Jews and Venetians in the Early Modern Eastern Mediterranean* (Leiden 1995); Olivia Remie Constable, *Trade and Traders in Muslim Spain: The Commercial Realignment of the Iberian Peninsula, 900–1500* (Cambridge, UK 1994); Steven A. Epstein, *Genoa and the Genoese, 928–1528* (Chapel Hill 1993). On trade across the Indian Ocean, see James C. Boyajian, *Portuguese Trade in Asia Under the Habsburgs, 1580–1640* (Baltimore 1993); Kirti N. Chaudhuri, *Trade and Civilisation in the Indian Ocean: An Economic History from the Rise of Islam to 1750* (Cambridge, UK 1985); Om Prakash, *European Commercial Enterprise in Pre-Colonial India, vol. II, 5: The New Cambridge History of India* (Cambridge, UK 1998); Sanjay Subrahmanyam, *The Political Economy of Commerce: Southern India, 1500–1650* (Cambridge, UK 1990).

36 Pierre Bourdieu and Jean-Claude Passeron, "Cultural Reproduction and Social Reproduction," in: Richard K. Brown (ed.), *Knowledge, Education and Cultural Change* (London

1977); Pierre Bourdieu, "The Forms of Capital," in: John G. Richardson (ed.), *Handbook for Theory and Research for the Sociology of Education* (Westport, CT 1986), 241–58.

37 Among possible examples, see Götz Freiherr von Pölnitz, *Anton Fugger*, 4 vols. (Tubingen 1958–71); Ekkehard Westermann and Marcus A. Denzel, *Das Kaufmannsnotizbuch des Matthäus Schwarz aus Augsburg von 1548* (Stuttgart 2011).

38 For an excellent, short introduction, see Franz-Josef Arlinghaus, "Bookkeeping, Double-Entry Bookkeeping," in: Christopher Kleinhenz (ed.), *Medieval Italy: An Encyclopedia*, vol. I (New York 2004), 147–50.

39 Westermann and Denzel's splendid critical edition of the 1548 notebook, kept by Matthäus Schwarz for the Fugger Firm, has little to offer this discussion, treating as it does a completely different, but no less important, source of information on mercantile practice in the sixteenth century. See Westermann and Denzel, *Das Kaufmannsnotizbuch des Matthäus Schwarz aus Augsburg von 1548*, passim.

40 Basil Selig Yamey, "Accounting and the Rise of Capitalism: Further Notes on a Theme by Sombart," *Journal of Accounting Research* 2 (1964): 117–36. See also Basil Selig Yamey, "Notes on Double-Entry Bookkeeping and Economic Progress," *Journal of European Economic History* 4 (1975): 717–23; Raymond de Roover, "The Development of Accounting Prior to Luca Pacioli according to the Accounts Books of Medieval Merchants," in: Julius Kirshner (ed.), *Business, Banking, and Economic Thought in Late Medieval and Early Modern Europe* (Chicago 1974), 119–80.

41 John J. McCusker and Cora Gravesteijn, *The Beginnings of Commercial and Financial Journalism* (Amsterdam 1991), 21–42. See also Wolfgang Behringer, *Im Zeichen des Merkur: Reichspost und Kommmunikaionsrevolution in der Frühen Neuzeit* (Göttingen 2003).

42 If one accepts the often-repeated formula that a horse and rider might travel as much as 50 kilometers per day, under ideal circumstances, then the journey from Antwerp to Augsburg might, for example, have required roughly two weeks. The *Reichspost* with its staged system of horses and riders moving throughout the day and night, increased the speed of overland communication to roughly 180 kilometers per day in the summer and 146 kilometers per day in the winter. The time for news to reach Augsburg from Antwerp would have shrunk accordingly to four or five days, depending on the season. See Behringer, *Im Zeichen des Merkur*, 50–64.

43 Pierre Bourdieu, *Outline of a Theory of Practice* (Cambridge, UK 1977); Pierre Bourdieu., *The Logic of Practice* (Stanford 1992).

44 Meder, *Handel Buch*, passim. See also Kellenbenz, *Handelsbräuche*, 9–62 and passim.

45 Kellenbenz writes that Meder became a teacher of arithmetic and reckoning, like his father before him, but only after periods of commercial service with the Imhof and Furtenbach family firms. See Kellenbenz, *Handelsbräuche des 16. Jahrhunderts*, 4.

46 Meder, Handel Buch, 1r.

47 Kellenbenz, *Handelsbräuche*, 71.

48 Ibid., 72.

49 Jacques Savary, *Le parfait négociant: ou instruction générale pour ce qui regarde le commerce des marchandises de France, & des pays étrangers*, edited by Edouard Richard ([Paris 1675] Geneva 2011).

50 Kellenbenz, *Handelsbräuche*, 72.

51 As a series of examples in a single volume, see the essays in Häberlein and Jeggle (eds.), *Praktiken des Handels*.

52 Mutschlechner and Palme, *Das Messingwerk in Pflach bei Reutte*, passim.

53 To offer but a single example, Ian Blanchard devotes 50 pages, most of which in fact discuss the trade in tin, of his monumental, three-volume, 1,500-page history of mining and metallurgy. See Ian Blanchard, *Mining, Metallurgy and Minting in the Middle Ages*, vol. III, 3 vols. (Stuttgart 2001/2005), 1525–74.

54 Georgius Agricola, *De re metallica*, translated by Herbert Clark Hoover and Lou Henry Hoover (New York 1950), 2.

55 Calamine is the traditional name given to the zinc oxide-containing minerals, hemimorphite (zinc silicate) and smithsonite (zinc carbonate). Until the eighteenth century it was essential for the production of brass, because metallic zinc does not exist in nature and the method of its production had not yet been discovered.
56 Theophilus, *An Essay upon Various Arts in Three Books*, translated by Robert Henrie (London 1847), 311.
57 The method was known to Roman craftsmen. Agricola offers an extended description of cementation for refining gold, but which also became the preferred process for brass-making. Agricola, *De re metallica*, 453–7, esp. 454.
58 It listed, among a vast number of things, 406 crucibles, along with funnels (good and bad) for the pouring of molten metals and alloys, and 186 lids. The lids suggest that the crucibles were intended to be closed and sealed, which would point toward use of the cementation process. See TLA, Inventar A 164/1. Inventarij des mössinghytwerkhs am Stainenperg, 17 November 1575.
59 Mutschlechner and Palme, *Das Messingwerk in Pflach bei Reutte*, 11.
60 The essential material was "*Passauer Erde*", a composite made of graphite and clay that originated in Obernzell on the Danube in Lower Bavaria. Metal workers could import the crucibles ready-made or import the raw material and fashion the crucibles on site. The surviving inventory from Pflach records a pottery building with all the required equipment to make crucibles at the foundry. Unfortunately, no documents preserve any record of the Höchstetters' traffic in *Passauer Erde*. Ibid.
61 OeStA. Haus- und Hof- Staatsarchiv, Reichsregisterbücher, 1507, 1515, 1516, 1517, 1518, 1519, 1529.
62 He notes that the Fuggers purchased several copper mines in the vicinity via the bankruptcy resolution and that the Höchstetters may have done likewise. Kern, *Studien zur Geschichte des Augsburger Kaufmannshauses der Höchstetter*, 12–13.
63 Cited in Jansen, *Jakob Fugger der Reiche*, 104ff.
64 Ibid.
65 Stadtarchiv Nuernberg (hereinafter StAN), B 14/II, Libri conservatorii des Stadt-, Bauern- und Untergerichts, Nr. Y, fol. 208v, 6 June 1511.
66 StAN B 14/II, Libri conservatorii des Stadt-, Bauern- und Untergerichts, Nr. 5, fol. 18v, 14 February 1514, fol. 19v, 20 February 1514, fol. 37r, 27 March 1514.
67 Hermann Kellenbenz, "The Organization of Industrial Production," in *The Cambridge Economic History of Europe*, Vol. V (Cambridge, UK 1977), 462–548, here 462–3, 478–9, 488–97.
68 The penetration of commercial companies into the mining industry of a territory, in this case Tyrol, was closely connected to credit transactions with that territory's regents. The repayment of loans from the proceeds of the mines developed into a fixed, quasi-traditional system of fiscal management.
69 TLA, Embieten und Befelch, 27 June 1511.
70 Mutschlechner and Palme, *Das Messingwerk in Pflach bei Reutte*, 21.
71 TLA, Embieten und Befelch, 5 July 1511.
72 Ibid., 11 November 1514.
73 Mutschlechner and Palme, *Das Messingwerk in Pflach bei Reutte*, 22.
74 TLA, Embieten und Befelch, 9 November 1514.
75 Mutschlechner and Palme, *Das Messingwerk in Pflach bei Reutte*, 22.
76 TLA, Bekennen, fol. 181, 10 November 1514.
77 According to Jakob Strieder, the cartel was created "*unter starker Anteilnahme, ja man darf sagen, unter dem Druck des Königs*" to prevent destructive competition between the two mercantile giants. Strieder, *Studien zur Geschichte kapitalistischer Organizationsformen*, 498.
78 TLA, Embieten und Befelch, 25 February 1518.
79 Ibid., 5 June 1514.
80 Ibid., 27 February 1517.
81 Ibid., 6 February 1522.

82 Ibid., 22 June 1523.

83 The *Fern Pass* is a mountain pass that lies at an elevation of 1212 meters in the Tyrolean Alps in Austria, between the Lechtal Alps to the west and the Mieming Mountains to the east. Today the pass serves as a busy connection via the Lechtal between Reutte and points north, including major South German cities.

84 TLA, Embieten und Befelch, fol. 124, 21 March 1514. The Fron was part of the state's assessment against minerals extracted in its territories, commonly referred to as Fron and Wechsl. The former was a duty on raw ore, usually calculated at 10 percent of the total value; the latter was a duty on refined metal, usually negotiated as a fixed price against the margin of profit, usually 12.5 to 25 percent of the total profit; both were rendered to the regent, from whose land the metal was mined.

85 The *Tonne* was an otherwise nondescript barrel or container for measuring and transporting goods, including ground minerals. The *Ster* was a bucket used to haul and measure ore in the mines of Tyrol, Bavaria and Styria. According to Grimm, it usually measured "*1 (Münchner) schuh 2 zoll lang, 1 schuh 2 zoll breit, 11⅝ zoll tief*". See Mutschlechner and Palme, *Das Messingwerk in Pflach bei Reutte*, 23.

86 TLA, Embieten und Befelch, 21 March 1514.

87 Ibid., 1 July 1517. A *Bergrichter* was an official experienced in the industry and knowledgeable of the region, who served as the government's agent in all matters relating to mining. He would be called upon to administer justice, collect taxes and gather information for the councils at Innsbruck.

88 TLA, Embieten und Befelch, 30 October 1517.

89 Ibid., 7 April 1524.

90 Mutschlechner and Palme, *Das Messingwerk in Pflach bei Reutte*, 24.

91 TLA, Embieten und Befelch, 22 September 1524.

92 TLA, Missiven 1524, fol. 428. See the discussion in Mutschlechner and Palme, *Das Messingwerk in Pflach bei Reutte*, 24–5.

93 Mutschlechner and Palme, *Das Messingwerk in Pflach bei Reutte*, 27–8.

94 Ibid., 29–31.

95 Ibid., 19.

96 Ibid., 31–2.

97 Ibid., 33–4.

98 Ibid., 29.

99 TLA, Geschäft von Hof 1524, fol. 124v.

100 StAN, Ratsprotokolle S I, Lade 207.

101 "*wo nun inen darüber gestattet werden, würde es dem gantzen Handwerk, Darauf sich meer dann Zweihundert Menschen nehrten, Zu verderben und unüberwindtlichen schaden raichen, Auch dadurch derselb Handel sovil lannger Jar bey diser Stat allain gewest und herkommen, inen entzogen*". StAN, Ratsprotokolle S I, Lade 207, Ratsbuch H, fol. 245.

102 "*Ist demnach in Betrachtung deß Handwerke Noturfft und zu Handhabung berürter Gesezes und herkommens ertaylt, den Personen, mit denen als oblaut von der Höchstetter wegen sy aufzupringen ist gehandelt, solch ir wegk Ziehen zuwehrn und dieselben auch allen andern gemelts Handwerks von neuem Zuverpitten. Mit den Aber, welche darüber sich von hinnen thon, den wöll man nicht meer einkommen lassen und soll mit Weib und Kindern draussen pleiben und fuiter alhie gemelts Handwerks und Bürgerrechtens beraubt sein, das auch ainichs Maister denselben keener mit Arbait alhie finden noch sagen soll krig aine nemliche Gelltstraf*". Ibid.

103 "*Item wiewol ain Erb. Rath auf ernstlich ansuchen, Herrn Paulußen vom Liechtenstain, Freyherrn zu Castellen Marschalken, von wegen der Höchstetter zu Augsburg Hüttenwerks an der Etsch Irn Knecht halben, so inen wider die Ordnung der Messingschlager und Dratziehen von hinnen zugeloffen seyen, mit wissen und zugeben der geschwornen Maister desselben Handwerks etliche mittel bewilligt und zugeschriben haben, wie solchs im Wankelbuch bey irer Ordnung verzaichnet, so ist doch den Herrn die zu aufnemmen der Bürger verordnet seyn, bevolhen, in achtung zuhaben, wenn hinfüro oder obgemelten Knecht ainer oder meer, so auf gemelter Höchstetter Hüttenwerk gezogen sein, oder sich fürter one wissen dahin thon würden, widerumb herkommen*

und deß Bürgerrechtens begern wolten, soll da kainer angenommen werden". Actum quarta post Andree 1512. StAN, Ratsprotokolle S I, Lade 207, Ratsbuch F fol. 69.

104 "*Item den Maistern und Gesellen der Messingschlager und Dratzieher, die auf der Höchstetter Hütten in der Pfleg Ernberg gearbait, und jetzo umb ir einkomen an Kaiyserliche Mayestät suppliciert haben, ist aus dem Rath geantworttet, das sy ain Rath nicht verhindern wölle, mögen auch one gefhar wol herein kommen, wo sy dann Arbait finden, oder sunst Irn Nutzen schaffen, laß ain Rath geschehen. P. Hannsen Volokhamer und Christoffen Furner. Actum quinta post Barnabe 1515*". Ibid., fol. 240.

105 StAN, B 14/II. Libri Conservatorii des Stadt-, Bauern-, und Untergerichts, Nr. 13, fol. 27r, 28 May 1519.

106 StAN, Ratsprotokolle, 1520, fol. 176v–183r.

107 "*darinn mer jrn selbsnutz und vortayl bedenck ungeachtet ob es den unnsern zu entlichen verderben raichet*". Ibid., 179v.

108 Ibid., 182v.

109 B. S. Yamey has pointed to the careless manner with which medieval Italian merchants, despite being masters of accounting methods and schoolmasters of European commerce, actually applied double-entry, making it a less than accurate tool for the measurement of profit and loss. The balance sheets of the Medici bank, to take one example, seldom actually balanced and, according to De Roover, preserve no clear evidence of attempted correction. See Basil Selig Yamey, "Accounting and the Rise of Capitalism: Further Notes on a Theme by Sombart," *Journal of Accounting Research* 2 (1964): 117–36; Basil Selig Yamey, "Notes on Double-Entry Bookkeeping and Economic Progress," *Journal of European Economic History* 4 (1975): 717–23; Raymond de Roover, "The Development of Accounting prior to Luca Pacioli According to the Accounts Books of Medieval Merchants," in: Julius Kirshner (ed.), *Business, Banking, and Economic Thought in Late Medieval and Early Modern Europe* (Chicago 1974), 119–80.

110 Häberlein and Jeggle define as practice those "commercial transactions that arise from the actions of [commercial] agents and structures that are a consequence of these actions" (*Handelsgeschäften vom Handeln der Akteure ausgehen und Strukturen als Ergebnis dieser Handlungen*). It is a useful definition for the purposes of identifying approaches to practice, but if offers little insight into the thinking and acting that underlie the practices themselves. To return to Bourdieu for a moment, it privileges *praxis* without regard for *habitus*. See Häberlein and Jeggle (eds.), *Praktiken des Handels*, 17.

3 Crisis and insolvency

Information management by and about the Höchstetters

At some point in 1528, Ambrosius I Höchstetter appealed to Anton Fugger for counsel and assistance.[1] The Fugger firm had long competed aggressively with the Höchstetters, but Ambrosius nonetheless addressed his counterpart as "friendly and dear cousin" (*Fraintlicher und lieber Herr Vötter*). It was, at best, a very distant connection, the evocation of which suggests the author's desperation.[2] "The time of day draws to its close", as he put it, "and I use every effort according to my reason to order daily my business and account". Despite all such efforts, the situation had put him in jeopardy (*geferdt*), and he saw no way out.

> As almighty God has thus weakened me, and I am more caught in this business, God knows how, as well as old, weak and in this completely stubborn and blind and, not unjustly, out of my sense, so has my need reached such a point that I no longer trust myself in the affair. Because I do not know how to help myself to my own advantage in this burdensome tribulation, such that alone I would be lost and not know what to undertake that might be advantageous or disadvantageous for myself or others, [I need] other good friends and advisors.[3]

His need had reached such a pitch that he had decided to "beseech three trusted, discrete, secret friends, who would reserve to themselves in stillness and secrecy and not reveal all my aforementioned business, whether they find it good or bad, as God ordains".[4] To this end Ambrosius promised to show these chosen three "all my property with truth and without exception", explicitly to allow them to examine all the necessary ledgers, accounts, books and whatever they felt was necessary to help him avoid the crisis.[5] Specifically, he hoped they would help him determine:

> First, in what manner and form one might make a workable and tolerable contract [with his creditors, tms], which I hope to God. Second, should no agreement be possible, that one suggests the best possible form of negotiation, such that I am not placed in jeopardy and no one suffers disadvantage because of me.[6]

In their function, these "secret friends" resemble unofficial *curatores bonorum*, a committee selected to manage the assets of an insolvent or bankrupt family or firm. Höchstetter claimed, however, to seek only their advice. To Fugger he insisted, "We must ensure that the aforementioned three [. . .] do not enter into serious negotiations with the creditors and damage both parties, and they would be completely wrong, in that they don't know what we have done".[7] "They don't know what we have done"; it seems he and Fugger had other, separate plans.

For his part, Ambrosius professed his need for help, his willingness to take advice to heart and his intention to follow it diligently. His was an extraordinary admission and an extraordinary action: Without consulting his partners, he violated the maxim of secrecy as generally practiced by all early modern capitalists and as specifically embodied in his family firm's charter of 1524. He admitted his own inability to master the misfortunes that had shaken his affairs and, accordingly, volunteered to place the family firm in receivership. He assigned blame neither to himself nor to his partners. Divine providence alone had placed him in jeopardy and rendered him defenseless.

How extraordinary that Ambrosius turned to Fugger! No evidence survives, nor would any testimony reveal in the course of the bankruptcy, that the senior Höchstetter ever took one of his partners or servants, any member of his firm or even his family into his confidence. It seems unimagineable that he would not have spoken of his worries to his wife or his sons. Yet, historical sources reveal nothing of the sort. He appears to have abandoned even the most intimate of networks at his disposal. Instead, he turned to Anton Fugger, nephew and heir of Jacob II ("the Rich") Fugger, *Regierer* of the largest and most powerful merchant-banking house in Augsburg, perhaps in all of Europe. In doing so, Ambrosius placed his fate and his firm in the hands of a determined opponent.

What had happened? Only four years earlier, "Ambrosius and Hans, the Brothers Höchstetter and Associates" had given no indication that its business was at risk, that "affairs were so badly compromised". In 1524, the partners had reorganized and renewed the family firm with proclamations of satisfaction on all sides. In the same year, their factor, Georg Hagen, had advised the government of Tyrol about its tariffs on calamine, sued the communities of Reutte and Breitenwang for the right to harvest timber and complained about the refusal of master brass-workers to teach their craft at the foundry in Pflach. In 1525, Ambrosius expanded his firm's enterprise from copper and brass to mercury. In 1526, the English crown had transferred to the Höchstetters, whom royal agents had described as equal in wealth and potential to the Welsers, its obligation to subsidize the embattled King of Hungary.[8] In 1527, Joachim I Höchstetter, a partner of the firm and its factor in Antwerp, had reached a ten-year agreement with the government of England to import and export goods between the continent and the island kingdom, the first South German firm to do so.[9] Given that harvest-related inflation was the order of the day in England, he had begun trading continental grain for English woolens with the brothers,

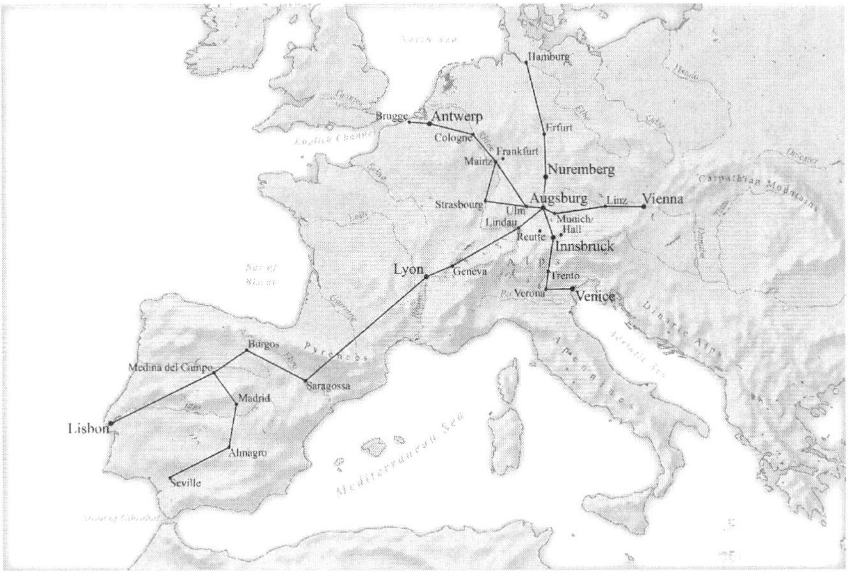

Map 3.1 Trade routes

John and Richard Gresham. Throughout the late 1520s, Wolfgang Vittl, their factor in Schwaz, Tyrol, had lent large sums of money to the House of Habsburg, secured with copper and textiles.[10] Their goods – textiles, spices, metals, foodstuffs, bijouterie, indeed, as Clemens Sender had suggested, anything of any value – were moving on all the major trade routes of Europe, north and south between Antwerp and Venice, east and west between Vienna and Lyons and beyond to Seville and Lisbon. Business was booming.

Ehrenberg speaks of the Höchstetters plunging into a "whirlpool of new ventures" (*Strudel neuer Geschäfte*) to outrun their impending ruin, but that characterization suggests an awareness of danger and a planned strategy, for which there is no evidence.[11] Ambrosius would later profess an inability to predict the outcome of his many interests and engagements. He would claim ignorance of the fact that many of his partners were engaged in activities that would destroy their company's *Trauen und Glauben*. He would later protest, reasonably enough, that he could not know and did not foresee the misfortune that would attend so many of his company's ventures, especially its commitment to the mercury trade. It would prove to be one speculation too many, a high-risk, high-reward enterprise that failed. He lacked information. He had no knowledge. His ignorance would cost him everything.

This chapter takes up the crisis and insolvency of firm and family to examine the flow of information and the effect of institutions on families and family firms. It seeks particularly to arrive at observations about knowledge in early modern economic life.

* * *

While historians have attended to the flow of information in the early modern and modern worlds, they have paid less attention to knowledge as a thing apart.[12] Common usage holds knowledge and information largely synonymous. According to the *Oxford English Dictionary*, information is "knowledge communicated concerning some particular fact, subject, or event".[13] Knowledge, on the other hand is "the fact or state of having a correct idea or understanding of something; the possession of information about something".[14] Upon closer observation, a subtle distinction appears: Knowledge tends to involve mental activity, "apprehension of fact or truth with the mind"; information signifies a thing, "that of which one is apprised or told" along the lines of intelligence or data.

Economists, especially those of the Austrian School, have attended to this difference in ways that may be fruitful for understanding economic life and behavior in the past. As Peter Boettke has pointed out, "knowledge is ever changing and is multifaceted, while information is something fixed".[15] Accordingly, information becomes a stock of facts, that which is known, while knowledge becomes discovery, "the flow of new and ever expanding areas of the known". This interpretive distinction grows immediately and familiarily out of the work of F. A. Hayek, whose essay "Economics and Knowledge" first pointed to it.[16] Though his argument concerned the creation of market equilibrium, the hypothetical state in which the quantity of goods a producer brings to market equals precisely the demand for that good in the market, he insisted that the knowledge required to create or achieve equilibrium does not exist *a priori* but must in every instance be ascertained by the producer. Thus, it depends upon the information which is available, which depends in turn upon the social and institutional contexts in which that process takes place. The question is always "to what extent and how [. . .] knowledge corresponds to the external facts".[17] It likewise cannot be separated from the past practical contact with facts or events of the individual person: "Experience creates knowledge".[18] It thus extends well beyond markets *strictu sensu* to concern all the circumstances of a particular setting that enable agents to make decisions and take actions.[19] It is "concrete and contextual and not abstract".[20]

Following Hayek, other scholars have taken up the inter-relationship of both information and knowledge to economic behaviors.[21] Rather than assume, as many modern economists do, that complete information is freely available and can be collected deliberately by agents in accordance with a standard cost-benefit calculation, the Austrian School has come to be identified with a distinct individualism that views quantification with skepticism in light of its insistence that knowledge and action cannot be abstracted from the broadly understood circumstances of the agent.[22] The point is to evoke not the radical anarcho-capitalism and political libertarianism that have laid claim to the Austrian tradition of economic thought and analysis, but rather the subjectivism that constitutes a single theme in much of its work.

The questions of what Ambrosius I Höchstetter knew and when he knew it must not be reduced, therefore, to the information that was available to him; it must extend to his experience in business and his grasp of the situation. Those questions must likewise assume that knowledge was both dynamic and incomplete. As noted in previous chapters, slowness and insecurity characterized communication in the sixteenth century. Even under the best of circumstances, news took a week at least to travel from Venice or Antwerp to Augsburg. This made necessary a degree of independence of action on the part of partners and factors, a fact clearly reflected in the Höchstetter charters of 1515 and 1524. Moreover, the degree to which merchant-entrepreneurs processed such news as they received remains indeterminate. Little evidence unequivocally supports the contention, as stated, that they practiced double-entry bookkeeping completely or consistently, a process that would suggest a swift processing of information, of discovering knowledge. Some scholars argue that the use of double-entry constitutes a touchstone of modern, rational economic life; its lack indicates, by contrast, a premodern, short-term, illogical approach to business.[23]

Hayek noted more than 70 years ago that rationality is not a postulate of economic analysis, but a consequence of economic institutions.[24] With this in mind, economic planning and action in the absence of timely, reliable information, confronted unique challenges. J. J. McCusker has argued it rendered effective coordination of enterprise a practical impossibility in the premodern period.[25] That necessitated rationality in a different key. Firms had to decentralize planning and decision-making; that fact transforms any notion of "the family firm", rendering it a fluid complex of semi- or completely independent enterprises run by loosely connected or autonomous agents. And the "rationality" that guided those agents may have corresponded only loosely to the maximization of subjective utility that most economic theories assume in common. Utility might have corresponded to narrow self-interest, but it might have extended to broader notions of acquired prosperity, power or status for one's self, one's firm and one's family. Most crucially, it might – probably did – vary among the partners of "Ambrosius and Hans, the Brothers Höchstetter and Associates". When Ambrosius lamented his lack of knowledge to Anton Fugger, he meant not only a lack of information concerning market trends in various marketplaces, but an inability to synthesize and grasp the changing political, social and familial currents that were about to sweep him and his firm aside.

The crisis that beset the Höchstetters' firm demonstrates the potential results of these qualities. The information sharing among the various partners and their factors was incomplete. The actions taken resulted from individual knowledge of local – even personal – circumstances, not from an over-arching conception of the firm, its resources or its goals. The reactions suggest the same situation-specific particularity.

What might be called the Austrian approach to economic knowledge liberates Ambrosius Höchstetter, his partners and his peers from such clumsy dichotomies as rational and irrational, modern and premodern. It emphasizes the cognitive environment in which he, his firm and his family rose and fell. It is impossible to reconstruct exactly what any of the persons involved knew. The evidence must be read against the grain, with a degree of skepticism, as their competitors and creditors did, but it cannot be rejected out of hand. Rather, the task is to attempt a reconstruction of their knowledge, to determine who understood what and when, given their experiences, situations and actions.

* * *

The move into mercury signaled both continuity and change. Already well-established as traders in copper and manufacturers of brass, the Höchstetters were well placed to diversify their interests in the mining and metallurgy industry. From this perspective, to begin trading in mercury was not a radical departure. Mercury was different, however. Its refining required different expertise, as did its transportation. It was also subject to different demand, offered different opportunities and posed different challenges. Success in its trade might depend on past experience, but it required a stock of new information and the discovery of new knowledge as well.

It also involved a different set of risks. No specific, financial obligations had accompanied the right to establish and operate a brass foundry at Pflach. By contrast, the contract of 1 January 1525, signed by Archduke Ferdinand I, representatives of the mine operators (*Gewerke*) and Ambrosius Höchstetter, granted "Ambrosius and Hans, the Brothers Höchstetter, and Associates" exclusive rights to purchase and sell all the mercury and cinnabar mined at Idria, located in present-day Slovenia, in exchange for large, fixed payments.[26]

Ferdinand's need for money to finance military operations against the Ottoman Empire and the operators' own entrepreneurial spirit created the circumstances for a highly speculative business. As early as 1524, they engaged in a series of transactions – payments to the prince in exchange for expanded mining rights, payments to the prince for arrears in various transactions – that set the stage for an even larger credit arrangement. On 19 December 1524, Ferdinand guaranteed that such transactions would continue into the future by reaching an agreement in principle with Ambrosius Höchstetter that established the terms of a monopsony.[27] "Ambrosius and Hans, the Brothers Höchstetter, and Associates" would become the sole purchaser of all Idrian mercury and cinnabar, not only its existing stockpile, but also its entire production over the ensuing four years at a fixed price of 30 fl for each Viennese hundredweight (*Wiener Zentner*) of mercury and 35 fl for each Viennese hundredweight of cinnabar.[28] This included existing quantities of both commodities that had already been sold to Hans II Paumgartner of Augsburg, Wilhelm Neumann of Villach and the heirs of his late partner, Hans Pfluegel of Salzburg; the agreement

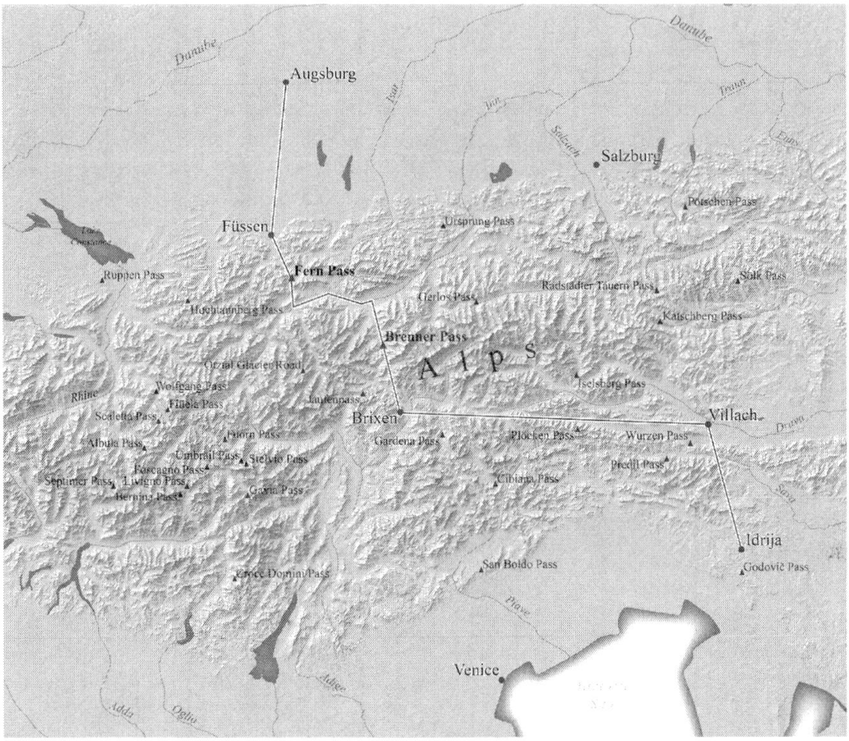

Map 3.2 Kärnten, showing Idria with Villach and Venice

compelled them to sell immediately to the Höchstetters at the contract price.[29] The contract set penalities in case Ferdinand or the operators sold mercury or cinnabar to any other firm. The Höchstetters were to assume all transportation and transaction costs for the metal they received, wherever they received it. They were also to pay all the customary tolls and duties; Ferdinand promised that such taxes would not be increased during the life of the contract. In exchange for monopsony control, the Höchstetters agreed to purchase mercury and cinnabar worth no less than 300,000 fl from the Idrian mine operators over the four-year period of the contract. The operators agreed to transfer this amount as a loan to Ferdinand. Their profit margin depended principally on interest from this loan as well as purchases of minerals beyond the contractually fixed minimum. These terms were formally accepted by all parties on 1 January 1525. With a single stroke, Ferdinand I received an extraordinary infusion of capital, the mine operators, who had previously organized production and sale, were reduced to the level of salaried managers and the Höchstetters gained control over all the mercury and cinnabar – and, by extension, over all operators and miners – at Idria.

How did Ambrosius choose this commodity, this market? In concluding the contract, he seems to have based his reasoning on indirect knowledge. The mining products of Idria had traded through Augsburg for years. The scarcity of mercury, especially in its pure, liquid state, and the richness of the deposits located in Idria had attracted merchant capitalists since the late-fifteenth century.[30] Initially, Venetian interests had dominated the scene, but Wilhelm Neumann from Villach – the future father-in-law of Ambrosius II Höchstetter – soon emerged as the dominant operator and trader.[31] When Maximilian I annexed Idria in 1509, at the conclusion of his war against the Republic of Venice, he seized the mine shares (*Kuxe*) held by Venetians, transferring some of them to Neumann, whom he also appointed *Bergrichter*. By the late 1510s, Neumann had established himself as the dominant buyer and seller of Idrian mercury, most of which traded via Venice to the East, but some of which moved north via Villach to Nuremberg and Antwerp. For this business, Neumann partnered with Hans II Paumgartner of Augsburg and Hans Tegler of Nuremberg. When, around 1520, mercury was discovered near Oberschönbach in Bohemia, Neumann and his partners moved to secure their monopoly on the Venetian market by purchasing the entire Bohemian production and selling it through Tegler in Nuremberg and Antwerp.[32] So profitable was this business that Ferdinand I decided to engage directly in it, rather than content himself with the various taxes and fees it remitted to him as archduke. In 1522, he ordered the digging of a new mine, the so-called Prince's Mine (*Fürstenbau*), in competition with the existing operations at Idria, an enterprise that proved so unprofitable – a money pit, rather than a mercury pit – that Ferdinand abandoned it the very next year.[33] The Höchstetters knew this history, being financial lenders and advisors to the Habsburgs, producers and sellers of metals in Austria as well as partners and competitors with Paumgartner. It convinced them to accept Ferdinand's offer of a monopsony, a means for both territorial prince and merchant-banker to profit.

The Höchstetters' mercantile practices appear to have changed little. They had relied consistently on political influence and patronage to reduce costs and risks, achieve market entry and limit price uncertainty at Pflach. Their contract in Idria spelled out precisely what kinds of influence and protection their financial services had purchased. It insulated them from unwanted competition that might influence the supply of mercury or cinnabar available to them. The operators would sell to no other firm than the Höchstetter brothers. If they produced more than the Höchstetters wished to purchase, that surplus would remain unsold in storage at the mine. It assured their control of mercury sales beyond the period of the contract. The Höchstetters received right of first refusal over an extension of the exclusive right to purchase mercury and cinnabar at Idria beyond 1528, provided their purchases worked to the benefit of the mine and its operators. Finally, and most importantly, it shielded their firm from prosecution as monopolists. Ferdinand promised "the aforementioned Höchstetters, their associates and heirs to be their gracious lord and representative and to keep them free of damage from the Imperial Majesty, our beloved lord and brother, or his and the Empire's government or its fiscal, as well as from anyone else who accuses them about this sale and thereby casts them in damages."[34] He made good on his promise: On 25 March 1525, little more than three months after the contract was signed, Emperor Charles V issued a mandate excluding the wholesale traffic in mineral ores from the antimonopoly legislation of the Empire.[35] Charles justified his action with an appeal to the need to foster the "common good" (*gemeinen Nutz*) of the mining industry. Whether the exception fostered the industry or not, it certainly promoted the interests of those capitalists into whose hands it had been sold.

The profitability of the 1525 contract lay for the Höchstetters in the possibility of selling mercury and cinnabar at prices higher than cost. Ambrosius was not content to suffer the ups and downs of unpredictable price trends on an open market, however. Like his predecessors in Idria, Neumann and company, he sought to be not only sole purchaser, but also sole seller; he sought to gain not only a monopsony but a monopoly position to set the price. He pursued his goal with "ruthless energy" (*rücksichtloser Energie*).[36] The contract at Idria was a first step.

Ferdinand also helped Ambrosius restrict his competitors. The mines in Oberschönbach remained a potential threat, as they had been a decade earlier to Wilhelm Neumann. So, in 1526, the Höchstetters followed Neumann's example and negotiated a deal with the Bohemian mine operator to limit his production to 800 hundredweight over five years, all of which the Höchstetters would purchase, thus eliminating competition. They then turned to Ferdinand with the request that the 800 hundredweight be counted against the 10,000 hundredweight they had contracted to purchase at Idria between 1525 and 1528.[37] The Höchstetters also convinced Ferdinand to prohibit the transportation of Bohemian mercury through the territory of the archduchy, thus limiting supply further. When Ferdinand became King of Bohemia in 1527, he exerted even more pressure, forcing the mine operators there into a cartel arrangement with the Höchstetters that amounted to a monopsony over the eastern European mercury supply.[38]

Only one source of mercury separated the Höchstetters from complete control of that commodity in all of Europe: the ancient mine at Almadén, in southern Spain.[39] In 1525, at the same time the Höchstetters began purchasing minerals at Idria, the Fuggers obtained rights to operate the mine at Almadén for a period of three years, making the two family firms competitors in this commodity as well as in copper and silver. As the expiration date of the Almadén agreement approached, in 1527, Ambrosius sought to end the competition and establish a monopoly in mercury by purchasing through Ferdinand the Fuggers' lease. In this case, political patronage displayed its limits. The attempt failed for two reasons: First, Ambrosius was outbid by other firms that were interested in Almadén – a consortium of the Fugger and Welser companies ultimately won the contract;[40] second, the Fuggers had reserves of mercury sufficient to prevent him from controlling supply. In the expectation that a worldwide monopoly was within his grasp, Ambrosius had purchased tremendous quantities of mercury. Once his plan for monopoly price control failed, these supplies had to be liquidated, now at prices lower than those at which they were bought. Sender chronicled the subsequent maneuvering:

> Ambrosius Höchstetter had bought up mercury in all kingdoms and lands at a higher price than was commonly asked, at 8 fl, so that he could oppress the other merchants with this trick. As soon as he had all the mercury in his hands, he demanded 14 fl for a hundredweight. God ordained, however, that the emperor in Spain and the king in Hungary found mercury in great quantities. And Höchstetter had purchased 200,000 fl worth of mercury of which he lost a third.[41]

Sender saw the failed attempt to create a worldwide mercury monopoly as one of the most important causes for the spectacular bankruptcy of the Höchstetter firm, an explanation that modern scholars have largely accepted.[42]

He knew it was not the only one, however. Among other things:

> [a] ship loaded with various herbs and spices was sunk at sea, several wagons enroute from the Low Countries to Augsburg were seized by bandits; and he suffered other losses. Yet, all of these misfortunes would not have damaged him, had his own son and his brother's son behaved in an upright manner and seen properly to their own, and had old Ambrosius Höchstetter taken an annual accounting and concerned himself with these things.[43]

Netherlandish authorities seized in 1528 a Höchstetter shipment of grain bound to the English firm of John and Richard Gresham in exchange for woolen cloth. Who or what prompted the seizure remains unclear.[44] Joachim I Höchstetter blamed the Gresham brothers for starting rumors of Höchstetter insolvency that resulted in the seizure of their cargo.[45] If doubts arose in England, they did not necessarily begin there, Joachim's accusations notwithstanding. As early as March of 1528, the Lyon factor of the Nuremberg firm of Tucher reported, upon information provided by the factor of the Augsburg firm of Manlich, that no one there would honor Höchstetter bills of exchange.[46] Though no reason was given, the likely explanation is the Höchstetters' inability to secure the Almadén contract. Indeed, one gets the impression of a campaign of information and innuendo, orchestrated to ruin the weakened firm.

Sender closed with the moral decay that was, for him, the ultimate cause of Höchstetter's failure: "For his son, Joachim and his son-in-law [Hans] Frantz Paumgartner [...] gambled away 10,000 or 20,000 or 30,000 fl at a time, young Ambrosius Höchstetter, the son of old Ambrosius Höchstetter, and Joseph Höchstetter, his brother's son, lived profligate lives, but not as bad as the other two". He claimed that the insolvency of the company could have been avoided, had "old Ambrosius" not been negligent. Had he kept careful track of profits and losses, especially losses due to misfortune, and exercised strict control over the behavior of his partners, specifically the gambling of his son and son-in-law, his fortunes would have recovered. Not fate, according to Sender, but foible determined the outcome. The company charter of 1524 called for a closing of accounts and a distribution of profits every three years. It further prohibited "dangerous games" on the part of the partners and threatened violators with immediate suspension from the firm. These prescriptions proved inadequate, according to Sender, because they were not properly followed. The Höchstetter firm suffered cash-flow problems. The losses it incurred from different events in different places – on the market for mercury, on the highway from Antwerp, on the high seas near England and on the gaming tables somewhere in Europe – prevented it from honoring its obligations. There is reason to doubt, however, that these problems could have been addressed by better oversight, whether in the form of accounting or of control.

Given the challenges of space and time, unavoidable information asymmetries existed in early modern markets. Local agents, the ones initially assessing the risks that adhered in most commercial or financial transactions, always knew more than their distant principals, who ultimately would pay for any consequences. Such a situation results in moral hazard, not as the chronicler Sender imagined it, but simply because the risk was displaced and incalculable. Moral hazard encourages opportunism in the narrow sense of the subversion of moral or ethical principles for the sake of profit, but market activity requires opportuneness in that broader sense of timeliness, the ability to seize a chance when it arises, without regard for planning. Because information asymmetries were intrinsic to the structure of early modern markets, especially when business was transacted over long distances or extended periods, moral hazard was a structural reality and opportunism a constant possibility. For this reason, the Höchstetters and their peers had to grant partners and agents broad freedom of action. The failed mercury speculation, the lost merchant cargo and the plundered wagon train might all be attributed to the miscarriage of freedoms necessarily granted partners and factors. Such losses could be portrayed as the unlucky, but innocent consequences of commercial fortune, which was undertaken "at profit and loss" (*auf gewinn und verlust*). An alert, but otherwise benign, opportuneness was essential to business conduct, but information asymmetries and their associated moral hazards also gave rise to malignant opportunism, frequently included under the rubric of principle-agent problems. The profligate lifestyles of Ambrosius II and Joseph Höchstetter, and especially the gambling debts of Joachim I Höchstetter and Hans Franz Paumgartner, constituted a sort of recklessness and, in the latter instance, violated the firm's own guidelines. Neither the firm's creditors nor the senior partner paid them much attention, however. Their opportunism resulted neither in the threatened suspension from the firm, nor in specific, legal or financial penalties.

This may reflect a structural characteristic of family firms. They encounter problems when the interests of certain members of the family do not align with those of the firm, for example, when an unqualified member wishes to be a manager. As de facto owners of the firm, family members who are active in it may be less subject to financial incentives or sanctions, because their capital is already invested in it. Moreover, the altruism that sometimes exists among family members may give those in the firm a positive reason to engage in opportunism or free-riding. Economists and business historians have pointed to the potentially negative economic effects of "altruism" in family life, including family business life.[47] (See Chapter 2.) It may have encouraged unsuitable behavior and discouraged corrective measures in the case of the Höchstetter firm.

The lack of sanctions against the junior partners may also have to do with the tension between information and knowledge. Given the illicit, unethical nature of their failures, these younger people may not have wanted to share the details of their lifestyles with their elders. Ambrosius I may have known they were wastrels, however, in much the same way he might have learned about the profits to be made in mercury trading: Just going about his business in Augsburg, rumor might have reached his ear. Having known three of them since childhood, he may have had a good idea about their strengths and weaknesses of character. In judging them, altruism may have played a role. He did not know, as he claimed, because the information was not forthcoming, because his experience taught him it would not matter, because he did not want to know. Ambrosius Höchstetter's disavowal ("God knows how") not only reflected the information flows and corporate structures of his day, but sought deliberately to shield himself, his partners and his firm from their worst consequences.

His appeal to Anton Fugger would call other knowledgeable persons into play. They reconsidered the available information about his affairs and came to very different conclusions about his prospects. It would set other forces in motion. His strategy, if that is what it was, would miscarry.

* * *

Whether or not Ambrosius was innocent of the problems and challenges that beset his firm in 1527 remains to be seen. Cognizant of the failure to gain control of the mercury mines at Almadén, he may nonetheless have been unaware of the recklessness of his partners or the reverses in England, the Netherlands and elsewhere. Surviving archival documents permit endless speculation about the difference between Ambrosius's information and his knowledge, between his awareness of the problem and his interpretation of failure. They leave no doubt that he possessed information that his bid for monopoly control of mercury had failed. Though it seems reasonable to assume that he was informed of the other reverses and problems as well, the evidence is incomplete. What sense he made of his situation can only be inferred from his actions. As his appeal to Fugger makes clear, by 1528 Ambrosius knew that he could no longer contain the damage on his own. With help, however, he still hoped to prevent ruin. He began to take immediate measures to shore up his and his firm's financial situation, creating liquidity by borrowing heavily.

In 1527, he engaged in 48 credit transactions, borrowing no less than 112,943 fl. A further 41 debts, accrued in 1528, netted the firm another 53,663 fl in capital, less than half of the amount borrowed the previous year. In the course of the bankruptcy that would open in Augsburg in 1529, the creditors pointed to this 166,606 fl in new debt as sure evidence of fraud. According to them, Ambrosius admitted "that he had entered into damage and decline in 1527 and borrowed money from the following persons, as indicated by his own debt contracts and handwriting".[48] They insisted he could offer no excuses, because he had formally declared before members of the City Council and many other persons that "he had foreseen and realized his deterioration two years earlier [i.e., in 1527, tms], but had hoped daily to recover that which he had a year and a day before [i.e., before the failure of his bid to control the mine at Amadén, tms] until he went bankrupt in France, around Easter, 1528".[49] They accused him of knowing as early as 1527, not that his circumstances were straightened, but that his firm was ruined, that he would never be able to repay these obligations. Moreover, they claimed that this list of new, fraudulent borrowing was incomplete, that it failed to include "several that were not recorded in the aforementioned interest registers (perhaps through laziness)".[50] Of the recorded debts, less than 10 percent involved persons or families with whom the Höchstetters had any other, verifiable relationship, whether social or professional. Thus, over 90 percent of these new creditors appear to have been strangers in the sense that they were not directly associated with the Höchstetter family or firm (see Appendix 2, Höchstetter Creditors).

If this is so, then it raises questions about capital markets in early modern Europe. How did the Höchstetters identify and approach these lenders? How did the lenders assess the credit-worthiness of the Höchstetters? More than 55 percent of the recorded debts involved persons or families who could not be identified as residents of Augsburg. As time passed, the frequency with which the Höchstetters borrowed from strangers and foreigners increased. And the success of his borrowing, measured in terms of the amounts obtained, decreased by more than 50 percent from one year to the next. Though far from conclusive, these patterns suggest that Ambrosius progressively sought capital from lenders who were less likely to know of his firm's vulnerability. It suggests a growing awareness of his firm's insolvency, not only on his part specifically, but also in capital markets generally.

The entrepôts and marketplaces of early modern Europe, such as Lyon, Antwerp and Venice, traded not only commercial commodities and financial instruments, but also business intelligence. The news of the Höchstetter insolvency traveled quickly. By 1528 at the latest, certain creditors began pressing Ambrosius for repayment. Sender sketched the immediate results:

> Many of the creditors, when they learned of the damages that Höchstetter had suffered and how the young [partners] had dissipated, demanded money from the company and were paid, so that he spent 400,000 fl in one year, though he did so unwillingly, because the creditors refused to wait any longer. Those creditors who were heedless, however, of whom there were some 300, found themselves in danger and instead of receiving their payment, principle and interest, were not paid at all.[51]

While Sender noted that some were paid and others were not, he omitted or mistook another aspect of these transactions. To preserve his "*trauen und glauben*" and to avert bankruptcy, Höchstetter willingly paid or arranged to have paid a series of creditors.

This was the point of his appeal to Anton Fugger. Ambrosius understood that he must at least satisfy the most important of his creditors, the ones who were powerful enough and whose obligations were large enough to relieve the pressure on the family firm. The less important creditors could be fobbed off somehow. Who these were to be and how they were to be placated was the task he set before Fugger.

According to the account Ambrosius provided to Fugger, the Höchstetter family firm held deposits at interest (*auff uns zinss gellt*) worth a total of 375,108 fl.[52] Of these assets, 221,574 fl originated "from good friends" (*von guten freunden*) and had not been recalled (*nit abkindt*) depite the rumors of insolvency. On the other hand, he identified 46 obligations worth 153,534 fl as "recalled money" (*abkindt Gelt* = *abgekündigtes Geld*), 108,501 fl payable in 1528 and a further 45,033 fl in 1529. Two involved organizations: 1,200 fl owed to the "Begging Purse" (*Bettelsack*), a possible reference to money deposited at interest by the Augsburg Alms Office (*Almosenamt*); 3,000 fl owed to the "*Pfleger des Hanstetters*", the official who administered the village of Haunstetten, located to the south of Augsburg, on behalf of the Benedictine Abbey of Sts. Ulrich and Afra. A further five were in the names of women, possibly widows, the most substantial of which was a 16,000 fl sum owed to "Frau Torsin", Anna Thurzo, the daughter of Hieronymus Fugger and wife of Georg Thurzo.[53] The remaining 39 debts involved diverse sums and persons, most of whom appear to have been members of the Augsburg elite but had no other, apparent connection to the Höchstetter family or firm. There were exceptions. The list identifies "Old Michel" as a servant in the household of Sigmund I Höchstetter, the son of Georg I and Ambrosius's nephew and partner from 1515 to 1519. Philipp Adler, the father-in-law of Joseph, the son of Hans I and Ambrosius's nephew and partner from 1524, had deposited more than 20,000 fl. Four members of the Rehlinger clan, closely associated to the Höchstetters via marriage and business, were owed more than 25,000 fl: Bernhard II, a former employee of the Höchstetter family firm; Hans I, his brother and a jurist in Imperial service; Wolfgang, his son, and Ulrich II, brother-in-law of Ambrosius. Several notable creditors, including Bernhart Walther, Andreas Grander and Georg Wielandt, maintained close connections to the Rehlinger famliy, which may help to explain their presence on the list. Two members of the "von Sparren" branch of the Langenmantel family, Augsburg patricians who were also connected to the Höchstetters through business and marital relations, appear as well: Joachim I, long-serving burgomaster of the city; and Markus, Bavarian governor (*Landpfleger*) in the neighboring town of Mering. All of the creditors on the list were well-positioned to hear rumors of his insolvency; Sender referred to them as the ones who "learned of the damages that Höchstetter had suffered and how the young [partners] had dissipated [and] demanded money from the company".

Of the 46 obligations acknowledged as recalled by Ambrosius, 17, which were worth 49,760 fl in total, also appear on the list of loans identified by the creditors as new and therefore fraudulent. This might confirm the suspicion that the other 29, the majority of the new lenders, were people with little notion of the Höchstetter insolvency, because they did not press for immediate repayment. It might also indicate that Ambrosius deliberately obscured the full nature of his indebtedness. His list constituted only a small portion of the loans he accepted between 1527 and 1528. The total of 375,108 fl might have been an under-valuation, just as 153,534 fl might have under-stated the amount that required immediate repayment. To the 153,534 fl in recalled obligations Ambrosius added a further 56,000 fl in moneys owed: 36,000 fl "to the Welsers to cancel the Spanish money" (*den Welsern auff den spanischen gellt auffzuheben*) and 20,000 fl "to the Lords Fugger on the purchase of Tauffer copper" (*den Herrn Fuggern auf den Taufferer kupffer kauff*). Whatever the true measure of his indebtedness, he assured Fugger: "We found that we are not otherwise indebted".[54]

Ambrosius also sent Fugger an assessment of Höchstetter holdings in mercury and cinnabar, not only his estimate of their market value, but also their exact quantities and locations.[55] In Salzburg and in transport from Idria, the Höchstetters had 713 *Fel*, weighing 1,070 Viennese hundredweight. Valued at 32 fl per hundredweight, this mercury was worth 34,240 fl.[56] In Augsburg or underway to Cologne, they had 1,031 hundredweight worth 33 fl each. There they also had 204 *Brot* (bread = loaves) of cinnabar, weighing 320 hundredweight at 38 fl each.[57] Ambrosius reckoned these goods at 46,183 fl. The list continued thus: In Venice, 59,603 fl in mercury and cinnabar; in Antwerp or on the road from Nuremberg to there, 9,900 fl in mercury; in Lyon, 4,400 fl in mercury and cinnabar; in Lisbon, 10,690 fl in mercury and cinnabar; in Frankfurt am Main, 606 fl in mercury and cinnabar; in Villach, in the hands of Wilhelm Neumann, the father-in-law of Ambrosius II, 570 fl in mercury and cinnabar. This inventory set the value of the Höchstetters' disposable mercury and cinnabar at 166,687 fl.

The list revealed as well the Höchstetter trading network. They transported and stored mercury and cinnabar from Idria to Salzburg, from Augsburg to Cologne, from Venice to Mediterranean ports and from Nuremberg to Antwerp. Lisbon was apparently an important market for the Höchstetters, accessible by sea from Antwerp and, perhaps, by land via Lyon. Lyon was another important trading station, serving as it did the financial and commercial needs of the Kingdom of France. Smaller amounts in Frankfurt, Vienna and Villach suggest further trading and transport locations. With this information, Fugger learned how much mercury his rival actually possessed and where he probably intended to dispose of it.

The inventory exposed Ambrosius's financial calculations. The Idria contract of 1525 set the price paid by the Höchstetters per hundredweight: 30 fl for mercury, 35 fl for cinnabar. When Ambrosius reckoned 33 fl per hundredweight of mercury in Cologne or 38 fl per hundredweight of mercury in

Lisbon, for example, he included the transaction costs of packing and shipping as well as his assessment of current market value on site. At no point, however, did his valuations for either mineral sink below the amounts he had paid per hundredweight at Idria. Given the circumstances of his own insolvency and the available supply, Ambrosius's round estimation of 166,687 fl may have been too optimistic.

That sum was not entirely disposable, being encumbered by a series of obligations, as Ambrosius made clear. Most importantly, his firm still owed an outstanding balance to the mine operators who had produced the minerals. Of the 300,000 fl in mercury and cinnabar, contracted in 1525, the operators had so far delivered 235,687 fl, for which the Höchstetters had paid only 131,000 fl. Hence, they still owed the operators 104,687 fl for what they had already received.[58] Set against his estimated valuation of those minerals, this left Ambrosius a surplus balance of 62,000 fl, according to his own accounting. From that 62,000 fl in mercury and cinnabar, Ambrosius deducted a further 44,736 fl from the "Venetian estimate" (*Venediger Überschlag*) and 2,058 fl from the "Nuremberg estimate" (*Nürnberger Überschlag*). Probably, some of the commodities in Venice and Nuremberg, which had initially been accounted as disposable capital, had already been sold to other parties. The remaining surplus balance of 15,206 fl in mercury and cinnabar, less than 10 percent of the gross reckoning, improved little with the addition of 5,500 fl owed them by Ferdinand I, which raised their total balance to 20,706 fl. Unmentioned, but probably not unnoticed by Fugger, were the remaining 64,313 fl of the contractual total still to be delivered to and paid for by the Höchstetters.

Anton Fugger may well have been less sanguine about the prospects of the Höchstetter family firm.[59] Ambrosius claimed 38,785 fl in cash (*parin gellt*), barely 10 percent of the total deposits his company held. As an experienced merchant-financier, Fugger knew that creditors would quickly demand the repayment of their deposits, principle and interest when news of a possible insolvency reached their ears, and that a liquidity of 10 percent would not satisfy them. The mineral inventory also left room for considerable doubt. The insolvency required that Ambrosius liquidate his supply of mercury and cinnabar, commodities he had purchased in anticipation of a monopoly and could sell now only at a loss. Moreover, Ambrosius made little mention of other business ventures or capital investments, such as the brass foundry at Pflach, of which Fugger had detailed knowledge via sales of copper, to say nothing of the purchase and sale of textiles, spices, foodstuffs and other commodities. Rather, he summarized 600,323 fl as the "extract in all lands that remains beyond all the debts that we have in all lands" (*die außzig jnn allen landen beliebt per rest uber alle shulden die zait lang, so wir aussin halb landen habend*). To this he added the 20,706 fl in unencumbered mercury and cinnabar from his earlier account, as well as "velvet cloths" (*samlin gewanndt*) worth 2,000 fl that were in transit from Antwerp to Cologne but that had not yet been seen (*dan wir nichts dar von gesecht haben*). Listed but unvalued were 100 woolens, "*lindisch Tuch*". Similarily unmentioned, but probably suspected, were any new debts that Ambrosius might have contracted in his desperate effort to raise funds. Fugger likely knew the information he had received was inadequate or incomplete.

Ambrosius did not offer Fugger complete business records, but rather incomplete crisis points, those parts of the Höchstetter enterprise that were under immediate pressure. The failure in mercury was becoming common knowledge, leaving him with over-valued commodities and investment capital that had to be liquidated. News would leak out eventually, leading investors to demand the return of their deposits. Fugger knew that those who had not yet heard of Ambrosius's insolvency, whom Sender described as "heedless", would then also rush to retrieve their capital. A run on the bank would be hard to avoid. Once it began, an opportunity would pass.

Fugger possessed information beyond that which Ambrosius provided. He mobilized his own company, calling upon his factors across Europe to track Ambrosius's affairs and, on occasion, to intervene in them. Throughout 1528 and into 1529, he received reports, including copies of contracts and inventories of goods from the Netherlands, Spain and Tyrol that described the collection of debts, the value of commodities and the sale of assets in Höchstetter hands.[60] Examining the information available to him, Fugger concluded by June of 1528 that matters were worse than his struggling competitior understood or admitted.[61]

With this in mind, Fugger extended resources to the Höchstetters and their embattled firm. Ambrosius supposedly, according to Sender, paid debts totaling some 400,000 fl in the course of his firm's insolvency. Anton Fugger played a large part in this process. In the year that passed between Ambrosius's appeal for help in 1528 and his declaration of bankruptcy in 1529, the Höchstetters managed with the assistance of Fugger and unnamed others to pay, whether by offering capital or surety, a total of 75 debts worth a total of 412,649 fl 14 sh. 6 hl, slightly more than the 400,000 fl Sender claimed. The larger share, 226,052 fl 12 sh 6 hl, had "otherwise been paid or consigned according to the inventory" (*sonnst allennthalben nach Ausswesung des Inventarii bezallt oder verwissen*), that is, they had been documented by Ambrosius as somehow settled during the period of insolvency. The remaining assets and assurances did not all come from the Höchstetters, however. According to documents filed during bankruptcy, they discharged only six debts, worth 20,050 fl 19 sh.[62] These they admitted in an extract "in the elder Höchstetter's handwriting" (*wölcher alter Höchstetters Handshrifft ist*). By contrast, according to the creditors, 49 debts, worth 166,546 fl 2 sh, were "relegated to or satisfied by the Fuggers" (*bey den Fuggern verwissen oder vergnugt*), "taken from the Fugger business" (*auss dem Fuggerischen Laden genommen*), located "in the paper concerning the business with the Fuggers" (*in dem Zedel die Hanndlung mit den Fuggern betreffend*), a reference to Ambrosius's appeal, or "consigned to Fugger or others, according to the information of an extract in the elder Höchstetter's handwriting" (*bey dem Fugger unnd annderst verwisen nach Ausweisung des Auszugs alter Höchstetters Hanndtschrifft*). Ambrosius and Fugger had secretly discharged 186,597 fl 2 sh worth of debts, according to "information outside the inventory" (*Aussweisungen ausserhalb des Inventarii*);

they had been settled under the table, so to speak, to the disadvantage of the creditors Sender referred to as "heedless".

Interestingly, Ambrosius and Fugger did not, for the most part, discharge the debts that appeared on the list of new debts, obligations contracted after 1527 and, therefore, assumed to be fraudulent by the creditors. Rather, they seem to have chosen to pay debts according to some measure of importance other than "last in, first out". Fugger paid 27 of the 46 debts that appeared on Ambrosius's list of "recalled money", 12 of which also appeared on the creditors' list of fraudulent debts. The majority of those he decided to pay were held by members of the Augsburg elite. Put another way, Fugger made sure that he satisfied those local lenders who might do the most damage to Ambrosius and himself or, by contrast, who might serve their interests best: 1,260 fl owed to Lucas I Schellenberger; 2,000 fl owed to Lucas II Welser; 1,500 fl owed to Bernhard Walther; 3,000 fl owed to Ulrich II Rehlinger; 13,000 fl owed to Hans I Rehlinger and 3,000 fl owed to Joachim I Langenmantel. Not all of the repaid lenders were local, however: 2,100 fl to "Doctor Farnbiller", a possible reference to the humanist Ulrich Varnbühler; 8,000 fl to Hans Thenn, the mint master of Salzburg, and Dr. Nicolaus Ribeysen, a jurist from Philippsburg by Speyer in the service of Cardinal-Bishop Matthäus Lang and, later, legal counsel for Ambrosius I.[63] Fugger also paid debts owed to persons or institutions that seem less obviously consistent with any instrumental, utilitarian principle, such as 1,400 fl owed to "Old Lady Walther" (*Alt Waltherin*) and 1,050 fl owed to "the wife of Rauscher" (*Rauscherin*) or the 1,200 fl owed to the Augsburg Alms Office and 3,000 fl owed to the administrator of the village of Haunstetten. Indeed, it is difficult to reconstruct any certain and consistent principle that guided the repayment of debts. Fugger – to say nothing of Ambrosius – left no written evidence of his thinking. The result is clear, however. This leverage made Anton Fugger the Höchstetters' largest creditor and put him in a position to dispose latter's fortune and fate.

The creditors of 1529 complained that Ambrosius had borrowed and concealed an additional, 87,186 fl 16 sh from Fugger, Paumgartner and others, quite apart from the more than 160,000 fl in debts assumed by Fugger on his behalf, "as one has no knowledge who was paid with it".[64] They clearly had received none of it. Moreover, a whole series of assets had been transferred to the Fugger firm at a considerable loss, removing them from the capital that could be used to satisfy outstanding debts.[65] With the leverage at his disposal, Fugger began to take control of the Höchstetters' fixed capital and moveable commodities. They mortgaged their copper mines on the Falkenstein near Schwaz in Tyrol, worth 20,000 fl, to him for 15,000 fl, a loss of 5,000 fl. Their share of copper mines in Joachimstal, Tyrol, worth 4,700 fl, passed to him for a mere 1,500 fl, a loss of 3,200 fl. They pawned him a variety of merchandise in Vienna for 23,141 fl 13 sh, 5,318 fl below its value. Likewise, merchandise in Augsburg, transferred to him for 59,183 fl 6 sh 11 hl, resulted in losses of 4,900 fl. Other companies took similar advantage, whether at the behest of Ambrosius or Fugger remains unclear. Thus, in 1528, Ferdinand's treasurer transferred thousands of marks of silver, owed to the Höchstetter firm, to the coffers of the Fugger and Welser companies.[66] Höchstetter copper passed into the hands of Hans II Paumgartner.[67] Their smelting works at Jenbach and Schwaz, both in Tyrol, and their mining interests at Idria came into Fugger's possession.[68] These and other transfers, which "should not have been alienated in this way" (*so nit gelost hatt muegen werden*), resulted in losses to the other creditors of 77,521 fl, in nominal value without taking into account their earning potential or current market value. The value of this sold or mortgaged capital, which included the mine interests in Steinfelden, Schwaz and Idria, notes obligatory from the King of the Romans, the Kingdom of Hungary, the Archduchy of Austria and commercial commodities in Venice, Tauffers, Linz, Antwerp and Lisbon, stood at 226,052 fl 12 sh 6 hl.[69] In the event of a Höchstetter default, it would all pass to the individual mortgage holders, the elite of South German capital. The leading merchant-financiers of Augsburg and Europe thus methodically striped one of their own of all his capital.[70]

What did Fugger get in return? To acquire more than 160,000 fl in bad debts – debts that might never be paid – seems to violate every modern principle of economic rationality. Reduced prices that totaled only 18,418 fl for a series of capital assets might seem inadequate compensation to the Fugger for more than 160,000 fl in debt relief. It might have been an act of Christian charity, aid given to a colleague in need, but this was not debt relief in the strict sense. Ambrosius's obligations to those creditors he acknowledged as having demanded their money had not been erased, but merely consolidated. Rather than 46 creditors, he now owed one, Fugger, who could dictate the future of his company.

In his biography of Anton Fugger, Götz von Pölnitz wrote of a *Kesseltreiben* or "battue", meaning a hunt organized by beaters who drive the game toward the hunters, and named the principal of the Fugger firm as the force behind it.[71] Fugger gathered sufficient information from a variety of informants, including Ambrosius himself, to arrive, by means of careful, comparative analysis, at accurate knowledge of the situation. If von Pölnitz's supposition is correct, that information proved highly effective: The game was driven to the hunter. Fugger received more than the value of Höchstetter assets; he received future profits from their productive capacity. He displaced them from a series of industries. Most importantly, the leverage he acquired, both financial and informational, put him in a position to determine the fate of one of his major competitors.

* * *

Whatever his arrangement with Ambrosius, whatever his ultimate goals, Anton Fugger appears to have had his own plans. According to Pölnitz, he saw an opportunity to rid himself and his company of one of its most dangerous rivals. Not only had their interests clashed in various commercial and industrial sectors, but Ambrosius represented to Fugger the chief stumbling block to power. His firm enjoyed a high degree of trust among the Habsburgs, especially with

Ferdinand I, King of the Romans and Archduke of Austria, who exercised immediate control over mineral wealth in large portions of the Holy Roman Empire and whose financial needs created profitable lending opportunities. Fugger intended to supplant the Höchstetter family firm with his own. As Pölnitz saw it: "The old seesaw policy [on the part of the Habsburgs, tms] that drew closer to one firm and abandoned another had to stop".[72] To achieve this end, Fugger relied not only on information supplied by the Höchstetters, but also on intelligence gathered by his own agents and a few, identifiable merchant-financiers.

In his 1528 appeal, Ambrosius had suggested seven colleagues to counsel him in his need: Fugger himself, Hans II Paumgartner, Lukas II Rem, Hans II Bimmel, Bartholomeus V Welser, Hans VI Lauginger and Hans I Herwart. Fugger could have exchanged information with any of them privately. They are an interesting group.[73] Like Ambrosius, all were engaged in long-distance trade and princely finance, and all were members of the merchant association Augsburg. Herwart and Welser were patricians and belonged to the city's *Herrentrinkstube*, while Bimmel retained his membership in the powerful weavers' guild (*Weberzunft*). Given their common engagement in commerce, all were probably associates and competitors of Ambrosius at one point or another: Rem partnered with him from 1515 to 1520, and, as events would prove, continued to support him long after his bankruptcy; Paumgartner and Fugger worked with him in joint ventures related to mining and finance; Herwart and Welser entered into at least one financial arrangement with him; only Bimmel appears never to have done business with the Höchstetters. Paumgartner, Herwart, Lauginger and Rem were all creditors of Höchstetter at the time of his insolvency. Only one had direct, albeit distant, social connection to Ambrosius: Hans II Paumgartner was a cousin of his partner, Hans-Franz Paumgartner.[74] All shared one characteristic: They were men on the make. All, without exception, declared large increases in tax liabilities, ranging from 30 (Bimmel) to 400 (Welser) percent, between 1522 and 1534.[75] All, without exception, engaged in the city's governance by taking active part in elective offices and by holding administrative positions in guild or civil administration. All, without exception, experienced rising social status. Emperor Charles V elevated Fugger to the rank of Count (*Grafenstand*) and named him an imperial counsellor in 1526; he would ennoble Welser in 1532 and Paumgartner in 1537. Paumgartner, Fugger, Lauginger and Rem would join Herwart and Welser as Augsburger patricians in 1538. Though Bimmel remained a weaver by association, his brother Anton I was already a guildmaster and would become burgomaster of Augsburg in 1529, and his sons Anton II and Hans III would join the merchant association.

In putting forward these seven names, men and families of varying political and economic potency but rising social, economic and political prominence, all of whom could claim success in commercial and financial affairs, Ambrosius appears largely to have ignored considerations of personal connection or familial affiliation. In a crisis, he reached beyond his more obvious social and economic relationships to create a council of men who could guide his affairs and, should the need arise, grant access to untapped capital markets and represent him to a wider community. He expressed a personal preference for Paumgartner, Bimmel and Rem, to whom he would refer his bookkeeper Thomas König and factor Georg Hagen, but he "would have you [Fugger] gladly, provided you wish to do this other business".[76] As with the composition of the larger group, the reasons for his preference for these three remain a matter of speculation. His personal relationship to any of them resists examination, leaving only partial, material considerations. At the time, Paumgartner was the wealthiest of the three and had extensive experience in the mining industry, including mercury mining and sales. Bimmel enjoyed political influence as well as a position in the textile trade, another sector in which the Höchstetters were heavily involved. Rem belonged to an established mercantile family and had personal knowledge and experience of the Höchstetters as a partner and investor. Each offered substantial advantages in the looming crisis.

No evidence indicates unequivocally that Fugger referred to or recruited any of the seven men or their peers among the *Kaufleuteschaft* of Augsburg. Rather, he seems to have acted on his own, gradually leveraging the Höchstetter family firm, gaining control of its assets and therewith its fate. By the Fall of 1528, guided by information that his factor in Antwerp, Conrad Mair, provided, he took a second decisive step after the Almadén monopoly in displacing his competitors as financiers to the Habsburg. He assumed the Flemish loan.

Despite their mounting losses, the Höchstetters had agreed in August 1528 to lend the government of Flanders 200,000 *Carolusgulden*, which it needed to pay the soldiers of the Imperial army.[77] They extended credit in the only form they possessed in surfeit, not the specified amount of cash, but their accumulated reserves of minerals: 3,507 hundredweight of mercury and 608 hundredweight of cinnabar. According to the monopsony contract of 1525, the Höchstetters must have paid 126,476 fl for these commodities; the difference in value between the loan and the minerals signaled both enormous losses for the court and liquidity problems for the firm.[78] Their inability to extend credit to the government of Flanders – the provision of commodities rather than coinage – provided everyone open, incontrovertible evidence of their deteriorating situation. It also provided Fugger with a golden opportunity to supersede the Höchsetter firm and simultaneously improve his stature with the Habsburgs.

In need of immediate funds to prevent the dissolution of its army, the Flemish court accepted Höchstetters' offer of 126,476 fl in mercury and cinnabar, rather than the contracted 200,000 *Carolusgulden* in cash, and commissioned Lazarus Tucher, a Nuremberg merchant and commission agent, resident in Antwerp, to sell the commodities. He was not the only one to become involved. A surviving report of 22 October 1528, written by Conrad Mair to his principal in Augsburg, reveals the full complexity of these arrangements.[79] It is, at best, an incomplete, one might say overheard, conversation, a couple of extracts from an on-going, two-sided correspondence.[80] It offers nonetheless some idea of the intelligence that was exchanged among a series of interested parties; it reveals much about the flow of information and the discovery of knowledge concerning the Höchstetters' insolvency.

Tucher and Gerhard Sterck, an Antwerp merchant and financial agent for the government in Flanders, acted on the government's behalf to transform the commodities into cash. They had received from the government copies of the original contract to lend 200,000 *Carolusgulden*. They had also received a series of mortgages against government revenues to assure partial repayment of the loan in five annual installments, beginning 1 September 1529: 10,000 fl per year for five years from the alum toll, for which Sterck was the collector; 3,000 fl per year for five years from the grain toll; 1,500 fl per year for five years from the office of the *Rentmeister* of Flanders and 1,500 fl per year for five years from the *Aprill* of Flanders. Thus, the Höchstetters could have assumed a fixed income of 16,000 fl per year for five years, a total of 80,000 fl, from the income of Flanders. So important was this transaction that the Flemish regent, Margaret of Austria, and seven members of her court, offered personal, written assurances, copies of which were also placed in the hands of Tucher and Sterck, that they would cover any shortfall up to 20,000 fl from their own private resources, should these revenues fail to generate the expected payments of 16,000 fl per year.

These documents were written in French and Flemish, and Mair, as he plaintively noted, could not understand them. So, he had them translated into German and promised to communicate with Fugger if he found any deficiencies.

Unwilling to brook any delay in receiving the urgently needed funds, the court now wanted to transfer the entire obligation, in exactly the terms originally negotiated with the Höchstetters, to Tucher and Sterck. Mair reported to Fugger: "And Paumgartner told me [that] to discharge the obligation of the court and lords (*anendadores*), Paumgartner, Gerhart Sterck and Lazarus Tucher should and would negotiate with the court and lords to such an extent that one would write and transfer the contract, in every respect as it stood for the Höchstetters or its bearer, to Gerhart Sterck and Lazarus Tucher or its bearer, thus the transactions regarding payment as detailed above should [be removed] from the hands of the Höchstetters and come into those of Sterck and Tucher".[81] Doubts clearly existed as to the Höchstetters' capacity to meet the terms of their agreement.

Mair later identified Paumgartner as Hans. He probably referred to Hans II Paumgartner, not only an Augsburg colleague and competitor of the Höchstetters and Fuggers, one of the men on Ambrosius's list of potential secret advisors and one of the wealthiest merchant-financiers in Europe, but an experienced trader in metals, including mercury, who had been engaged in the business since the first decade of the sixteenth century with Wilhelm Neumann. His expertise made him an obvious choice to assist Sterck and Tucher in selling off the mercury and cinnabar that the court had received from the Höchstetters. It does not explain, on the other hand, his readiness to share his knowledge of events with Fugger. He even provided Fugger, via Mair, with copies of all the relevant contracts, including the original loan, the government mortgages and other letters. This exposure raises the possibility that the "Hans Pangartner" of Mair's report is not Hans II Paumgartner, principal of his own family firm, but Hans Franz Paumgartner, the son-in-law and partner of Ambrosius Höchstetter and a shadowy figure in his bankruptcy. Though the likely choice remains Hans II, the surviving documents do not permit a conclusive identification.

Mair made no mention of compensating the Höchstetters for the minerals they "loaned" the government. He informed Fugger that the transaction would be renegotiated with Sterck and Tucher, the sellers of goods that were not theirs, listed as creditors. Sterck and Tucher, Paumgartner, Mair and Fugger all had immediate, detailed access to the terms of the Höchstetters' agreement with the government of Flanders. They knew precisely the commitments made by each side, and they knew the expectations each side had of the other. It was clear to all that the Höchstetters could not and would not deliver 200,000 *Carolusgulden* in cash. It was likewise clear, by implication, that the Höchstetters did not expect payment for the mercury and cinnabar they had loaned. It seems likely that some undisclosed third party had discounted the Höchstetters' debt for an undisclosed amount of money. Given the roles played by each of these merchant-financiers, the likely third party was Anton Fugger.

The Flemish court provided security in the form of mortgaged revenues for 80,000 fl of 200,000 *Carolusgulden*. It also intended, according to Paumgartner, to transfer to Sterck and Tucher a further 50,000 fl in mercury and cinnabar that it had received from the Höchstetters.[82] Had the Höchstetters still been creditors, Sterck and Tucher would then have provided them written assurance not to sell or transfer the minerals until they had received written assurances from the government that it would secure repayment of the 50,000 fl by mortgaging more of its revenues. Sterck and Tucher were unable to provide such assurance, according to Paumgartner, because the Höchstetters themselves had not yet received – and, so, not yet transferred to the government of Flanders – the minerals in question. Only when Sterck and Tucher received written reports that the mercury and cinnabar were, in fact, being produced and delivered did they draft and sign the required security. This they transferred not to the Höchstetters, as originally arranged, but to Conrad Mair on behalf of Anton Fugger. Sterck and Tucher pledged "that they had received to their hands from the government of the land 50,000 courant or *Carolusgulden* in mercury and cinnabar and swear on oath to you, Lord Fugger, not to let them go until you receive from the court security sufficient to your own satisfaction that one shall and will repay you the 50,000 fl over the next five years, each year 10,000 fl beginning on 1 September next year [1529]".[83]

Mair assured his principal that he held this written agreement to be as binding as a formal, notarial instrument, though he would have such a document created, should Fugger wish it. He obviously felt this to be a complicated, risky transaction. As he put it, "And should I not have gotten the matter right in one way or another, which I do not think, just let me know your will, and I will act accordingly".[84] Following the instructions of his principle, Mair recognized the complexity of the transaction and worried about risk and loss.

With all the documents in hand, Fugger stood creditor for 130,000 fl of the 200,000 *Carolusgulden*, promised by the Höchstetters to the government of Flanders. Of that 130,000 fl, 80,000 would be repaid in cash from specified government revenues, and 50,000 would be repaid in revenues yet-to-be-determined, with the equivalent value in mercury and cinnabar held by Sterck and Tucher as security until these details were settled. That left 70,000 fl unaccounted, as Paumgartner and Mair both recognized. Mair professed confusion on this point: "I don't know whether I should speak or act on this matter, as your [Anton Fugger's] letter was suddenly interrupted and indicated absolutely nothing about this 70,000 fl, whether it is reserved for the Höchstetter or would pass to someone else". To clarify the matter, Mair asked Paumgartner to locate the missing 70,000 fl, and Paumgartner reported that "the younger Ambrosius [II Höchstetter] told him he had sold them in another manner and assigned them to other people shortly before his departure [from Antwerp, tms]".[85] It is the first clear indication that these transactions had, in fact, been undertaken at Fugger's direction.

The dating of Ambrosius's appeal to Fugger becomes critical at this point. It is impossible to determine whether this resolution of the Flemish loan was part of Fugger's response to Ambrosius or a separate stratagem to profit at his competitor's expense. It seems possible that Ambrosius referred to this exchange when he warned Fugger in his appeal that "they don't know what we have done". Be that as it may, this information seems to indicate that Fugger acted with the Höchstetters' knowledge and consent, that he assumed part of their obligation and left them to discharge the remainder.

Mair closed his report with details of 15,000 fl payments to Tucher and to Paumgartner that were to be rendered at two of the great Brabantine trade fairs, the *Koudemarkt* (*Kaltenmarkt* or Cold Market) in Bergen op Zoom and the *Bamismarkt* (*Bavonmarkt* or St. Bevo's Market) in Antwerp.[86] Funds were drawn from a series of currency exchanges in Seville. A following letter from Mair, dated 28 October 1528 suggests that he had made the promised payments to Tucher and Paumgartner "for the Höchstetters", as he put it. He added "God grant that they can satisfy their creditors and get by at these two markets, but I worry truly that it will not be enough".[87] The nature of these payments, whether on behalf of the Höchstetters of for some other purpose, remains unclear.

Anton Fugger's reply to Ambrosius's appeal does not survive, but a directive to Mair, dated 7 November 1528, contains his reactions to the factor's reports of 22 and 28 October.[88] His words reveal something of both the information he possessed and the knowledge upon which he based his actions.

Much of his letter concerned contractual security: Fugger wanted every stage of this complex transaction guaranteed in best legal form. As he repeatedly instructed Mair, "Have them put in our name and transfer it to you in the presence of a notary and witnesses, according to local custom, so that it has authority".[89] He was unwilling to arrange details according to informal agreements, whether written or oral. With regard to the 80,000 fl in mortgaged state income, he noted that Mair had not indicated, whether Paumgartner has provided notarized contracts transferring those funds from Sterck and Tucher to him. The factor was to waste no time providing them. He pointed out that no guarantee had been made against furture Höchstetter claims: "On the same point, the Höchstetters should and must acknowledge that they have been satisfied with such money (*sollichs Gelts*) and that they once and for all can and may have nothing further to do with it".[90] Sterck and Tucher should, according to Fugger, assure that this had indeed taken place. To this end, Mair should "conduct [himself] toward those two in a friendly manner, so that they indicate as much to you the more completely and cooperatively".[91] The same practice applied to the 50,000 fl in mercury and cinnabar, which had been subject to delay and confusion. As the commodities were being delivered in Venice, Fugger expressed confidence that this part of the transaction was secure, but he insisted nonetheless that the personal notes of Sterck and Tucher be recast as formal contracts, notarized and witnessed. Likewise, the Höchstetters must again give assurance in writing that they had received compensation and renounced all further interest in this business.

Fugger was alert to confusion that might signal risk or opportunity. The guarantee of 20,000 fl per annum, offered by Margareth of Austria and other members of her court, made little sense applied to the promised 16,000 fl in Flemish incomes. Fugger realized this immediately, and assumed it was meant to apply to the total obligation of 200,000 fl. "Now with regard to the security of the lords of 20,000 fl annually, I noted that it is placed on the 16,000 fl, which you [should] not have indicated to me, but rather on the entire sum of 200,000 *Carolusgulden*; if it is in fact on the 16,000 fl, then in the name of God do everything you can to have it [. . .] put in our name".[92] The possibility of 20,000 fl in surety for 16,000 fl in capital was too good to pass up.

Finally, he reassured his factor that the supposedly missing 70,000 fl were of no real consequence: "Now I am of the opinion that is does not matter whether we know what has become of [the 70,000 fl] or not; so long as we have the contract for the entire sum of 200,000 fl payable to the bearer and the transfer of the aforementioned 130,000 fl, it is a correct thing".[93] The Höchstetters had vacated the Flemish loan; Fugger's firm held nearly two-thirds of the capital and, most importantly, all the legal documentation. What did the Höchstetters receive in exchange? "That you have satisfied the host (*den Wirt*) with 30,000 fl is good." Can it be that the "the host" was Ambrosius I Höchstetter or someone acting on his behalf? It seems Fugger paid 30,000 for a credit transaction worth 200,000 fl and still was not entirely satisfied: "I think you should not have paid him so much". Yet, "Now I think he has other things to do, so that once we have security for this sum, he would not longer be able to interfere with us, which would be preferable to me".[94] In essence, Fugger discounted the Höchstetters' Flemish transaction at 30,000 for 200,000 fl, an astonishing rate of 14.3 percent that captured not only his profit, but Höchstetter's loss. Once word got out, his advantage would be lost, and creditors would crowd forward demanding repayment.

Conrad Mair's correspondence with his principal evokes Ambrosius's appeal. All written in 1528, perhaps within months of one another, they reveal how information flowed as the insolvency deepened. Höchstetter provided specific information to Fugger. Fugger directed his factor to act upon it: He obtained copies of all relevant contracts; he oversaw the transferal of the obligation; he maintained carefully correct relations with his intermediaries and colleagues; he guaranteed that Höchstetter was excluded from further involvement.

Despite the need for secrecy, the correspondence demonstrates a remarkable level of detailed information shared among colleagues and confederates. By October 1528, Steck and Tucher, Paumgartner, Mair and Fugger all knew that the Höchstetters would never provide the funds required in Flanders. They knew precisely the financial details, and they possessed the legal documentation. This may help to explain Fugger's repeated, anxious admonitions: "Conduct yourself with them [Sterck and Tucher] in an even more friendly manner, so that they complete [the deal] completely and quickly"; "I would be pleased, if you would speak with Tucher in good faith, how we are secured and whether it is a good security".[95] The secret was no longer secret. Its communication was no longer limited to rumor. These men traded in official copies of contracts that contained explicit financial details: What was owed to whom, and when and where payments were to be made.

There remained points of obscurity and confusion, to be sure. Were the Höchstetters engaged in double-dealing? What was the full extent of their indebtedness? In the final analysis, knowledge remains elusive, distinct from information. That information flowed at a slow pace by modern standards, but it was remarkable in its regularity and completeness, the problems of time and space notwithstanding. It intimates the knowledge these merchant-financiers discovered, in Hayek's sense of the term, that is, the sense that they made of it and the purpose to which they put it.

* * *

In 1528, the exact date being difficult to determine, "Hans and Ambrosius, the Brothers Höchstetter and Associates" was insolvent. Though its meaning is commonly understood, the strict definition deserves consideration. Insolvency refers quite simply to an inability or lack of means to pay one's debts. It describes, according to *Black's Law Dictionary*, "the condition of a person who is unable to pay his debts as they fall due, or in the usual course of trade and business".[96] Deceptively simple, a deeper meaning revolves around the word, "unable". Experts distinguish two forms of inability: Cash-flow insolvency, which involves a lack of liquidity to pay debts as they fall due; and balance-sheet insolvency, in which liabilities exceed assets.

This distinction illuminates the tactics of both Ambrosius and Anton Fugger. The former believed his problems arose from a temporary lack of liquidity, arising from an unsuccessful attempt at a monopoly in mercury as well as other business failures. Some of Ambrosius's problems appear to have arisen from miscalculation; the vast quantities of mercury and cinnabar purchased by the Höchstetters in advance of their monopoly had to be liquidated at a loss afterward. Others resulted from sheer bad luck: Highway robbery or maritime piracy occurred regularly but unpredictably. Others stemmed from reckless and unprofessional behavior that reflected poorly on the reputations of the partners and their firm; the gambling and profligacy of the younger partners worked to the detriment of all. Still others may have resulted from a growing awareness of the Höchstetters' plight. Convinced that his problems could be resolved with infusions of cash, Ambrosius borrowed heavily in 1527 and 1528 and appealed to Fugger for further counsel and capital. As his appeal made clear, he believed that the total assets of his firm sufficed to cover his obligations, both old and new, even though he lacked the cash to honor them as they came due. Selective payments and careful negotiations formed the key to his approach. Fugger apparently extended resources to Ambrosius, though whether in support of his competitor or of himself remains unclear. His evaluation of the insolvency, based on secret information provided by Ambrosius and business intelligence gathered by his agents, led him to the conclusion that the crisis arose from negative net assets. Ambrosius lacked not only the cash but also the assets to pay all his debts. Bluntly put, his expressed hope to avoid bankruptcy – "that I am not placed in jeopardy and no one suffers disadvantage because of me" – was vain. Thus convinced, Fugger began to pay off certain creditors and purchase certain assets, acquiring the Höchstetter firm's debt leverage and displacing it in certain markets. Whether Fugger intended these various machinations to help or harm the Höchstetters is, in the final analysis, irrelevant. By the time the remaining unpaid creditors turned to the city government of Augsburg for protection, in June 1529, Ambrosius lacked the means to meet his obligations. A reputed monopolist, accustomed to pushing competitors and debtors to the wall, he found himself now in the hands of his peers.

These machinations reveal something of the flow of information and the discovery of knowledge in early modern business life. Hayek's distinction between the two – and his caveat against an essentialist construction of rationality – proves particularly useful at this point. The correspondence between Ambrosius and Fugger and between Fugger and his agents offer rare glimpses of the scope of business intelligence they exchanged. The modern, scholarly discussion of information in politics and business, in public life, centers on emergent technologies, such as moveable-type printing, and formal knowledge, such as handbooks.[97] It connects thus tacitly to modernization narratives that insist on a clear distinction between that which constitutes modernity and that which preceded it. The premodern world supposedly relied on tacit knowledge and traded informally by word-of-mouth or line of sight. There is a certain truth to this, but it remains incomplete. Modern business continues to rely on learning by doing; apprenticeships and internships in place of or in addition to formal training have grown in frequency and importance over the few last decades. It also relies on informal means of communication, such as letters, conversations and rumors, affecting markets and politics in ways that are highly reminiscent of so-called premodern business life. Though it moved slowly by modern standards, sometimes taking a week or two to travel from Antwerp to Augsburg or from Augsburg to Lyon, Fugger's information demonstrated a level of detail that occasionally astonishes.[98] Exact legal and financial data changed hands, extending even to proprietary information that should have remained secret. It was a dense market in facts. Yet, it stops short of knowledge, which Ambrosius and Fugger "discovered" on the basis of the available facts. Lack of documentation makes it difficult to reconstruct what Ambrosius might have known about his firm's condition. It is unclear how much he knew of events in his far-flung trading network. And even his creditors remarked the "lazy" nature of his firm's accounting. To what extent was he fully cognizant of the losses that accrued in various marketplaces and gaming tables? Whatever facts were at his command, the sense he made of them appears overly optimistic, whether colored by altruism or desperation remains clear. By contrast, Fugger's point-by-point arithmetical analysis is lapidary. His own disciplined review of Höchstetter finance left no doubt that the firm was doomed, ripe for the picking. Yet, even in this case, where knowledge seems clearly documented, it would be a mistake to assume that his tactics resulted from rational calculation alone. To what extent might he have been motivated by resentment toward a highly successful competitor? Whatever facts were at his command and however clearly his actions reveal his conclusions, no linear continuum exists between facts and interpretation, information and knowledge.

Rationality, as Hayek argued more than half a century ago, is an historical construct. He considered misguided the assumption on the part of many economists (and historians) that it is an element of human nature, unchanging over space and time. Perfectly capable of pursuing their own advantage and utility, Ambrosius and Fugger understood their motives and their goals in ways that defy exact description, except by the attribution of characteristics or qualities assumed to be universal. Undisputable is the fact that Ambrosius did not accurately describe the crisis that engulfed his firm. Whether he misrepresented or misunderstood it, and why he might have done so, simply defy analysis. Fugger seized the essence and the moment, but how he managed his information, a crucial step in the process of making sense of it, and why he did so, remain similarly obscure.[99] Only the effects are clear.

The additional leverage of 1527 and 1528 failed to ease the plight of "Hans and Ambrosius, the Brothers Höchstetter and Associates". Quite the contrary. It had the long-term consequence of convincing their creditors that they had been the victims of fraud, that Ambrosius and his partners had sold assets and borrowed money in the full knowledge that they would not be able to meet their obligations. Over the short term, it would do little to solidify their *Trauen und Glauben*.

As news of the developments in Augsburg, Antwerp and elsewhere spread, confidence in "Ambrosius and Hans, the Brothers Höchstetter and Associates" was badly shaken. Rumors of financial reverses, compounded by the appearance of recklessness and mismanagement, quickly eroded the credit and credibility that Sender claimed the elder Höchstetter enjoyed. That personal reputation reflected not only credit-worthiness, the trust that arises from an ability to repay one's debts and a history of having done so, but also and equally a stature that comes from business success and the good fortune and controlled discipline that were thought to lead to it. Sender pointed to the heart of the problem: The monetary damages from unsuccessful plans and commercial mishaps, even from wasteful living, mattered less than the partners' failure to "act in an upright manner" (*sich rechtgeschaffen gehalten*) and to "concern themselves with these things" (*sich geben lan* [sic], *wer solichs auch fürkommen worden*). News began to circulate in many trading centers that the Höchstetters lacked the capital reserves to honor their obligations. Once word of their liquidity crisis leaked out, their creditors pursued them, no longer confident that they would or could pay up. Writing from Antwerp to Christian II, exiled King of Denmark, on 16 January 1529, Lazarus Tucher showed how suspicions had hardened: "I will have nothing large or small to do with him (Joachim I Höchstetter, a close associate of the king, tms), the causes for which I will tell your Royal Wisdom".[100]

Notes

1 Richard Ehrenberg set the date of this appeal for assistance in the spring of 1529. Available documents indicate that it was sent a year earlier, sometime in 1528. See Richard Ehrenberg, *Das Zeitalter der Fugger: Geldkapital und Kreditverkehr im 16. Jahrhundert*, I, 2 Bde. (New York 1990), 217.

2 Fugger had recently married Anna Rehlinger, a daughter of the same Augsburg patrician clan as Höchstetter's own wife. The fathers of the two Annas shared little more than their name. See Wolfgang Reinhard, et al. (eds.), *Augsburger Eliten des 16. Jahrhunderts: Prosopographie wirtschaftlicher und politischer Führungsgruppen 1500–1620* (Berlin 1996).

3 Fürstlich und Gräflich Fuggersches Familien- und Stiftungsarchiv Dillingen (hereinafter FA), Handel 2, 2, 1, Gemischte Korrespondenz der Administration der gemeinen Handels, 1527–1638; u.a. betr. Hoechstetter-Konkurs, 1527–1542, fol. 1. Also quoted in full in Ernst Kern, *Studien zur Geschichte des Augsburger Kaufmannshauses der Höchstetter* (Berlin 1935), 35–7.

4 Ibid.

5 Ibid.

6 Ibid.

7 Ibid.

8 Ehrenberg, *Das Zeitalter der Fugger*, I: 214.

9 Ibid.

10 TLA, Bekennen 1521, fol. 70–1; Bekennen 1523, fol. 51–2.

11 Ehrenberg, *Das Zeitalter der Fugger*, I: 214.

12 A cursory examination of titles in the bibliography of John J. McCusker and C. Gravesteijn, demonstrates the point. See John J. McCusker and C. Gravesteijn, *The Beginnings of Commercial and Financial Journalism* (The Hague 1979).

13 "information, n.," OED Online, June 2017. Oxford University Press. Available at: http://proxy.library.upenn.edu:2946/view/Entry/95568?redirectedFrom=information (accessed 6 December 2017).

14 "knowledge, n.," OED Online, June 2017. Oxford University Press. Available at: http://proxy.library.upenn.edu:2946/view/Entry/104170?rskey=87sPFR&result=1&isAdvanced=false (accessed 6 December 2017).

15 Peter J. Boettke, "Information and Knowledge: Austrian Economics in Search of Its Uniqueness," *The Review of Austrian Economics* 15 (2002): 263–74, here 266.

16 F.A. Hayek, "Economics and Knowledge," *Economica*, New Series 4 (1937): 33–54.
17 Ibid., 46.
18 Ibid., 46.
19 F. A. Hayek, "The Use of Knowledge in Society," *The American Economic Review* 35 (1945): 519–30.
20 Boettke, "Information and Knowledge," 268.
21 Their refinements and extensions speak to issues of entrepreneurship and markets. See Israel Kirzner, *Competition and Entrepreneurship* (Chicago 1973); Donald Lavoie, *Rivalry and Central Planning* (New York 1985).
22 See Ludwig Lachmann, *Capital, Expectations and the Market Process* (Kansas City, MO 1977); Murray Rothbard, *Man, Economy and State*, 2 vols. (Princeton 1962).
23 See, for example, Jacob Soll, *The Reckoning: Financial Accountability and the Rise and Fall of Nations* (New York 2014). The techniques of double-entry booking were commonly known in the mercantile community of the late-fifteenth and sixteenth centuries, but I have found few unequivocal examples of its practice in German account books of the period.
24 Hayek, "Knowledge and Economics," passim. See also Boettke, "Information and Knowledge," 268.
25 See John J. McCusker, "Introduction," in: John J. McCusker and C. Gravesteijn, *The Beginnings of Commercial and Financial Journalism*, 21–41.
26 Helfried Valentinitsch, *Das landesfürstliche Quecksilberbergwerk Idria, 1575–1659. Produktion – Technik – rechtliche und soziale Verhältnisse – Betriebsbedarf – Quecksilberhandel* (Graz 1981), 287. See also Jacob Strieder, *Studien zur Geschichte kapitalistischer Organisationsformen*, 2nd ed. (Munich 1925), 292–309. Strieder also provides the text of the 1525 agreement. See, ibid., 458–63.
27 Strieder refers to the agreement as a monopoly contract (*Monopolvertrag*), a usage that is commonplace in the historical literature. It was, in fact, a monopsony, in so far as it created a sole purchaser of the commodities in question. See Strieder, *Studien zur Geschichte kapitalistischer Organisations*formen, 295.
28 "*die all fur sich selbs und als gwalthaber annderer jrer mitverwannten und gwerckhen des berckhwerchs jn Ydria mit zeytigen rat unnd wolgedachten muet fur sich jr erben unnd nachkomen gnedig unnd unterthenigklich mit ainander veraint auch entschlossen unnd den vessten furnemen Ambrosien unnd Hannsen den Hochstettern gebruedern zue Augspurg unnd jren mitverannten ainen q. s. und zinober kauf von unns unnd aus dem berckhwerch Ydria gegben und kaufsweyss zugestellt haben, wissenntlich jn crafft dit brieffs, also das den gemelten Hochstetern unnd jren mitverwannten von der F. Mt. unnd den gewerckhen zue sten unnd ervolgen soll, nemlich aller q.g. unnd zinober, sovil des auff heutigen tag gemachts guets vorhannden ist unnd zusambt den selbenn von denen g.s. unnd zinobern die jm negstgeenden 4 jaren gemacht werden, benanntlich jn ainer suma umb dreymall hundert tausennt gulden wert guets an q.s. unnd zinober, also und der gestalt das sollichs q.s. unnd zinober den Hochstettern und allen gwerckhen gemachts guets unnd auch von abberurt Fl. Mt. fronn unnd wexl unnd anndern der berurten gwercken q.s.und zinober so sy in Ydria haben werden by gedachten berckhwerch jn Ydria sollen uberanntworten unnd zuestellen nach gerechten geschwornen zenntner wiennisch gericht ain jeden zenntner q.s. umb 30 fl Rh unnd ain jeden zenntner zinober umb 35 fl Rh als mit gueter gemainer lanndsgebreuchlichen Muntz nachvolggender gestalt zu bezallen oder mit abziehung der fell und vossl soll es gehoben worden, wie des bisher unnd vormals mit den Pfluegl Neumann oder anndern kaufleuten gehalten worden ist*". FA, Gemeiner Handel und Auslösung, 2.2.1 ½,V–17.
29 Strieder, *Studien zur Geschichte kapitalistischer Organisationsformen*, 296–7.
30 Valentinitsch, *Das landesfürstliche Quecksilberbergwerk Idria*, 286–7.
31 Heinrich Blank, "Der Villacher Bürger Wilhelm Neumann als Kaufmann und Gewerke in Idria," in: Gotbert Moro (ed.), *700 Jahre Stadt Villach* (Villach 1940), 116–37.
32 Richard Klier, "Der Konkurrenzkampf zwischen dem böhmischen und dem idrianischen Quecksilber in der ersten Hälfte des 16. Jahrhunderts," *Bohemia: Jahrbuch des Collegium Carolinum* 8 (1967): 82–110, esp. 88f.

33 Strieder *Studien zur Geschichte kapitalistischer Organisationsformen*, 293–6.

34 "*gemelten Hochsteter jren mitverwannten unnd erben gegen der Ky Mayt. Unnsern genedigisten lieben Herrn unnd Brueder oder seine Kay.Mayt. und des Reichs Regiment oder derselben Viscul auch sonnst gegen menigklich, von welchen sy sollichs Kauffs halben angesprochen und der durch jn schaden zu furen unnterstannden wurden jr gnediger herr und vorsprechen sein auch deshalben gatz schadlos halten*". FA, Gemeiner Handel und Auslösung, 2.2.1 ½,V–17.

35 Strieder, *Studien zur Geschichte kapitalistischer Organisationsformen*, 298–9. See also Ulrich Klinkert, "Die Augsburger Handelsgesellschaft der Höchstetter. Zusammenbruch 1529, Gläubiger und soziale Verflechtung" (Hausarbeit, University of Augsburg 1983), 22.

36 Strieder's use of the term "*rücksichtlos*" suggests not only ruthlessness, but recklessness. Whether he wished to suggest a lack of diligence on the part of Ambrosius cannot be determined. It is interesting to consider, however, in light both of the outcome of the business and of Ambrosius's own protestations of innocence. Ibid., 303.

37 "*Nun wyssen wir kain anndern weg, dann dass dass Bechmysch Bergkwerckh dem Pergkwerckh Jdria mecht verwannt unnd zu gestalt werden, damitt E. Ku. Mt. dess hohem Ansuchen so von den Pehammen umb ain Pass die Sylber durch E. Ku. Mt. Erbland auff Venedig zufueren soll absein mecht. So haben wir doch mitt dem Wigkell, der dann sollich Perkwergkh zu Behaim in Hannden hatt, sovill gehanndellt, dass er alle sein Quecksylber, so er in funff Jarenn machte, doch solt er uber acht hundert Zentner die funff Jar nitt machenn, wolt kaufflich zu stellen. Der Kauff wer dennocht leydennlich, allain yst es in unnserm Vermugenn nit, die weyl wir vorhin ain grosse uberschwengliche Soma auf ain klain Zeytt habenn. Wa aber E. Ku. Mt. mitt sampt den Wergkenn gnediglichenn wolte darain sehen, unnd umb sovil auff den ganntzen Kauff der dann yst zehen tausent Zenntner unns amm dysser Suma die 800 Zentner, wie vorstett, gnedigklich erlassen, dass wir der selben 800 Zentner jn Jdria sovil minder schuldig were zu erpharen*". Österreichisches Staatsarchiv Wien, Innerösterreichischen Miszellen und Briefe (hereinafter ÖStA, IÖMuB) 134/1. See also Kern, *Studien zur Geschichte des Augsburger Handelshauses der Höchstetter*, 15; Klinkert, "Die Augsburger Handelsgesellschaft der Höchstetter," 22.

38 Strieder, *Studien zur Geschichte kapitalistischer Organisationsformen*, 303.

39 Klinkert, "Die Augsburger Handelsgesellschaft der Höchstetter," 23.

40 Kern mentions Genoese and Spanish entrepreneurs without naming names. See Kern, *Studien zur Geschichte des Augsburger Handelshauses der Höchstetter*, 16. Despite heavy competition of this sort, the Fuggers managed to renew their contract at Almadén in 1528 by joining financial forces with the Welser. See Kern, *Studien zur Geschichte des Augsburger Handelshauses der Höchstetter*, 15; Konrad Häbler, *Die Geschichte der Fugger'schen Handlung in Spanien* (Weimar 1897), 96.

41 Sender's price information differs widely from those demanded by the Idria contract of 1525. The disparity cannot be finally explained. It seems possible he intended 8 fl and 14 fl to indicate a price in the marketplace, not at the mine head, reflecting the seller's profit margin. Clemens Sender, *Die Chronik von Clemens Sender von den ältesten Zeiten der Stadt bis zum Jahre 1536. Die Chroniken der schwäbischen Städte. Augsburg*, vol. IV (Leipzig 1894), 220.

42 See also Kern, *Studien zur Geschichte des Augsburger Handelshauses der Höchstetter*, 31; Klinkert, "Die Augsburger Handelsgesellschaft der Höchstetter," 24.

43 Sender, *Die Chronik*, 220–1.

44 Ehrenberg, *Zeitalter der Fugger*, I: 215. See also StAA, Literaliensammlung, Höchstetter-Selekt II, fol. 301; Kern, *Studien zur Geschichte des Augsburger Handelshauses der Höchstetter*, 8, 32.

45 Ehrenberg is unclear about the grounds for the seizure of the ships bearing a cargo of grain bound for England. See Ehrenberg, *Das Zeitalter der Fugger*, 214–15.

46 Ehrenberg, *Das Zeitalter der Fugger*, I: 216.

47 On altruism in economic life, see Gary Becker, *A Treatise on the Family* (Cambridge, UK 1981); Howard Margolis, *Selfishness, Altruism and Rationality* (Cambridge, UK 1982); Edmund S. Phelps, *Altruism, Morality and Economic Theory* (New York 1975); Oded Stark, "Altruism and the Quality of Life," *American Economic Review* 79 (1982): 86–90.

48 *"das er jnn Shaden unnd Verderben des 27 Jars unnd hernach gewachsen wei und jnn woelchem Jar er vonn nachgeshriben Personen Gellt uffgenommen hat als seine Schuldbreiff unnd Hanndtshrifften ausweisen*". StAA, Literaliensammlung, Höchstetter-Selekt I, EE, Wievil Hoechstetter in Zeit seines Verderbens Gellt auffgemenn [aufgenommen?] unnd von wem, s.d, s.a.

49 "*er habe voe zway Jaren sein Abfal gesehen unnd befunnden doch tagliche Hoffnung gehapt zu sampt dem das er vor Jar unnd Tag ehe er hie beclagt worden jnn Franckhreich falliert, nemblich des 28. Jars vor oderumb Ostern ungefarlich*". Ibid.

50 "*One etlichs so nit jnn gemelte Zinsbucher (vileicht durch Unfleiss) nit eingeshriben worden, als Graff Haugen Sebastian Widenmans*". Ibid.

51 Sender, *Die Chronik*, 221.

52 FA, 2.2.1: Gemischte Korrespondenzen der Administration des Gemeinen Handels: Höchstetter-Konkurs. Von Ambrosius Höchstetter an Anton Fugger, s.d., 1528.

53 Reinhard, *Augsburger Eliten des 16. Jahrhunderts*, 155.

54 "*Also befunden wir daß wir auf kaine ardt mer shuldig sendt*". FA, 2.2.1: Gemischte Korrespondenzen der Administration des Gemeinen Handels: Höchstetter-Konkurs. Von Ambrosius Höchstetter an Anton Fugger, s.d., 1528.

55 FA, Handel 2,2,1, fol. 5–7. "Auszug von Quecksilber und Zinnober," "Beschluß alter Handlung" and "Abgekündigtes Geld." Also cited in Klinkert, "Die Augsburger Handelsgesellschaft der Höchstetter," 45.

56 By virtue of its liquid state and its amalgamating quality, mercury had to be shipped and stored in leather "skins" (*Fel*) that were placed in barrels, two to a pack animal.

57 The term "loaves" suggests that cinnabar traveled as a ground mineral, compacted and shipped in solid shapes.

58 *"benanntlich jn ainer suma umb dreymall hundert tausennt gulden wert guets an q.s. unnd zinober, also und der gestalt das sollichs q.s. unnd zinober den Hochstettern und allen gwerckhen gemachts guets unnd auch von abberurt Fl. Mt. fronn unnd wexl unnd anndern der berurten gwercken q.s.und zinober so sy in Ydria haben werden by gedachten berckhwerch jn Ydria sollen uberanntworten unnd zuestellen nach gerechten geschwornen zenntner wiennisch gericht ain jeden zenntner q.s. umb 30 fl Rh unnd ain jeden zenntner zinober umb 35 fl Rh als mit gueter gemainer lanndsgebreuchlichen Muntz nachvolggender gestalt zu bezallen oder mit abziehung der fell und vossl soll es gehoben worden, wie des bisher unnd vormals mit den Pfluegl Neumann oder anndern kaufleuten gehalten worden ist*". FA, Gemeiner Handel und Auslösung, 2.2.1 ½, V–17. Ambrosius worked to minimize the meaning of this obligation to the mine operators of Idria. Against the 104,687 fl, he set 58,000 fl in "*fronn unnd wexl*", the taxes on minerals rendered to the Archduchy of Austria. The inventory refers to sealed agreements between Ambrosius and the mine operators that are no longer extant. It seems possible that the operators agreed to assume the tax liability. For whatever reason, he deducted the 58,000 fl in taxes owed from his firm's total obligation at Idria, leaving a debt no higher than 46,487 fl, payable over two years.

59 Götz, Freiherr von Pölnitz, *Anton Fugger*,vol. I, 4 vols. (Tubingen 1958–86), 132–3.

60 FA, 2.2.1: Gemischte Korrespondenzen der Administration des Gemeinen Handels: Höchstetter-Konkurs. Georg Hörmann to Anton Fugger, 17 June 1529; Anton Fugger to Georg Hörmann, 9 July 1529; Wolf Haller to Anton Fugger, 15 August 1529; Wolf Haller to Anton Fugger, 11 December 1529.

61 FA, 2.2.1: Gemischte Korrespondenzen der Administration des Gemeinen Handels: Höchstetter-Konkurs. Höchstetter, 8 Junio 1528.

62 StAA, Literaliensammlung, Höchstetter-Selekt I, Dok. 1, "Welcher Glaubiger von den Hoechstettern oder jrn Hausfrawen vergnug und verwisen zu woelcher Zeit bei wem und umb was Gellt."

63 Johann Sallaberger, *Kardinal Matthäus Lang von Wellenburg (1468–1540): Staatsmann und Kirchenfürst im Zeitalter von Renaissance, Reformation und Bauernkriegen* (Munich 1997), 181–5.

64 "*Jnn disem Ausszug werden demnach nit gemeldt die 87186 fl. 16 sh. 0 hl. so Hoechstetter [. . .] von Fugger Paumgartner unnd annders uffgenommen, dann man nit Wissen hat, were damit bezallt worden*". StAA, Literaliensammlung, Höchstetter-Selekt I, Dok. 1, "Welcher Glaubiger von den Hoechstettern oder jrn Hausfrawen vergnug und verwisen zu woelcher Zeit bei wem und umb was Gellt."

65 StAA, Literaliensammlung, Höchstetter-Selekt I, Dok. 4, "Was die Hochstetter an allen Orten verpfendt, versetzt unnd mit Shaden verkhaufft haben."

66 Pölnitz, *Anton Fugger*, I: 133, 489.

67 Ibid, I: 497.

68 FA, Handel, 2,2,1 fol. 17–20; Handel 40, 1. See also Pölnitz, *Anton Fugger*, I: 498.

69 StAA. Literaliensammlung, Höchstetter-Selekt I, Dok. 1 "*Welcher Glaubiger von den Hoechstettern oder jrn Hausfrawen vergnug und verwisen zu woelcher Zeit bei wem und umb was Gellt. Wer sonnst allennthalben nach Aussweysung des Inventarii bezallt oder verwissen*".

70 StAA. Literaliensammlung, Höchstetter-Selekt I, Dok. 4, "*Was die Hochstetter an allen Orten verpfendt, versetzt unnd mit Shaden verkhaufft haben*".

71 Pölnitz, *Anton Fugger*, I: 131.

72 Ibid. Also cited in Klinkert, "Die Augsburger Handelsgesellschaft der Höchstetter," 25–6.

73 The following discussion relies substantially on prosopographic data published in Reinhard, *Augsburger Eliten des 16. Jahrhunderts*, passim.

74 Bimmel and Herwart had indirect connection via common ties to the Rehlinger clan. See Klinkert, "Die Augsburger Handelsgesellschaft der Höchstetter," Abb 5, S 114.

75 The city of Augsburg taxed wealth, as opposed to income or property. Every seven years, it required its citizens to submit a sworn declaration of their worth, which it then assessed at rates of 0.50 percent for moveable and 0.25 percent for immoveable capital. As a result, recorded tax liabilities indicate a range of wealth, depending on how an individual's property was distributed. See Claus-Peter Clasen, *Die Augsburger Steuerbücher um 1600* (Augsburg 1976).

76 "*Nun wer ich der Mainung Hannsen Bongarten, Lauxen Remen Hanns Pummel für die frey zunemen, ich hett Euch auch geren, so irs annderst geschafft halben thon mecht*". FA, Handel 2, 2, 1, Gemischte Korrespondenz der Administration der gemeinen Handels, 1527–1638; u.a. betr. Hoechstetter-Konkurs, 1527–1542, fol. 1. Also quoted in full in Kern, *Studien zur Geschichte des Augsburger Kaufmannshauses der Höchstetter*, 35–7.

77 Ehrenberg, *Das Zeitalter der Fugger*, I: 212, Kern, *Studien zur Geschichte des Augsburger Kaufmannshauses der Höchstetter*, 20; Strieder, *Studien zur Geschichte kapitalistischer Organizationsformen*, 305.

78 Ehrenberg, *Das Zeitalter der Fugger*, I: 215, Kern, *Studien zur Geschichte des Augsburger Kaufmannshauses der Höchstetter*, 32; Strieder, *Studien zur Geschichte kapitalistischer Organizationsformen*, 307.

79 FA 2.2.1: Gemischte Korrespondenzen der Administration des Gemeinen Handels: Korrespondenz mit Antwerpen. Conrad Mair to Anton Fugger, 22 October 1528; 28 October 1528.

80 Pölnitz, *Anton Fugger*, I: 134–5.

81 "*Und pangartner hat mir zu gesagt die Corta und anendadores jrer Verschreibung ledig zu zellen und so das beschechen, sollen und wollen als dann pangartner, gerhart sterck und lassarus tucher so fiel zu hoff und bei den anendadoresen handlen, das man die brief allen massen wie die auffs hochstetter oder bringer der brieff gestanden, auffs gerhart stercken und lassarussen tucher oder bringer der brieff schreiben und stellen solle, also das die handlung umb die posten wie die hie vor gemelt gar aus den hochstetters handen und auff den stercken und tucher kommen soll*". FA 2.2.1: Gemischte Korrespondenzen der Administration des Gemeinen Handels: Korrespondenz mit Antwerpen. Conrad Mair to Anton Fugger, 22 October 1528; 28 October 1528.

82 "*Als aber sterck und tucher umb 50,000 fl quecksilber und zinober von der Corta jnn handen solten haben und sich gegen hochstetter verschrieben haben, die selben guetter nichts aus jren henden zu geben bis zu vor die hochstetters umb sollich 50,000 curant gulden von der Corta auff gwisse*

einkommen versichert seien, das man sy deren jn den negsten 5 jaren bezallen und mit der ersten frist auf primo septenber des 29 jars anfachen wolle, so solt jr doch wissen das die hochstetter vom stercken und tucher kain solche verschreibung nit gehapt haben, aus der ursach die zween starck und tucher haben kain solche verschreibung der hochstetter geben wollen bis sie zu vor schreiben haben das die guetter als quecksilber und zinober von den hochstetter zu vor zu jren handen gelibert seien". Ibid.

83 "*Das sy von der Regierung disser land umb 50,000 curant oder Karlus gulden quecksilber und zinober jnn handen haben und geloben euch dem hern fuggern die nichts aus jren handen zu lassen bis jr von der Corta umb sollich 50,000 fl bis an wuer benuegen versichert und verwissen sein werdet, das man euch die jn den negsten 5 jaren ain jedes 10,000 fl bezallen solle und wolle und anzufachen primo setember negstkunfftiges jar*". Ibid.

84 "*Und ob jch jn ain oder anderm die sach nit recht von mir hett als jch doch nit acht so welt mich euren willen laussen wissen, so handl ichs darnach*". Ibid.

85 "*Ich hab woll den hans pangartner darumb angesprochen, ob man mir nit die verweissungen umb die selben 70,000 fl auch zustellen werde, so gipt er mir zu antwurt, den jung ambrosii hab die vor seinem wegkziechen hie jn ander weg verhandlt und andern leith zu gestalt*". Ibid.

86 Donald J. Harreld, *High Germans in the Low Countries: German Merchants and Commerce in Golden Age Antwerp* (Leiden 2004), 23–4.

87 "*Gott woll das si disse zwen merckt jr Creditori darmit zu friden stellen und auskommen konden. Ich sorg aber warlich, es werd nit so ferr raichen*". FA 2.2.1: Gemischte Korrespondenzen der Administration des Gemeinen Handels: Korrespondenz mit Antwerpen. Conrad Mair to Anton Fugger, 22 October 1528; 28 October 1528.

88 FA, 2.2.1: Gemischte Korrespondenzen der Administration des Gemeinen Handels: Höchstetter-Konkurs. Anton Fugger to Conrad Mair, 7 November 1528.

89 "*lassen sie es nochmal unnser namen stellen, euch uberschreiben, vor nottari und gezeugen unnd inn der furm dem lanndprauch nach, dz es krafft hab*". Ibid.

90 "*am selben ort, sollen unnd muessen sich hechsteter bekennen dz sie sollichs gelts vergnuegt seyen, unnd dz mans auff die stell damit sie wie ain mal garnichts darmit zu thun mer haben kunden noch mugen*". Ibid.

91 "*halt euch mit den selben 2 desto freuntlicher, damit sie euchs voll unnd furderlicher anzaichten*". Ibid.

92 "*Item von wegen der Verschreibung vonn den Hern umb die 20,000 fl jerlich, vernume ich dz nun auf jerlich 16,000 fl ist, dz hanndt sie mir gleuchwoll nit annzaigt, sonnderst auf die gannz Summa der 200,000 Currentgulden, so es dann nun auf dise 16,000 send, in namen gots aber secht jnn allweg das man die selben auch ob der wirt namen stell, und deucht mich am furderlichesten, dz mans auf unnsern namen stellet*". Ibid.

93 "*nun main ich dz nit darann lig, an dem 70,000 wir wissen dz oder nit, so wir den brief umb die ganntz suma haben und dz er leu tuff wirt oder pringersbrieffs und haben nochmaln die obangemelt ubergab der 130,000fl, so sey es also ein richtig ding*". Ibid.

94 "*So habt jr dem wirt die 30,000 fl vergnuegt ist gut [. . .] jch maint jr sollt jnn nit also vill zalt haben [. . .] nun jch halt er hab sunst auch zu thun, so wir einmal mit diser summa versichert wern, dz er uns nichts kundt darjnn eintrag thun, dz wer mir am liebsten*". Ibid.

95 "*halt euch mit den selben 2 desto freuntlicher damit sie euchs voll unnd furdlicher aussrichten [. . .]*"; "*Doch lass ich mir gefaln dz ij mit dem Thucher jnn gutem vertrawen davon redt, wie wir versichert sein unnd ob es also ein gute versicherung sey*". Ibid.

96 "https://thelawdictionary.org/insolvency/"title="INSOLVENCY">INSOLVENCY.

97 The argument concerns "propositional knowledge", knowledge about a given thing, which signifies information and ignores Hayek's distinction that supposedly could be more broadly and reliably communicated via print media. See, for example, Joel Mokyr, *The Gifts of Athena* (Princeton 2002), 4–5; Fritz Machlup, *Knowledge: Its Creation, Distribution, and Economic Significance*, vol. 1 (Princeton 1980), 30–1.

98 Historians have yet to address the range and reliability of networks in business communication. Scholars of business and management have examined these themes in contemporary settings. See, for example, Gunnar Dahl, *Trade, Trust, and Networks: Commercial Culture in Late Medieval Italy* (Lund 1998); James Murray, "Of Nodes and Networks:

Bruges and the Infrastructure of Trade in the Fourteenth Century," in: Peter Stabel, Bruno Blondé and Anke Greve (eds.), *International Trade in the Low Countries (14th-16th Centuries)* (Leuven 2000); Walter W. Powell, "Neither Market nor Hierarchy: Network Forms of Organization," *Research in Organizational Behavior* 12 (1990).

99 The journal *Media History* recently devoted an entire issue to the topic of information and its management, a topic the editors claim with right has been addressed insufficiently, especially in the case of economic life. Among the examples cited are these: Ann M. Blair, *Too Much to Know: Managing Scholarly Information Before the Modern Age* (New Haven 2010); Simon F. Davies and Puck Fletcher (eds.), *News in Early Modern Europe: Currents and Connections* (Leiden 2014); Brendan Dooley (ed.), *The Dissemination of News and the Emergence of Contemporaneity in Early Modern Europe* (Farnham 2010); Brendan Dooley and Sabrina Baron (eds.), *The Politics of Information in Early Modern Europe* (London 2001); Andrew Pettegree, *The Invention of News: How the World Came to Know about Itself* (New Haven 2014); Joad Raymond (ed.), *News Networks in Seventeenth-Century Britain and Europe.* (Abingdon 2006). See Michiel van Groesen and Helmer Helmers, "Managing the News in Early Modern Europe. 1550–1800," *Media History* 22, 3–4 (2016): 261–6.

100 Otto Nübel, "Das Augsburger Kaufherrengeschlecht Höchstetter und die Restitution König Christians II. Von Dänemark," *Zeitschrift des historischen Vereins für Schwaben* 73 (1979): 139.

4 Bankruptcy

Local institutions and their consequences

On 26 September 1531, Ambrosius I Höchstetter stood accused and at bay before the City Court of Augsburg. The crisis he had sought to avoid with the assistance of Anton Fugger in 1528 had swept his family firm away. The rumors of insolvency had proven unmanageable; a run on the bank had ensued. On 1 July 1529, he had petitioned the City for bankruptcy protection. When the private negotiation and official mediation that are the topics of this and the following chapter failed to resolve the dispute, to say nothing of the secret machinations that preceded and accompanied them, he and two of his partners, son Ambrosius II and nephew Joseph, suffered arrest and confinement. Efforts to locate and sequester his property proved difficult, despite his promise of full disclosure and cooperation. Now, his creditors and the authorities wanted what had thus far eluded them: Clear answers.

Above all, the authorities and creditors wanted to know what Ambrosius knew and when he knew it.

> [A]s he, the old Höchstetter, had seen and known his ruin two years ago [1529, tms], as he himself admitted before the authorities, [why] had he fraudulently run up such huge debts in 1527 and 1528 and raised a sum to the ruin of rich and poor alike, fully aware that he knew he would not be able repay?[1]

He responded that he had had no knowledge of any insolvency in 1527; on the contrary, his "estimate" (*Überschlag*) of that year had shown assets in excess of 100,000 fl. They wanted to know why he had asked his creditors for an 18-month period of grace to continue in business, which he maintained would enable him to repay his debts with interest and remain an honorable, propertied man, when he had been aware that he had no possible means of doing either. He answered that he had had no idea his spokespersons had made any such offer, no knowledge that his affairs had been so badly compromised and no reports from the Netherlands or similar locations. They accused him of fraud, borrowing money that he could not repay with the intention of absconding with it, misrepresenting the state of his finances to the disadvantage of his creditors.

The interrogation – the first of several – extended to 26 articles and must have lasted hours. Most of their questions and answers circled around the current value and location of his capital, all of which was now subject to seizure and redistribution. "Fourthly, ask and insist strongly, what is openly rumored, whether [men of] the counts of Ortenburg took substantial property, which belonged to the Höchstetters, from the house of Philip I Gassner and transported it via backways out of the city, where, how, when and such like it has gone".[2] Ambrosius responded, "[he] knows nothing about this, insists sincerely, if he had so much as three pennies, he would give two to his creditors and keep only one for his sustenance; should one find it to be otherwise, they should punish him corporally (*an Leib und Leben*), as the law requires".[3] He claimed ignorance, blamed others and begged clemency.

The old Höchstetter of the interrogation stands in sharp contrast to the image of his younger self as Sender presents it, the "fine, lordly, tall, large and strong man, of princely appearance, considered of great credit and credibility". He and his family firm were not only insolvent, but now bankrupt, that is, not only unable to pay debts due to excess liabilities, but now engaged in legal action to protect themselves and meet their obligations. Unable to withstand the continued pressure of his creditors and pay his debts, Ambrosius now fulfilled "the condition of one who has committed an act of bankruptcy and is liable to be proceeded against by his creditors therefor, [sic] or of one whose circumstances are such that he is entitled, on his voluntary application, to take the benefit of the bankrupt laws".[4] The suddenness and depth of the fall were astonishing to contemporaries and to Ambrosius.

Rumors of secret payments to favored creditors had begun to circulate almost as soon as he and Fugger began to correspond. From the summer of 1528 to the summer of 1529, as doubts crystallized about his solvency, the unpaid creditors, the ones Sender described as "heedless" (*hinlessig*), became increasingly desperate. Again, Sender recorded the growing conflict:

> As these other creditors became aware of Höchstetter's ruin, they wished also to be paid, but he was no longer able to do so. They lodged a complaint against him before the [City] Council and demanded, that he be imprisoned in the tower until he paid them. The council refused to do this, saying it went against ancient custom and city law. The creditors heard this answer with consternation, whereupon the council summoned Höchstetter and made him swear an oath neither to leave the city nor to flee anywhere, until he had paid his creditors.[5]

On 1 July 1529, Ambrosius I Höchstetter, his son Ambrosius II and his nephew Joseph appeared before the council and swore the required oath to cease business and cooperate with the creditors. This, their public declaration of insolvency, constituted the initiation of formal bankruptcy proceedings and sealed their firm's fate. From this point, the bankruptcy became a legal matter to be argued and resolved before the Augsburg City Court.[6] The proceedings would involve oaths, petitions, arguments, interrogations and judgments, many of which would revolve around the questions of risk awareness, assessment and management. The bankrupts would plead the limits of certainty and security. The creditors would argue the assumed safety – indeed, sanctity – of their credit and investment. The authorities would question the dangers of finance. None possessed the tools or the language to evaluate risk; these would begin to emerge a century later. Yet, they all had a quotidian experience of it, of the uncertainties of everyday exchange, the possibility that any undertaking might have positive or negative results, might turn out better or worse than expected. How they expressed and applied this experience reveals something of the ways in which people understood risk before risk could be calculated.

This chapter traces the initial, local course of the bankruptcy proceedings against "Hans and Ambrosius, the Brothers Höchstetter and Associates". The narrative attends to institutions and the role they play in managing the risks of economic life at the time. The court documents and merchant correspondence generated by the proceedings record the daily calculation and negotiation that demonstrate how expedient behaviors guided by self-interested motives, how rationality and opportunism, far from being deterred, remained constitutive of daily market life, influenced by prevalent institutions, but constantly evading and, so, shaping them as well.[7] In this chapter, the bankruptcy of the house of Höchstetter offers thus a perspective on the function of institutions.

* * *

Douglass C. North argued that "institutions", those social constraints that make certain behaviors more predictable in certain situtations, encourage economic interaction by limiting uncertainty.[8] Though North's theory has attracted the attention of a generation of scholars, an awareness of the role of institutions in economic life is by no means new. As early as the mid-nineteenth century, German opponents of Smithian, classical economics, the so-called Old School or German Historical School, rejected any notion of isolated individuals acting in accordance with unchanging, selfish economic motives that failed to account for the influence of religion, politics or ethics. North managed thus to wrestle institutions from the grip of the *Methodenstreit* and to endow their study with new relevance and rigor.

Since the publication of North's seminal work, economists and economic historians have embraced his definition of institutions with enthusiasm. Many recent works attend to the means and methods by which the "rules" are enforced, particularly with regard to property rights and contract disputes. Many of these authors follow North's lead, arguing, for example, that strong territorial states held the key, supposedly because they alone possess the military might and legal authority to protect foreign trade and adjudicate commercial disputes.[9] These assertions do not account for the early expansion of trade, especially in Europe, where state authority and bureaucracy were under-developed. To explain economic growth in circumstances of political fragmentation, others focused on the development of private- or public-order responses to opportunism, multilateral reputation mechanisms enforced by coalitions of merchants as opposed to legal contracts enforced by courts of law.[10] To this debate, Oscar Gelderblom contributed another element, arguing that "open access" institutions, developed by urban magistrates for any and all traders within their jurisdiction, made possible the concentration and expansion of commerce between the thirteenth and seventeenth centuries: "[T]he very problem of Europe's political and legal fragmentation also produced its solution, in the form of competition between urban governments that tried to attract trade through the continuous adaptation of their legal, commercial, and financial institutions".[11] Because traders could vote with their feet, so to speak, taking their commerce elsewhere, if local conditions proved disadvantageous, political authorities struggled to protect trade and traders and yielded to their coercion. Institutions do not simply exist, a fact often overlooked in institutional histories, but are created and altered over time.

The issue of institutional adaptations to defend property rights and to settle contract disputes moves to the heart of the scholarship on institutions. Why are institutions created and how do they change? The language of competition suggests a consciousness of markets and their function that is compelling, but may also be problematical, when applied to premodern commerce or politics.[12] The historical evidence for Augsburg seems inconclusive on this point. Despite governing a center of manufacturing, commerce and finance, which competed actively with other commercial centers in the Holy Roman Empire, city authorities hesitated to adapt its economic institutions throughout much of the fifteenth and sixteenth centuries. They never, as noted, introduced laws to govern the organization of the firm[13] and were dilatory in establishing legal guidelines to settle bankruptcy.[14] In these and other respects, Augsburg lagged behind other economically important, free imperial cities, such as Nuremberg and Frankfurt.

An examination of conflict resolution, not of the legislative but of the legal process, offers a counterweight to the top-down approach of much institutional scholarship. Urban magistrates were, in fact, often merchants themselves, drawn from an elite actively engaged in commerce and finance. The regulations they created had, at best, uneven influence. The legal statutes and procedures that shaped the Höchstetter bankruptcy offer a case in point.

The documents of the Höchstetter bankruptcy contain frequent reference to the customary law and usage of the city. Yet, the traditional practices that articulate the early, established institutions of Augsburg were seldom fixed in writing. The City Council passed ordinances to regulate bankruptcy resolution in the late-sixteenth century. Their timing suggests that the council reacted to catastrophical business failures that shook the city's merchant community, first and foremost the collapse of the Höchstetter family firm.[15] It would seem in this case that economic organizations – the structures that articulate and thus make tangible institutions, according to North – emerged from the quotidian necessities and practices of economic agents.[16] That is to say, they rose from the bottom up, and their formalization into fixed "institutions" was reactive.

Merchants and authorities felt their way along, learned by doing. The institutions themselves existed at the metalevel of meaning, that is, at a level of abstraction behind the organizations and processes that are the object of actual study.

In modern Europe, bankruptcy is understood as a condition in which a debtor is declared insolvent before a court of law, at the request of either the debtor or the creditor(s). In direct consequence, the court usually appoints from among the creditors a committee of representatives as curators – the *curatores bonorum* in civil law – who sequester and inventory the bankrupt's remaining capital for the purpose of either administering it for or distributing it among the creditors.[17] In premodern Europe, however, bankruptcy had a more ambivalent meaning. Jurists and merchants distinguished not only between insolvency and bankruptcy, but also between innocent and fraudulent bankruptcy, between bankruptcy that resulted from circumstances beyond the normal control of the bankrupt and bankruptcy that resulted from his or her deliberate carelessness or dishonesty. Moreover, some legal communities limited bankruptcy to certain trades or professions.[18] Artisans, for example, could acquire debt and become insolvent, but only merchants could declare bankruptcy. In effect, some regulatory regimes denied tradesmen and their creditors the legal protections of a court-ordered and -controlled remedy to insolvency.

Such particularities notwithstanding, the legal treatment of bankruptcy emerges from Roman Law and retains to this day a series of characteristics first mandated by this ancient code.[19] Before the promulgation of the Twelve Tablets Law, around 450 BCE, no distinction seems to have been made between insolvency and bankruptcy, and bankruptcy was a personal and private matter between creditor and debtor. In lieu of proper payment, a creditor could, in an act of private execution, seize the property or person of the debtor to compel the discharge of the obligation. The Twelve Tablets mitigated bankruptcy proceedings, in so far as they shielded the debtor from immediate, arbitrary detention or death. To reduce further the violent and disorderly consequence of insolvency, Caesar Augustus decreed the *lex Julia*, which introduced the *cessio bonorum*, the ceding or surrender of property. Whoever became insolvent through no personal fault and declared bankrupty had the opportunity to surrender all his or her property without exception to the creditors. This act spared the bankrupt any penalty or dishonor and supposedly made possible a new beginning in trade or business. In the Middle Ages, when courts and magistracies treated bankruptcy like larceny, because the bankrupt had in effect stolen the creditors' money, a *cessio bonorum* permitted the bankrupt to save life and reputation.

Augsburg possessed no clearly articulated bankruptcy ordinance before the second half of the sixteenth century. The earliest codification of local law, the *Augsburger Stadtbuch* of 1276, which includes the first "City Law" (*Stadtrecht*) of 1176 as well as its many emendations, remained for more than two centures determinative for the city's legal practice, prescribing measures and sanctions for nonpayment of debt.[20] These provide the point of departure for a centuries-long evolution of official procedures in cases of default.[21] What becomes clear upon examination of the case record is that the magistracy reacted to the practices of debtors and creditors. Their rulings occurred in the course of specific disputes and became established over time as customary practices that were fixed in the sixteenth century as legal regulations.[22]

The Augsburg code offered creditors no right of summary execution in cases of default. Rather, they had a claim to pledge and surety (*Anspruch auf Gewett und Pfand*), from which to satisfy their demands.[23] The defaulting debtor had to appear before the magistrate, either the *Vogt* or the *Burggraf* of Augsburg, pledge payment and offer adequate surety to meet the obligation within eight days.[24] Should the debtor refuse to appear or flee the city, the magistrate could order seizure of the debtor's property as surety of payment. If the debtor paid within the first eight days, the surety was returned, and the matter settled. If not, then the creditor received permission to sell the surety in satisfaction of the debt after a second period of eight days, during which the debtor received another chance to settle his obligation.[25] A court official (*Waibel*) carried out the valuation and auction of the surety and distributed the proceeds to the creditor. As the earliest case records make clear, the magistracy mediated each step in the proceedings: The parties had to appear before the appropriate official and appeal for permission before action was taken by an official.

This presupposed that the debtor had at least some means with which to satisfy the creditor. When this was not the case, severe consequences followed.[26] The propertiless debtor would be laid in irons for eight days, after which he had to offer proof of his utter poverty and swear to turn over any future earnings, beyond 30 *Pfennig* and the clothing on his back, until all debts were paid.[27] Or the creditor might demand that the debtor work off his debt, a legal form of debt peonage. Augsburg appears to have abandoned these practices in the late-fifteenth century, but banishment or imprisonment until payment remained the penalty for defaulting and dishonest bankrupts.

The proceedings appear straightforward in the case of a single creditor. What if multiple creditors demanded payment of debts owed, especially if the debtor's property did not extend to full payment of all obligations, as was clearly the case with the Höchstetters? This created a situation in which creditors sued not only the debtor, but also one another. It encouraged conflict, opportunism and violence. The early law codes of Augsburg did not permit private execution or summary settlement, but the authorities could not entirely prevent such individual, extralegal actions. Over the course of the fourteenth and fifteenth centuries, procedures developed that tried to impose order on cases of bankruptcy. These included elements that characterize bankruptcy litigation and settlement to this day: equality of creditors, priority of payment, representation by committee.

Initially, the principle of "first come, first served" seems to have determined the priority of payment, though no edict officially mandated this practice.[28] The creditor who first registered a legitimate claim against a debtor was the creditor who was offered first payment.[29] Understandably, creditors strove to be the first to register their claims with the magistracy, to evoke a summons for the debtor to appear before the magistrate *(Fürgebot)* or, in cases of flight, to appeal for the seizure or arrest of the debtor's property (*Verbieten*). Over time and of necessity, the magistrates granted equal claim to proportional payment for all those creditors who registered their debts on the same day.[30]

Further steps followed in the fifteenth and sixteenth centuries. The Augsburg magistracy established a single, open *Gewett* in the presence of the *Stadtvogt*, at which point all creditors were required to submit their just claims in person and to receive a pledge of payment from the debtor.[31] Announced by edict and conducted in common, this procedure generated pressure to end what had been a common practice of individual suits and private seizures, carried out despite their extralegality by single creditors, and brought an abrupt end to the system of "first come, first served". The resort to a single, common *Gewett* emerged in legal practice without official sanction and was well established by the time it occurred in the case of the Höchstetter bankruptcy on 10 July 1529.[32]

The cessation of "first come, first serve" and the creation of common proceedings helped to promote equality among the creditors but failed to clarify their order of payment. If priority was no longer to be determined on the basis of timing, how would the magistracy distinguish between multiple creditors with various claims against the debtor? Several compilations of Augsburg law contain formal priority guidelines that are difficult to date.[33] These vary in small, but significant ways. One lists in order of precedence: government fees, employee wages, property rents, guaranteed loans, dependent support, wife's property and common loans. Another lists government fees, dependant support, employee wages, property rents, guaranteed loans and unguaranteed loans. In other words, the second list gives preference to dependant care, such as the moneys held in trust for children or elders, before all other claims except those of the state. Also, it makes no mention of the property of wives, a particularly contentious issue in many cases of bankruptcy, including that of the Höchstetters.

In general, wives enjoyed a privilege, known as the "wife's freedom" (*weibliche Freiheit*), which made repayment of their marital property – any property they brought to their marriages, received from their husbands at the time of their marriages or inherited from their families during their marriages – a priority before the claims of all other creditors. A wife might voluntarily yield her "wife's freedom" to help meet her husband's obligations, but, if she allowed her property to be invested in her husband's business or involved herself directly in the conduct of that business, her freedom was automatically forfeit, and she was understood to be fully liable for all his debts. The Höchstetters' wives did both over the course of the bankruptcy: They offered to surrender their privilege, and they collectively defended their property against the claims of their husbands' creditors by swearing in court that it had never with their knowledge and consent been invested in the bankrupt family firm.[34] Over the course of the sixteenth century, Augsburg authorities limited the *weibliche Freiheit* until it applied only to the husband's gifts to his wive at marriage.[35] This seems consistent with the long-term effort to create summary proceedings that avoided unnecessary formalities; it obviated the complexities of distinguishing the wife's property from the husband's.

The efforts to create summary proceedings in cases of bankruptcy by establishing common meeting dates and fixed payment priorities set the stage for further development. Stricter procedures for the settlement of disputes among plaintiffs emerged.[36] Creditors were required to legitimate their claims at the time of the *Gewett* by attending the proceeding and producing the original debt contract. Court dates were separated by periods of four weeks, rather than the earlier, more expeditious eight days.[37] The involvement of multiple creditors, some of whom might not reside in Augsburg, led authorities to appoint one or more *curatores litis et bonorum*, persons charged with representing the creditors in bankruptcy proceedings and administering the bankrupt's property to their benefit. Over the course of the sixteenth century, the court gradually adopted an elected committee of creditors to carry out the same functions.[38]

For resolution of the Höchstetter bankruptcy, the creditors elected jurist Heinrich Peringer, councilor Matheiß Langenmantel and notary Franz Frieß to represent their interests.[39] Committing representation and administration to one or more elected rather than appointed representatives appears to have been a cost- and time-saving move: The legal and personal expenses of curators appointed by the court had to be born by the city that appointed them; those of a committee elected by the creditors were paid out of the bankrupt's property, that is, by the creditors themselves. Moreover, the creditors had to swear to accept the committee's representation and cease all individual actions against the bankrupt, thus reducing the likelihood of single appeals and private seizures. It remained possible for a minority of creditors to appeal decisions or actions of the committee that it considered unfair or illegal, but such opposition remained within the context of the court-ordered, summary proceeding. All of these considerations would have direct bearing on the Höchstetter bankruptcy, shaping its course and future regulation.

During the course of the sixteenth century, between 1564 and 1590, the Augsburg City Council passed a series of ordinances in response to a wave of bankruptcies among merchant houses that totaled more than 70 between 1529 and 1580.[40] Confronted with a challenge that overwhelmed the customary practices of the city, the authorities reacted by instituting greater uniformity in the resolution of bankruptcy by enshrining those practices in law.[41] By the end of the sixteenth century, that law prescribed an orderly, efficient settlement of bankruptcy through the official announcement of court hearings, the creation of a creditors' committee, the equal treatment of all creditors, the examination of bankrupts' account books and the collective management of the bankrupt's capital. The role of the City Council became more aggressive over time: It prescribed sanctions; it defined procedures; it encouraged negotiation. But these measures constitute post hoc attempts to enforce institutions in the Northian sense. Reactions, they reveal an empirical process that sought to steer economic life, not determine it.

Yet this is precisely what failed to occur in the case of the Höchstetters. Their bankruptcy, which preceded these civil edicts, but may have helped to prompt their passage, was shaped by partially unwritten, customary practices, which permitted all parties a broader range of action. Ambrosius I applied every means – fair and foul, because the distinction was open to interpretation – to escape insolvency and avoid bankruptcy. The creditors acted likewise: They seized property to settle individual debts; they opposed the court-appointed *curatores litis et bonorum*; they frustrated attempts at an orderly prioritization of payments; they ultimately made impossible any regulated settlement. This failure was too massive to be regulated by fluid organizations and practices, created for other, simpler situations. In consequence, the Höchstetter bankruptcy of 1529–1532 sheds light on financial practice and business law and raises questions about economic institutions.

* * *

On 5 July 1529, less than a week after his public declaration of bankruptcy, Ambrosius I lodged a formal protestation before the Augsburg City Court.[42] His ever more alarmed creditors had become ever more insistent in their demands for repayment. One of them, *Reichserbmarschall* Hans von Pappenheim, a member of an ancient aristocratic family and a high imperial official, could not be ignored or forestalled. Speaking through his representative to the City Court, Ambrosius declared his inability to meet Pappenheim's demand for immediate payment in full. Given the large number of creditors and the large sum of his debt, he could not mobilize so much capital in so little time.[43] He would be unable to pay his other creditors were he to show partiality towards Pappenheim. Settlement must follow the principle that "one creditor's demand cannot be granted with right without the others and in prejudice to those absent".[44] Moreover, many debts deserved payment first because of their longer term (*magnam prerogativuam temporis*); these creditors could claim priority of payment before Pappenheim.

> Because everything that would be negotiated or contracted to the disadvantage, ruin, fraud or prejudice of the creditors is without force or value and as all such contracts or agreements by law are rescinded and made void, so much less should Your Wisdom recognize or rule in favor of what is contrary to law, and were it so ruled, it must be rescinded, and by so doing a nullity avoided at all cost.[45]

From this point onward, the Höchstetters' creditors confronted a single question: How to recover as much of their capital as possible out of the Höchstetters' ruined firm. On 10 July, nine days after their public declaration of bankruptcy and five days after his protestation to treat all creditors equally, Ambrosius I, Ambrosius II and Joseph Höchstetter offered pledge and surety (*Gewett und Pfand*) of payment.

The surety took the form of a complete *cessio bonorum*. Though not prescribed in Augsburg before the late-sixteenth century, it was not unknown.[46]

By voluntarily surrendering all their property to their creditors, the Höchstetters hoped to avoid personal dishonor and imprisonment. That would have remained the case but for the suspicion of fraud and the size of the debt. Even when debtors and creditors reached a mutual agreement about repayment, bankruptcy could still bring with it a demoralizing loss of status, a fact which could prove fatal to the bankrupt in an economy based substantially on personal relationships and individual honor, on *Trauen und Glauben*. A 1527 amendment to articles of the Augsburg *Kaufleuteschaft*, the city's merchant corporation, prescribed an immediate and permanent loss of all rights of membership for any merchant who declared bankruptcy without proof of innocent cause, arranged with his creditors to settle their claims but failed to make payment or extended payment beyond three years.[47] Innocent insolvents, by constrast, who reached agreement with their creditors to pay within three years, retained full rights as merchants. This seems to have been Ambrosius's hope and plan, to which his 1528 arrangements with Anton Fugger with their appearance of favoritism would prove a severe hindrance.

The *Gewett* was an established feature of debt settlement in Augsburg. Since the fourteenth century, debtors had appeared before the appropriate magistrate in the presence of their creditors to promise under oath to meet their obligations and to offer surety of payment, whether in the form of moveable or fixed capital. The court record for 1529 no longer exists, but a later entry described the proceeding as follows:

> Item on the 10th day of July in the 29th year [. . .] Endril Perstl as fully empowered attorney and procurator of Ambrosius Höchstetter the Elder, burgher of Augsburg, on behalf of him and his associates, pledged with the following hereinafter named honorable persons and creditors, absent and present, for their acknowledged debts, on the basis of their letters and scripts, according to the law of the city, whereupon the same hereinafter named creditors, some for themselves and others through their empowered counselors Matheus Langenmantel and Franz Frieß, citizens of Augsburg, and others hereinafter named, on the basis of the pledge and their debts, obtained their legal rights according to city law against Ambrosius Höchstetter the Elder and his associates on the 6th day of July in the current 31st year.[48]

This brief, cryptic statement preceded a list of 95 creditors, whose claims amounted to 293,071 fl 15 kr.

The Höchstetters offered pledge and surety in 1529. Two full years had passed. The creditors acknowledged that they had "obtained all their rights according to city law" in 1531. The phrase appears frequently in the court records related to debt settlement in Augsburg. It indicates, not that payment had been made, but that the formalities of settlement have been observed and that enforcement (*Vollstreckung*) of the debtor's claim can proceed.[49] In this case, it signaled that the Höchstetters had offered pledge and surety, proven unable to fulfill its terms and, in consequence, forfeited their property. Sequestration and sale could now take place, with the proceeds to be distributed among the creditors.

What had happened?[50] The record speaks of city law, which makes frequent reference to the *Gewett*, but no clear description of the procedure appears in any archival records of Augsburg.[51] The case law of the Augsburg city court, as well as its Civil Code (*Stadtbuch*) of 1276 and Public Auction Ordinance (*Gantordnung*) of 1447 described procedures for establishing legitimate claims for debt and selling the defaultor's property at auction. They do not indicate what form the pledge and security took or how payment was to be made, beyond placing the procedure in the hands of the magistracy, specifically the *Stadtvogt*, and they offer no information about the method or order of repayment. In the Höchstetter case, however, the records of the city court (*Stadtgerichtsbuch*) provide a tantalizing clue that suggests the creation of a prioritized list, according to which the creditors might expect to be paid.[52] In the left-hand margin, next to the name of each creditor, a small square that contains a specific number of spots, one to six, was carefully drawn. No explanation or clarification accompanies these small images, 93 in number, but in their pattern they resemble strikingly the up-turned face of a cast die. Given the uncodified state of bankruptcy procedure in Augsburg, it remains entirely possible that the creditors actually wagered, setting priority of payment by some form of cleromancy, that is, a determination by means considered to be random, such as rolling dice.

In the case of the Höchstetter *Gewett*, the following results obtained: One spot, 11 times; two spots, 12 times; three spots, 27 times; four spots 14 times; five spots, 20 times; six spots, nine times. If the creditors simply rolled the dice to see who among them would be paid first, assuming the process to be random, then those who rolled a one would go first, those who rolled two would go second and so forth. Or, the number of spots might correspond to some formal, prescribed order of priority.

The Augsburg court secretary, Franz Kötzler, transcribed two lists of priority in 1529, the very year of these proceedings, either of which might have governed the Höchstetter *Gewett*.[53] One of those lists contained six categories, corresponding to the number of sides on a die.[54] Were this list used, the following priorities would have been observed: One spot would signify fees owed to governments, such as unpaid taxes, tolls, penalties, etc.; two spots would signify dependant wages, money loaned or invested on behalf of minors, orphans, widows or any other persons considered unable to support themselves or manage funds; three spots would indicate unpaid wages or commissions to employees of one sort or another; four spots would represent rents and fees related to landed property; five and six spots would signify guaranteed and unguaranteed loans, respectively. The court record lists only the names of the creditors and their representatives; it makes no mention of the nature of their debts. Hence, any final determination remains speculative, a matter of guesswork.

The list is frustratingly inconsistent.[55] Of the 11 debts marked with a single spot, which might indicate moneys owed to governments, only one mentions a government official, Jerg Gawel, the Bürgermeister of Speyer, though whether by virtue of his office or by dint of personal finance remains unclear. Another debt marked by a single spot was 5,800 fl owed to Sigmund I Höchstetter, son of the late Georg I and nephew of Ambrosius, who never occupied a government office. All others refer to amounts of money owed to individuals, such as 5,000 fl due Jacob von Landau zu Waal or 6,000 fl owed to the Munich residents Hans Ridler and his mother. Also marked with one spot were debts of 3,200 fl owed to the heirs (*Erben*) of the late Blasien Hultzel and of 2,000 fl pledged to "the Kuffners heirs in Rotenburg am Inn". The mention of heirs might suggest category two, moneys owed to dependents of various sorts, but of the 12 debts so identified, only four of these make specific reference to heirs and one to a woman. It is not an entirely convincing result. Indeed, one of the entries with two dots lists the Bishop of Freising as a creditor who received surety of payment for a debt of 706 fl.[56] The Lords of Alms (*Almosenherren*) of Augsburg, whose funds might conceivably have been loaned on behalf of dependants, the poor or disabled, received surety for a debt of 400 fl, but their obligation was marked with three spots, indicative of unpaid wages to employees. Three spots appeared most frequently on the list, 26 out of 93 times, suggesting that arrears in wages might have made up the larger part of those debts still owed by the Höchstetters, but few of the creditors in the list can be positively identified as their employees or agents. Two creditors who were also long-term employees were Sigmund Kunderskofer and Lienhart Riederer the Elder. They were owed 1,400 fl and 3,600 fl respectively, but those debts were marked with two spots. Given the amounts in question, it seems possible that these debts might have represented legacies invested on behalf of their descendants but might also have been back-wages owed them or funds deposited by them. The remaining 24 entries involve persons with no verifiable connection to the firm "Ambrosius and Hans the Brothers Höchstetter and Associates". Conversely, employees with claims against the firm, such as their factor Wolf Vittel and their bookkeeper Thomas König, do not appear at all. Four spots, which mark 14 entries on the list, might signify rents and fees from landed property, but these are similarly difficult to identify consistently. Did the 1,400 fl owed to Dr. Nicholas Ribeisen of Salzburg (who would serve as the Höchstetters' advocate during the course of the bankruptcy), or the 1,000 fl owed to Matheus Besser (the Bürgermeister of Dinkelsbuhl), or the 1,800 fl owed to Arnold von Segen (the Bürgermeister of Cologne) or the 1,000 fl owed to the city of Wörth near Nuremberg represent unpaid rents or fees for real estate? Neither the list itself nor surviving business accounts offer any indication. Least problematical in some respects are the final, fifth and sixth, categories, the guaranteed and unguaranteed loans, possibly marked by five or six spots. These appear 20 and 9 times, respectively, and constitute what might be thought of as common loans or deposits. What distinguishes them is the guarantee, that is, the promise of some third party, whether an individual person, a private entity or a government agency to repay the obligation in the event that the borrower defaults. Yet, once again, these loans involve a wide array of persons or entities and sums, few of which can be reconstructed in their entirety. The 8,600 fl owed to the step-children (*Stiefkinder*) of the aforementioned Dr. Ribeisen of Salzburg received a five-spot notation. What did it have in common with the 44,722 fl owed to the mercury-mine operators of Idria, the 11,598 fl owed to Karl Villinger (an Augsburg merchant-financier also engaged in mercury trading), or the 35,444 fl owed to the merchant-financier and Höchstetter relation Philipp Adler? The first might have been some form of legacy, invested in trust, but the others were major business obligations, moneys owed for mercury and other commodities delivered per contract, as well as familial investments of various sorts.

It is impossible to reconstruct the nature of the debts that the Höchstetters pledged to pay in the 1529 *Gewett*. As a legal procedure, it served to reassure creditors that their debts would be paid. In the presence of multiple claimants, it also served to establish some order of payment. Despite Ambrosius's promise to treat all creditors equally, equality had not yet been established as a principle of law. Nor, indeed, were all debts considered to be equal, as the surviving priority lists make clear. Some obligations took priority over others; some creditors could claim payment ahead of others, depending not on the nature of their persons, but on the nature of their obligations.

Yet, the spots one through six that adorn each entry on the list of participating creditors correspond in no obvious manner to any surviving list of priority, and their distribution appears to be random, the result of a simple cast of a die. Some logic that cannot be reconstructed appears to have been at work. The Northian institution in this case seems to correspond to the ancient brocard of civil and canon law, *pacta sunt servanda*, that is, that contracts must be honored. In this instance, debts must be paid. Some were to be repaid first, in preference to others. That order appears to have been utterly idiosyncratic, an order negotiated among the creditors, possibly with the mediation of the city magistracy, but not in accordance with any surviving precedent. Institutions might function, in other words, but they were subject to the dictates of circumstance.

The debts owed to the Idrian mine operators, Karl Villinger and Philipp Adler form a case in point. The list represents each alike with five spots, suggesting that they were guaranteed loans, the result of obligations secured by contracts and, perhaps, by the guarantees of third parties. Yet, though the contract for the mine operators survives, those for Villinger and Adler do not. Moreover, these merchant-financiers had familial as well as business relations with the Höchstetters. Villinger was himself a mine operator in Idria, holder of shares (*Kuxe*) in the mines that he had inherited form his father, Jacob. Jacob Villinger was Imperial Treasurer (*Reichsschatzmeister*) under Maximilian I, from whom he received those shares. A merchant from Freiburg im Breisgau, Jacob settled in Augsburg in the early-sixteenth century, where he eventually married Ursula, the daughter of Philipp Adler. Another daughter of Philipp Adler, Benigna, was the wife of Joseph Höchstetter, who stood in the dock with his cousin and uncle during the *Gewett*.[57] It seems likely, therefore, that these business obligations combined with familial commitments of various sorts, not only material and financial, but also social and emotional. The settlement of debt relied in all probability not only on the "institutions" of law, which focused on the nature of the debt, but also on the identity of the creditor and his, her or its relationship to the debtor. Of this, more in the following chapter.

⋆ ⋆ ⋆

From this point onward, the law might have run its appointed course. As part of the *Gewett*, the Höchstetters had pledged all of their property to settle their outstandings debts to the satisfaction of their creditors. These totaled 293,071 fl 15 kr, according to the City Court's 1531 resumé.[58] Having done so, on 10 July 1529, they would have received a fixed period – anywhere from eight days to four weeks – within which to honor their pledge or forfeit their fortune. They appear to have had other plans.

The pace suggests summary proceedings. From a formal declaration of bankruptcy on 1 July, with an accompanying oath against flight or fraud, parties moved to pledge and surety on 10 July. Accordingly, payment or execution would have followed on or around 18 July, but the records for that date are no longer extant. What happened next, how the resolution of the bankruptcy proceeded, remains unclear. On or around this point in time, the creditors would have received access to the Höchstetters' business records.

Armed with this information, they eventually arrived at a clear evaluation of their actions and began to press for information about their money. They realized that Ambrosius's protestation to *Reichserbmarschall* Pappenheim was empty. His tactics gave the lie to such florid promises of fair and equal treatment, including his recently sworn oath "to alter recklessly neither his person nor his property inside or outside the city to the disadvantage of his creditors".[59] Efforts to resolve the bankruptcy and to return to business quickly collapsed. His collusion with Fugger had become common knowledge, leading many of the unfavored – and unpaid – creditors to fear rightly that Höchstetter resources had been distributed discretely to "insiders", in clear violation of his oath and protestation, and that whatever remained would not be sufficient to meet their demands.

They viewed the capital that Ambrosius had transferred into the hands of the favored creditors, Anton Fugger above all, as lost. They put the matter concisely:

> If the Höchstetters wished, as they claimed, to handle all creditors to equal advantage, they would not have sold the aforementioned capital and paid their friends and those others, whom it pleased them, before the rest, but rather would have let these properties lie to be divided among the creditors in common.[60]

Indeed, it would have been much better for all the creditors had they "just sold it, rather than transferred it in this manner".[61] But, no, "once he had realized his ruin, Höchstetter (as the one who paid little attention to his creditors' good) preferred to pay his friends, relatives and employees twice the damage [done to] the creditors, rather than hold to his infamous claim of equality".[62]

An interrogation of Ambrosius I on 26 September 1531 made mention of an 18-month moratorium, during which the creditors permitted him to conduct his business without interference, in return for which he promised to pay all his debts with interest.[63] Whether this moratorium constituted a "winding down" of "Ambrosius and Hans the Brothers Höchstetter and Associates" or a continuation of the firm for the sole purpose of discharging its debts cannot be determined. Whether it meant a temporary end to prosecution for default, while the *curatores bonorum* assumed direction of the company is similarly unclear. What is clear is that any accord among creditors and bankrupts proved short-lived.

Ambrosius and his partners appear to have done nothing to disarm the hostility of their creditors, nothing to promote a settlement. Sender sketched the deteriorating situation:

> In the meanwhile [after the public declaration of 1 July, tms], Ambrosius Höchstetter took the most valuable treasures that he had and hid them in bales [of textiles] and put a foreign trademark on the bales and ordered that these be moved out of Augsburg, which was done. The creditors learned of this and went before the council and demanded that all of Höchstetter's property, real and moveable, be inventoried with whatever he had in his house. The inventory was made, but nothing proper was found there, and it was once a large house full of fine ornaments like a prince's palace. At that the creditors were furious, such that the noblemen and Dr. Ribeisen [Höchstetter's attorney, tms] exchanged angry accusations, and they demanded that payment be made.[64]

The creditors wanted to know about the vanished, supposedly hidden wealth in luxuries. They knew that, shortly before Höchstetter declared bankruptcy, "great credenzas, silver plate, jewels, [. . .] silk hoods, precious coats, gold rings and jewels, gold chains and precious tapestries, much good cloth and textiles, grand horses and much more were seen" in his house.[65] Where had it all gone in so short a time, so that nothing appeared in the inventory? Höchstetter responded that all the silver in his house "belonged to his wife" and that is was "never worth more than 1,000 fl".[66] Moreover, many of "the things that should profit the creditors and the city had been used to support his household since his bankruptcy". The clothing and tapestries were still there, so far as he knew. Chains he never had.[67]

It was not just a matter of preferential treatment or lost value, however, substantial as these issues were. With access to the Höchstetters' account books, the creditors quickly realized just how costly these insider arrangements and perjured dealings had been. They valued the purchase of debt and the transfer of credit at more than 690,000 fl, capital that should have been used to repay all creditors, rather than a few friends, as they complained. Most suspicious in their eyes were the capital transfers, however, the exchange or mortgaging of fixed and moveable capital that extended from mines and smelteries to commodities and notes, amounting to nearly 280,000 fl, more than one-third of the lost capital.

The creditors claimed that some or all of these sales may have been fictitious (*Scheinkäufe*) rather than real, an attempt on Höchstetter's part to prevent the seizure of his property by temporarily transferring ownership to someone else. Grimm describes this kind of deal as a form of pledge that resembles a derivative known as a futures contract.[68] A "purchaser" promises to buy a given commodity at a certain, set price, but neither pays the price nor takes possession of the commodity. Rather, at the end of a mutually agreed time, he either receives from "seller" the excess or pays to "seller" the deficit between what he offered for the commodity and what it is actually worth. The more familiar futures contract differs from a ficticious sale in three ways: First, the contracting parties pay a bond, known as a margin, which is an agreed percentage of the value of the contract, to prevent one or the other from walking away, if the deal goes against them; second, settlement occurs at the close of the contracted time either by physical delivery of the commodity or by cash payment of the loss or gain related to the contract; third, a third party, either a person or an organization, such as an exchange, holds the margin and mediates the settlement to assure compliance by both parties. Profit or loss in a futures contract, as in a ficticious sale, depends on the difference between agreed value and market value at the close of the settlement.

Regardless of the specificities, "purchaser" and "seller" do not engage in a game of pure chance. Rather, they rely upon their experience in the market, producing or trading the commodity in question, to give them some indication of the likelihood that it will rise or fall in value over the agreed period. Ambrosius I and his partners in these transactions could not calculate probabilities, but they could weigh them. They knew the prices of various commodities as they traded on the markets of Europe. They knew the productivity of various industries, be they woolen weaving in the Southern Netherlands, fustian manufacturing in South Germany or mineral mining in Tyrol. They knew the policies of the governments that regulated commerce and industry and determined the financial requirements of both. A degree of uncertainty remained, as is always the case in futures trading, but it was not a matter of blind luck. Fortune depended also upon the acuity of those who would seize it.

How the *Scheinkäufe* were organized in this case remains uncertain. Perhaps the Höchstetters and their "purchasers" agreed that the various properties would be transferred to the new owners for a certain price at a certain point in time, the classic commitment to buy a thing for a certain sum on a certain date that is the essence of any financial derivative. Perhaps the "purchasers" were also substantial creditors, as can be confirmed in many instances, in which case these "sales" might have depended upon the Höchstetters' future capacity to repay all or part of the sums that they owed them. In the meanwhile, the Höchstetters could claim that these properties were reserved by virtue of "contracts" of sale and, accordingly, could not be seized legally by the creditors. If they dared to play one group of creditors off against another, they might even use the properties as security for repayment of other debts, hoping that communication between the various parties would not reveal the manipulation.

The creditors identified as a "*Scheinkauff*" one transaction in particular.[69] At some point around Easter, 1529, before his declaration of bankruptcy, Ambrosius I transferred "in a fiction" (*jnn einem Shein*) capital in the city of Linz, which included commercial commodities and notes obligatory, to Philipp I Gassner, "so that he [Gassner, tms] could transfer them from there to [Augsburg] and do with them as he pleased". Gassner had been a partner in the Höchstetter family firm from 1515 until 1520. Despite nearly a decade without direct business relations with the bankrupts, suspicion that they were somehow in league still dogged him. The creditors claimed that Gassner had removed the Höchstetter trademark from the goods, replacing it with his own, and placed some 43 negotiable instruments in his own name. They noted that he paid nothing for this "purchase". Once the capital arrived in Augsburg, Katharina Neumann, the wife of Ambrosius II, entered into another *Scheinkauf* with Gassner.[70] She "purchased the goods from [him], giving in exchange her note obligatory for 3,000 fl". Interestingly, this capital already acted as security for Neumann's claims against her father-in-law and husband, probably to cover her dowry, which was part of their firm's capital. No real money changed hands at any point, but the change in formal ownership prevented immediate seizure by the creditors. The ficticious sales permitted Ambrosius I to transfer capital safely from one city to another and to retain its financial benefit. Gassner apparently benefitted, too.[71] The creditors noted that he had invested at profit or loss 2,000 fl in the Höchstetter mine at Steinfelden, which Ambrosius had declared "a great loss". Gassner should have shared this loss, but instead "Höchstetter secured the entire sum, because he [Gassner, tms] was a friend".

What had occurred with some could have involved others. The creditors interrogated Ambrosius's employees, whether they "had been given goods or capital through ficticious sales or in some other form".[72] They questioned merchants from Augsburg and Nuremberg, including Anton Fugger, Hanns Georg Herwart, Hans Welser, Matthis Manlich and Bastian Neidhart, along similar lines. Clearly, they suspected widespread use of the maneuver.

Ambrosius insisted adamantly that he knew nothing about any *Scheinkäufe*. No commercial goods had been hidden from the creditors. In keeping with this principle, Gassner had acted on his behalf in Linz, gathering 3,000 fl in textiles and a further 8,000 in notes obligatory, not hiding them for Höchstetter's benefit, but using them to pay some of his creditors.[73] These payments occurred in 1529, but before his oath to transact no business with the knowledge and consent of the creditors.

Yet such assurances and explanations, like Ambrosius's oath and protestation, lacked conviction. The creditors alleged an entire series of fraudulent behaviors, of which the *Scheinkäufe* were but a single example. They quoted a letter of instruction, in which Ambrosius wrote, "And what is more, I am confident that they will permit our wives, attorneys and Dr. Marshalkh [Ambrosius I's procurator, tms] to visit us after we are removed from our house [i.e., imprisoned, tms], but as I cannot be certain of this, we should see to our accounts and registers as a precaution, which concerns my wife".[74] In the same letter, he advised his wife and daughters-in-law, the spouses of the named partners, to resist intimidation by the creditors and to claim that they have nothing.[75] The creditors saw such statements as proof that Höchstetter anticipated arrest for debt long before he declared bankruptcy. They cited financial records that revealed many instances of Höchstetter withholding information from the creditors: The identities of silent partners; the transfers of capital to family, friends and associates; the location of commercial commodities; the liens on various real properties.[76] No fewer than 16 individuals denied Höchstetter's claims that they owed him money, while nine of them insisted contrarily that he owed them.[77] The complaints of obstruction and swindle seemed to rise with each passing day.

Ultimately, the Höchstetters' *Gewett* failed. Some creditors were unable to participate. The bankrupts lacked the capital to satisfy those who did. Nor were the creditors able to compel even partial payment. Moreover, the bankrupts did not abide by it themselves. They, especially Ambrosius I, seized every means possible to preserve what they had for themselves and their families. It formed a pattern of prevarication and obstruction that persisted for years.

From the early stages of the bankruptcy to its bitter conclusion, Ambrosius protested his ignorance and promised cooperation. He swore before the City Court and in the presence of many of his creditors "to alter recklessly neither his person nor his property [. . .] to the disadvantage of his creditors". The creditors responded with a list of his transactions that they found duplicitous, if not fraudulent: The leverage of Anton Fugger; the transfers to friends and family; the *Scheinkäufe* to associates; the concealment of luxuries. The City Court delayed decisive action, pleading that either to dismiss the creditors' claims or to imprison the defaultors would be "contrary to our ancient custom and city law" (*es wer wider iren alten prauch und wider ir statbuch*).

Yet, the city's customary law and usage offered insufficient guidance in this case. It did not supply a common standard to govern the behavior of debtors and creditors. Its procedures in cases of default existed in the form of case law, a set of specific rulings that might be cited as precedent, not as statutory or regulatory laws, codes enacted by legislative or executive bodies to direct procedures. Given the growing importance of civil law in Augsburg, the accumulated case law of bankruptcy proved inadequate to resolve the Höchstetter failure.

The law, the courts and the magistracy serve as instruments to settle conflict and maintain order in a society. Understood thus, it follows that they change over time to reflect altered social realities and imperatives. Examples might be a shift in social or political power: A new ruling elite might staff the courts or alter the laws to suit its purposes. Likewise, changing economic goals or circumstances might incline a society to establish new tribunals or alter regulations, as Oscar Gelderblom has documented. Strictly speaking, therefore, the law and its attendant structures are not institutions in the Northian sense, but rather organizations that articulate the "rules of the game". Those deeply held principles or standards that direct human behavior may become visible in the functioning of the law, but they exist in the consciousness of social and economic agents.

In this respect, they fulfill a role analogous to that of *habitus* in Pierre Bourdieu's logic of practice.[78] Bourdieu understood practice as *praxis*, actions based on an implicit sense of what is appropriate in a given setting or situation. *Habitus* functions both consciously and unconsciously as patterns of feeling, thought and action, acquired in response to real social experience, accumulated by individuals over time. Bourdieu's theory seeks to show that social agents develop both reflected and unreflected strategies that are adapted to the needs of their social settings, their social lives.

Bourdieu's notion that action results from a sense of what is situationally appropriate in a specific social setting introduces a useful specificity and dynamism to North's theory of institutions. It opens the possibility of multiple perspectives and interpretations of historical events. The opportunism of Ambrosius I inhered to his own sense of what was appropriate for a merchant-financier. It violated no fixed legal standard of Augsburg, but clearly contravened the creditors' sense of a debtor's proper, honorable behavior. The creditors insisted that he hold to his oath and observe customary practice in the settlement of his obligations, but neither he nor the authorities acknowledged that he had failed to do either, that his actions were in any regard illegal. The court initially refused to intervene, either by seizing Höchstetter property or imprisoning the partners, though instances of both could be found in the case law of Augsburg. No formal law, statutory or regulatory, identified specific violations.

How, indeed, were the judges to determine whether Ambrosius had "recklessly" practiced his business or violated his oath? No common, consensual definition existed. This opened to a multiplicity of interpretations not only the specific legality of his actions but also the general assessment of his management. This lack of uniform clarity suggests the possibility that such institutions as Augsburg might have applied to the fall of the House of Höchstetter were as yet incomplete or insufficient. It also suggests the possibility that such "institutions" as the actors in this drama evoked – ancient custom, reckless behavior, etc – were no more than instruments consciously manipulated by parties in pursuit of their interests.

★ ★ ★

Through most of July 1529, the Augsburg City Council took no action to protect the creditors or to sanction the Höchstetters. When Ambrosius I declared bankruptcy and swore to cooperate, the authorities refused to arrest him and his partners, as the creditors demanded, because it would be "contrary to our ancient custom and city law".[79] Neither Augsburg law nor local custom, as noted, made non-payment grounds for immediate imprisonment of person or seizure of property. Nor did repeated accusations and mounting proof of fraudulent – or at least unethical – business practices.[80] The failure of the *Gewett*, the pledge to pay and the offer of surety should, on the other hand, have resulted in immediate sequestration of his property by the magistrates.

The official attitude of *laissez aller* changed on 25 July 1529. Sender picks up the story at this point:

> As the council took cognizance of all this [Höchstetter's efforts to conceal his wealth and frustrate his creditors, tms], on Saint Jacobs Day it summoned Ambrosius Höchstetter, his son Ambrosius and his brother's son Joseph – his older son Joachim and his son-in-law Franz Baumgartner had secretly fled, taking with them much capital, as the rumor went. When these three Höchstetter appeared before the Council, it ordered all three imprisoned together in a room in the City Hall, and it stationed 10 men outside the door to prevent them from fleeing or anyone going to them without knowledge of the Council. One allowed their wives and servants to go to them. More than enough food and drink and all essentials were taken to them from their homes.[81]

Flight to avoid prosecution proved too much. It constituted not only a clear violation of a sworn oath, but also irrefutable evidence of intent to avoid payment. That the two absconders reportedly took capital with them worsened the situation for the remaining three.

What became of Hans Franz Baumgartner is not known. By contrast, Joachim's movements are well documented. He managed to slip out of Augsburg in a diplomatic retinue.[82] Dispatches sent to King Christian II of Denmark by Johan, Archbishop of Lund, who represented the king in the matter of a debt of 30,000 fl owed him by the Höchstetters, reported that the Höchstetters were insolvent and their creditors, led by aristocratic investors, demanded imprisonment by the city. When the Council refused, Johan summoned Joachim, who had served as the firm's factor in Antwerp, where he had provided financial services to the king. Ambrosius's son claimed to be no longer a partner in the company and wished to negotiate a private settlement for himself. As a result, Johan helped him escape the city, bringing him to the Netherlands, beyond the grasp of the other creditors. Though a settlement was eventually negotiated, it remains unclear whether the debt with Denmark was ever paid. Joachim later used commercial connections as well as ties to German émigré miners and managers to become a Master of Mines (*Bergmeister*) to Christian in 1532, an indication that the king was satisfied with him, and eventually to enter the tin-mining industry of England, where his descendants survive.[83] Of these developments, more later.

Compelled to act, the City Court began to function as arbitor in the bankruptcy with the City Council ready to act as the court of appeal of first instance. They appointed a group of three men to represent the creditors as a group, effectively making them *curatores litis et bonorum*, the expectation being that under such leadership the creditors would act in an orderly and expeditious manner.

The creditors were deeply divided against themselves, however. Höchstetter's collusion with Fugger probably made this inevitable by emphasizing the social and economic distinctions among them and by indicating that only a favored few could expect payment in full. The demands for priority on the parts of certain aristocratic creditors, such as *Reichserbmarschall* Pappenheim, further complicated matters. It seems reasonable that the higher a creditor's loss and the greater her or his need, in general, the less likely she or he would be to compromise on full payment. These divisions made themselves known soon after the imprisonment and delayed for years such settlement as was still possible. According to Sender:

> On Saint Michael's Day [29 September 1529, a month after the Höchstetters' imprisonment, tms], the creditors gathered here for counsel and justice and negotiated openly against the Höchstetters. As the Höchstetters now could not pay, some of the creditors thought to forgive one-third [of the debts owed them, tms], some more, some less and some nothing at all but payment in full.[84]

The bankrupts rejected all these options, insisting on a complete *cessio bonorum*, that is, a voluntary surrender of all their property in favor of the creditors.[85] In light of the fact that much of it had already been settled on favored creditors or secured in various other ways, this high-sounding offer did not promise much: The bankrupts themselves had little or nothing left to relinquish. The creditors knew it.

> The creditors did not want to do that for this reason: their [the bankrupts', tms] wives, had taken out their dowries, morning gifts, grants and transfers and wanted to give nothing toward the debts of their husbands to the creditors. In response to this freedom of the wives, the noblemen among the creditors were very displeased that they would not help their men gain release from prison and from the creditors, but rather (wished) to live well on the creditors' capital, practice pomp, pride and courtliness, and moreover, when they had profited with the creditors' money, the creditors would have inherited none of it, but rather the (bankrupts') wives and their children, for which reason they should now properly repair the damages.[86]

The "wife's freedom" (*weibliche Freiheit*), once again, referred to the immunity that protected the property of a wife from seizure by her husband's heirs or creditors. Although the city government of Augsburg worked to limit the definition of this property, thus making more available to creditors, the Höchstetter women apparently insisted on a much broader interpretation. They applied it not only to the dowry and gifts exchanged at marriage, but also to any property inherited or received during their married lives. Though their husband enjoyed usufruct, the wives remained the proprietors. In principle, therefore, the Höchstetter husbands bore responsibility for the preservation and eventual return of their wives' capital intact. It could not be consumed during their lifetimes or settled on other claimants afterwards. Accordingly, the Höchstetter wives claimed a priority that ran contrary to the emerging, but as yet uncodified, legal practice in Augsburg. The creditors objected, not because the wives had no rights in the matter, but rather because they would practice an offensive ostentation with the creditors' capital and, worse still, would pass it and its earnings on to the bankrupts' heirs, thus depriving the creditors twice. The efforts to defraud the creditors, in which the wives supposedly participated, must have made the claims of the bankrupts' wives particularly offensive.

The City Council yielded to the obstruction and bitterness with an offer to tighten the Höchstetters' arrest. They had hitherto been held under guard in a chamber of the City Hall, with wives and servants granted free access. Now, they would be transferred to one of the city's towers and laid in irons. The creditors, especially the nobility, saw no point in this gesture, just as empty as the Höchstetters' oath. At this point,

> they didn't care much, if one chained the Höchstetters or not, because one did not hear and accept their pleas in the first place, when the property was still at hand and before Joachim Höchstetter and [Hans] Franz Baumgartner fled secretly with much of it; they want to see to it that they recover their principle and damages.[87]

They understood that the city's proposed methods for resolving a bankruptcy would have little effect.

For the city's magistrates, however, flight altered the facts of the case. Whereas severe treatment of the bankrupts would have been "contrary to our ancient custom and city law", direct action was now justified. For the creditors, the city's intervention was now irrelevant. It would not help them regain their capital. Other, more effective means would have to be found.

* * *

The three Höchstetter partners – Ambrosius I, Ambrosius II and Joseph – remained under house arrest in the Augsburg *Rathaus* for two more years. The creditors remained divided among themselves, unable to agree as a group how best to resolve the bankruptcy and recover the moneys owed them. The bankruptcy proceeding would soon shift to a different level of adjudication, passing out of the city's jurisdiction to be mediated by territorial and imperial appointees. Seen from this perspective, the city's legal organizations and institutions failed to end the dispute or even to uphold the city's sovereignty.

Yet, such a conclusion fails to do justice to the law's historical complexity. The traditional practices and case laws that governed the resolution of bankruptcy in Augsburg developed from instances of individual default, one debtor unable to pay what was owed a single creditor. Even as these simple practices changed over time to address more complicated situations – multiple creditors demanding payment of different debts – no evidence exists to suggest that the city's courts and magistrates had ever confronted a case as large and complicated as the Höchstetter failure. Certainly, there were bankruptcies before the sixteenth century, but it seems there were none quite like this one. It presented many creditors, more than the 93 who participated in the *Gewett*, not only single individuals and family groups, but corporate bodies and commercial organizations, ecclesiastical establishments and political entities, aristocratic clans and merchant elites, demanding in sum hundreds of thousands of *Gulden*. The sorting and prioritizing of so many different claims, to say nothing of the management of capital on this scale, must have posed an unusual challenge for curators and officials alike. The efforts of Ambrosius I and his partners, to say nothing of those alleged of their families, friends and employees, exceeded anything that local custom and legal practice were prepared to address. Nothing in the extant case law of the city makes specific reference to *Scheinkäufe* and the like. The legality and ethicality of leveraged buyouts, such as Anton Fugger appears to have practiced at the Höchstetters' request and at their and their creditors' expense, corresponded to no category of unacceptable, financial behavior. It is not that local organizations and institutions failed in this instance but that they were not intended to address such situations.

Much of the historical scholarship tends to reify economic institutions. Too often they become fixed and concrete, cease to be situational and, above all, instrumental. They cease to be responses to economic actions that seek to channel those actions into more profitable, more orderly channels. Taking on a life of their own, they instead determine those actions. Too often they displace human behaviors as the object of study, becoming not the consequence, but the cause of commerce.

As creditors jostled, bankrupts maneuvered, and as all negotiated in this first phase of the Höchstetter bankruptcy, they exposed the inadequacy of the "rules of the game". The notion that agreements should be honored appears to have motivated all parties. None openly questioned or denied it. Ambrosius went so far as to evoke it specifically in response to the demand for preference on the part of highly placed creditors. The existence of prioritized lists of debts demonstrates clearly, however, that not all agreements had equal status or equal protection. They were not to be "honored" at the same time and, consequently, to the same extent. Some, such as the "wife's freedom", were not universally understood to be agreements that should be honored. The presence of the die-like symbol that accompanied the name and claim of each creditor at the *Gewett* suggests something more: Any agreement was open to negotiation; whether it was honored depended upon the interest and influence of the parties to it. Those parties – agents in the strict sense – created and recreated the "rules of the game" to fit the circumstances as they understood them. To the brocard, *pacta sunt servanda*, should perhaps be added *caveat emptor*. As will become clear, most "buyers" denied the necessity of "caution". They argued uniformly and unanimously that the Höchstetters bore sole responsibility for shielding them from risk and loss.

Notes

1 "*da er alter Hochstetter sein Abfall vor zway jarn gesehen, und gewiss, wie er selbst vor den Herrn bekhanndt, das er erst darnach jm 27 und 28 Jar so gross Shulden betrugenlich gemacht, und ain solliche Summa zu Verderbung reicher und armer uffpracht, und doch wol gewist, das er die alten Shulden zubezalen nit gehapt hab*". StAA, Literaliensammlung, Höchstetter-Selekt I, Dok. 24, Erste Hochstetters Fragstuck.

2 "*Zum viersten fleyssig anzuhalten und zufragen, das offennlich gesagt wurtt, dass des Graven von Orttenburg ain mergklich Gut den Hochstettern zugehorig in Phillip Gassners Behausung uffgeladen unnd uff Ruckhwerchk auss diser Statt getragen haben, wo wie, wann und solchs hingewandt fleissig vekundden*". Ibid.

3 "*Zum 4. Articul, wise nichts Darvon zu sagen, neme es auf hochst, wann er etwas gehapt alls nur drei Pfennig welt er zwein den Glaubigern geben und den ain zu Zerung gehalten haben, ob mamns aber anders finde, sol man jne an Leib und Leben, und was das Recht auf jn trag, straffen*". StAA, Literaliensammlung, Höchstetter-Selekt I, Urgicht, Actum auf 26 Tag Septembris Anno 31, Jn praesentibus Herrn Hofmann, Sighart, Paler, Schollenberger, Ambrosi Hochstetter der Elter sagt an gutlichen Frag wie hernachfolgt.

4 The formal definition of bankruptcy as it appears in *Black's Law Dictionary*. Available at: "https://thelawdictionary.org/bankruptcy/"title="BANKRUPTCY">BANKRUPTCY.

5 Clemens Sender, *Die Chronik von Clemens Sender von den ältesten Zeiten der Stadt bis zum Jahre 1536. Die Chroniken der schwäbischen Städte. Augsburg*, vol. IV (Leipzig 1894), 221.

6 By the end of the fifteenth century, bankruptcy proceedings in Augsburg could be initiated by the bankrupt or by one or more creditors. Regardless of agent, the action began formally with an appeal to the civil magistracy. In the case of the Höchstetters, it is impossible to reconstruct whether the actions taken by the unfavored creditors on 1 July 1529 or some unrecorded earlier complaints initiated the process. See Friedrich Hellmann, *Das Konkursrecht der Reichsstadt Augsburg* (Breslau 1905), 32, 120f.

7 Thomas Max Safley, "Die Frage einer frühneuzeitlichen Standardisierung des Rechtsprozesses in Bankrottsfällen am Beispiel des Höchstetter Konkurs 1529," in: Thomas M. J. Möllers (ed.), *Vielfalt und Einheit. Wirtschaftliche und rechtiche Rahmenbedingungen von Standardisierung* (Baden-Baden 2008), 107–26.

8 Douglass C. North, *Institutions, Institutional Change and Economic Performance* (Cambridge, UK 1991).

9 Douglass C. North, *Violence and Social Orders: A Conceptual Framework for Interpreting Recorded Human History* (New York 2009).

10 Avner Greif, *Institutions and the Path to the Modern Economy: Lessons from Medieval Trade* (New York 2006). His critics, chief among whom was Sheilagh Ogilvie, responded that he had failed to demonstrate either the existence of reputation mechanisms in the hands of Eastern coalitions, the private-order option or the efficacy of contract enforcement in the hands of Western courts, the public-order option, in his explanation of how the West grew rich. See Sheilagh Ogilvie, *Institutions and European Trade: Merchant Guilds, 1000–1800* (New York 2011). For a rejoinder to both, see Jessica Goldberg, *Trade and Institutions in the Medieval Mediterranean: The Geniza Merchants and Their Business World* (Cambridge, UK 2012).

11 Oscar Gelderblom, *Cities of Commerce: The Institutional Foundations of International Trade in the Low Countries, 1250–1650* (Princeton 2013), 2–3. See also Thomas Max Safley, "Institutions and Their Discontents," *Tijdschrift voor Sociale en Economische Geschiedenis* 11 (2014): 61–73.

12 According to the *Oxford English Dictionary*, "competition" in its commercial sense indicates a "rivalry in the market, [a] striving for custom between those who have the same commodities to dispose of." "competition, n.," OED Online, March 2018. Oxford University Press. Available at: http://proxy.library.upenn.edu:2817/view/Entry/37578?rskey=yhGhBD&result=1&isAdvanced=false (accessed 13 April 2018).

13 Cf. Katharina von Ciriacy-Wantrup, *Familien- und erbrechtliche Gestaltungen von Unternehmen der Renaissance: Eine Untersuchung der Augsburger Handelsgesellschaften zur frühen Neuzeit* (Münster 2007).

14 Cf. Sabina Birnbaum, *Konkursrecht der frühen Augsburger Neuzeit mit seinen gemeinrechtlichen Einflüssen* (Münster 2014); Hellmann, *Das Konkursrecht der Reichsstadt Augsburg*.

15 Mark Häberlein, *Brüder, Freunde und Betrüger: Soziale Beziehungen, Normen und Konflikte in der Augsburger Kaufmannschaft um die Mitte des 16. Jahrhunderts* (Berlin 1998), 323–6, 331–7; Reinhard Hildebrandt, "Zum Verhältnis von Wirtschaftsrecht und Wirtschaftsprazis im 16. Jahrhundert: Die Fallitenordnungen des Augsburger Rates 1564–1580," in: Anita Mächler, et al. (eds.), *Historische Studien zu Politik, Verfassung und Gesellschaft: Festschrift für Richard Dietrich zum 65. Geburtstag* (Frankfurt Main 1976).

16 This argument was published in Safley, "Die Frage einer frühneuzeitlichen Standardisierung des Rechtsprozesses in Bankrottsfällen am Beispiel des Höchstetter Konkurs 1529".

17 Cf. Peter Hertner, "Bankrott," in: *Handwörterbuch zur deutschen Rechtsgeschichte*, I: 429–32.

18 Cf. Jan P. H. Duffy, "English Bankrupts, 1571–1861," *American Journal of Legal History* 24 (1980): 283–305; Sheila Marriner, "English Bankruptcy Records and Statistics Before 1850," *The Economic History Review* 33, 3(1980): 351–66.

19 Cf. Roman Obenchain, "Roman Law of Bankruptcy," *Notre Dame Law Review* 3 (1928): 169–200.

20 Bayrisches Hauptstaatsarchiv München (hereinafter BHStA), Reichsstadt Augsburg Literalien, Lit. 32. See also Christian Meyer (ed.), *Das Stadtbuch von Augsburg, insbesondere das Stadtrecht vom Jahre 1276, nach der Originalhandschrift zum ersten Male herausgegeben und erläutert* (Augsburg 1872); Rolf Schmidt, "Zum Augsburger Stadtbuch von 1276," *Zeitschrift des historischen Vereins von Schwaben* 70 (1976): 80–179.

21 Birnbaum, *Konkursrecht der frühen Augsburger Neuzeit*, 6.

22 Hellmann, *Das Konkursrecht der Reichsstadt Augsburg*, passim.

23 Ibid., 17.

24 From the eleventh century, the *Burggraf* represented the authority of the Prince-Bishop of Augsburg in matters of feudal rights and law. By the twelfth century, the function of this office had shifted slightly to matters of lower justice and trade regulation, while the *Vogt* exercised authority in matters of high justice. This official was originally also a representative of the Prince-Bishop, although he became a gauge in the struggle for authority between bishop and emperor until the thirteenth century, when the city seized control and made him a *Stadtvogt*. As Augsburg established its independence as a free imperial city, during the Late Middle Ages, both offices lost their original function and significance to the *Stadtgericht*. By the fifteenth century, the *Burggraf* finds no further mention in the city's legal ordinances, while the *Stadtvogt* served certain notarial and executive functions. During most of the Middle Ages, however, either official could oversee proceedings for insolvency. See Eugen Liedl, *Gerichtsverfassung und Zivilprozeß der freien Reichsstadt Augsburg* (Augsburg 1958); Rolf Kießling, *Bürgerliche Gesellschaft und Kirche in Augsburg im Spätmittelalter* (Augsburg 1971), 54–7, 67 f; J. Zeller, "Das Augsburger Burggrafenamt," *Archiv für die Geschichte des Hochstifts Augsburg* 5 (1916/19): 321–410.

25 Hellmann, *Das Konkursrecht der Reichsstadt Augsburg*, 20.

26 Ibid., 28.

27 Ibid.

28 Birnbaum notes what Hellmann observed nearly a century earlier that no official ordinances mark the early development of insolvency and bankruptcy regulation in Augsburg. Rather, the historian must rely on "Randvermerke und Nachträge". Birnbaum, *Konkursrecht der frühen Augsburger Neuzeit*, 5.

29 Ibid., 22.

30 Hellmann, *Das Konkursrecht der Reichsstadt Augsburg*, 43.

31 Ibid., 66.

32 StAA, Reichsstadt Strafamt, 47. Stadtgerichtsbuch, 1531, 59r–65v. Hellmann quotes it, marking both the legal formality of the procedure and the unprecedented importance of the case Hellmann, *Das Konkursrecht der Reichsstadt Augsburg*, 69–70.

33 Hellman cites two in particular, both copied in the seventeenth century from the 1529 compilation by the Augsburg court secretary, Franz Kötzler. This makes an exact dating of the ordinances impossible. It shows clearly, however, that they predate and, thus, might have guided the Höchstetter proceedings. Ibid., 104–5. Cf. Birnbaum, *Konkursrecht der frühen Augsburger Neuzeit*, 9–10.

34 Again, Hellmann cites Kötzler, this time his compilation of 1540. Hellmann, *Das Konkursrecht der Reichsstadt Augsburg*, 106.

35 Ibid., 85.

36 Ibid., 72.

37 The extended timeframe probably reflects the greater complexity of financial practices and bankruptcy settlements that developed over time. The increasing number of creditors from all levels of society and all points on the map made an extension of the periods between hearings essential.

38 Hellmann, *Das Konkursrecht der Reichsstadt Augsburg*, 74.

39 The appropriate entry in the records of the Augsburg City Court names "Matheusen Lanngenmantel" and "Franntz Friesen" as the "fully empowered counselor and procurator" (*vollmechtige Anwaldte und Procuratoren*). StAA, Reichsstadt Strafamt 47, Gerichtsbuch 1531, fol. 59r. Cf. Hellmann, *Das Konkursrecht der Reichsstadt Augsburg*, 76.

40 Scholars attribute the series of commercial failures to the state bankruptcies that shook European finance and politics in the second half of the sixteenth century, beginning with the French cessation of payments in 1557 and peaking with the Spanish defaults of 1557, 1560 and 1575. (Largely ignored in this context is the last and most serious of the Spanish defaults, that of 1596.) Certainly, Augsburg merchant-financiers extended substantial credit to these and other princes, but this unicausal explanation for a large series of bankruptcies appears to rest on little more than chronological coincidence. That creditors called debts and capital markets tightened notably in the second half of the sixteenth century is not open to question. Proof would require a close analysis of accounts, however, which has not occurred in most cases. See Christel Warnemünde, *Ausburger Handel in den letzten Jahrzehnten des 16. Jahrhunderts und dem beginnenden 17. Jahrhundert* (Freiburg/Br. 1956); Reinhard Hildebrandt, "Zum Verhältnis von Wirtschaftsrecht und Wirtschaftspraxis im 16. Jahrhundert: Die Fallitenordnungen des Augsburger Rates 1564–1580," in: Anita Mächler, et al. (eds.), *Historische Studien zu Politik, Verfassung und Gesellschaft: Festschrift für Richard Dietrich zum 65. Geburtstag* (Bern 1976), 154 ff; Jakob Strieder, *Das reiche Augsburg: ausgewählte Aufsätze Jakob Strieders zur Augsburger und süddeutschen Wirtschaftsgeschichte des 15. und 16. Jahrhunderts* (Munich 1969), 44 ff; Wolfgang Zorn, *Augsburg: Geschichte einer europäischen Stadt* (Augsburg 2001), 262 ff.

41 StAA. Ordnungen und Statuten. Fallitenordnung, 1564, 1574, 1580. Cf. Häberlein, *Brüder, Freunde und Betrüger*, 323–37.

42 StAA, Literaliensammlung, Höchstetter-Selekt I, fol. 9, Des allten Ambrosien Hoechstetter Protestation wider Hannsen Marschalk von Bappenhaim auf Montag den 5. Julii Anno 29 beshehen jn unnsern Acta.

43 "*dann dieweil also offennlich am Tag unnd vor Augen ist, das sich etwo vil Glaubiger unnd zum Thail ja nicht wenig, mocht shier sagen dess merer Thails, auf sein des Marschalckhs Hoertt dringenden unmitleidenlichen verderblichen Ubertreiben unnd Ubersturtzen verursacht unnd bewegt unnderstanden unnd wollen uberhaupt von Ambrosien Hoechsteter seinem Principal entricht unnd bezalt sein, das in so kurtzer Zeit in ainer so hochschaetzigen Summa unmuglich ist, unnd also mit dem unnd annderer durch jne verursachter Glaubiger Anlauffen umb Bezalung der Schulden zu seinen Guetern unnd Warn nit on wenigen Nachtail aller Glaubiger nach dem Unwerdt gedringen unnd gegriffen will werden, wie dann jetzemaln vor Augen unnd wie man spricht an der Tag ist*". Ibid.

44 "*So kan unnd mage eins Glaubiger allein ausser der anndern unnd in Prejuditium der abwesenden begern mit keinem Rechten nit stat getan werden*". Ibid.

45 "*Darumb dieweil dann alles das jhenig, so zu Nachtail Abbruch unnd in fraudem oder preiuditium der Creditorum gehanndlet oder contrahiert wurdet ohne alle Krafft unnd Wurden ist unnd also das all sollich contract unnd Vertrag durch Erkanntnus der Rechten crafftloss gemacht unnd rescindiert werden, so soll auch durch ewr E. W. vil minder mit Recht erkannt, oder in Recht gestatt nich zugelassen werden, das wider recht ist unnd das so es vor geschehen were mit Recht muesst wider rescindiert werden, unnd also die Nichtigkait zum hoechsten zuverhueten*". Ibid.

46 Hellmann, *Das Konkursrecht der Reichsstadt Augsburg*, 95.

47 Ibid., 97.

48 "*Item diser hernachgeschriebenen erbern Hern Personen und Gläubigern abwesenden und gegenwertigen hat uf Sambstag den 10 Tag monats Juli der mindern Jarzal Christi jn 29 Jar Endris Perstl als ain vollmechtiger Anwaldt und Procurator Ambrosii Hochstetters des Elltern Burgers zu Augspurg für sich selbs und seine Mitverwandte umb jr bekanntlich Schulden laut jr Brief und Handschriften verwettet nach diser Stattrecht unnd darauf dieselben nachbenannten Gläubiger zum tail durch sich selbs und ettlich durch jre vollmechtige Anwaldte benanntlichen Herrn Matheusen Lanngenmantel und Franntz Friesen Bürger zu Augspurg unnd ander hernachbenannt, uff beshehen verwetten und bekennen jrer Schulden, uff obgenannte Dornstag den 6 Tag Juli dies lauffender 31ter Jahr, alle Recht nach diser Stattrecht an denselben Ambrosii Höchstetter der Elltern und seinen Mitverwanndten behaist und erlanngt*". StAA, Reichsstadt Strafamt 47, Stadtgerichtsbuch, 1531, fol. 59r–69v.

49 Hellmann, *Das Konkursrecht der Reichsstadt Augsburg*, 32.

50 For a full discussion of the topic, see Safley, "Die Frage einer frühneuzeitlichen Standardisierung des Rechtsprozesses in Bankrottsfällen am Beispiel des Höchstetter Konkurs 1529."

51 Concerning customary law that in some cities became fixed in written statutes, but not in Augsburg, see Clemens Bauer, *Unternehmung und Unternehmungsformen im Spätmittelalter und in der beginnenden Neuzeit* (Jena 1936); Hermann Kellenbenz, "Handelsgesellschaft," in: *Handwörterbuch zur deutschen Rechtsgeschichte*, vol. I (Berlin 1971), 1936–42; Elmar Lutz, *Die rechtliche Struktur süddeutschen Handelsgesellschaften in der Zeit der Fugger*, 2 vols. (Tübingen 1976).

52 StAA, Reichsstadt Strafamt 47, Stadtgerichtsbuch, 1531, fol. 59r–69v.

53 Hellmann, *Das Konkursrecht der Reichsstadt Augsburg*, 104–5. Cf. Birnbaum, *Konkursrecht der frühen Augsburger Neuzeit*, 9–10.

54 See ch. 5, p. 16. Cf. Hellmann, *Das Konkursrecht der Reichsstadt Augsburg*, 104–5; Birnbaum, *Konkursrecht der frühen Augsburger Neuzeit*, 9–10.

55 StAA, Reichsstadt Strafamt 47, Stadtgerichtsbuch, 1531, fol. 59r–69v.

56 This obligation may have had something to do with the fact that Ambrosius's two elder brothers, both named Ulrich, were cathedral canons in Freissing.

57 Reinhard identifies Benigna as the daughter of Philipp Adler, but Höchstetter leaves the father's identity open to question. Cf. Hoechstetter, *Stammtafel der Hoechstetter*, 4; Wolfgang Reinhard, *Augsburg Eliten des 16. Jahrhundert. Prosopographie wirtschaftlicher und politischer Führungsgruppen 1500–1620* (Berlin 1996), 312.

58 StAA, Reichsstadt Strafamt 47, Stadtgerichtsbuch, 1531, fol. 65v.

59 "*weder jr Leib noch Guet ausser noch jnner der Statt gevarlich oder zu Nachtail der Glaubiger zuverenndern*". Ibid.

60 "*Wann die Hochstetter (jrm Erbieten nach) zu gleichen Nutz aller Gleubiger wolten gehanndlt haben sollten sy di angezaigten Warn unnd Pfenwerdt nit also verkhaufft unnd Freundt und annder so in darzu gefallen vor anndern bezallt haben sonnder die Guetter under die Gleubiger jnn gemain auszutailenn ligen lassen hetten sy nit dermassen Nachtail unnd Shaden daran erlitten*". StAA, Literaliensammlung, Höchstetter-Selekt I, Was die Hochstetter an allen Orten verpfendt, versetzt unnd mit Shaden verkhaufft haben.

61 "*Dann dess Geschafts halben wo sy redich damit handlen wollen nit sollten dermassen gemainen Gleubigern zu unwiderbreinglichen Shaden versetzt haben, sonnder gleicherweiss wie anzaift ist ligen lassen ob sy aber je nit dess Willenns gewessen sollten s yes vile he gar verkhaufft dann der Gestallt versetzt haben, woliches den Gleubigern vil nutzlicher gewessen. Dann er were khen so mergklich jnteresse darauf verlegenn und denn Gleubigern aller Preiss (wo sy annderst den nit verstegkht) zu gut khomen*". Ibid.

62 "*Aber Hochstetter, nach dem er sein Verderbenn gesechenn, hatt er (als der auf der Gleubiger Gut wenig Achtung gehabt) vil lieber seine Freundte Verwanndte unnd Diener mit zwifachem der anndern Gleubigern Shaden bezalen wollen, dann sein erdichtenn Beruemen nach Gleichait hallt*". Ibid.

63 The creditors would later pose the question how Ambrosius I could have proposed such a thing when he knew that "his representation [of his affairs] was untrue and that he did not have enough to pay even the tenth part [of his debts], creating the suspicion that he wished to commit himself with others and to stray into fraud". He repeated his ignorance and his innocence. He "did not know at that time that his affairs were in such a bad state". Fugger had suspected as much: Höchstetter either misunderstood or misrepresented the extent of his insolvency. To the creditors, Höchstetter explained that he "might well have promised to do his best to pay as much as he could in eighteen months, but if his representative promised more, it was not at his command". StAA, Literaliensammlung, Höchstetter-Selekt I, Actum auf 26 Tag Septembris Anno 31. Jn praesentibus Herrn Hofmann, Sighart, Paler, Schollenberger Ambrosi Hochstetter der Elter sagt an gutlichen Frag wie hernachfolgt.

64 Sender, *Die Chronik*, 222.

65 "*Zum achtenden, das kurzlich davor er Hochstetter valliert, bey jm in seiner Behausung gross und hoch Credennzen, Silbergeshirr, Edelgestain, Maderrock und Seydenshauben, cosstlichs Fuettern, gulden Ring und Edelgestain, gulden Kettin, kosstlich Tappezereyen, vil gutter Tuch und Gewanndt, hochen Pferden unnd annders gesehen, wa das in so kurzer Zeyt vershwunden, so doch nachmals jn Jnventori nit gefunden seye*". StAA, Literaliensammlung, Höchstetter-Selekt I, Erste Höchstetters Fragestuck.

66 "*Zum 8. sagt, alles das Silbergeschirr, das in seiner Haus gewesen seie, hab seine Eewurtin zugehort, benamlich auf jr Hochzeit gebracht von Freunden ererbt, hab jr nit uber 200 Gulden Wert Silbergeschirr alls lang er sie gehapt gemacht, achte auch solhs Silbergeschir sey nit uber 1000 Gulden Wert gewessen, zaigt ferner an, so er Hochseti oder ander Ladschaften gehapt haben er unn sein Hausfraw Silbergeschir von Freunden entlehnet, also je zu Zeiten ein Credenz zusamen getragen, mer zaigt jr Silbergeschir seie auf allen [. . .] alls [. . .] Fursten Potschaften versprochen unnd sampt ander Sachen des den Blaubigern und gemeiner Stat zu gueter komen, auc auf 3 Jar underhaltung gewendet worden seins Haushabens die weil er falliert gewendtworden, dessgleichenn die Claigung, Tappecirei seien seines Achtens vocal er gehapt noch verhanden. Ring seien auch alle Sachen halb wie ob alut verkauft und verbracucht worden, hab kein Ketin nie gehapt, dan sein Hausfraw sonst kain Abclag dann das er jr ncht solichs gemacht hab, wol hab sie ein Ketin biss jn 80 Gulden Wert das hab sie seiner Dochter gebenn, hab am letzten kain Tuch oder Gewand gehapt, waist Riederer gutten Beschaid zu geben, dann er die jn Raitung gehabt, er hab kein Hoch Pferd sonder allein ein clein Rosslin gehapt hab sein Sone vil Pferd gehapt lass er jne verantwurten, hab kein Wissen darvon*". StAA, Literaliensammlung, Höchstetter-Selekt I, Actum auf 26 Tag Septembris Anno 31. Jn praesentibus Herrn Hofmann, Sighart, Paler, Schollenberger Ambrosi Hochstetter der Elter sagt an gutlichen Frag wie hernachfolgt.

67 StAA, Literaliensammlung, Höchstetter-Selekt I, Erste Hochstetters Fragstuck.

68 Wilhelm Grimm, *Deutsches Wörterbuch von Jacob und Wilhelm Grimm*, 16 vols. (Leipzig 1854–1961, Quellenverzeichnis Leipzig 1971). Available at: www.woerterbuchnetz.de/DWB?lemma=scheinkauf (accessed 14 October 2016).

69 "*Der allt Ambrosy Hochstetter hat jnn der Zeit seins Verderbens, nemblich des 29 Jars, etwo umb Ostern oder hernach, die Warn, Schulden unnd Pfennwerdt, so jme noch zu Lynntz uberbeliben unnd die er (als hernach verstannden wurdt) seins Gefallenns nit einziehen oder verstecken mogen,*

seinem Vettern Philipp Gassner jnn einem Shein zugestellt oder zukauffen geben, damit ers jnn bemelter Gassners Namen dessen boss von Lynntz herauff fiern unnd alhie sein Will damit verbringen, als zum Theil beshehen. Dann als pald darauff gevolgt, dass Gassner alle Warn unnd Pfennwerdt zu sein Hannden genomen, der Hochstetter Marckh herab gethon, das sein jnn die Statt gemacht unnd sie dermassen one etlich thuch als herauff gebracht. Darzu die Shuldbrief, so umb die Linzer Shuldenn verhannden, wolher bei 43 oder darob gewesen, all uff sich stellen lassen, wie man austruckhennlich jnn jungen Ambrosy Rechenbuch seins Einnemens und Aussgebens No. 22 fol. 100 [jst seine aigne Handtshrifft] befundt". StAA, Literaliensammlung, Höchstetter-Selekt I, Des allten Hochstetter und seiner Mitverwanndten betruglichen Hanndlung.

70 "*Nochmaln ist jungen Ambrosi Hochstetters Hausfraw jnn bester Form darauss verwesen worden, dabei wol verstannden mag werden, als dann an jme selbs auch war ist, das die vorig Verweisung des Kaukffs halben mit Gassner beshehen allein ain Shein gewesen, dann jme seind die Guter keufflichen zugestellt, daran hat er nichts bezallt, wie jnn vorbemelltem Rechenbuch No. 22 fol. 188 der jung Ambrosy selbs bekennt, unnd hat die Newmennin (als gut zugedencken) mit Gassner umb bemelte Gueter abermals ain Sheinkauff troffen, dann nach dem sie (wie angezaigt ist) verwisen darauff, hat sie mit Gassner lassen hanndlenn, er soll jr di Gueter umb ain zimblichs widerfarn lassen, das er, als der on das khein sonder Gerechtigkheit darzu gehapt, leichtlich gethon, jr di umb 3000 fl. [jnn jungen Ambrosius Rechenbuch No 22, fol. 107] sampt den Shuldbreif zugestellt, Sendbrief darumb auffgericht worden, darunder hat sich Gassner und Catharina Newmennin auch zu mererm Schein die alt Fraw selbs unndershriben, jnn krafft desselben Kaufbrieffs vermaint di jung Fraw die Guter zu verkauffen*". Ibid.

71 "*Hochstetter bekennt jm Jnventario fol. 46 Philipp Gassner hab auff dem Berckhwerckh Steinfeld Zugewinn und Verlust 2000 fl. gehapt. Nun zaigt Hochstetter grossenn Verlust an, den er an disem Berckhwerckh erlitten, wer je billich Gassner sollt sampt dem Hochstetter ain Shaden sien Theil gehapt haben. Unangesehen des (gleich wie mit Georgen Hochstetter) verweist er jne umb sein ganze Summa das eer ain Freundt ist*". Ibid.

72 "*ob jme nit dergleichen Waren oders anders durch Scheinkeuff oder jn ander Gestalt zugestellt sei*". StAA. Literaliensammlung, Höchstetter-Selekt I, Verhörsprotokolle, 1531–1532.

73 "*Zum 5. Articul sagt, als Gassner jm 29 Jar gen Lintz gezogen, hab er jne gebeten dieweil er vil Kinder hab unnd ob sich die Sach anderst sein Hochstetters halb zu [. . .] dan Guet wie damit er dannoch seiner Shuld auch bezalt Weichnacht uff das er demselben Gassner die Gueter laut des Articuls so bei 3000 Gulden Wert gewesen umb seins Enthalts sambt den Schulden jnn Lintz gemacht biss jnn 8000 Gulden kauflich zugestelt besagenn versichert [. . .] jme gebenn dermas sich Philip Gassner selbs danen zu bezalen und folgends den jhenen die er auch darauf verwisen benamlich die junge Ambrosy Hochstetterin jres Heuratguts, Herrn Burgermaister Rechlinger, Lucas von Stetten und der allt Hochstetterin sein Hausfrawen die Ubermass zu geben benamlich die seins Frawen umb jr Heiratgut, sein Hausfrawen, Herrn Burgermaister unnd Lucas von Steten biss jn 1600 Gulden ongefarlich herruerends des Gellts von der Einnemen*". StAA, Literaliensammlung, Höchstetter-Selekt I, Actum auf 26 Tag Septembris Anno 31. Jn praesentibus Herrn Hofmann, Sighart, Paler, Schollenberger Ambrosi Hochstetter der Elter sagt an gutlichen Frag wie hernachfolgt.

74 "*Unnd hernach, jch bin gutter Hoffnung, wan wir auss disem unnserm Hauss verfuert werden, das man dannocht die Weiber zu unns last geen, auch unnsern Gewalthaber und Doctor Marshalkh, doch waiss jch das nit, auff ain Fursorg so muss man dannocht die Biecher unnd Register versehen, was mein Hausfrawen an geet*". StAA, Literaliensammlung, Höchstetter-Selekt I, Des allten Hochstetter und seiner Mitverwanndten betruglichen Hanndlung.

75 "*Bevilicht er jr unnd der Newmennin sonnderlich sie sollenn nit mer Gellts aus jnen shreckhen lassen, sonnder sagen sie habenselbs nichts, unnd jnn Summa vast ubel gehaben*". Ibid.

76 StAA, Literaliensammlung, Höchstetter-Selekt I, Was die Hochstetter gemainen Glaubigern gevarlicher weys verhallten.

77 StAA, Literaliensammlung, Höchstetter-Selekt I, Weliche Personen Hoechstetter jm Jnventario als Schuldner furgeben, die desselben nit gestenndig.

78 See Chapter 3. Cf. Pierre Bourdieu, *Outline of a Theory of Practice* (Cambridge, UK 1977); Pierre Bourdieu, *The Logic of Practice* (Stanford 1992).

79 Sender, *Die Chronik*, 221.

80 Birnbaum, *Konkursrecht der frühen Augsburger Neuzeit*, 22; Hellman, *Das Konkursrecht*, 32.

81 Sender, *Die Chronik*, 222.

82 Christian C. A. Lange, C. R. Unger, H. J. Huitfeldt-Kaas, Gustav Storm, Alexander Bugge, Christopher Brinchmann, and Oluf Kolsrud (eds.), *Diplomatarium Norvegicum*, vol. 8, 21 vols. (Christiana [Oslo] 1847–[1995]), 630–33, Nos. 546–7.

83 Staatsarchiv Schleswig-Holstein, Bergwerksrechte in Schweden 10, Urkunde aus dem Jahre 1532 betr. Bestellung Joachim Hoechstetters I. zum Bergmeister: 250r-255r: "Privilegia der Beckwerck aus Schonn / Joachim Hoechsteder gegeben / Anno etc. 1532.

84 Sender, *Die Chronik*, 222–3.

85 Ibid., 223.

86 Ibid. Sender speaks particularly of the objections of "the nobility of the creditors" (*der adel der glaubiger*) in this context. It is unclear whether he refers to the aristocrats among the creditors or the speakers of the group, the *curatores bonorum* appointed by the City Council.

87 Ibid., 223.

5 Bankruptcy

Financial markets and credit networks

The Höchstetter bankruptcy had never been a strictly local affair. Parties to it came from all corners of the Empire and beyond, from Antwerp to Vienna, Brandenburg to Bavaria, from Madrid and Lisbon to Lyon and Venice. Sender gave a sense of the affair's scope when he wrote that "[p]rinces, counts, noblemen, burghers, peasants, servants and maids deposited such money as they had with him", an enthusiasm shared by "many peasants and those who had not more than 10 fl".[1] These depositors had not invested capital *auf Gewinn und Verlust*, but rather "deposited it with him [Ambrosius I, tms] in his company and thought it very well secured". All who could attended the proceedings or sent representatives.

It was common practice in the late medieval and early modern periods to apply local law in cases of default, but the customary procedures of Augsburg had proven unable thus far to resolve this spectacular failure. The bankrupts were imprisoned in the *Rathaus*, but they were well-attended by their servants and wives; their families continued to live in style, as the creditors freely complained; and the creditors themselves were divided as to how they should proceed. Not least, the bankrupts themselves were far too important to be treated as common – or uncommon – criminals. The Höchstetters were not mere wholesale traders but important industrialists and financiers, who occupied the centers of far-flung capital networks that included princely houses. Their accusers included highly placed Imperial officials and landed aristocrats. It was inevitable that other, higher authorities would eventually become involved.

Sender chronicles this turn as follows:

> King Ferdinand sent Dr. [Johann, tms] Zott to the Höchstetters as a counselor and Duke William of Bavaria [sent] Doctor Augustein Lesch, his chancellor, in order to bring the creditors and the Höchstetter together and release the latter from prison. Nothing could be achieved, however, without considerable payment. At last, these two commissioners agreed and called together all the Höchstetter wives and all their friends and relatives and asked them whether they wished their husbands and friends to be helped (to honor themselves), to share and put forward their property, so that they could leave prison and the creditors be satisfied. At this, they took

> time until All Saints Day [1 November 1529, tms] to consider, which was granted them. During this time, the Höchstetters remained under guard at the Rathaus as before.[2]

Mediation began sometime in October 1529. Sender believed that the intention was to assist the bankrupts. The princes' reliance on them for financial support, quite apart from any desire to avoid disturbances among Europe's greatest merchant-financiers, gave them an interest in a speedy resolution. The means to it were obvious to no one, however.

Negotiations resumed on 1 November 1529, but an outbreak of epidemic disease prevented most of the foreign creditors from attending,[3] and the commission recessed until 6 January 1530. Sender records the etiquette of that meeting:

> When the creditors came together here to take counsel or to go to city hall, the nobility were the first to go, followed by the burgher, women and men, servants and maids, poor and rich, each person according to their estate, and the foreign common folk went before the Augsburgers.[4]

Neither equality among the creditors, nor priority of payment, both of which had hitherto been points of dispute among bankrupts and creditors, appear to have had any place here. The social hierarchy brooked no leveling, but even the lowest foreigner preceded the highest burgher.

During the two-month delay, the commissioners worked to hammer out a compromise among the bankrupts, their supporters and the creditors. Wives, relatives and friends of the Höchstetters had apparently agreed to use their own funds as the means to a settlement; a bare majority of the creditors made their peace with a partial repayment of their loans, deposits and investments; nearly as many refused any settlement short of payment in full.

Among the recalcitrant were the Swabian, landed aristocrats, Konrad von Buhel and his sister-in-law, Dorothea von Buhel, née von Fronhofen. Konrad had notified Ambrosius I on the Friday after St. Martins (11 November), 1528, of the death of his mother, to whom the Augsburg merchant owed "a gallant sum of money", the exact amount of which he could not give. He had asked, not that the partners remit the deposit, but that they "not release such money without my particular knowledge, consent and notification, but keep it with you until further instruction".[5] Ambrosius had reassured him on 15 November 1528 that no money would change hands, but "could not withhold the fact that the brothers of your brother's wife [Dorothea, tms] had already written, demanding the same thing as he, also with legal justification".[6] According to an edict from Ludwig XV, Count of Oettingen, dated 15 December 1528, at stake was Konrad's maternal inheritance, which he shared with his late brother, Christof.[7] When Christof died, his share passed to his children, Christof and Apollonia, who were represented by their mother, the widow Dorothea. Konrad and Dorothea disagreed over the exact division and called on Ludwig to mediate a settlement. After long and difficult negotiation, Ludwig awarded certain annuities to Konrad, but the Höchstetter deposit to Dorothea's children. Apparently, the mediated settlement satisfied neither party.

On 22 April 1529, with his insolvency a matter of common knowledge, if not yet a legally declared bankruptcy, Ambrosius had responded to Dorothea's demand for immediate payment, promising to comply by St. Michael's Day (29 September), but stating, in light of his communication with her brother-in-law, that he could not do so until he received sufficient instruction and proof of what was due both of them in capital and interest.[8] Von Buhel's answer is lost, but she appealed again to Ludwig of Oettingen in June.[9] She had received instruction to register her claim with the Augsburg City Court, to whose authority she declared herself not subject. She argued further that she would receive little of what was owed her if her debt was but one of many. It was, as she noted, not an investment at venture in the business, but a deposit at 5 percent interest. Ludwig should intervene, as her lord, to compel Ambrosius to render immediate payment in full.

Many wished by one means or another to compel him to pay. This chapter takes up the questions, who they were, what they invested and how their investments happened. The bankruptcy records of "Ambrosius and Hans the Brothers Höchstetter and Associates" leave little doubt that lending occurred across late medieval and early modern society. Lenders clearly possessed capital and knew to invest it. Less clear is exactly how they came to possess capital. How could "peasants and those who had not more than 10 fl" have acquired such sums in the first place? Similarly unclear is exactly how they located investment opportunities. How did investors locate and evaluate potential borrowers before banks and exchanges, organizations created to foster such mediation, existed? And how did they understand what they were doing? In attempting to answer these and related questions, this chapter examines the emergence of financial markets *avant la lettre*.

* * *

Sender drew sweeping attention to all those who had evem small amounts of disposable capital to deposit at interest with merchant-banking houses, where "it would be secure and provide them an annual income".[10] He hinted at their sheer numbers, when he wrote of those who got paid and the some 300 who were left empty-handed by Ambrosius. Such quantities have inspired speculation about premodern financial markets. Scholars, such as Richard Ehrenberg and Jacob Strieder, have spoken of the Höchstetter firm as paradigmatic of early capitalistic enterprises, both in its monopolistic practices and in its financial structure.[11] As Ehrenberg put it, with evident reference to Sender, "They drew, so one says, capital in the form of small deposits and used it to dominate the market in specific commodities".[12] Pölnitz characterized the Höchstetter firm as "a bank of small-scale savers and speculators", and a generation of scholars repeated his portrayal in one form or another.[13] Ulrich Klinkert posed the question explicitly in an unpublished thesis.[14] Were the Höchstetters among the first to draw capital from beyond the circle of immediate family and friends to seek investment from a broader market in a manner reminiscent of a modern joint-stock company?

This presupposes the existence of financial markets in one form or another. In modern economies, these usually resolve themselves into two basic forms. Capital markets direct the flow of wealth from savers to borrowers, who can make productive use of it, through the purchase and sale of long-term debt (bonds or debentures) or equity-backed securities (stocks). Bond- or debenture-holders become creditors of whatever entity issued the debt, it could be a state (bond) or a firm (debenture), whereas equity-holders become owners of the entity that issued the equity. Capital markets usually have both primary and secondary sectors, the first selling new bond or stock issues to investors, the second reselling existing securities among investors. In contradistinction to capital markets that meet long-term capital needs, money markets exist to address the need for short-term capital, usually in the form of loans that are expected to be paid back quickly. This kind of capital is often used to meet general operating or brief liquidity requirements. Lending of this sort, usually provided by banking houses, differs from capital market transactions, even when the loans are extended over longer periods of time, in a number of respects that go well beyond their term. Money-market lending, whether in the form of bank loans, peer-to-peer lending or factor financing, is usually not securitized, that is, it does not take the form of a resaleable security (i.e., a share, debenture or bond) that can be traded on the market.[15] It tends to be more heavily regulated than capital-market lending, and its lenders tend to be more risk-averse. These differences make money markets preferable, not only for short-term loans, but also for certain small- and medium-scale borrowers.

Generally speaking, financial markets gather capital from investors and direct it to enterprises that use the capital to fund operations and achieve growth. Without these markets, borrowers might struggle to locate capital for themselves. Hence the need for mediation. In modern money markets, this function is carried out by banks of one sort or another that take deposits from those who have money to save and lend from these deposits to those who need capital. Such credit transactions usually take the form of mortgages or loans, the difference being that the former is secured with real property as collateral, while the latter can be either secured by other forms of guarantee or unsecured. In capital markets, where transactions involve larger sums and longer terms, exchanges bring together lenders and borrowers for the purposes of generating new credit-debt transactions or selling existing commitments, in the form of shares or bonds.

These rudimentary distinctions, familiar to most people, become important in the context of late medieval and early modern companies and economies. Family firms in the fifteenth and sixteenth century could not rely on fully articulated financial markets to meet their capital needs. They turned in the first place to family and friends, usually the partners themselves, as the Höchstetter contracts of 1515 and 1524 make clear. Bankruptcy records reveal that other sources of money expanded this initial investment. The Höchstetters and their peers accepted deposits at fixed interest from a wide range of third parties. They were suspected also of offering the essential equivalent of shares, exchanging a portion of their company's eventual profits, if any, to so-called good friends or silent partners, in return for substantial investments of capital.

To this point, it seems that rudimentary money markets existed in the medieval and early modern periods. Many individuals loaned at interest money that they had earned, received or saved. When they deposited their capital with merchant-banking houses, they expected a secure return – the "five Gulden on 100" that Sender described – over the period of the deposit. Regardless of term, merchant-banking houses "loaned" these deposits to other parties or to the house itself.[16] Whether capital markets also existed before the fifteenth century depends on the existence of "shares" that could be issued and resold, a murkier question altogether. Professional money-lenders came in all sorts and sizes, from pawnbrokers to shop-keepers to merchant-bankers, whether Jewish, Muslim or Christian, and they not only loaned money to individuals and companies, but also discounted and traded debts with one another, and bought and sold government debt issues.[17] By the fourteenth century, Venetian lenders traded in debt issues from many governments, making them among the first European investment brokers.[18] Richard Goldthwaite has argued for a similar development in Florence.[19] Scholars generally hold, on the other hand, that official shares, such as could change hands, did not exist before the late-seventeenth century, though other kinds of instruments functioned to bind entrepreneur and financier and to generate incomes much as stocks now do.[20]

Insofar as capital flowed from lenders to borrowers, a financial market can be said to have existed. It operated without the fundamental organizations associated with modern finance, however. Commodity and stock exchanges that brought together borrowers and lenders for the purposes of large-scale, long-term capital transactions emerged as discrete, dedicated spaces only in the sixteenth century and only in a few commercial centers. Antwerp may claim the first stock exchange, founded in 1531, where brokers and lenders met to trade in the entire range of debt issues, from promissory notes and bonds, but not in stocks. Merchant-banks offered small-scale, short-term credit to borrowers as early as the fourteenth century, but these lacked the authority, stability and credibility of larger, church- or state-based organizations. Not until the early seventeenth century did the archetype for modern, commercial banking appear. The Amsterdam *Wisselbank* (Exchange Bank), founded in 1609, originally served to lend money to the Dutch government, but expanded its service to private individuals by the end of the century. Over time, similar organizations emerged elsewhere.

Yet most commercial and industrial centers lacked the fundamental organizations necessary for a well-functioning financial market until sometime in the eighteenth century. How did markets like Augsburg compensate? Without bourses or banks, certain challenges had to be overcome by other means. These included both the creation of a supply of capital that could be used for financial purposes and the mediation of contact between lenders and borrowers. The availability of lending and investment capital appears to have reached across the social spectrum, showing no obvious sign of a lack of circulating specie.[21] It raises the question, however, how relatively modest earners – Sender's "peasants, servants and maids" – managed to accumulate. Banks provide but one means of pooling savings. Individuals without access to such organizations could avail themselves of other organizations or strategies. Various kinds of corporations, such as guilds and charities, accepted deposits from their members. Savers could also choose not to entrust their money to any third party, locking it in a box, burying it in a garden or hiding it about the house. The German saying, "*etwas auf die hohe Kante legen*" (to place something on the high ledge), may capture this, insofar as it commonly refers to saving money and has been associated with a time when "banking" was done at home. Whether poor or rich, potential lenders had to find and evaluate potential borrowers. In Augsburg, no organization existed for this express purpose, leading to the assumption that word-of-mouth functioned across both social and geographical spaces that were as extensive as the servant populations in merchant homes and the factor networks of family firms.

Though lacking in banks and bourses, sixteenth-century Augsburg was not entirely without an organizational basis for financial life. Word-of-mouth could facilitate lending and borrowing through a variety of social networks. Tavern-keepers, for example, might have played an intermediary role similar to that of hostelers in Bruges, as portrayed by Oscar Gelderblom.[22] The city also possessed officials and organizations that could assist financial transactions through information and mediation.

The local *Unterkäufler* might have provided such information and services for lenders and borrowers by virtue of their knowledge of local market conditions.[23] *Unterkäufler* were intermediaries (*Makler*) who brought together foreign and local merchants for the purposes of financial or commercial transactions.[24] Foreigners without experience in Augsburg and its markets might turn to the services of an *Unterkäufel* to locate suitable trading partners. In this respect, they assumed some of the functions of a bourse, as other scholars have noted, before one existed as a physical locus of economic life and information in Augsburg.[25] They served a fiscal function as well: They were civic officials, appointed by the city council to oversee all commercial and exchange transactions, to arrange a fair price and to assure the quality of the goods traded and the range of trade relations for the principal purpose of guaranteeing the city its tax (*Ungeld*) revenue.[26] The position and function of these intermediaries was well established by the time of the Höchstetter bankruptcy, having been subject to legal regulation since the thirteenth century. A separate *Unterkäufelordnung* of 5 March 1524 placed practically all wholesale goods and foreign exchange in the hands of two appointed *Unterkäufel*.[27] They received sales goods from the seller, assessed their quality and established their value, received the sale price from the purchaser, levied the tax to be paid by both seller and purchaser and transferred the goods only when the money had changed hands. Likewise, the sale of real capital, precious metals and financial instruments fell within the *Unterkäufels* purview, as did currency exchanges. They served thus the purpose of reducing risk in long-distance or large-scale transactions as well as extending the city's fiscal regulation.

Though no direct evidence exists, the meeting halls of Augsburg's elite corporations almost certainly functioned as an *ersatz* bourse. The *Kaufleutestube*, founded in 1479, was the corporate and social center of the *Kaufleutestubengesellschaft*, which was founded in the same year. Despite its name, suggesting a place and group dominated by long-distance, wholesale traders, the *Kaufleutestubengesellschaft* was open to members of all guilds in Augsburg until 1548, when the constitutional changes demanded by Emperor Charles V transformed the members of the *Kaufleutezunft* into a closed corporation.[28] Formed in the fourteenth century, it had never encompassed all long-distance trade, which appealed to many groups and many individual.[29] Patricians, shop-keepers and weavers all might engage in it and, by so doing, earn the name of *Kaufleute* without membership in the *Kaufleutezunft*. The Höchstetters themselves entered into long-distance trade as bleachers and textile retailers (*Gewandschneider*). For this reason, perhaps, the *Kaufleutestube* played a less central role as a place where merchant-bankers might meet, a place that might assume some of the functions of a bourse. Elite *Kaufleute* found that place in the *Herrentrinkstube*, the meeting place of the *Herrenstuben-Gesellschaft* from the early-fifteenth century. Eligible for membership were all descendants of patrician ancestors (*Patrizier*) as well as those who married into patrician families, the so-called Patrons of Society (*Mehrer der Gesellschaft*).[30] The *Herrentrinkstube*, the social, political and economic meeting point of the city's elite, was ideally suited to serve merchant-bankers as a bourse.

The Höchstetters frequented the *Herrentrinkstube*. It seems likely that they gathered business intelligence and encountered at least some potential investors and depositors there. The financial market of Augsburg remained essentially decentralized, however. The surviving record of their *Gewett* indicates as much. For capital they turned to sources both local and foreign, elite and common, institutional and individual. The lack of a single source or location for financial capital or financial information probably raised the transaction costs of lending and borrowing. It probably also increased the risk.

The records of the Höchstetter bankruptcy unfortunately shed little light on these functions. On the one hand, they demonstrate the existence of a lively financial market, capable of complex transactions without organizational development. Though lacking banks and bourses, parties engaged in sophisticated book transfers, derivative instruments and debt discountings. The multiple, secret arrangements between Ambrosius I Höchstetter and Anton Fugger, and the evidence later produced by the *curatores*, leave no doubt on this score. This market relied heavily on written, contractual agreements, not the oral bargains of small-scale credit relations.[31] Augsburg legal practice required all creditors in bankruptcy proceedings to document their claims, regardless of size, by submitting the signed contract of debt (*Schuldbrief*). As we have seen, these

Schuldbriefe could be exchanged and discounted like debentures. On the other hand, the functions of this market remain in many respects remarkably obscure. The records say little about mediation. How the bankrupts sought, found and evaluated lenders, or vice versa, especially in distant or marginal locations, is not discussed. The following discussion will address, therefore, only certain aspects of financial markets and their function in the fifteenth and sixteenth centuries, before both the emergence of central organizations and the distinction between capital and money markets. It will examine the lenders and their capital, asking who they were, what, if any, relationship they had with the Höchstetters and what they chose to lend. These questions should lead to the larger issues of information and risk.

★ ★ ★

The von Buhel brother and sister-in-law struggled for control of their inheritance, but it had a different meaning – and different value – for each of the contestants. Those differences altered their understandings of the transaction with Ambrosius I Höchstetter and the risks that it involved. For Konrad, at stake was his share of his maternal inheritance, part of which passed to him and part of which passed to his late brother, Christof. It was a "galant" sum of money, as he put it, one that might alter his quality of life. For Christof's widow, Dorothea, that capital constituted her husband's estate, possession of which would affect her ability to support herself and her children. It was not a matter of quality of life, but of life itself.

To preserve it intact, she mobilized a group of aristocrats to put pressure on the Augsburg city court and council. Her brother, Christof von Fronhofen, appealed on her behalf to Georg "the Pious", Margrave of Brandenburg-Ansbach. Georg, in turn, wrote to the city government of Augsburg in June 1529, insisting that it permit Ambrosius to pay his debt to von Buhel, oath and arrest notwithstanding.[32] Brothers Eucharius and Georg von Fronhofen, joined Christof in their sister's support and pointed out to the Augsburg authorities how Ambrosius had failed to make the most recent interest payment and had responded to repeated requests with dismissive answers. "It would be a shame were poor children, who do not have much, to be thus deprived of their own".[33] The magistrates acknowledged receipt of these petitions, noting that they had taken the Höchstetters into custody and would proceed with payment to the extent that the city's sovereignty and law permitted.[34] Far from settling the matter, the suggestion that Augsburg would proceed according to its own standards, refusing to take into account the petitioner's status as a noblewoman and widow, prompted further and more dramatic gestures. In August 1529, no fewer than 29 noblemen signed a letter to the city government, stating their absolute conviction that the *Gewett* "does not concern and has nothing to do with [Dorothea von Buhel], also she and her children are not subject to [Augburg's] jurisdiction and to [its] supposed, meaningless sovereignty, whether you or your judges would ignore an obvious debt and legal document".[35]

Susanne, the widow of Casimir, Margrave of Brandenburg-Bayreuth and wife of Ottheinrich, Count Palatine of Palatinate Neuburg, joined the campaign at about the same time, noting that von Buhel's "acknowledged and documented debt was loaned to Ambrosius at interest, not invested at profit or loss like others in his business" and requesting a "not dismissive answer".[36]

Acknowledging this support, von Buhel submitted her own rendering of events and petition for aid to the Augsburg authorities.[37] In 1527, her mother-in-law had deposited 1,300 fl in gold at 5 percent interest with the Höchstetters. That principal and interest had been promised and transferred to her as her wedding dowry and gift in 1528 by virtue of a negotiated inheritance settlement. Ambrosius had acknowledged the obligation and promised in writing to pay it, but requested that she agree to delay until 1529. He later refused payment with reference to the claim of her brother-in-law that the deposit was, in fact, his inheritance. Given that this claim had been dismissed in the inheritance settlement, as Ambrosius knew, his refusal constituted a swindel. She had since learned of the Höchstetters' insolvency, which forced her as a poor widow with nothing else in the world to support herself through service and to appeal to her noble friends and relatives, including the Margrave Georg. She proclaimed herself willing to leave her capital in the hands of the city and creditors until all claims had been settled, provided the Höchstetters offered sufficient assurance of payment in full. Failing that, the bankrupt should be held in jail.

The authorities' insistence that von Buhel must submit to the *Gewett* and accept its eventual outcome, like all other creditors, local and foreign, common and noble, male or female, unleashed another, even angrier flurry of letters and petitions. Her brothers wrote to the city again, referring to "this inconvenient and unlawful day that one refers to as a pledge, better known as a 'swindle' day" (*diesenn vermeinten unbequenen auch unrechtlichenn tag den man ein wethe [. . . ja ein betrueg tag] nennt*).[38] Well-informed, they referred to the flight of the two of the partners, Joachim I Höchstetter and Hans Franz Paumgartner, and the removal of capital from the city. They rehearsed the rumors of payments to certain favored creditors, over the protestations and petitions of the nobility, saying that the bankrupts would have been imprisoned had the authorities acted properly, "which you neither did nor wished to do". They repeated their earlier demand that their sister be paid in full immediately and concluded on a sinister note that "we mean to demand and to have this from you and the city with the help of our lords and friends". The possibility of an aristocratic vendetta (*Fehde*) against the city and its burghers remained unmentioned, but it could not be dismissed.

It did not come to that. Countess-Palatine Susanne of Palatinate Neuburg and Margrave Georg of Brandenburg-Ansbach continued to apply steady pressure but without thinly veiled threats. Georg's brothers, Archbishop Wilhelm of Riga, Archbishop Johann Albrecht of Magdeburg and Friedrich, a canon in Würzburg, all entered the correspondence with firm, but mild pleas on behalf of von Buhel.[39] The Augsburg magistracy also found ways to avoid direct confrontation. It continued to defend the city's custom of a pledge as their effort to create a level playing field in which the many interested parties receive equal – or, at least, fair – opportunity of having their claims met.[40] At the same time, they opened the possibility of direct negotiation. The further course of events becomes clear in a letter from Margrave Georg to the Augsburg council.[41] He appreciated as well "that you permitted her to visit the Höchstetters in order to discuss her need and, as she reported to us, in other ways demonstrated your good will to her". Although she still could not participate in the forthcoming pledge, "not knowing what sort of thing it is", she would send a representative to Augsburg to act on her behalf. It seems the possibility of some sort of settlement that preserved her separate status as an aristocrat and simultaneously upheld Augsburg law had arisen.

That resolution proved elusive, however. Communication continued through the end of 1529 and into 1530 without effect. Von Buhel continued to object to the city's procedures, and her supporters kept up a steady drumbeat of letters on her behalf.[42] According to such records as survive, she never took part in the *Gewett*. She would be party to no lesser settlement than payment in full.

To prosecute her case, von Buhel mobilized a network of aristocratic family, friends and patrons who shared her dim view of Augsburg's claim to jurisdiction. They were well-informed about her financial situation and the Höchstetter bankruptcy. They grasped the formal distinction between deposits and investments and viewed with apparent consternation any suggestion that the security of the former could or might be compromised. The failure to resolve the stalemate indicates that despite a degree of information and sophistication in matters financial, they did not have access to organized, third-party mediation and securitization of the sort that a bank or bourse might have offered.

What did the efforts of royal and ducal commissioners offer von Buhel and the other creditors that the bankrupts' pledge did not? Certainly, it superseded any limits set by local jurisdiction, preserving thus the legal and social status – and privileges – of foreign creditors, noble and common. It also engaged the capital of the bankrupts' friends and families, including their wives, removing what had been a controversial issue and increasing thus the probability of eventual payment at better terms. Sender included its text verbatim in his chronicle of Augsburg history.[43] It provides a window into the economic, social and cultural contexts of early modern credit-debt relations.

The compromise document opened with a review of the situation. Warned by the commissioners to "make an accurate, well-founded report and indication of all their property, real, moveable, debts, commodities and everything, excluding nothing, so that all conflict may be better negotiated to a good resolution",[44] the bankrupts produced writings and extracts from their records and accounts. As of 1 January 1530, the Höchstetters and company had unmet obligations totalling more than 300,000 fl, as well as numerous bills of exchange to fulfill.[45] Moreover, they owed the mine operators (*Gewerke*) at Idria approximately 75,000 fl for quantities of quicksilver and cinnabar received. Their urban palaces and landed estates had all been alienated to secure their wives' "brought, inherited and owned property, also legacies and marriage gifts beyond their moveable property, such as clothing, jewelry, silver plate, household goods and such like, as has been declared their own in their marriage agreements".[46] This property amounted to 50,000 fl. A further 50,000 fl in debts and commodities were likewise promised to the wives as surety for repayment of their dowries. Accounts revealed that Ambrosius I and his partners would be able to collect no more than 180,000 fl in total for all the debts, commodities and goods that remained in their possession. Of this sum, no more than 70,000 fl "could be considered certain" and 50,000 fl of that much smaller amount had, as noted, already been mortgaged to the women. That left only 20,000 fl to meet the demands of the creditors and, as the agreement stated baldly, "[this sum] took the form not of cash but of debts that must be gathered with difficulty and expense, and it remained doubtful whether they were certain or uncertain".[47]

To make up the dramatic shortfall, the commissioners turned to various friends of the Höchstetters, urging them to commit funds to help meet the demands of the creditors, "so that a goodly agreement would succeed, and peace and unity follow". Various persons, including former partners of the Höchstetter offered to contribute 20,000 fl within a year. The wives of the Höchstetters agreed "out of heart-felt love and to free their husbands" to release 40,000 of the 50,000 fl in family real estate and to surrender their rights to 50,000 of the 70,000 fl in the firm's secure debts, commodities and goods. By so doing, the wives "surrender their wife's freedom in best, finest form to the advantage of the creditors".[48] These unmortgaged assets and negotiated agreements promised a settlement of less than 50 percent under the best of circumstances, only 130,000 fl in payment of more than 300,000 fl in outstanding debts.

In response to this undeniable fact, the commissioners proposed a series of arrangements. First, to the mine operators in Idria, to whom Höchstetter owed some 75,000 fl, they offered a payment of 10,000 fl from Ferdinand I and a promise of thousands more "so that His Majesty's mines might be promoted, dispute and resentment be prevented and goodness be fostered".[49] The Höchstetters would pay nothing at all. The operators who were present promised only to transmit the agreement to those absent and expressed hope that it might be accepted. Second, to the Augsburg creditors, "who were friends with the Höchstetters", whose claims exceeded 100,000 fl, the commissioners offered the 50,000 fl that constituted the wives' claim to the firm's 70,000 fl in secure debts and commodities. This they would divide among themselves and all the other creditors without exception. They would also receive a further 18,000 fl that would come from the three younger Höchstetters and Paumgartner.

That 18,000 fl constituted a penalty to be paid to the creditors by the junior partners after all available means had been exhausted. Having completely surrendered (*gentzlich cedieren*) to the creditors all his present and future property of whatever sort, the imprisoned senior partner, Ambrosius I, would retain nothing beyond what was his wife's property. The Höchstetters and their creditors agreed that Ambrosius II and Joseph Höchstetter, who had also been imprisoned, would each be permitted to keep whatever they might earn or inherit, except for 3,000 fl, "because they excused themselves and claimed not only that they had little or no property of their own but also that they were not responsible for the ruin [of the company]".[50] Joachim I Höchstetter and Hans Franz Paumgartner, who had fled the bankruptcy, taking considerable capital with them, and who "gave greater cause to the Höchstetter ruin and wasted the company's money", would each be required to pay 6,000 fl.[51] If they managed to earn or receive more than 2,000 fl, that amount would be taken by the creditors and the balance left to them until they had paid the fixed amount of 6,000 fl.

Finally, to the remaining creditors, the commissioners proposed to give the 20,000 fl promised by the good friends and former partners, their share of the 70,000 fl in secure debts minus 10,000 fl reserved for the wives and all the remaining 110,000 fl in bad debts that they might collect.

To summarize briefly, the bankrupts lost all property and had future income garnished to varying degrees. Their immediate families, represented by their wives, but including their children, retained only 10,000 of 100,000 fl in various forms of capital that they called their own. Those "friends" who promised 20,000 fl to the settlement, despite having claims against it worth 100,000 fl, would receive no more than one-third of what was owed to them, or one-fourth when their promised payment was subtracted. All the others, those creditors with no recognized connection to the bankrupts, would receive at least half and possibly more, depending upon the collection of outstanding, mostly bad debts.

Leaving aside the bankrupts themselves, the terms of the proposed agreement fell hardest on the abandoned wives and children. They stood to endure the financial, social and psychological consequences of actions they may have abetted but did not commit. The wives of Hans Franz Paumgartner and Joseph Höchstetter, Ottilia Höchstetter and Benigna Adler, respectively, died shortly after the proposed agreement, early in 1530; both succumbed to grief, mortification or despair (*unmüt*), according to Sender.[52] The survivors, Anna Rehlinger, Katharina Neumann and Anna Langenmantel von Sparren, the spouses of Ambrosius I, Ambrosius II and Joachim I Höchstetter, respectively, would struggle for decades to protect what remained of their properties from the unfulfilled demands of the creditors, appealing some of the claims against them as high as the Imperial Chamber Court (*Reichskammergericht*). Of the enduring impact of the bankruptcy on the members of other Höchstetter family, more later.

Why, in light of such difficulties, did the wives agree to part with 90 percent of their property, retaining only 10,000 fl? Despite the reduction in material circumstances, they would benefit in several ways. Contributing directly to the resolution of the bankruptcy increased their own honor and status, as the wording of the agreement made clear.[53] The 90,000 fl that the wives released constituted the vast majority of the total 138,000 fl in secure capital available to settle the bankruptcy, which made any resolution more likely to be accepted by the creditors. With the conflict ended and their husbands freed, they might eventually regain the wealth and status that had been theirs.

The "friends," who promised to contribute 20,000 fl to the settlement, may have had similar motives. Like the wives, the "friends" might have enhanced their own honor by coming to the aid of imprisoned debtors. The available information identifies them further as "especially old and former partners of the Höchstetters" and "Augsburg creditors". Of the former partners who were still alive in 1529, Stephen Gabler, Philipp I Gassner, Georg II Höchstetter, Sigmund I Höchstetter, Wilhelm Höchstetter, Lukas II Rem and Hans II Ungelter, only Sigmund I Höchstetter and Lukas II Rem appeared with claims of 5,800 fl and 7,184 fl, respectively, among the creditors. By paying into it, they improved their chances to get something out of it. These "friends" may well have gained other benefits from the release of the bankrupts. The creditors suspected some of them might be silent partners of the bankrupt Höchstetters and, according to the terms of unlimited liability, accountable for payment of their obligations. They specifically accused Philipp I Gassner, for example, of abetting the Höchstetters in the matter of the *Scheinkäufe*. Acceptance of the agreement ended all disputes and controversies among bankrupts and creditors.

The "other creditors from the nobility, foreigners and locals" (*andern glaubigern vom adel, auslendern und hiesigen*) had little interest in assisting the Höchstetters. As the long negotiation with Dorothea von Buhel makes clear, they wanted repayment without reduction or delay. The commissioners convinced at least some of them to compromise, however, to accept less than a complete return, rather than no return at all, given the lack of available capital. Dated 6 February 1530, the proposed settlement breathed a spirit of balanced financial interest and social solidarity. The commissioners spoke consistently in terms of renewing group honor, restoring peaceful relations and reestablishing communal harmony. Self-interest and individual objectives were not set aside, but the individual and communal were brought into tenuous equilibrium. The creditors were given two months to sign individual, notarized papers accepting the agreement. Those who refused the agreement would lose their claim to a portion of the private property surrendered by the Höchstetter wives.

That possibility might have had little meaning for creditors like Dorothea von Buhel, who insisted on payment in full. That her name had disappeared from the roll of creditors in 1531 has to do with an individual arrangement reached shortly after the deadline for acceptance of the proposed settlement. On 22 April 1530, Anna Rehlinger declared herself willing to settle von Buhel's claim of 1,200 fl in gold, half in 1530 and the balance in 1531 on behalf of her husband and his company.[54] The two women never closed the deal. As Rehlinger complained to the magistrates, she had paid 1,000 fl at considerable disadvantage, but she could not pay the balance, because the creditors refused to release her seized property.[55] In a letter dated the Monday after St. Lucie (13 December) 1533, Georg von Fronhofen wrote once again on behalf of his sister and asked the Augsburg authorities once again to compel Rehlinger to fulfill her contractual promise to pay.[56] Failing that he threatened "to take into consideration ways to prevent [his sister] being dangerously and fraudulently denied her own". The final outcome of this long dispute is not recorded.

The commissioners' efforts failed as well. In spite of the incentives they constructed to encourage compromise and resolution, a substantial number of creditors, like Dorothea von Buhel, refused to yield. Sender noted, "[H]ardly half of the creditors wanted to consent to the contract, but rather wanted all or nothing, and so they parted from one another divided".[57] His chronicle indicates repeatedly that internal differences among the creditors determined their attitude toward the bankrupts and the settlement. The nobles were determined to get back their money but had no interest in imprisoning the Höchstetters. The friends, most of whom were merchant-bankers, were prepared to accept a partial return, rather than risk losing it all, in order to end the long dispute without further damage to themselves or their community. Perhaps market experience better enabled certain creditors to compare the uncertainties involved with demanding full payment against those of accepting a limited loss. A distinction might also be made between stakeholders, who had reason not to become involved in the bankruptcy proceedings and might be more anxious for a settlement, therefore, and depositors, who had reason to insist on full repayment. (See Chapter 2.) A distinction might also be made on the basis of the nature of the capital involved. Dorothea von Buhel referred repeatedly and heatedly to the poverty she and her children would suffer if their inheritance – her dowry – were not repaid in full. For her brother-in-law, by contrast, the deposit was merely a "gallant sum of money". The role that capital played in the lifecycle of a family and its planning for the future altered their risk averseness and influenced accordingly their readiness to hold, deposit or invest. All wanted to profit, but the stakes were not the same for all. No one wanted to lose their money, but some understood the risks involved differently.

The 1530 Imperial Diet (*Reichstag*) that convened in Augsburg on 15 June offered another chance at mediation and resolution. The chronicle of events continues:

> The part that accepted the contract cited that part that had not wanted to accept it before the court in order to compel them to accept it. Whereupon the court decreed that that part should not be forced to accept the agreement, unless their good will was present. The creditors who accepted the contract appealed this verdict to the Emperor.[58]

Not the bankrupts this time, but rather the creditors who had accepted the commission's proposal, appealed directly to Charles V, who responded by setting 15 July as the day he would judge the case. After a substantial hearing (*gnugsamer verhör*), and "because his Imperial Majesty was burdened with other difficult affairs", the Emperor named Christoph von Stadion, Prince-Bishop of Augsburg, as his commissioner and judge in the case.[59] The bishop set his hearing for 15 December in Augsburg. The parties appeared, but refused to agree, despite the fact that "the bishop mediated among them with great industry, effort and work for eight days".[60] Having so far failed, the bishop recessed the proceedings until 14 March 1531, when he would hold another hearing at his court in the town of Dillingen.

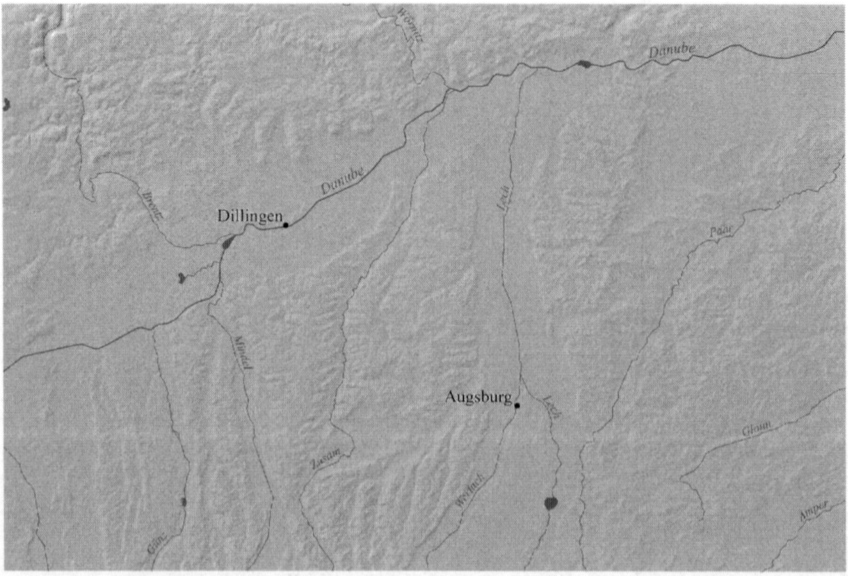

Map 5.1 Diocese of Augsburg

On 9 August 1530, nearly 13 months after the original pledge of payment, the creditors complained to the magistrates:

> Your foresightful, honorable Wisdom knows well how long ago, now a whole year past, Ambrosius Höchstetter the Elder pledged on behalf of himself and all his associates with all his creditors in open court here in Augsburg, upon which pledge the required actions were to be executed in accordance with city custom, but in what manner we have with great assurance, good-natured negotiation and agreement since been impeded.[61]

For the remainder of the year and into the next, while waiting for the bishop's second attempt at mediation, the creditors continued to disagree amongst themselves, press the imprisoned bankrupts for payment and petition the authorities for action. Like Dorothea von Buhel, some worried that they risked losing dowries or inheritances, funds that had substantial significance in the lifecycles of their families. Dr. Jacob Kreel, a jurist at the Imperial Chamber Court (*Reichskammergericht*) in Speyer, appealed to the Augsburg council, "Because the above mentioned sum [1,700 fl, tms] constitutes the greater share of my wife's paternal and maternal inheritance as well as her dowry, the loss of which would cause unavoidable, ruinous and everlasting damage to me, my wife and my dear children".[62] A petition from Dietrich von Knöringen, whose estate was near

Burgau in Swabia, to the west of Augsburg, revealed how complicated such familial finance could be:

> In the first place the matter is as follows: As the late Moritz von Altmanshoven, my beloved brother-in-law of blessed memory, whose surviving widow is the legitimate sister on both sides of my wife, during his lifetime invested 2,000 *Gulden* with the aforementioned Höchstetter and his partners in consideration of the fact that he had three unmarried daughters, as the mother still has in her keeping, should he ever have the good fortune to arrange the marriage of one or two of them, he could assure them on the basis of his investment that the union would not be refused because of his poverty. Of the same 2,000 Gulden my late brother-in-law received from the beginning as he deposited it not one *Heller* of profit or interest.[63]

Disposable capital of 2,000 fl. may not indicate "poverty", but its importance for the futures of the unmarried daughters is unmistakable. Anna, the widow of Anton Nagl, a Viennese clock-maker, enlisted the assistance of a city secretary to plead for repayment of 1,000 fl, a considerable sum, that constituted her and her children's fortune.[64] In terms reminiscent of Dorothea von Buhel, she objected to Augsburg's legal customs, especially to the *Gewett*, which would result in the "destruction and disadvantage of my capital". Unlike von Buhel, however, no records survive of payments, partial or otherwise, to these claimants.

While the creditors continued to agitate before the Augsburg magistracy and press their defaulting debtors, the Imperial commissioner reconvened on 14 March 1531 at his seat on the Danube. As the opposition between the two groups of creditors remained unbroken, Bishop Christoph "sat in court with his counselors and decreed with verdict and right that the council of Augsburg had judged well: The party that had accepted the contract had appealed wrongly".[65] No creditor could be forced to accept less than payment in full. There would be no negotiated settlement of the Höchstetter bankruptcy.

It had continued for nearly two years without resolution. As the creditors' resentment and distrust increased, conditions worsened for the bankrupts and their families. Since late July 1529, the three imprisoned offenders had remained under loose arrest, confined to a single room in the City Hall, guarded round the clock by ten men, but permitted unlimited visits from wives and servants and boarded and supplied from their own homes. A proposal to lay them in irons had been refused by the creditors. With no prospect of a voluntary settlement, on 28 June 1531, city magistrates ordered them removed from the City Hall to Ambrosius's own house, presumably his palace in the Grottenau section of Augsburg's elite Upper City.

> Around midday on the eve of Sts. Peter and Paul, the council here ordered the three Höchstetters led under arrest by the *Stadtvogt* and four city guards from the city hall to the elder Ambrosius Höchstetter's house, where they were imprisoned together in a single room, and 12 men guarded them

> day and night, and this room served all three as chamber and toilet, and it stank badly. And in this room one laid beds on the floor, upon which they had to sleep. And all other chamber doors in the house were sealed by the *Stadtvogt*, so that the Höchstetters could not flee in secret.[66]

Apart from the demeaning circumstance of having to live together in a single room without sanitary facilities, the entire change signaled a social descent. Father, son and nephew were led through the streets by the city bailiff and four guards. The family's representative dwelling was transformed into a prison with doors sealed and guards stationed.[67] Augsburg demonstrated that the Höchstetters had ceased to be honored members of the community.

Yet the legal tradition of the city – its institutions and organizations – had failed to resolve the bankruptcy. Its *Gewett* had yielded nothing. A single, summary procedure had proven impossible. Much of the capital the Höchstetters possessed had already been sold to pay certain, favored creditors or hidden to escape the claims of the rest. Some, like Dorothea von Buhel, achieved some satisfaction through private appeal and negotiation. The rest were left to wonder what had become of the fantastic wealth of Ambrosius I Höchstetter.

That wealth grew from a rudimentary financial market that existed by virtue of relatively robust information flows, allowing lenders and borrowers to find one another and conclude credit relations. To speak thus generally of "credit relations", however, obscures their variety and fluidity. Certainly, networks played a crucial role in late medieval and early modern finance. Their vitality and importance become apparent in von Buhel's efforts to enforce payment or the commissioners' efforts to reach compromise. They are less apparent over distances and across hierarchies. Without more highly developed organizations to articulate across social and geographic space, the institutions that governed finance, lenders brought to the Höchtetter bankruptcy a variety of assumptions about what capital was and how capital and money markets should function. That institutional failure, the disparity of assumptions about capital, finance and financial markets, doomed to failure all efforts to resolve the Höchstetter bankruptcy.

* * *

Who were the creditors? Sender insisted that they came from all social stations, anyone with a bit of money to deposit or invest. He also identified two groups of creditors: Those who "recognized the damages" and promptly demanded (and received) payment; those who were "careless" and, consequently, demanded payment too late to receive it. His are interesting distinctions. They suggest, on the one hand, that early modern society was generally alert to the opportunities presented by financial markets, and, on the other hand, they were not equally alert to the uncertainties. Sender seems to imply that Höchstetter's insolvency was common knowledge – that the risk of failure and non-payment was known – and only negligence prevented more of the creditors from getting their money.

In an unpublished thesis, completed in 1983, Ulrich Klinkert collated the various lists of persons owed money by the Höchstetters and determined that 193 creditors were owed 470,500 fl in total.[68] There is every reason to believe that these numbers remains incomplete; they exclude creditors who registered their demands too late; they cannot include any creditors who did not come forward at all. It is, in fact, impossible to determine the exact number of creditors or the exact level of debt, because the available sources are incomplete or contradictory.[69] Sender spoke of more than 300 creditors and reckoned the total liability of the Höchstetters to all the creditors, those who were paid and those who were not, at some 1,000,000 fl, an astronomical sum.[70] Ambrosius I set the negative balance at 375,100 fl in his 1528 appeal to Anton Fugger for assistance.[71] According to the creditors' reckoning, Fugger and Ambrosius managed in 1528 and 1529 to pay or guarantee no less than 412,649 fl 14 sh 6 hl, which left 279,904 fl to be settled in bankruptcy proceedings.[72] Hence, taking the creditors' accounting, which was based on Höchstetter's business records, his total indebtedness at the outset of his insolvency amounted to 692,153 fl 14 sh 6 hl, a figure that may still undervalue the total, given the probability of unregistered claims.[73] The creditors expressed bewilderment at the complexity of the calculation and the uncertainty of the result.[74] This fact likely fueled later accusations of fraud.

Klinkert's careful prosopography of the Höchstetter creditors can serve nonetheless as a basis for answering questions about their social relationships and individual identities.[75] He used it to demonstrate his thesis about the centrality of social networks in economic life, specifically to determine the degree to which "foreign capital",[76] that is capital from persons outside the family as defined by lineage and marriage, played a role in late medieval and early modern family firms. It can also serve to shed light on the function of late medieval and early modern financial markets. (See Appendix 2, Höchstetter Creditors.)

Of the 193 creditors from whom Ambrosius and company drew funds and who registered their claims with the city magistracy in 1528 and 1529, 87 (45.1 percent) were resident in Augsburg. Of the Augsburg creditors: 62 (33.5 percent) were members of the "elite",[77] who deposited 217,081 fl (46.2 percent) of all foreign capital; 19 (10.2 percent) were commoners, who deposited 23,924 fl (5.0 percent) of all foreign capital; 6 (3.2 percent) were employees of the firm, who deposited 10,450 fl (2.2 percent) of all foreign capital. In addition to the 87 local creditors, a further 80 (41.5 percent) were not resident in Augsburg. They can be distinguished as follows: 49 (26.5 percent) were commoners, who deposited 94,927 fl (20.1 percent) of all foreign capital; 28 (15.1 percent) were aristocrats or officials, who deposited 97,166 fl (20.6 percent) of all foreign capital; 3 (1.6 percent) were members of the clergy, who deposited 13,600 (2.9 percent) of all foreign capital. Eighteen (10 percent) depositors could not be further identified as to relationship, residence or status.

Of those who registered their claims in 1528 and 1529, 47 percent were local and held 53.4 percent of the firm's capital, while 41.6 percent were foreign and held 40.7 percent of the capital. [78] This represents the Höchstetter dependence on foreign capital, for example, as 20 percent greater than that of the Fugger firm, headed by Anton Fugger.[79] The figures confirm Sender's claim that the creditors came from all ranks of society. It also confirms what scholars have long suspected: The Höchstetters, like other South German capitalists, organized their businesses as family firms, but they relied to a greater than usual extent on foreign capital. Augsburg elites, which included business associates and social connections, contributed substantially to the firm's capitalization, but nonelites did so as well. Nineteen individuals, constituting over 10 percent of all creditors, contributed 23,924 fl, or 5 percent, of the firm's capital, testifying to the widespread resort to financial markets in late medieval and early modern society.

Mercantile companies of that era commonly resorted to foreign capital in the form of fixed-interest deposits. As Robert Schmied noted, however, a degree of caution governed their acceptance and utilization.[80] The financial policies of Jacob II ("the Rich") Fugger make this quite clear.[81] He consciously avoided large, individual deposits and limited the total value of deposit finance. That these policies shaped Fugger capitalization emerges clearly from an inventory completed by Anton Fugger in 1527.[82] Against a family capital of about 2,000,000 fl stood foreign deposits worth only 290,780 fl, of which more than 70 per cent came either from persons related by blood or marriage or from employees of the firm. Clearly, the Fuggers accepted deposits to a restricted extent and preferred deposits from relatives and employees. In 1527, the Fuggers' reliance on foreign capital stood at 15 per cent; the Höchstetters' reliance stood at roughly 84 percent.

The Höchstetters exercised far less caution in this regard. Assuming that Klinkert's accounting of their creditors is correct and that most of their debts took the form of deposits, they held 193 deposits of capital valued at 470,500 fl compared to just under 90,000 fl in start-up capital from the partners at the outset of their insolvency.[83] And the vast majority of these deposits came from persons with no obvious connection to the family or the firm, persons who were neither relatives nor employees. Regrouping the categories makes the discrepancies clearer.[84] The Fugger firm accepted far more deposits from employees than did the Höchstetter, by about 5:1: 27 deposits worth 56,742 fl, compared to 6 deposits worth 10,450 fl. The Fugger firm depended far more on local money markets than did the Höchstetter: 108 deposits worth 508,761 fl, compared to 87 deposits worth 252,175 fl. The Höchstetter firm turned more to foreign money markets: 80 deposits worth 205,643 fl, compared to 46 deposits worth 131,722 fl. Somewhat fewer elites deposited their capital with the Fugger than with the Höchstetter, but their capital was worth more: 74 deposits worth 502,572 fl, compared to 90 deposits worth only 314,967 fl. On the other hand, commoners deposited with both firms to about equal extent: 73 deposits worth 121,889 fl in Fugger accounts, compared to 74 deposits worth 129,301 fl according to Höchstetter records. Unlike the Fuggers, the Höchstetter family firm drew the majority of its capital from outside their immediate circle.

Klinkert stresses the commonalities, however.[85] Like the Fugger and, supposedly, other family businesses of the day, the Höchstetter firm relied essentially on a narrow circle of select investors made up of family members, business associates and local elites. That the Höchstetters drew relatively less of their capital from this group had to do, according to Klinkert, not with a policy of targeting foreigners, as scholars have alleged, but with the fact that the Höchstetter themselves were outsiders, that is, marginal to their social network. The marriage of Ambrosius I to Anna Rehlinger, for example, connected him to a robust network that involved the Rehlingers, Langenmantels, Laugingers and a group of other families – the Arzts, Königsbergers, Wielands and Vogels – that were already intensively linked to one another through social and economic relationships of long standing. The 1527 marriage of his son, Ambrosius II, to Katharina Neumann of Villach, solidified a long-standing commercial relationship with her father, Wilhelm Neumann, an important *Gewerke* and merchant, who maintained active relations with another group of families that were already intensely connected among themselves.[86] Neumann's long-term associate, Hans Pflügl of Salzburg had been married to Neumann's sister. After her death, Pflügl remarried the daughter of Jacob Thenn, the Salzburg *Münzmeister*, who later married the Salzburg jurist, Dr. Nikolaus Ribeisen, who represented Ambrosius in his bankruptcy. All of these men appear among the Höchstetters' creditors. In both instances, through the Rehlinger and Neumann marriages, the Höchstetters became connected but not central to their respective networks, as measured by the relative lack of multiple relationships with families other than Rehlinger and Neumann. As a result, according to Klinkert, the Höchstetters enjoyed less success at raising local capital for their enterprise. They did not choose, but were compelled by a lack of intensely networked relationships, to seek foreign capital. Theirs was not a step toward future possibility, but a concession to present necessity.

Such network-based explanations assume broadly that reliance on close relatives and associates – their familiarity and solidarity – reduced the transaction costs and associated risks of capital investment. The collapse of the Höchstetter family firm can be understood in terms of a smaller social network that compelled them to accept higher costs and risks. At first glance, taking into account only the connections, it would seem to be true. Of those 193 creditors, who were owed no less than 470,568 fl, according to Klinkert, only 30, whose claims totaled 185,679 fl, also had some other form of relationship to the Höchstetters, be it marital or commercial. Put in other terms, 15.5 percent of the creditors, with embedded, that is, multiple and inter-connected relationships to the debtors, claimed 39.4 percent of the total liability. Two were themselves members of the Höchstetter family: Barbara, the daughter of Jacob Höchstetter, who was not involved in the firm, claimed 1,260 fl; Sigmund I, the son of Georg I and a partner from 1515 to 1519, claimed 5,800 fl.[87] Twelve creditors from four families could claim some sort of relationship by marriage to the Höchstetter partners. Wilhelm Neumann, an associate of Ambrosius I and the father-in-law of Ambrosius II, claimed a debt of 8,520 fl.[88] Joachim and Markus Langenmantel, distant relatives of Anna, the wife of Joachim I Höchstetter demanded payment of 7,000 fl and 6,000 fl, respectively.[89] Philipp Adler, the father of Benigna Adler, the late wife of Joseph Höchstetter, claimed 34,100 fl. Most deeply involved were the Rehlingers, the family of Anna, the wife of Ambrosius I. No fewer than nine members of this family, with claims totaling 55,022 fl. appear among the creditors.[90] Five creditors from three families were associates with a variety of social and economic ties to the Höchstetters. Of these, two appear among Ambrosius's suggested, secret advisors. Hans II Paumgartner, a frequent business associate and competitor of the Höchstetters, claimed 23,000 fl owed him.[91] His nephew, Hans Franz Paumgartner, an absconding partner in the insolvent firm and a son-in-law of its principal, demanded payment of 2,000 fl.[92] And Lucas II Rem, distantly related to the disgraced bookkeeper, Bartholomäus III, and a partner of the Höchstetters from 1515 to 1519, joined his brother Andreas to demand repayment of 7,184 fl.[93] The Höchstetters had many dealings with the Fugger firm and family, to whom they owed more than 27,000 fl in 1527, long before Ambrosius I sought Anton's aid.[94] And 12 former partners or employees of the firm or the family claimed a total of 64,250 fl.[95]

Network analysis constitutes, perhaps, the best-established method among economic historians to examine *praxis*, that is, practice within a social setting, and to demonstrate thus indirectly the possible workings of emotional and mental dispositions among economic agents. It relies on the reconstruction of kin and social relationships, often based on detailed prosopographical or transactional compilations, to create formal models of social systems that connect people without acknowledging that the connections themselves might vary in quality or intensity over time.[96] In addition to revealing the spatial and social, network analysis can shed light on such diverse, important issues as mercantile training, business ethics, rational techniques, information exchange and risk management.[97] In these activities, *habitus* and field, individual disposition and social setting, give concrete shape to the social interactions that accompany economic behaviors. Ignoring the dynamic quality of a system of relationships, however, the construction of networks still fails to capture *praxis*.

Given the multiplexity of the Höchstetters' connections – creditor and debtor who were also employer and employee, father- and son-in-law, uncle and niece or husband and wife – the corollary should, according to its advocates, hold: Connected individuals would be more likely to support one another by reducing demands for payment or petitioning the court for mercy. That proves not to be the case, however. Networks are artefacts, constructions created after the fact. At their best, they reveal connections at a single point in time. They say little, however, about the quality of those connections or about their fluidity over time. Even in those instances where a high degree of embeddedness based on a multiplicity of over-lapping connections can be firmly established – for example, when relatives by blood or marriage are also partners or associates in some enterprise – the essential quality of the connection, its intensity and intimacy, its degree of solidarity or trust, the things that determine its meaningfulness, cannot be measured or, in many instances, even assessed. To complicate matters further, connections are diachronic, changing over time, but the construction of networks from them, based on individual transactions, renders them synchronic. Philipp Adler was to prove one of the Höchstetters' most steadfast advocates, helping to transfer their resources and pleading for mercy in their case, despite the size of the debt they owed him. The Rehlingers, patricians with the closest social connections to the Höchstetters, were divided amongst themselves, with some members defending and others attacking the bankrupts. Fugger and Paumgartner, as noted, seized the opportunity of their competitor's insolvency to acquire his capital. Connection does not constitute a relationship; relationship does not explain behavior.

The Höchstetters' reliance on foreign capital complicated the resolution of their bankruptcy. Those creditors who did not reside in Augsburg would be the last to know of their risk and the last to react against it. Residents of the city might have had more immediate, more intimate knowledge of the situation. Sender differentiates the alert from the inattentive, the paid from the unpaid, but such distinctions provide only a partial explanation.

Ambrosius I's 1528 appeal for assistance from Anton Fugger set in motion what the creditors would come to view as a conspiracy that changed everything. Records indicate that, beginning in 1528, Fugger made payments or offered security on the Höchstetters' behalf to no fewer than 45 named individuals, some of whom held multiple notes obligatory. Given that certain accounts are described as being in Ambrosius's hand, it appears that he personally placated a further five. Surviving accounts also refer to some 20 others, unnamed persons or groups who also received payment or surety in this way, raising to 70 the total number of creditors paid in 1528, and rendering unreliable any final analysis of the preferred creditors. They had information about Höchstetter's precarious finances and acted upon it; they were the ones whose demands for payment forced Höchstetter and Fugger to react with payment or surety. As a group, the identifiable, preferred creditors display interesting characteristics. Apart from three members of the landed aristocracy of Swabia and and four members of artisanal guilds, all others, nearly 85 percent, belonged to the political or economic elite of Augsburg. Within this group, the Rehlingers play a central role. Not only were their own members well represented, but more than half of the others, including such names as Arzt, Baumgartner, Eggenberger, Grander, Herwart, Königsberger, Langenmantel, Lauginger, Schellenberger, Walther, Welser and Wieland, maintained ties of blood and marriage to this ancient and extensive patrician clan. The Rehlingers constituted Höchstetter's most important social connection. Yet this alone does not explain why they and their friends loom so large among those preferred creditors who received payment before the bankruptcy. These families were also connected directly to the Fuggers, far more so than to the Höchstetters. Between 15 September 1528 and

10 July 1529, total payments reached 412,649 fl 14 sh 6 hl, as noted.[98] As Anton Fugger made the vast majority of these payments, it seems reasonable to infer that he acted in his own interest. As he systematically leveraged Ambrosius's outstanding debts, acquired capital assets and weakened a dangerous competitor, he also solidified connections within his own social network at the expense of his weakened peer and prey.

Fugger's strategy appears to have extended beyond local elites.[99] He also took care to pay Höchstetter's employees. Specifically named were Hans II Ungelter, a long-term partner, and Thomas König, the bookkeeper. He likewise discharged debts owed to Wilhelm Neumann, not merely father-in-law to Ambrosius II, but a central figure in the mercury trade and the Höchstetters' link to the Salzburg elite.

If as many as 70 creditors received payment in 1528 and 1529, before the start of formal bankruptcy proceedings, then at least 123 did not. Of these, 95 had participated in the *Gewett* of 1529 and reappeared in court to declare the pledge failed and the security forfeit. The non-preferred creditors, those who received no payment, form a far more diverse group than the preferred creditors, who belonged overwhelmingly to the local elite.[100] They cannot be described as common, because they included more than 25 members of the Augsburg elite and more than 20 landed aristocrats and Imperial officials. Nor can the non-preferred creditors be described as unprivileged, because many claimed some sort of special entitlement to immediate payment. These included no fewer than 28 women who tried to enforce repayment on the basis of the "wife's freedom". Seven groups of heirs appealed on the basis of a similar privilege applied to the inheritances of minors. Four civic and ecclesiastical organizations instrumentalized the weight of state and church to make sure that their capital was returned, even if nothing else was. If they were neither common nor unprivileged as a group, the non-preferred and therefore unpaid creditors were also not local. The majority of them lived at a distance from the center of events and the source of information, and this distance seems to have worked to their disadvantage.

Among the 123 nonpreferred creditors, no fewer than 75 had deposited funds with Ambrosius I and company in 1527 and 1528, even as rumors had begun to spread regarding the firm's questionable finances.[101] Characteristics of this group suggest both some of the ways in which financial information circulated in early modern Europe and some of the ways financial risk was assessed and managed. Twelve of these persons were women who invested in their own name and appealed in their own right; six were representatives of testimentary estates, speaking on behalf of groups of heirs; the remainder were men, acting on their own behalf. Of these 57 men, 13 were members of the landed aristocracy and 45 were identified as commoners. Six were Augsburg patricians not engaged in commerce.

These patterns indicate broader recourse to financial markets in late medieval and early modern Europe than is commonly assumed. They reveal that much investment capital was linked to lifecycle events and that access to precise, timely information, upon which the management of risk depended, was not evenly distributed. Rumor of the Höchstetters' decline would have become known first among those persons with most direct access to market information, namely merchants and patricians. These groups are notablely absent among the late depositors, apart from the six patricians who did not get the news. Nobles and commoners, arguably, would have been less likely to have heard of the Höchstetters' difficulty and more likely to continue to deposit with them on the basis of their established reputation for success and solvency. Many of these, all 16 nobles and 23 commoners, were foreigners, further reducing the chances that they would have gotten information on the Höchstetters' changing fortunes. In an age before probability, risk assessment and management turned essentially on the quality of information; foreign capital ran a higher risk due to the greater likelihood that the information guiding it was neither accurate nor current.

By late 1528, the rumors had become harder to miss or to dismiss, and a few depositors and investors – only 41 of the 193 or more identifiable persons, groups or organizations that had extended funds to Höchstetter and 19 of the 75 who had placed money with him at the last minute – sought to withdraw their funds.[102] The majority of these cautious creditors were male Augsburgers of common stock. Four of the six patricians who had invested in 1527 or 1528 likewise sought to rescue their capital before it was too late. One would expect Ambrosius I to have responded to these requests quickly and positively in order to create an appearance of solvency and to prevent a more general panic. One would expect further that he would have urged Fugger to do the same. To refuse demands for repayment of capital and interest would have been tantamount to admitting the validity of the rumors, announcing his bankruptcy and thus reducing any possibility of financial survival. It is interesting to note, therefore, that only 24 of the 41 received payment.[103] Ambrosius saw to Ulrich and Lucas Welser, who received payments in full, totaling 2,000 and 600 fl, respectively.[104] Their demands were relatively modest, but their family was powerful in city hall and marketplace. Fugger purchased the debts of the remaining 22. He did not always pay the full amounts they claimed. In 11 instances, involving two patricians, two merchants and seven commoners, all from Augsburg, he discounted the debts. Dr. Johann Rehlinger, for example, the Augsburg *Stadtsyndikus*, a potent figure in Augsburg and closely connected to the Höchstetters, received from Fugger only 7,000 of the 14,750 fl he demanded in 1528 and 1529.[105] Six of those underpaid creditors would continue to press their claims years into the formal bankruptcy; of the other five no clear information exists. By contrast, Fugger overpaid to acquire four debts. Philipp Adler, whose close connections to Höchstetter would involve him in the later course of the bankruptcy, sought in 1528 repayment of 8,100 and received in 1529 26,000 fl, a spectacular difference.[106] In only seven instances did Fugger pay exactly the amount demanded by the creditor. One noteworthy example, Anna Thurzo, née Fugger, claimed and received 16,000 fl.[107] Questions of reasoning cannot be answered with finality. It seems clear that some discounting occurred. Other assets or social considerations may have played a role in individual instances.

The pattern of his payments strengthens the impression of self-interested motives on Fugger's part. In a manner reminiscent of the financial structure of his family firm, he preferred to assume the debts of those Höchstetter creditors who were themselves socially or politically prominent. That pattern also confirms the advantage of local over foreign creditors. Customary bankruptcy procedures in Augsburg specified that any creditors who did not appear in court to register their claims on the first day of proceedings would be excluded from participation, unless they could show to the magistrate's satisfaction that they had not known of the proceedings or had been unable to attend.[108] Unlike developments in the Low Countries, as demonstrated by Gelderblom, Augsburg undertook no legal reforms to ease the plight of foreigners engaged in commerce or finance in the city. That this increased the costs and risks for foreigners in Augsburg's markets or its courts seems likely.

The reasoning that guided investment in the past may lie beyond the historian's – to say nothing of the economic historian's – ken. Why did Ambrosius I and Fugger seek capital beyond the resources of their own extended families? A rationalist answer would probably include references to ambitious enterprises, planned growth and increasing costs. Why did depositors invest their capital with merchant-bankers? Again, a rationalist response would probably include references to a reputation for profit or a miscalculation of risk. These are not historical explanations, however; few documents – none in these cases – contain direct answers.

The risks associated with foreign capital raise a further set of questions. How did foreigners come to know about the Höchstetter or Fugger firm? How did the firms solicit their funds? The surviving records provide likewise few direct answers to any of these questions. Some of depositors indicated that they invested dowries or inheritances, funds that had substantial significance in the lifecycle of persons or families, in so far as they were needed to assure the future marriage of daughters or the survival of widows and orphans.[109] Given that such investors were likely to be risk-averse, unwiling to jeopardize the future survival of their families, their willingness to deposit funds with a firm rested at least in part on the reputation of the firm and its partners, whatever other considerations might have come into play. Yet documents speak only indirectly to the mechanics of investment, that is, to the flow of information, the assessment of risk and, consequently, the selection among options. Dorothea von Buhel offers a case in point. The very fact that nearly half of the depositors resided in places outside Augsburg indicates, however, that the dangers of foreignness – the chance that geographical distance might distort or delay information, the likelihood that alien status might endanger repayment – might influence but did not determine their calculations.

Many factors shaped credit-debt relations in early modern Europe. Social relationships played a substantial role – so did information, especially in long-distance transactions. That Höchstetter depositors came from as far away as the Mark of Brandenburg or the Archduchy of Austria suggests much about the expansion and penetration of financial markets. Clearly, institutions and organizations existed to create and enforce the obligations of credit over space and time, but they remained far from efficient. Are these factors unique to early modern finance? New technologies have reduced distance and time to matters of milli-, even nanoseconds. Yet, profits and losses recorded on global exchanges still capture the effects of foreign versus local transactions. Differing legal structures continue to make some capital markets riskier than others. Insiders – those who possess special knowledge of or connection to particular traders or transactions – continue to profit beyond the winnings of open-market investors or depositors. Even moral considerations play a role in modern finance by virtue of their influence on regulation, if not on behavior. In many ways, the Höchstetter bankruptcy captures the modern in premodern capitalism.

★ ★ ★

Economists and historians usually define family firms in terms of a single family's engagement in a given enterprise; a family firm is privately held and owner managed. In other words, a single family holds all or the majority of its capital and provides all or the majority of its direction. In consequence, a family firm affected all members of the family, not only those immediately engaged in it, and could be affected by members of the family not immediately engaged in it. At only one point does the Höchstetter firm correspond to this definition: It provided the majority of the management. Most of the firm's resources came from beyond the circle of the family and its immediate relations. In fact, the majority of Höchstetter family and friends were not engaged in the firm or affected by its fate in any obvious way. The Höchstetters had a family firm only if the definition of family is reduced anachronisitically to the isolated, nuclear household.

Most of their operating capital – most creditors – came from outside the family, from persons other than relatives by blood or marriage. And most of them suffered loss due to the Höchstetter bankruptcy. Of 193 identifiable creditors, of whom approximately 70 were paid either by Ambrosius I or Anton Fugger in 1529, no fewer than 123 gave no indication of any payment at all. At least 95 of the 123 creditors who gave no indication of any payment at all continued to demand it throughout the bankruptcy proceedings. These individuals, groups and organizations coalesced into the body of creditors that petitioned the City Government of Augburg in July 1529, seeking remittance of their debts and arrest of their debtors.

These nonpreferred creditors do not correspond, as a group, to the expected pattern of finance in the age of merchant capitalism.[110] The majority are neither elite nor local. Some claimed ordinary business debts, such as the Idrian mine operators, who demanded over 70,000 fl for delivered mercury and cinnabar. The vast majority appear to have been depositors, however, who came from all levels and all groups of society and who expected a safe return on their accumulated capital. That fact should surprise no one; it certainly did not surprise contemporaries. Writing in 1523, in response to a proposed prohibition on depositing money in mercantile companies, the Augsburg jurist Conrad Peutinger wrote:

> Common law forbids no one to accept money in his business, whether against interest or in some other way, unless it be an investment at profit and loss. In these hard times, not everyone wants to get into shares at profit and loss or to purchase real estate, but finds it more comfortable to invest their money at an appropriate rate of interest, in order to be able to withdraw it at will and to use it according to their own convenience to endow sons and daughters. There are many upright people, from various social strata, even noblemen, burghers, orphans and others, who neither practice nor understand any trade, who do not serve, nor are in a position to provide their own sustenance, apart from the interest and usage of their capital [sic]. And when they have cash left lying about that they might wish to invest in real estate, they cannot easily purchase the same, because where real estate is offered for sale, it is always snapped up at such high prices that one can very seldom acquire real estate at tolerable prices [. . .]. Were one to place these decent men at a disadvantage by such a godless measure as to forbid them to invest their money at interest with merchants and thus to force them to consume their own capital or to slide into loss, it would be contrary to the common good and the the ruin of many estates of the German nation.[111]

Noteworthy is Peutinger's observation that so many people, even very humble persons, placed funds in financial markets and that they did so after reckoning the benefits and costs – the risks – of various forms of investment. They understood the dynamism of capital, took advantage of it, and the "nation" profited from it. Here is a reflection on the lived experience of financial capitalism that extended beyond the mercantile elite and involved complex calculations and mechanisms long before such things were supposed to have existed at all.

The behaviors of the bankrupts and their creditors, their often-tenuous connections and obscure relationships among one another, all reveal much of the workings of financial markets and financial capitalism in late medieval and early modern Europe. What they reveal does not conform to expectation. Financial activities penetrated further and involved more people than expected: Foreign and local, low and high, female and male. Accumulated earnings and lifecycle transfers provided much of the capital. Investments did not always yield profits, but they resulted from some sort of rational calculation. Sender appears not to have exaggerated. In consequence of these observations, three, what might be called structural, characteristics begin to crystallize. First, the relative importance of social networks in shaping credit-debt relations appears to have been overdrawn in relationship both to financial markets and to family firms. Networks play a substantial role to be sure, but that role has less predictive and less explanatory value than has been recently argued, especially over distance or across society, where personal connections might be attenuated. More important, second, was information. Financial markets turned on information that traveled widely, but slowly and imperfectly. On the basis of that information, financial techniques were surprisingly sophisticated. One touchstone of modern economic life, at least according to some recent scholars, double-entry bookkeeping, appears not to have been widely practiced, but late medieval and early modern merchant-financiers achieved nonetheless a surprisingly accurate sense of cash flow and current value, even over time and space. They engaged in leveraging, discounting and options trading as a matter of course. In doing so, third, they displayed a sense of risk without any mathematical assessment of it. It appears that they learned this by experience, watching and emulating their colleagues. They learned through practice, not solely or even necessarily by studying, but by doing.

Notes

1 Clemens Sender, *Die Chronik von Clemens Sender von den ältesten Zeiten der Stadt bis zum Jahre 1536. Die Chroniken der schwäbischen Städte. Augsburg*, vol. IV (Leipzig 1894), 219.
2 Ibid., 223–4.
3 Sender records an outbreak of the "*englischer Schweiß*" that killed many in Augsburg. Also known as "*englische Schweißkrankeit*" and "*sudor anglicus*," it appeared for the first time in 1485 in England – hence the name – and recurred throughout Europe five times before disappearing suddenly in 1551. The symptoms were flu-like in the first stage, followed by massive sweating, a racing pulse and great thirst, usually ending in death. The exact causes of the disease remain unknown, although recent research points to a strain of Hanta virus. See Ibid., 224.
4 Ibid., 224.
5 StAA, Schuld-, Klag- und Appellationsakten, Teil 2, Karton XIV, Doc. 5.
6 Ibid., Doc. 6.
7 Ibid., Doc. 7.
8 Ibid., Doc. 8.
9 Ibid., Doc. 9.
10 Sender, *Die Chronik*, 219.
11 Richard Ehrenberg, *Das Zeitalter der Fugger: Geldkapital und Kreditverkehr im 16. Jahrhundert*, vol. I, 2 vols. (Jena 1896), 212–18; Jacob Strieder, *Das Reiche Augsburg: Ausgewählte Aufsätze zur Augsburger und süddeutschen Wirtschaftsgeschichte* (Munich 1938), 95–101.
12 Ehrenberg, *Das Zeitalter der Fugger*, I: 212.
13 Götz, Freiherr von Pölnitz, *Anton Fugger*, vol. I, 4 vols. (Tubingen 1958–86), 652. See also Hartmut Schiele and Manfred Ricker, *Betreibswirtschaftliche Aufschlüsse aus der Fuggerzeit* (Berlin 1967), 26; Wolfgang Zorn, *Augsburg: Geschichte einer deutschen Stadt* (Augsburg 1972), 175; Günter Ogger, *Kauf die einen Kaiser: Die Geschichte der Fugger* (Munich 1980), 75.
14 Ulrich Klinkert, "Die Augsburger Handelsgesellschaft der Höchstetter. Zusammenbruch 1529, Gläubiger und soziale Verflechtung" (Hausarbeit, Universität Augsburg 1983), 6.
15 Peer-to-peer lending is exactly what the term indicates: The extension of credit between equals, be they companies or individuals. Factor financing is a type of debtor finance in which a business raises short-term capital by selling its accounts receivable to a third party (called a factor) at a discount.
16 Herein lay the risk that risk-averse depositors seemed unable to comprehend. Should these secondary loans fail for whatever reason, the merchant-banking house might not be able to repay deposit and interest within the specified term.

17 Nial Ferguson, *The Ascent of Money: A Financial History of the World* (New York 2008); Fritz E. Heichelcheim, *An Ancient Economic History*, 2 vols. (Leiden 1965); Charles P. Kindleberger, *A Financial History of Western Europe* (London 1984).

18 Reinhold C. Mueller, *The Venetian Money Market: Banks, Panics, and the Public Debt, 1200–1500* (Baltimore 1997), esp. Pt. IV, 359–450.

19 Richard A. Goldthwaite, *The Economy of Renaissance Florence* (Baltimore 2009), 408–83.

20 Violet Barbour, *Capitalism in Amsterdam in the 17th Century* (Ann Arbor 1963); Jonathan Barron Baskin, "The Development of Corporate Financial Markets in Britain and the United States, 1600–1914: Overcoming Asymmetric Information," *Business History Review* 62 (1988): 199–237; P. G. M. Dickson, *The Financial Revolution in England: A Study of the Development of Public Credit, 1688–1756* (New York 1967); Kindleberger, *A Financial History of Western Europe*; Larry Neal, *The Rise of Financial Capitalism: International Capital Markets in the Age of Reason* (New York 1990); George David Smith and Richard Sylla, *The Transformation of Financial Capitalism: An Essay on the History of American Capital Markets* (Cambridge, MA 1993); Woodruff D. Smith, "The Function of Commercial Centers in the Modernization of European Capitalism: Amsterdam as an Information Exchange in the Seventeenth Century," *Journal of Economic History* 44 (1984): 985–1005; J. Sperling, "The International Payments Mechanism in the Seventeenth and Eighteenth Centuries," *Economic History Review* 14 (1961): 446–68; Charles Wilson, *Anglo-Dutch Commerce and Finance in the Eighteenth Century* (Cambridge, UK 1966).

21 It is interesting to consider this apparent surfeit of capital in light of the recently argued thesis that this period was marked by economic deflation caused in large part by a decreasing money supply, itself caused in turn by a decreasing supply of monetary silver. Cf. Philipp Robinson Rössner, *Deflation – Devaluation – Rebellion: Geld Im Zeitalter Der Reformation* (Stuttgart 2012).

22 Oscar Gelderblom, *Cities of Commerce: The Institutional Foundations of International Trade in the Low Countries, 1250–1650* (Princeton 2013), 45–53 and passim.

23 Friedrich Blendinger, *Zwei Augsburger Unterkaufbücher aus den Jahren 1551 bis 1558: Älteste Aufzeichnungen zur Vor- und Frühgeschichte der Augsburger Börse* (Stuttgart 1994).

24 For further discussion of the *Unterkäufel* and their role in financial markets, see Friedrich Blendinger, *Zwei Augsburger Unterkaufbücher aus den Jahren 1551 bis 1558*; Bernd Fuhrmann, *Mit barer Münze: Handel im Mittelalter* (Darmstadt 2010); Peter Geffken, "Kaufleutestube," in: *Augsburger Stadtlexikon Online* (Augsburg 2010). Available at: www.wissner.com/stadtlexikon-augsburg/artikel/stadtlexikon/kaufleutestube/4359; Gerhard Hetzer and Wolfgang Zorn, "Augsburger Börse," in: *Augsburger Stadtlexikon Online* (Augsburg 2010). Available at: www.wissner.com/stadtlexikon-augsburg/artikel/stadtlexikon/boerse/3374.

25 In Augsburg, wholesale merchants and merchant-bankers traditionally met to conduct business in the arcade that stood at the foot of the Perlach, the city's bell tower near the City Hall. This was too public a venue for sensitive conversation and negotiation, however. When the merchant association (*Kaufleutestubengesellschaft*) acquired its "drinking hall" (*Kaufleutestube*), first in rented rooms near the city's wine market around 1480, then in a dedicated house in 1548, that place assumed many of the functions of a bourse. See Pius Dirr, "Kaufleutezunft und Kaufleutestube in Augsburg zur Zeit des Zunftregiments," *Zeitschrift des Historischen Vereins für Schwaben* 35 (1909): 132–51.

26 Blendinger, *Zwei Augsburger Unterkaufbücher aus den Jahren 1551 bis 1558*, 14.

27 Ibid., 17–18.

28 Pius Dirr, "Kaufleutezunft und Kaufleutestube in Augsburg"; Wolfgang Zorn and Leonhard Hillenbrand, *Sechs Jahrhunderte schwäbische Wirtschaft: 125 Jahre Industrie- und Handelskammer Augsburg; Beiträge zur Geschichte der Wirtschaft im bayerischen Regierungsbezirk Schwaben* (Augsburg 1969), 54–65.

29 Anton Mayr, *Die großen Augsburger Vermögen 1618 bis 1717* (Augsburg 1931); Jakob Strieder, *Zur Genesis des modernen Kapitalismus: Forschungen zur Entstehung der großen*

bürgerlichen Kapitalvermögen am Ausgange des Mittelalters und zu Beginn der Neuzeit, zunächst in Augsburg (Leipzig 1935); Götz Freiherr von Pölnitz, "Augsburger Kaufleute und Bankherren der Renaissance," in: Hermann Rinn, et al. (eds.), *Augusta 955–1955: Forschungen und Studien zur Kultur- und Wirtschaftsgeschichte Augsburgs* (Munich 1955), 187–218; Friedrich Blendinger, "Die wirtschaftlichen Führungsschichten in Augsburg 1430–1740," in: Herbert Helbig (ed.), *Führungskräfte der Wirtschaft in Mittelalter und Neuzeit, 1350–1850*, vol. I, 2 vols. (Limburg an der Lahn 1973), 51–86; Gunther Gottlieb, et al. (eds.), *Geschichte der Stadt Augsburg: 2000 Jahre von der Römerzeit bis zur Gegenwart* (Stuttgart 1985), 166–71, 171–81, 258–301.

30 Pius Dirr, "Zur Geschichte der Augsburger Zunftverfassung 1368–1548," *Zeitschrift des Historischen Vereins für Schwaben und Neuburg* 39 (1913): 144–243; Pius Dirr, "Kaufleutezunft und Kaufleutestube in Augsburg"; Olaf Mörke and Katharina Sieh, "Gesellschaftliche Führungsgruppen," in: Gunther Gottlieb, et al. (eds.), *Geschichte der Stadt Augsburg*, 302 f.; Fritz Peter Geffcken, "Soziale Schichtung in Augsburg 1396–1521" (1995, München Diss. 1983), 223 ff., 227–30; Jörg Rogge, *Für den gemeinen Nutzen. Politisches Handeln und Politikverständnis von Rat und Bürgerschaft in Augsburg im Spätmittelalter* (Tubingen 1996), 184–209.

31 Scholarship has brought forward the importance of oral promises and the consequent reliance on reputation and the problem of enforcement for quotidian, consumer lending in early modern communities. The capital needs of wholesale, long-distance commerce had to be met in more formal ways. Cf. Craig Muldrew, *The Economy of Obligation: The Culture of Credit and Social Relations in Early Modern England* (London 1998).

32 StAA, Schuld-, Klag- und Appellationsakten, Teil 2, Karton XIV, Doc. 10, 11.

33 "*dann es je zuerbaremen wer das die arme kinder die sonnst nit vil habenn umb das jr also kommen sollten*". Ibid., Doc. 12.

34 Ibid., Doc. 13.

35 "*sollchs gewette sie nichts angeen oder damit zuschaffenn hab auch sie unnd jre kinder unter euren gerichtszwanng nit gehoren auch euer vermainte nichtige freyhait ob jr oder euer richter wider ganntz offenbar schulden unnd rechtmessige verschreibung hetten ganntz nichts pinde*". Ibid., Doc. 14.

36 Ibid., Doc. 16.

37 Ibid., Doc. 17.

38 Ibid., Doc. 19.

39 Ibid., Doc. 21, 30.

40 Ibid., Doc. 25.

41 Ibid., Doc. 22.

42 Ibid., Doc. 27, 28.

43 Sender, *Die Chronik*, 224–34.

44 Ibid.

45 Ibid., 224.

46 Ibid., 225–6.

47 Ibid., 226.

48 Ibid.

49 Ibid., 227.

50 Ibid., 230.

51 Ibid., 231.

52 Ibid., 234. The German, *Unmut*, possesses multiple meanings that range, according to both Duden and Grimm, from vexation to discomfort to embarrassment to despair. Senders use of the term signals that the the wives' deaths resulted from the shattering emotional or psychological impact of the bankruptcy, the absence of their husbands and the loss of their property.

53 Ibid., 224.

54 StAA, Schuld-, Klag- und Appellationsakten, Teil 2, Karton XIV, Doc. 31.

55 "*wie woll wir sollichs zuthun nit schuldig gewesen auch dessen kainen nutz gehapthaben jr auch daran wiewoll mit grossem mercklichen Schaden und Nachtail tausent Fulden entricht und bezalt und wolten noch nichts liebers thun dann sy zu friden stellen und entrichten dann wiewol die endtmitl zwischen den Herrn Glaubigern und unser Ergangen so haben wir doch kainer Execution derselben noch ainicher Relaxierung und entschlagung unserer verbottnen gueter bisher bekommen noegen*". Ibid., Doc. 32.

56 Ibid., Doc. 33.

57 Sender, *Die Chronik*, 234.

58 Ibid., 235.

59 It is, in fact, remarkable that Charles agreed to hear this dispute at all, because he truly had "other difficult affairs" to manage. He requested the 1530 Diet of Augsburg to resolve three issues: The defense of the empire and of all Europe against the Ottoman Turks; the policy of the empire concerning welfare; and the currency and the resolution of the schism within Christianity. Under Suleiman the Magnificent, Ottoman forces had nearly seized Vienna in 1529, and Charles needed a united Christendom to defend against this rising power. Unity had proven elusive, however, since the condemnation of Luther's teachings after the Diet of Worms in 1518. Distracted by his wars against France and his commitments elsewhere in his vast Empire, Charles had failed to focus on the German religious problem. The 1529 peace with France permitted him to turn his attention to this situation. One result was the formulation of The Augsburg Confession by Philipp Melanchthon, which was read at the Diet and intended to be a basis of reconciliation between Evangelical reformers and Roman eccclesiastics.

60 Sender, *Die Chronik*, 235.

61 "*Ewer fursichtige ersame weysheit ist gut wissen wie lang jetzung ain gantz jar verschinen das Ambrosius Höchstetter der Ellter für sich und seine Mitverwandten allen jren Gläubigern vor offnen Statgericht allhie zu Augsburg verwettet hatt, auf sollich Gewett hette sich nach der Stat Gebrauch geburt, furderlichen Volziehung zuthun, welcher Gestalt aber wir allweg mit grosser Vertrosstung gutiger Hanndlung unnd Vereinigung von einem Tag auff den andern mit grosem unnsern Nachtail unnd Schaden aufgehallten worden ist*". StAA, Schuld-, Klag- und Appellationsakten, Teil 2, Karton XIV. Supplik, 9. August 1530.

62 "*Dieweil dann sollich ob anzaigt gelt der mertail meiner lieben hausfrawen vätterlich und muterlich erb unnd ir zupracht heyratsgut ist, und wo ich darumb komen sölt, mir meinem weib unnd lieben Kinden zu unwiderbringklichem verderplichem unnd ewigem schaden raichen würde, so ist [. . .] mein ganz fraintlich unnd underdiennstlich pit sie wölln [. . .] hilff unnd beystannd thun*". StAA, Literaliensammlung, Höchstetter-Selekt, II, fol. 181. Also cited in Klinkert, "Die Augsburger Handelsgesellschaft der Höchstetter," 118.

63 "*Unnd hat erstlich dise sach die gestalt, als weilendt Moritz von Altmanshoven seliger gedechtnus, mein freindtlicher, lieber schwager, dess verlassen eeliche Wittfrau, meiner Hausfrauen eeleipliche Schwester vonn baiden Bannden ist, inn Zeit seins lebens zzway tausent guldin zu gemellten Höchstettern unnd seinen mitverwanndten inn ansehnung das er dreie gewachsen Döchter, bey Ime vorhannden gehapt unnd die muter noch bey Ir unverheurat hat, ob jme etwan ain glückh mit ainem heurat der ainen oder zwayer döchtern zugestannden, das er sy dar auff zu versichern, damit der Heurat nit auß anseung seiner armut, sich entschlagen möcht, von denselbigen zwaytausent guldin Hauptguts, hat mein Schwager seliger von anfang, wie er die erlegt werden, keinen Heller nuts, noch Zins nie empfangen*". StAA, Literaliensammlung, Höchstetter-Selekt, II, fol. 398. Also cited in Klinkert, "Die Augsburger Handelsgesellschaft der Höchstetter," 118.

64 StAA, Schuld-, Klag- und Appellationssachen, Teil 2, Karton XIV, Dok. 40. Antonio Urmachers Wittib gegen Hochstetter, 6 December 1530.

65 Sender, *Die Chronik*, 235.

66 Ibid., 235–6.

67 The city recorded the costs of this new imprisonment. Expense accounts refer to 20 guards, rather than 12, at 14 fl for eight days. See StAA, Baurechnungen, 1531, fol. 71r.

68 Klinkert, "Die Augsburger Handelsgesellschaft der Höchstetter," 47.

69 No master lists, as would be preserved in the *Geheim* or *Zinsbücher* of any firm survived the bankruptcy. Ambrosius I created three lists for Anton Fugger, an "*Abgekündigtes Geld*", an "*Auszug von Quecksilber und Zinnober*" and a "*Beschluß alter Handlung*", in 1528, as part of his appeal for Fugger's aid in avoiding bankruptcy. Also, a 1529 deed of sale of the estate Jenbach by the Höchstetters to the Fuggers lists the creditors the Fuggers committed to pay as part of the price. These are located in the FA, 2,2,1 / 5–7 and 40, 1. Other surviving documents are extracts from materials seized by the Augsburg City Court in 1529: Lists of depositors in 1527 and 1528, list of depositors paid by the Fugger or provided security in 1528 and 1529, a list of creditors who demanded payment in 1528, a supplication by foreign creditors in 1529, an attestation in 1529 by foreign creditors of their demands and a list of creditors in 1531. These documents are located in StAA, Literaliensammlung, Höchstetter-Selekt I, fol. 329–32, Literaliensammlung, Höchstetter-Selekt II, fol. 2–7, 13–20, 362 and Reichsstadt Strafamt 47, Stadtgerichtbuch 1531, 59–65.

70 Sender, *Die Chronik*, 219.

71 FA, Handel 2,2.1, fol. 6.

72 The Augsburg City Court recorded that the total, unpaid claims of all creditors, who had participated in the *Gewett* of 1529, stood just over 293,071 fl in 1531. StAA, Reichsstadt Strafamt, Stadtgerichtsbuch, 1531, fol. 65v.

73 StAA. Literaliensammlung, Höchstetter-Selekt I, Dok. 1, Welcher Glaubiger von den Hoechstettern oder jrn Hausfrawen vergnug und verwisen zu woelcher Zeit bei wem und umb was Gellt.

74 "*Jnn disem Ausszug werden demnach nit gemeldt die 87186 fl. 16 sh. 0 hl. so Hoechstetter uff Ausweisungen von Fugger Paumgartner unnd annders uffgenommen, dann man nit Wissen hat, were damit bezallt worden*". Ibid.

75 Klinkert, "Die Augsburger Handelsgesellschaft der Höchstetter," 45–120.

76 A word about terminology: "Foreign capital" is in many ways an inadequate, misleading term. While a direct translation of the German cognate, *Fremdkapital*, it lacks the breadth of application, the multiplicity of meanings. In the context of financial history, "foreign capital" can refer to capital that comes from all external sources, e.g., beyond the biological family/lineage (exogenous capital), beyond marital alliances (non-marital capital), beyond social equals (non-peer capital), beyond residents of the same political entity (in the strict sense, foreign capital) or from political persons or entities (state capital) to name be a few possibilities. Each of these distinct sources of capital suggests possibly distinct aspects of financial markets that merit examination and comparison. With particular reference to the Höchstetters and their bankruptcy, "foreign capital" refers solely to exogenous and non-marital capital, capital from outside the family. It leaves aside all other possible meanings, e.g., capital from foreigner. The use of "foreign capital" in this work is thus a term of art, the limitations of which are here acknowledged.

77 Klinkert defined elites as those who paid 10 fl or more annually in taxes, claimed the right as patricians or members of the more powerful guilds – *Kaufleute, Salzfertiger* and *Weber* – to a place in the city government or belonged to the recognized prestige groups, the *Herren* and *Mehrer der Gesellschaft*. See Klinkert, "Die Augsburger Handelsgesellschaft der Höchstetter," 106. This definition is not original, however, relying on the work of other social historians. See Ingrid Batori, "Das Patriziat der deutsche Stadt: Zu den forschungsergebnissen über das Patriziat besonders der süddeutschen Städte," *Zeitschrift für Stadtgeschichte, Stadtsoziologie und Denkmalspflege* 2 (1975): 5; Rolf Kießling, *Bürgerliche Gesellschaft und Kirche in Augsburg im Spätmittelalter: Ein Beitrag zur Strukturanalyse der oberdeutschen Reichsstadt* (Augsburg 1971), 44f.

78 Klinkert, "Die Augsburger Handelsgesellschaft der Höchstetter," 45–120.

79 Anton Fugger and company display a different profile. They drew funds from 173 foreign depositors of whom 108 – far more than the Höchstetters – were resident in Augsburg:

52 (30 percent) were elites, who deposited 428,024 fl (65.2 percent) of all foreign capital; 29 (16.7 percent) were commoners, who deposited 23,995 fl (3.6 percent) of all foreign capital; 27 (15.6 percent) were employees of the firm, who deposited 56,742 fl (8.6 percent) of all foreign capital. Another 46 were foreign: 17 (9.8 percent) were commoners, who deposited 41,152 fl (6.2 percent) of all foreign capital; 22 (12.7 percent) were aristocrats or officials, who deposited 74,598 fl (11.3 percent) of all foreign capital; 7 (4.0 percent) were members of the clergy, who deposited 15,972 fl (2.4 percent) of all foreign capital. Twenty depositors could not be further identified. See Klinkert, "Die Augsburger Handelsgesellschaft der Höchstetter," 107–8.

80 Robert Schmied, *Kapitalbeschaffungsformen des Frühkapitalismus. Die Formen der Kapitalbeschaffung und der Vergrösserung des Eigenkapitals der frühkapitalistischen Kaufleute und Handelsgesellschaften des 15. und 16. Jarhunderts* (Berlin 1936), 72.

81 The loss of capital that followed the death in 1509 of Cardinal Melchior von Meckau, who had deposited more than 200,000 fl with "Ulrich Fugger and Brothers" in 1496, which had to be paid out to his heirs, brought the company to the verge of collapse and convinced Jakob II to limit the degree to which his family firm relied on such resources in the future. See Götz Freiherr von Pölnitz, *Jakob Fugger und der Streit um den Nachlaß des Kardinals Melchior von Brixen* (Bonn 1940).

82 After 1527, under the leadership of Anton, the Fugger firm loosened its policy regarding deposits. The number of foreign depositors rose from 82 worth 290,780 fl in 1527 to 173 worth 656,356 fl in 1533. See Klinkert, "Die Augsburger Handelsgesellschaft der Höchstetter," 102–3; Jakob Strieder (ed.), *Die Inventur der Firma Fugger aus dem Jahre 1527* (Tübingen 1905), 65ff.

83 The difference between depositors and investors needs to be kept in mind. Depositors deposited a fixed sum of money for a fixed period of time in the hands of a merchant-bank, for which they received a fixed rate of interest. At the conclusion of the set period of time, capital and interest were repaid. Investors, by contrast, invested a fixed sum. Their capital was at risk of profit or loss, according to the fortunes of the merchant-bank. Investors in the Höchstetter firm would have been hesitant to claim their investments, because the limited liability which would have protected them from the claims of other creditors had not yet been introduced in Augsburg. Klinkert, "Die Augsburger Handelsgesellschaft der Höchstetter," 104.

84 Ibid., 107–8.

85 Ibid., 119–20.

86 Ibid., 116.

87 StAA, Reichsstadt Strafamt 47, Stadtgerichtbuch 1531, 62v, 64v. See also Klinkert, "Die Augsburger Handelsgesellschaft der Höchstetter," 66.

88 StAA, Reichsstadt Strafamt 47, Stadtgerichtbuch 1531, 64r.

89 FA, 2,2,1/7; StAA, Literaliensammlung, Höchstetter-Selekt II, 13–16; StAA, Reichsstadt Strafamt 47, Stadtgerichtbuch 1531, 62r, 65v.

90 FA, 2,2,1/7; FA, 40,1; StAA, Literaliensammlung, Höchstetter-Selekt II, 2–7, 13–16, 17–20; StAA, Reichsstadt Strafamt 47, Stadtgerichtbuch 1531, 62r, 65v.

91 StAA, Literaliensammlung, Höchstetter-Selekt II, 2–7.

92 Ibid.

93 Ibid.

94 Höchstetter, *Stammtafel der Höchstetter*, 77, 83.

95 FA, 2,2,1/7; StAA, Literaliensammlung, Höchstetter-Selekt II, 2–7; StAA, Reichsstadt Strafamt 47, Stadtgerichtbuch 1531, 63v. See also Klinkert, "Die Augsburger Handelsgesellschaft der Höchstetter," 49–101.

96 Mark Häberlein, *Brüder, Freunde und Betrüger. Soiale Beziehungen, Normen und Konflikte in der Augsburger Kaufmannschaft um die Mitte des 16. Jahrhunderts* (Berlin 1998); Margrit Schulte Beerbühl, et al. (eds.), *Spinning the Commercial Web. International Trade, Merchants, and Commercial Cities, c. 1640–1939* (Frankfurt Main 2004).

97 See, for example, Franco Angiolini and Daniel Roche (eds.), *Cultures et formations négociantes dans l'Europe moderne* (Paris 1995); Natacha Coquery, et al., (eds.), *Ecrire, compter, mesurer. Vers une histoire des rationalités pratiques* (Paris 2006); Martin Fiedler, "Vertrauen ist gut, Kontrolle ist teuer: Vertrauen als Schlüsselkategorie wirtschaftlichen Handelns," *Geschichte und Gesellschaft* 27 (2001): 576–92; Ute Frevert (ed.), *Vertrauen: Historische Annäherungen* (Göttingen 2003); Wolfgang Kaiser and Biagio Salvemini (eds.), "Informazione e scelte economiche," *Quaderni storici* 42 (2007); Paola Lanaro (ed.), *La pratica dello scambio. Sistemi di fiere, mercanti e città* (Venice 2203); Craig Muldrew, *The Economy of Obligation: The Culture of Credit and Social Relations in Early Modern England* (New York 1998); Katia Occhi, *Boschi e mercanti. Traffici di legname tra la contea di Tirolo e la Repubblica di Venezia (secoli XVI-XVII)* (Bologna 2006).

98 StAA, Literaliensammlung, Höchstetter-Selekt I, Dok. 1.

99 Ibid.

100 Klinkert, "Die Augsburger Handelsgesellschaft der Höchstetter," passim. The following discussion is based largely on his findings, supplemented by my own researches in the same archival documents.

101 StAA, Literaliensammlung, Höchstetter-Selekt I, fol. 13–16, 17–20.

102 The highest figure of 190 is based on the painstaking research of Ulrich Klinkert in the social connections among Höchstetter's creditors. It represents the totals drawn from all the surviving nominal lists of creditors. The lesser figures were drawn up by the unfavored creditors as part of their prosecution of the Höchstetters in bankruptcy. See Klinkert, "Die Augsburger Handelsgesellschaft der Höchstetter," 45–101. See also StAA, Literaliensammlung, Höchstetter-Selekt I, fol. 2–7, 13–20; FA, Handel 2, 2.1, fol. 7.

103 StAA Literaliensammlung, Höchstetter-Selekt I, fol. 2–7.

104 FA, Handel 2, 2.1, fol. 7; StAA Literaliensammlung, Höchstetter-Selekt I, fol. 2–7.

105 Ibid.

106 Ibid.

107 Ibid.

108 Hellmann, *Das Konkursrecht der Reichsstadt Augsburg*, 72.

109 "*Dieweil dann sollich ob anzaigt gelt der mertail meiner lieben hausfrawen vätterlich und muterlich erb unnd ir zupracht heyratsgut ist, und wo ich darumb komen sölt, mir meinem weib unnd lieben Kinden zu unwiderbringklichem verderplichem unnd ewigem schaden raichen würde, so ist [. . .] mein ganz fraintlich unnd underdiennstlich pit sie wölln [. . .] hilff unnd beystannd thun*". StAA, Literaliensammlung, Höchstetter-Selekt II, fol. 181. Also cited in Klinkert, "Die Augsburger Handelsgesellschaft der Höchstetter," 118.

110 StAA, Reichsstadt Strafamt 47, Stadtgerichtsbuch, 1531, 59r-110r; Klinkert, "Die Augsburger Handelsgesellschaft der Höchstetter," 45–110.

111 Cited in P. Hecker, "Ein Gutachten Conrad Peutingers in Sachen Handelsgesellschaften," *Zeitschrift des historischen Vereins von Schwaben* 2 (1875): 211f. See also Klinkert, "Die Augsburger Handelsgesellschaft der Höchstetter," 43–4.

6 Ruin and recovery

The question of resilience and the Höchstetter "family firm"

With the failure of mediation, formal bankruptcy proceedings drew to an end. A further appeal by the creditors, who came together in Augsburg during the summer of 1531, achieved nothing. Confronted with their demand for payment of all outstanding debts, the Höchstetters refused to answer. They alleged instead that "Emperor Charles and King Ferdinand had granted them the privilege to give and receive justice nowhere but before the Imperial Chamber Court".[1] Those who remained unpaid could only try to salvage what they could from the ruin.

The city's magistracy, sensitive about its legal independence and jurisdiction, responded promptly and severely.

> At that, on 23 September, a Saturday at midday, it had the three Höchstetters – the elder Ambrosius, the younger Ambrosius and Joseph Höchstetter – led from the chamber in the elder Ambrosius's house to the city prison by four city guards. There they laid them in irons, the elder Ambrosius Höchstetter in a small cell (*Stüblein*) and the other two Höchstetters just outside bound with chains in a cellar. (*Gewölbe*)[2]

A citation from the Manlich Chronicle records the event as well, adding to its drama the ringing of church bells and the presence of the *Reichsvogt*, as the procession made its way through the streets from house to prison.[3] Their legitimate debts were unpaid; their brilliance was all but forgotten. The 1527 regulation of the Augsburg *Kaufleuteschaft* took effect: An insolvent merchant, who failed to pay an obligation, lost all rights as a merchant, was expelled from the corporation and was not to be readmitted.[4]

The creditors were not finished with them, however. Over the following months, they re-examined the records of the Höchstetter family firm, interrogating the prisoners and their former employees closely and repeatedly. The suspicion of dishonest, even fraudulent dealings gradually hardened into a firm conviction. With their debtors in chains and their evidence gathered, they realized further proceedings would yield little.

On 2 March 1532, the city of Augsburg acted to close the bankruptcy proceedings that had struggled onward without resolution for nearly three years. Some creditors had received payment, but most remained unsatisfied. Some had acted on their own, seizing Höchstetter property in private execution to satisfy outstanding obligations. The *cessio bonorum* promised in July 1529 by the bankrupts themselves to all the creditors in common had yielded nothing. The magistracy now ordered the seizure and sale of all remaining Höchstetter capital.

> On the Saturday after *Reminiscere* [2 March, tms] anno domini 1532, the court declared with right that all remaining property, real and moveable, of the three Höchstetters should be sold and such money be deposited with the *Stadtvogt* until further announcement and notice, and in the meanwhile, according to a decree of the Council, the wives and children of the Höchstetters shall be detained.[5]

Nothing would be spared, not even the private property of the wives. Their "wife's freedom", which had long delayed any settlement, had now lost its validity. The creditors thanked the magistrates and withdrew. The Höchstetter wives asked for and received a recess of six weeks and three days to consider this latest development. Sender remained censorious:

> They later appealed to the Chamber Court and other procedures followed that one as well. There the matter remains still. The women created a great deal of confusion [*Irrigkait*] und caused the creditors much injury.[6]

A note to the text indicates that the wives appealed so often that the ensuing legal procedures and negotiations ended up costing all parties "more than the Höchstetters ever possessed".[7] Yet their struggle to retain ownership of their property, their homes and their incomes ultimately assured the survival of their families, if not the release of the prisoners.

The bankrupts themselves remained in jail. Some two years later, on 7 July 1534, Ambrosius II and Joseph were transferred from the cellar to the tower of its Holy Cross Gate, where they were to remain in prison.

> In the fall thereafter, the elder Ambrosius Höchstetter died in chains in the little chamber. And, he had such terrible injuries to his feet that he truly stank, so that no one could stand to be with him, and he had to suffer the stench with great hardship. He had *den wolf*.[8]

The disease marks the harshness of his treatment. Ambrosius I was chained constantly and denied care. In the usage of the sixteenth century, especially in Swabia, according to Grimm, "the wolf" (*der Wolf*) referred to an aggravated and dangerous skin disease, usually *lupus vulgaris* or intertrigo that, left untreated, could spread and develop into ulcers.[9] This condition manifests itself as open, superating wounds, usually associated with chafing of the skin, where it is constantly covered or restricted in motion. It was an ugly, painful death.

Sender wrote his chronicle with some degree of literary art. With the words "den Wolf", the monopolist, who reputedly treated competitors and consumers with predatory rapacity, passes from Sender's chronicle of Augsburg history as the victim of a rapacious disease, having occupied it for nearly 20 pages, longer than any other single person or event. Gone was the "fine, lordly" Ambrosius of 1527. Reduced to a prison and lost to creditors was the "large house full of fine ornaments like a prince's palace". In their place, the reader encountered a man of no means, covered in oozing sores, chained to a prison wall. It emphasized the moral of Sender's story, a "good Christian", doomed by his own avarice.

It is hard to imagine any kind of resilience or recovery from such a fall. This chapter addresses the topic nonetheless. The Höchstetter family not only renewed its fortune, it even achieved a certain fame, if not the notoriety of Ambrosius and his partners. New family firms arose in the place of – and possibly with the capital of – "Ambrosius and Hans, the Brothers Höchstetter and Associates". This raises questions about and offers insights into the nature of the family and the firm in early modern Europe, suggesting both possess greater vitality and dynamism, especially in the face of ruinous crises, than the historiography has recognized.

* * *

Though well established in the English language, resilience is a neologism of social science.[10] In the seventeenth century, it described "the action or an act of rebounding or springing back", but in the mid-nineteenth century, it expressed also "the quality or fact of being able to recover quickly or easily from, or resist being affected by, a misfortune, shock, illness, etc."[11] In the twentieth century, systems theorist seized upon those qualities of robustness and adaptability to describe resilience as "the ability of a system to withstand changes in its environment and still function".[12] In the twenty-first century, the modern business community took up this concept and the attendant issues of security, preparedness, risk and survivability.[13] Theorists commonly understand an organization's resilience, its ability to survive crises and thrive in uncertainty, in terms of several sets of factors – some internal and others external, some measurable and others not – that render any business more or less resistant.[14] The ability of leadership to balance risk-taking and -aversity, allocate resources to strengthen security and encourage commitment in the workforce plays a role. Staff and workers contribute to resilience by embracing accountability and supporting a firm's goals. Effective record- and book-keeping techniques that allow managers to monitor current performance and diagnose emergent risks are essential to an organization's resilience. Smooth, efficient communication among multiple workplaces as well as redundancy in record-keeping are also frequently cited. In addition to such factors, which might be generally described as internal to the firm, there are external considerations, such as effective partnerships that promote communication and cooperation – tantamount to embedded relationships with the larger business community. So understood, a resilient company appears proactive rather than reactive: It focuses on inherent strengths, it promotes risk awareness, and it emphasizes adaptation rather than stasis.[15] The question is to what extent the Höchstetter family firm – or any other late medieval or early modern enterprise – shared any of these characteristics.

The question of resilience dogs family firms particularly. They are notorious for their assumed inability to survive challenges over time. Indeed, that inability has been captured in the platitude: "Shirt-sleeves to shirt-sleeves in three generations".[16] (See Chapter 2.) Experts hold them to be particularly susceptible to problems of succession, discipline and efficiency precisely because the interests of the family do not always align with those of the firm. The Höchstetters had confronted crises in the past. Their former employee Bartholomäus III Rem posed an extended and violent challenge that could easily have destroyed their firm and did alter its structure. Their response, as suggested by changes to their 1524 charter, appears to have been largely defensive and to have strengthened their connection to and reliance on the family. They restricted the practice of accepting non-family members as partners. Rather than alter established accounting and reporting practices, rather than recruiting new partners or factors, they explicitly bound partners and employees to secrecy about internal affairs, blind acceptance of the firm's accounting and eschewal of any external appeal of its decision-making. The Höchstetters also contended with issues that were more immediately familial in nature. (See Chapter 4.) The alleged misbehavior of the younger partners – the gambling of Joachim I and Hans-Franz Baumgartner and the profligacy of Ambrosius II and Joseph – should have resulted in their immediate separation from the firm, per the terms of its charter, but these disciplinary actions never took place. All of these issues seem to have placed the Höchstetters squarely among the many family firms that have suffered the so-called Buddenbrooks Syndrome.

The records of the Höchstetter bankruptcy provide a different perspective. In the period following the laying in irons of the partners and the ending of formal procedures, from September 1531 to March 1532, the creditors examined the books and interrogated the prisoners and their employees. Intent on recovering as much of their loaned capital as possible, they asked where the resources were and, by extension, how they got there. In so doing, they uncovered some of the causes of the Höchstetters' fall and some of the means of their eventual recovery.

* * *

Interrogation records possess complications of their own. Even when they are reasonably complete, including questions, answers and observations, they are not transparent. Interrogators formulated their questions in advance. Officials of the court, usually three or four patricians of the city, posed the questions, and a court secretary recorded the answers, which were given under oath and with a warning. Unconvincing or untruthful responses might prompt the application of force, as the respondents knew full well. The questioning occurred in prison with the instruments of torture in full view. As a result, answers were seldom free or frank. They must be read "against the grain", that is, contrary to general custom, practice or inclination. In the case of Ambrosius I and his two remaining partners, their answers were explicitly instrumental, intended to excuse them from any responsibility in the bankruptcy and to achieve their release from prison. With a few noteworthy exceptions, as will be seen, they consistently expressed ignorance and innocence, claims the creditors found unconvincing.

After two frustrating years of failed negotiations and partial payments, the creditors and authorities had become increasingly aggressive. Quite apart from the ever harsher terms of confinement they imposed on the bankrupts, their final questions presumed falsehood and fraud. They were particularly direct in their interrogation of Ambrosius I. Why, for example, did he continue to borrow large amounts of money and accept deposits at 5 percent annual interest in 1527 and 1528, when he knew that his firm faced bankruptcy and he would not be able to repay his debts?[17] When he claimed that he had no idea his firm stood on the brink of insolvency – quite the contrary, in 1527 it had a positive balance in excess of 100,000 fl – they asked him why he insisted on lying when his own business correspondence explicitly contradicted him.[18] Given that he promised to pay his debts with interest, if his creditors would give him an 18-month period of grace, and given that he knew he would never be able to cover more that 10 percent of his obligations, had he not always planned to gather what properties he could and flee? And again, the follow-up question, why he insisted on lying, when his earlier words and deeds, all matters of court record, contradicted his current statements. The creditors demanded to know what had become of the capital and property that lacked clear accounting. What had become of the cash in his firm's strongbox? What had become of the goods removed from his house under the seal of the Count of Ortenburg to the house of the late Philipp I Gassner and from there out of Augsburg? What had become of the bales of textiles and other commercial wares transported from Linz, Austria, to Augsburg and eventually sold by the same Philipp Gassner? Who ordered their removal? Who received all this money? The creditors clearly implied that these goods or the proceeds from their sale should have – but had not – been placed in the hands of the *Stadtvogt* to be applied to their claims. What did the Höchstetters, not only Ambrosius, but also his wife, their children and children-in-law, do with all their private property, commercial goods and household furnishings, which neighbors had seen being carried away from their homes in the middle of the night? Expensive silverware, jewelry, clothing, tapestries and textiles, worth hundreds if not thousands of *Gulden*, had simply disappeared. Rumors abounded that these valuables had been hidden, sold, buried, anything but surrendered, as the bankrupts had sworn an oath to do. Again and again, the creditors directly accused Ambrosius of withholding property he had sworn to cede to them.[19] Why did he violate his oath to conduct no further business without their knowledge and consent: Collecting debts on his own to pay his legal fees and jailhouse expenses; mortgaging properties to pay favored creditors? Why did he claim ignorance of these matters, blaming his wife, when she would have reported all her actions to him? Why did he insist on lying, when it was common knowledge? "Höchstetter should give clear, honest answers and evidence".[20]

And that is exactly what he did not do. He professed ignorance not only of his dire financial straits, but of most aspects of his business. Of the reverses suffered in the Low Countries and elsewhere, "he had no report until he was confined in the *Rathaus*".[21] Not only had he received no reports from his factors in the most important trading centers of his day, he had no knowledge of what goods they stored in the various, far-flung warehouses of his company. Of the contents of his own cellars in Augsburg he "knew nothing more to say about them, than that all their contents had been sold to pay creditors".[22] He had no knowledge of what his wife did with her own property, much less other members of his family: "If the wives carried anything away, he knew nothing about it".[23] He had never violated his oath by borrowing money, collecting debts or selling goods without the knowledge of the authorities and his creditors.

Ambrosius possessed extraordinarily detailed information about a number of major deals, as he readily admitted, that he had made after his insolvency emerged but before his oath to cease business. To raise funds, he mortgaged real properties, first and foremost the Höchstetter estate Burgwalden, located roughly 25 kilometers south-southwest of Augsburg, for 10,000 fl at 5 percent from Anton Fugger.[24] He mortgaged 3,000 fl worth of supplies and commodities at the brass foundry at Pflach, Tyrol to his factor, Georg Hagen, then sold the property, all buildings and rights, to the von Freyberg family for 7,000 fl.[25] Asked about shipments of brass manufactured at Pflach, he explained that he had 20 containers (*Fesslen*) scattered between Augsburg and Venice.[26] Eight of these, stored at Neumarkt, South Tyrol, he "sold" to Conrad Rehlinger, instructing his factor in Trent, Hans Noll, to ship the goods wherever Rehlinger instructed him. Noll transferred another eight containers to Hans II Paumgartner's factor in Trent. Ambrosius did not know the location of the remaining four containers.[27] At the close of 1528, he sold Anton Fugger 3,000 hundredweight of copper, 1,000 per year, for 15,000 fl.[28] The funds were used to pay his creditors. Because he could not deliver the copper all at once, he offered Fugger security by transferring to him his share of the mine at Schwaz, Tyrol. Their agreement specified that Ambrosius would recover his share of the mine in proportion to the copper he delivered. He also disposed of his surfeit of mercury and cinnabar, not only to the regency government of Flanders (see Chapter 3) but also to several of his colleagues, merchant-bankers in Augsburg and elsewhere.[29]

His interrogators particularly wanted to know what was meant by the use of the terms, "trust" (*Vertrawen*) and "confidential" (*vertrewlich*), suspecting that these might be fictive transactions (*Scheinkäufe*), designed simultaneously to provide Ambrosius financial support and to preserve his capital from the just demands of his creditors. (See Chapter 4.) Ambrosius explained trust, in this case, meant that "he trusted his lenders to return the minerals or their sales price in the event that he paid his debts".[30] He also recalled his lenders had bargained hard: At the time, mercury brought 31 fl and cinnabar 36 fl per hundredweight on the Venetian market, but they were prepared to offer no more than 20 fl and 24 fl, respectively.[31] In various locations and with various commodities, Ambrosius ordered that capital be made liquid – sold or mortgaged – to pay his debts. His actions and orders were, in his own telling, consistent and honest; he could not and would not speak for the actions taken by his relatives or employees.

His private arrangements with Anton Fugger in 1528 also remained clear in his mind. (See Chapter 3.) Fugger had loaned him roughly 100,000 fl, which the two of them in turn paid to his creditors. In return, Ambrosius guaranteed repayment with a variety of capital (*Guetern*): silk and woolen textiles in Austria; mercury, silk and wool in Nuremberg and the Netherlands; sums of money "auf den Zellen" in the Netherlands, Seeland, Holland, Brabant and Flanders; silk, wool, mercury and copper in Venice and mining shares in Schwaz, all of which "he sold to Fugger on trust".[32] The payments occurred in 1528 and 1529, before his formal pledge and cessation, but he could not recall who and how much was paid.

Quite apart from any question of its credibility, Ambrosius's interrogation suggests several circumstances that bear negatively upon the question of resilience. It demonstrates that his firm was highly leveraged, that is, that he and his partners had borrowed heavily in their futile attempt to avoid insolvency and that this borrowing had ultimately proven fatal. Ambrosius later "claimed in his inventory of damages, among other causes that brought him to ruin, the fact that he had to pay 5 percent interest on the accepted deposits".[33] He had also disposed of fixed and moveable capital at discounted rates. Such a high level of leverage, that is, the use of credit to enhance one's speculative ability, significantly weakens the resilience of any business both by limiting further credit operations and by expanding the influence of creditors. The interrogation further indicates that his firm was highly decentralized: Ambrosius offered little evidence of collaboration among himself and his partners, of centralized planning and decision-making. Finally, questions and answers show that strategic information did not circulate freely, indeed seems to have circulated selectively, if at all. The charter of 1524 indicates that this situation was deliberately constructed and fostered: Partners were given freedom to conduct whatever business they pleased; they were not required to share information about their business. (See Chapter 1.) This structure encouraged the creation of "silos", to use the modern term for units within which information circulates that is not transmitted to other parts of the sytem or organization, a condition inimical to coordinated, unified planning and action.

The interrogation of Ambrosius also suggests unexpected strengths. The Höchstetter family firm practiced a high degree of financialization. Its debt-to-equity ratio appears to have been unusually high (see Chapter 5), but it readily engaged in complex financial transactions, discounting debts, liquidating commodities, mortgaging assets, all of which enabled the ready transfer – and preservation – of its capital. These actions began long in advance of the crisis that finally destroyed the firm, suggesting that they were part of a purposeful strategy of resilience, just as the creditors expected. The transformation and survival of the Höchstetter family firm was not a matter of good fortune, much less superior heredity.[34] Finally, the Höchstetter family firm was deeply embedded in a social community of partners, employees, relatives and servants, all of whom played a role in transferring capital from place and one form to another. In the course of insolvency and bankruptcy, the Höchstetters relied on the active support of persons outside the firm and the family, putting themselves in a position to leverage not only capital but also information. The extent to which this proved to be the case for the bankrupts became a focal point of a second set of interrogations.

* * *

In the second half of 1531, the authorities interrogated a wide range of Höchstetter employees, associates, relatives and servants. The nature of their questions varied little, despite the diversity of persons questioned, and suggests dissatisfaction with the information Ambrosius I had provided. What was their relationship to the Höchstetters? What did they know about the Höchstetters' affairs? What had become of the Höchstetters' vast wealth, both their business capital and their personal property? What transactions on behalf of the Höchstetters had they undertaken since the insolvency became common knowledge and the bankruptcy began? The level of detail suggests that the creditors already possessed specific information, whether from the Höchstetters' documents, unrecorded evidence or common knowledge. The answers they received were frequently defensive; the various respondents strove to avoid personal guilt either by action or association. As a group, however, they provided further information about the Höchstetters' response to bankruptcy, and they revealed a key to the Höchstetters' resilience: Their social community.

The questioning began with the factors and employees of the firm on 23 October 1531. The creditors petitioned the authorities particularly to warn these Höchstetter associates to tell the truth. If they failed to testify honestly, the truth "would be wrung out of them with painful questioning", that is, with torture.[35]

> On this point, one does not wish to deceive them, for they will lose not only their bodily health (which would be worth more than all riches), but they might also lose their lives and fortunes, bring slander to themselves for the rest of their lives and in all eternity as well as to their children and relatives, for which no one could compensate them.[36]

The persons to be questioned were not merely witnesses, but potential accomplices.

The first questions addressed matters of work relations. The answers enabled the creditors and authorities to confirm a core group of employees, whom they refer as "confidential employees" (*Geheimdiener*) nearly all of whom had worked in responsible positions for the Höchstetters for more than a decade: Wolfgang Vittel, Thomas König, Wolfgang Preischuch, Hans Doll, Markus Rot, Matthäus Rem, Simon Noll, Georg Hagen, Leonhard I Riederer, Joachim I Gassner, Conrad Rehlinger, Erasmus Villsecker, Georg Noll and Anton II Nusshart.[37] (See Chapter 1.) Such questions make sense in the context of a loyalty that might lead the employee to act on his employer's behalf even to the extent of dishonesty or illegality. Georg Hagen, for example, explained that he had sworn his oath to Ambrosius I and Hans I Höchstetter, the two named partners, but volunteered that "for several years he had earned through his own trade in Nuremberg something beyond his service, for which he thanked God".[38] In other words, he had sworn service but was self-employed at the same time. Such was the case for many of the other *Geheimdiener* as well.

Hagen and his colleagues refused to admit any knowledge of their employers' business during the insolvency and bankrupty. Though they could describe their duties in positions of trust that would have made them privy to all kinds of sensitive, business information, their nearly unanimous response to over 60 questions was "[I] don't know" (*Wiss nit*). Every *Geheimdiener* insisted that he had rendered complete accounts of all his transactions to the Höchstetters. Yet, when asked about accounts and payments before and during the bankruptcy, all denied any knowledge.[39] Even the bookkeeper, Thomas König, claimed to "know nothing other than how matters lay in the chancery".[40] He likewise had no knowledge of changes in accounting practices, removal of account books or mortgaging of capital assets, all matters that would normally have passed under the eye and hand of a bookkeeper. The others answered in chorus. Though factors, individually responsible for the conduct of all business at important locations, they had no knowledge of the removal or sale of property or goods, whether commercial wares and financial notes, in their individual factories and warehouses. They had no knowledge of an impending bankruptcy until it was formally declared. They did not know the names of partners, investors or depositors; they did not know about specific enterprises or transactions; they did not know about preferential payments to certain creditors; they did not know about any business conducted after the bankruptcy declaration and the *cessio bonorum*. They appeared to know – or were willing to divulge – only the terms of their employment and the back wages owed them. Riederer, for example, knew nothing of the insolvency before it became "common knowledge" (*dz Geschrai*), but he was sure that "Ambrosius I had pledged him 3,600 fl" (*der Hochstetter hab jm gewet umb 3600 Gulden*).[41]

The interrogation of these employees yields conflicting images of the family firm. On the one hand, long service might have fostered solidarity; these employees might have refused to disclose damaging details about the men and family that had provided their livelihoods, masking their knowledge behind a façade of ignorance. Were this the case, "Ambrosius and Hans, the Brothers

Höchstetter and Associates" might seem a tightly united company, the response to crisis of which cannot be measured only in terms of the outcomes. On the other hand, these employees were subject to individual service agreements and wage regimes, and they worked individually and independently, each uniquely responsible for his own task or enterprise in widely dispersed locations. They claimed to receive little or no information from the firm and recalled few but the most personally relevant details about it. Their ignorance of its financial situation and the senior partner's ignorance of local developments reinforce the impression that the principle decision-makers neither shared nor managed information effectively. Accordingly, "Ambrosius and Hans, the Brothers Höchstetter and Associates" might seem a highly decentralized holding company, which combined individual businesses that worked for themselves as well as for the family firm. The internal realities are difficult to unpack. The creditors probably found the employees' professed ignorance unconvincing, even conspiratorial. The employees had little reason to lie, however. The bankruptcy had damaged their individual interests. Some of them, like Leonhard Riederer, were owed not only wages for service but deposits at interest. The interrogators further warned them, prevarication promised pain and more, the loss of health and honor. As independent merchants whose business activities could survive the bankruptcy of their past employer, they could afford neither.

The creditors inquired particularly about the independent business interests of the confidential employees, whether these might have been instrumentalized, either to abscond with Höchstetter capital for their own purposes or to connive with the Höchstetters in their efforts to shield capital from the creditors. Had Leonhard Riederer and son Christoff, who transacted their own business in Austria and Bavaria, aided the Höchstetters in their capital flight? Riederer replied unequivocally, "What he and his son had transacted to this end [debts collected in Bavaria and elsewhere, tms] had been his own affair".[42] Did Hans II Ungelter, a former partner who separated from the firm in 1528, early in its insolvency, help Ambrosius to raise credit in Augsburg?[43] Ungelter dismissed both issues. These relatively minor inquiries testify to the fluidity of capital in late medieval and early modern family firms. Employees' relationships to the firm as well as their independent capital could increase resilience, as the creditors clearly understood.

Another confidential employee, Wolfgang Vittel, had recently become involved in large-scale enterprises of his own. The creditors imagined he might have assisted his employers in selling, mortgaging or otherwise alienating capital without the creditors' knowledge and consent. This was true of all the *Geheimdiener*, whom the creditors questioned closely in this regard, but Vittel may have taken matters a step further: "As he had inherited nothing from his parents, from what [capital] has he managed [to live in] such splendor, and where did he get the money to build such a magnificent house in Hall as well as a considerable trade in all kinds of wares and good?"[44] The creditors believed that Vittel had taken possession, whether by theft or agreement, of a large amount of Höchstetter capital that was theirs by right. To all their questions, Vittel answered that his transactions on behalf of the Höchstetters had been recorded in his accounts, which were now in the hands of the creditors, and that he could explain the splendor and building in Hall, if need be.[45] The creditors questioned other employees: All denied involvement. Thomas König went so far as to say he was not liable to reveal (*des mer er sye nit schuldig anzuzaigen*) what anyone else has invested in Vittel's enterprise.[46] Georg Hagen, who had transferred large sums in worked metals and financial instruments to Vittel, denied all knowledge of the enterprise. The building and its "splendor" (*Pracht*) were undeniable facts, nonetheless. It was a large undertaking, one that would eventually help restore the Höchstetters to better fortune. Of these developments more later.

The testimony of the *Geheimdiener* reminds us of several aspects or resililence in late medieval and early modern family firms. First, merchant-bankers of the period relied on a community of persons, connected to them in multiplex and complex ways, to carry out their business in good times and bad. The notion of a network with its implication of reciprocal relations among social equals fails to capture fully the range and density of this interaction. Second, the nature of these relationships, set as it is in a distant, only partially recoverable past, proves remarkably resistant to historical analysis. Even direct testimony seldom confirms unequivocally the intimacy or intensity of emotions that bound people together; it seldom explains unequivocally the motives behind their actions. Third, the fluidity of capital, meaning both the many forms it could take and the ready transfer of it from one form and place to another, points to the financialization of economic life, a quality that at turns helped and harmed the Höchstetters, expanding their business and leveraging it at the same time. Their experience suggests a kind of trial-and-error empiricism, learning the ropes of finance by doing it, in an age when financial markets were just beginning to develop. Any attempt to explain the resilience of late medieval and early modern, family firms must keep in mind the deliberate actions and strategies pursued in this historical context.

* * *

At the end of October 1531, questioning shifted to a different category of witnesses: Persons who transferred and disposed of capital as a trade or profession. This included a wide range of individuals, male and female, artisanal and mercantile, rich and poor, official and unofficial. They and their services were an essential aspect of finance and financial markets in late medieval and early modern Europe. The Höchstetters made full use of them, and their creditors knew precisely where to find them.

They had questions for Leonhard Pfister, the *Unterkäufel* of Augsburg. (For a discussion of these officials and their functions, see Chapter 5.) He testified that he had undertaken a number of transactions that involved the Höchstetters, but all had been legitimate exchanges before their declaration of bankruptcy. On 5 June 1527, he appears to have loaned them two sums at 5 percent interest: 400 fl (*die Warn Hartmann Sulzers*) and 600 fl (*die Warn Ulrich Welsers*). And, on 28 August 1527, he loaned them a further 1,500 fl (*die Warn Fraw Lenhart Beckin*).[47] That these appear to have been third-party loans secured with commercial goods or commodities (*Warn*) of one sort or another, rather than simple sales transactions, is suggested by the mention of the 5 percent interest charged. Moreover, Sulzer and Welser appear among the creditors in 1529, demanding repayment of the amounts they had secured. Beck, by contrast, did not appear, leading to the assumption that she either received payment or surrendered her claim. Since 1527, Pfister testified to no further business with the Höchstetters, apart from the usual traffic in bills of exchange.

> The aforementioned three persons asked him to take the money to the Höchstetters for them, and he has had no further dealings with the Höchstetters from that day to this apart from charging them no more or less than the acknowledged 5 percent; beyond all this he worked between the Höchstetters and [their] partners and local merchants who trusted the Höchstetters, making exchanges to a value of 47,000 fl, 6,900 Ducats and 2,850 Marks silver.[48]

Pfister's services as intermediary extended beyond financial instruments and capital, however. He had also undertaken to sell real estate on behalf of the Höchstetters. With the knowledge and consent of Ambrosius I and his daughter-in-law, Anna Langenmantel, the wife of the absconded Joachim I, he sold Joachim's house for 800 fl to Georg Wieland, the husband of Katharina Langenmantel, Anna's aunt. This might have been an attempt to keep the house occupied by Anna and their children in sympathetic hands. Pfister also sold three properties in the village of Wertingen that belonged to Anna Rehlinger for 600 fl, which he paid to Anton Fugger, to whom they had already been mortgaged. All of these transactions were suspect, despite the transparency assured by the services of a civic official. Pfister accentuated that assurance by disclaiming any further knowledge of or role in the unravelling of the Höchstetters' affairs.

Another figure who engaged in the buying and selling of various new and used goods was the so-called servant of the Shopkeepers' Guild (*Kramerzunftknecht*). Blendinger notes that this official served a similar fiscal function as the *Unterkäufel*, that is, he collected the city's tax (*Ungeld*) on all retail sales that involved members of the Shopkeepers' Guild.[49] Accordingly, a wide variety goods passed through this official's hands, giving him not only the opportunity to levy tax but also knowledge of current retail prices and making him an ideal intermediary for the liquidation of goods. Otmar Fugger fulfilled this function in 1530. Questioned by the authorities, he provided an lengthy inventory of wares – spices and textiles for the most part – that he had received in May 1530 from Philipp I Gassner and sold for 901 fl 32 kr on behalf of Katharina Neumann, the wife of Ambrosius II.[50] When interrogated, Ambrosius II would shed further light on this transaction, highlighting the fluid boundaries between a family and its firm.

Tax assessors of various kinds were not the only persons in late medieval and early modern cities, whose access to information and capital made them potential business intermediaries. Gelderblom identified hostellers as agents who served a similar purpose in Bruges, Amsterdam and Antwerp, where they "provided accommodation and storage facilities [. . .] acted as brokers and commission agents, and [. . .] even acted as guarantors for debts outstanding".[51] In Augsburg, gold- and silversmiths fulfilled such roles as well, especially in the buying and selling of precious metals.[52] Their traffic in gold and silver, their knowledge of current prices and their accumulated capital made them valuable figures in the financial market, sources of ready cash and credit, ersatz pawnbrokers and bankers.[53] Joachim Nitzel admitted purchasing various silver pieces – jewelry and tableware – worth 298 fl from Anna Rehlinger in 1529.[54] Her maid brought him the items, but Anna collected the money.

Testimony reveals another, somewhat obscure group, the *Käuflerinnen*, that is, women who bought and sold goods of all sorts, whether as street peddlers or stall holders.[55] The creditors wanted to question all "common, female peddlers, whose names the police (*Stadtknecht*) know well".[56] On 31 October and 4 November 1531, the authorities questioned five women, most of whom appear to have been unmarried or widowed. Like the *Unterkäufel* and *Kramerzunftknecht*, they functioned as intermediaries on the basis of their knowledge of the market in first- and second-hand wares of various sorts, which made them useful for liquidating personal items and housewares in order to raise quick cash. Appolonia Wech, also known as "Angel" (*Engel*), kept a shop across from the house of Hans Lauginger, and Elisabeth Dillbau had her place just off the city watchtower, the "Perlach", beneath Bernhard Walther's house.[57] Anna Zimmerman, Dorothea Frohlich, also known as "Schadenfrohin" and a peddler known only as "Bechin" completed the list. Only these last three had anything to do with the Höchstetters, according to their testimony.[58] They worked with the bankrupts and their wives to sell a wide variety of personal and household items, everything from clothing and jewelry to silver plates and cups and lengths of luxury textiles, such as satins, velvets and silks, to modest, quotidien items, such as dishtowels, blankets and underwear. The more expensive goods found individual buyers, often among the elite. Anna Zimmermann, for example, seems to have specialized in an elevated clientel; the Imperial Diet (*Reichstag*) of 1530 had brought to Augsburg a large number of aristocratic persons and their entourages, potential buyers for luxury goods.[59] Silverware often went to goldsmiths, who could reuse or resell it.[60] Whatever else they did, all of the *Käuflerinnen* peddled cheaper goods at the jumble markets, the Osterdult, and the *Michaelidult*, also known as the St. Michael's *Kirchweih* on 29 September, or at the St. Ulrich's *Kirchweih*.[61] They consistently claimed to have paid the proceeds of all the sales, less a small commission, to the rightful owners of the sold goods, either the individual partners or their wives. None of the *Käuflerinnin* knew anything about the family firm, its capital or its bankruptcy.

An illustrative pattern emerges from their otherwise innocent testimony. The *Käuflerinnen* dealt directly with the Höchstetters and their wives. They came into the family's houses, where they received the goods to be sold and, after the sale, paid the proceeds to the former owners in face-to-face transactions. The same may be said of *Unterkäufel*, *Kramerzunftknecht* and *Goldschmied*: They dealt openly with the owners. The bankrupts made no effort to conceal these dealings from the creditors. Nor did these intermediaries know anything about the bankruptcy. Indeed, they considered these small transactions to be a thing apart: Private property could be used to meet private needs and expenses, a view the creditors did not share. This kind of transparency contrasts sharply with the secret disposal of company and family properties, of which the creditors suspected them. It also contrasts sharply with the nocturnal movements of servants and employees in and out of the various Höchstetter dwellings.

* * *

Georg I Ratold and Ulrich III Artzt, both figures in the Augsburg merchant community, both informants of the creditors, possibly neighbors of the bankrupts, testified to highly suspicious activity.[62] According to Artzt, "It happened four or five times, at night between 10:00 PM and midnight as he went home: He would go past the house of the elder Ambrosius Höchstetter and see a handcart come out of the doorway that led to the chancery; he could not tell what was in the cart or who was pushing it, because it was night".[63] Nor was such activity limited to the senior partner. Ratold reported:

> At some point in the past, which year he could not recall, he saw Joseph Höchstetter's young servant took a traveling chest with two locks on a hand cart out of the St. Jacob's Gate at around the fifth hour of the evening. Whether the trunk was placed on a barge in the river or somewhere else and what was in it, he could not say. He also did not recall the exact time, except that it occurred while the Höchstetters were detained.[64]

Their testimony, which confirmed common knowledge, opened another avenue of inquiry.

The creditors formulated a set of questions for 20 current and former servants of Ambrosius I, Ambrosius II and Joseph Höchstetter.[65] They wanted to know what the servants had moved out of the various Höchstetter houses. The creditors asked specifically about items moved to the houses of Lucas II Rem and Jobst Meuting, who were established Augsburg merchants and Höchstetter associates, as well as the houses of Thomas König and Hans Doll, former employees of the Höchstetter firm. The specificity of their questions – references to chests or bales of goods, contents that made klinking or rattling sounds, specific destinations for specific goods – indicate clearly that the creditors possessed information and entertained suspicions.

Nearly all the servants denied any knowledge of goods removed from the houses of their owners. Either they did not concern themselves with such things, because they served in other capacities, or they were not told or trusted with such information and duties, or they were not in service at the time the transfers in question occurred.[66]

Anna Schmidin and a woman identified only as Walpurga, both formerly in service to the late brother and partner of Ambrosius, Hans I Höchstetter, admitted freely that they had carried bales of goods two or three times to the house of Lucas II Rem.[67] When questioned, Rem indignantly denied any involvement. He was in Salzburg when his wife agreed to a request by Hans's widow to keep several things of his in her house (*jne etlich Beraitschaft zu behalten*).[68] When he returned home and learned of the situation, he was sorry and opposed to it (*jme auch vast laid und wider gewesen*). He saw nothing other than clothing and housewares and a closed trunk, the contents of which he guessed were silverware. Summoning a notary and witnesses, he ordered his and the Höchstetter servants to return all of the transferred items. At his command, this was done that very night. He later went to the widow Höchstetter with the notary and witnesses and asked her whether she had received back all the items that had been taken to his house. She responded affirmatively and signed a notarized statement to that effect, which he kept. Rem's servant, Berlin Mair, who had accompanied his master to Salzburg, confirmed this testimony almost verbatim.

Magdalena, a nurse in the household of Ambrosius I, also claimed that one of his daughters had ordered her to take clothing to the home of the widow Ubelhörin, a *Käuflerin*, but that the clothing had later been returned.[69] The Höchstetter wives later confirmed that they had sent everything from clothing to silverware to chests of letters via their houshold servants to the widow Ubelhörin for sale or safekeeping. The widow admitted that she had received a chest of silverware from Anna Rehlinger.[70] The removal was for the purpose of safe-keeping, as Rehlinger later testified, because all of this had happened before the bankrupts were first confined, that is, before formal bankruptcy proceedings, when she had feared sudden seizure by the creditors, not legal surrender through the courts.[71] What Rehlinger did with the silverware, Ubelhörin could not say, only that she had reclaimed it.

The creditors questioned servants not only to track the movement of property that might be used to meet their demands, but also to track the movement of the bankrupts themselves. Joachim I Höchstetter had managed to avoid prison by escaping the city and taking 30,000 fl with him. Though he was out of their reach, the creditors sought to trace his movements in the hope of attaching liability to any who had assisted him or received funds from him. To this end, they questioned Anna Scholhörin, formerly a servant in Ambrosius I's household and currently in service to Matheus Langenmantel. She revealed that Joachim had returned to Augsburg in 1530, around the time of the *Reichstag*, during which time he had remained in his house, never going out, but receiving visitors, including a "bishop from Denmark", presumably Johan, Archbishop of Lund, the representative of King Christian II of Denmark.[72] (See Chapter 4.) She also offered a clue as to the means by which the Höchstetters might have smuggled capital out of Augsburg and away from the creditors:

> She heard from her mistress [Scholhörin served the wife of Ambrosius I, Anna Rehlinger, at the time, tms.] that Joachim had melted down and

> taken away both her and his silverware, as he had a melting oven in his household. Moreover, she heard further of the serving maid, Magdalena, [presumably the nurse in the Höchsteter household, tms] that she had a man in Adelsried who sewed the legs of Joachim's trousers full of *Gulden* when he went away. More she does not know.[73]

This kind of testimony contrasts sharply with the thinner evidence provided by most of the other servants. Its tattling tone serves as a reminder that the mere existence of a social networks does not predict the kinds of relationships that comprise it.

What emerges from this widespread investigation is the image of a family and firm embedded not in a network, but in a community. Discussions of networks in economic life tend to emphasize the horizontal connections and relationships among equals. Yet the testimony of the Höchstetters' employees, servants, collaborators, spouses and acquaintances reveals a much more complex situation. To liquidate and transfer capital, to ensure the survival of the family and its ability to recreate the firm, the partners and their wives relied on a multidimensional community of relationships, vertical as well as horizontal, with social and economic superiors, equals and inferiors. These relationships were not in any sense equal in intensity or intimacy. Some were openly supportive of the Höchstetters; others were not. Some were of long standing and experience; others developed solely out of the necessities of the moment. Some were more engaged in the bankruptcy and its consequences; other claimed complete ignorance and detachment. Yet, creditors and bankrupts all understood alike that this community was essential to the resilience of the family and its firm.

* * *

Toward the end of 1531, the investigation entered its final stage: The creditors questioned the families of the bankrupts. They started with Georg II, the son of Georg I, Ambrosius's elder brother and partner until his death in 1514. Georg II joined the family firm in 1515 along with his two brothers, Sigmund I and Wilhelm. He attracted the attention of the creditors and the authorities because of information that he had removed property from his uncle's house. He replied stoutly that he had taken nothing, complaining that "he was being treated unjustly" (*jn geschicht unrecht*).[74] Indeed, he claimed to "have not fiddled with the Höchstetters since 1519" (*er hab seidther 1519 Jar mit den Hochstettern gar nichts zu handtiern gehapt*). The flatness of the statement and the choice of terms in reference to his uncle and cousins might suggest tensions within the family. Georg I had been the eldest son and, likely, the heir presumptive to Ulrich II and his business. (See Chapter 1.) Though he was succeeded as partner by his three sons, Georg II, Sigmund I and Wilhelm, they all left the firm in 1519, to be replaced by Ambrosius's sons and associates. Only limited evidence exists of any further contact or cooperation among the descendants of the two brothers.

Of greater and more central interest were the surviving wives of the partners. Ottilie Höchstetter, the wife of Hans Franz Paumgartner, and Benigna

Adler, the wife of Joseph Höchstetter had both died in 1530 at the height of the bankruptcy. The creditors put a long list of questions to Anna Rehlinger, Katharina Neumann, Anna Langenmantel and Katherina Ehinger, the wives of Ambrosius I, Ambrosius II and Joachim I Höchstetter and the widow of Hans I Höchstetter, respectively.[75] Most turned on the liquidation of valuable, private property, such as the silverware of Ambrosius I, to which the wives had little to say. They all admitted, for example, that Ambrosius had possessed "prestigious silverware" (*namhaft Silbergeschirr*), but only Rehlinger could provide any details about its fate. She admitted to selling it for about 700 fl out of "pressing need" (*verobligenden Not*) and "used the same money for her housekeeping and the support of the legal proceedings" (*dz selb Geld jr Haushaltens und Underhaltens der Rechtfertigung verpraucht*).[76] The silver, as she pointed out carefully, had been hers, not her husband's, inherited from her family and brought as part of her trousseau at the time of her wedding. Langenmantel testified that Joachim had melted down and sold their silverware, from which she received roughly 135 fl, money used to support herself and her family because "they had received nothing from the firm for the last three years", that is, since 1528.[77]

Ehinger confirmed the lengths to which merchant wives could be driven to preserve their own property as a thing separate from that of their husbands. When the bankruptcy process began in 1529,

> she removed from her household all those things that belonged to her or were transferred to her under contract and seal to her advantage under the conviction, as one says, one would go to her house. At that she was concerned [literally, had care, tms] that her own property would be dealt with to her disadvantage, which gave her cause to remove those things and only those things that belonged to her.[78]

She documented and sent her property to Thomas König, Hans Doll, Leonhard Pfister and other employees of the firm, because she feared that the creditors would plunder her household to recover their capital. Clearly, the possibility of private execution for debt remained a reality in the minds of merchant wives, even if it had been banned by the letter of the law. The wives all confessed to treating their property as their own to use as they wished for whatever purpose they wished. They did the same with their husbands' personal property, clothing, jewelry and the like. Ehinger, again, "sold her late husband's clothing as her own property to her pressing need" (*Jres Ewirts seligen Claider hab sy als jr zustendig verschriben gut zu jrer obligenden Notdurft verkauft*).[79] Likewise Rehlinger: She sold her husbands clothing and jewelry to pay various, minor debts related to her housekeeping after the bankruptcy. In all of these transactions, that shadowy complex of dealers in second-hand goods – *Goldschmiede, Käuflerinnen, Kramerzunftknecht* and *Unterkäufler* – were indispensible. Likewise the numerous servants who carried the goods back and forth among households and shops played a crucial role, shielding the maneuvers from the public authorities and the maneuverers from public censure.

And those manuevers could be extreme. The creditors had information that the Höchstetter wives had concealed valuable property by burying it in their garden, which lay outside the city walls, along a stream known as the Lauterlech. They had also buried housewares in a "large, deep trench" (*ain grosse tieffe Gruben*) behind the house of Hans I Höchstetter.[80] The wives were capable of transferring all sorts of property in all sorts of ways, but they denied resorting to such methods.[81] Their resourcefulness kept the possibility of buried treasure nonetheless alive in the fantasies of the creditors.

Of their husbands' capital in that larger, financial sense – of their various, business dealings – they knew little or nothing. Yet they had reason to recall their various stakes in the firm. They were all heavily vested in it. Though her husband had died in 1527, upon which event the surviving partners were to pay his share of the firm to his surviving heirs over a period of years, Ehinger claimed all her money (*all jr Barschaft*) was still invested, though she could not say how much it was.[82] Rehlinger testified, "Everything that she received from her father, was made subject to her husband and not a cent came to her".[83] Similarly, Neumann's dowry was in the firm; more she could not say.[84] Langenmantel did not know exactly how much money she had in the firm, but could confirm that "her husband had received her dowry of 4,000 fl from Georg Wiclandt and, so far as she knew, deposited it in the firm, as he told her".[85] All had substantial interests in the firm; all would suffer substantial losses; all would insist that their dowries be repaid. All understood their dowries to be their own capital absolutely, funds discrete from the resources of family and firm, regardless of the purposes to which they might be put.

This put them on a collision course with the creditors in common. (See Chapter 5.) Augsburg law was not clear on this point. (See Chapter 4.) The "wife's freedom" gave priority to the repayment of their marital property – any property they brought to their marriages or received from their husbands at the time of their marriages – before the demands of any other creditors were met. Only if a wife allowed her property to be invested in her husband's business or involved herself in the conduct of that business was the privilege forfeit. The Höchstetter wives sought to defend their property from the creditors demands, swearing that their husbands had invested their dowries in the bankrupt family firm but without their knowledge and consent.[86] Their testimony under interrogation affirms that position. Their successful preservation of their property in a series of disputes that would extend to the Imperial Chamber Court contributed to the resilience of the Höchstetter family and its firm.

The wives' testimony, like that of the other witnesses, suggests a lack of communication. The near universality of ignorant innocence raises the suspicion that all testimony had been carefully coordinated and rehearsed. Taken at face value, however, without more concrete evidence of collusion, what each had to say confirms the general impression of isolated individuals, acting and reacting on their own without a conceived strategy, without even a common interest.

The mass of information provided by these interrogations makes possible two observations. First, the resilience of the Höchstetter firm and family was not a matter of chance but the product of purpose. Though lack of communication and information rules out any *a priori* plan or strategy, the actions of family members and associates testify to an iron determination to survive. Though not proactive, they reacted with a vigor that did not shy from extralegal or illegal means. Second, the family firm cannot be strictly identified with a single, nuclear family. An extended clan of Höchstetters had interests in the firm, extending even to cadet branches, albeit to varying degrees. The ability to draw capital from an extended family and to move it among its various branches becomes a central aspect of premodern resilience.

* * *

In April of 1532, the creditors submitted another set of questions to be put to the bankrupts, Ambrosius I, Ambrosius II and Joseph.[87] The creditors clearly remained suspicious of the information they had received, but they turned their attention to the organization of the Höchstetters' business, especially the investors and the secrets of the firm. Though still interested in recovering every bit of capital they could from the ruin of "Ambrosius and Hans, the Brothers Höchstetter and Associates", the creditors showed now an increased concern for the causes and context of its failure.

The partners' responses display a certain degree of unanimity. Questioned about the "good friends" who invested at profit or loss of the company, Ambrosius mentioned his younger brother, the textile retailer Jacob, but insisted that all the others could be found in the firm's *Geheimbuch*, which the creditors had in their possession. None of the investors, with the sole exception of Jacob, had been listed as creditors.[88] Ambrosius II replied that he had no knowledge of any investors, it having been his father's business.[89] Joseph likewise denied all knowledge.[90] Questioned about various transactions, they replied only to those they had themselves undertaken. Ambrosius I could say nothing about 8,000 fl in customs duties, collected in Antwerp and Mechelen in Flanders: "Young Ambrosius handled it".[91] Similarly, Ambrosius II and Joseph claimed ignorance of all dealings in mercury; this had been the provenance of the elder Ambrosius exclusively. Asked repeatedly about various transactions carried out by their wives, they all claim ignorance beyond the assertion that the women sold or mortgaged only their own properties, not the firm's capital.[92]

Ambrosius II offered further details about his wife's dowry, revealing the complex ways in which the property of family and firm might become imbricated.[93] His father had transferred all the company's business on the Linz market to Philipp I Gassner in payment for the 6,000 fl Gassner had on deposit. Gassner was to liquidate these goods and notes; any value beyond the sum owed to him would be transferred by Gassner to Katharina Neumann, because the capital in Linz also secured her dowry. Gassner accepted the arrangement and had all promissory notes transferred to his name, but he refused to give an accounting and refused to transfer any cash, notes or goods to Ambrosius II's wife. After long, tense negotiations, Gassner agreed to give the Höchstetter wives collectively 3,000 fl in commodities. The *Kramerzunftknecht*, Otmar Fugger, received these goods from the wives and managed to sell roughly 800 fl worth, for which Ambrosius II had a receipt dated 8 June 1530.[94] Gassner's heirs received the balance and gave Katharina Neumannin a promissory note, which constituted her dowry.[95] Dowries took a variety of forms and flowed into and out of the family firm. Their availability expanded a firm's capital base even as it complicated the the dowry's separate status. The "wife's freedom" not only protected the interests of wives, but also provided the partners of family firms with a degree of security, that is, a means to shield part of the family fortune from the demands of creditors.

The bankrupts seem, whether as a result of consensus or coordination, to have divulged as little about themselves or their families as they could. They expanded on other aspects of their business, however. Why had a general accounting not occurred as prescribed in 1527? Ambrosius II did not know, but his father revealed that a disbursement (*Raitung*) had occurred in 1524, at which time profits of 9 percent were distributed among the partners and, one assumes, their "good friends", the anonymous investors. No accounting (*Rechnung*) had occurred in 1527, because of the mercury monopoly: "It had been so confused that one did not know what to make of it".[96] Joseph went a step further, asserting that the Höchstetter firm had conducted no general accounting at all in the last 21 years.[97] This astonishing statement seems unlikely, given the extended legal and financial difficulties that surrounded the dispute with Bartolomäus III Rem, but it accords with the general impression of lax financial and incomplete information management in the house of Höchstetter. The practice of secrecy appears to have been no more closely observed than accounting. The creditors wanted to know, "as the most recent company charter expressly required among other things that the partners and employees keep secret in good faith various transactions and accounts, which ones were so confidential that they could become thus entangled?"[98] Ambrosius II and Joseph replied in chorus that they they "knew nothing other than to keep secrecy in business dealings".[99] Ambrosius I explained that "it was the common practice of all companies to keep their trade secrets, so that they were not hindered in buying and selling".[100]

Comparing the various statements of Ambrosius I, Ambrosius II and Joseph, a more complete picture of the firm in crisis emerges. They indicate what appears to have been a surprising lack of communication among the stakeholders, as noted, a state of affairs that the firm's charter enabled. Each seldom knew – or was unwilling to discuss – what the others were doing. In those instances where knowledge was common, it was frequently incomplete, a matter of scuttlebutt rather than confirmed fact. Not only had they little knowledge of one another's doings, they present themselves as incompletely informed about their employees and servants. Even their wives appear as free agents, acting on their own to protect themselves. This lack of information management – directed communication, intended to inform key decision-makers of the company's commitments and to enable them to coordinate the firm's activities and, more importantly, to respond to crisis and change – may have reflected the structural realities of early modern commercial and financial markets and may have resulted from the particular qualities of this family firm, but it cannot have aided the Höchstetters in their efforts to respond to their insolvency. A lack of contact or coordination raises questions about solidarity. At no point do the bankrupts speak openly in defense of one another. This sits uneasily with received notions of the affective ties of family, if not of the firm.

It is even more surprising, given the interpenetration of the two. The creditors' interest in personal property, not just the dowries of the bankrupts' wives and daughters, but also their clothing and jewelry, not just the real properties of the bankrupts, but the moveable property of very member of the extended Höchstetter family, demonstrated their recognition of a double truth. First, business assets could be and were stored not only in the form of capital investments but also in the form of personal possessions, whether cash, goods, buildings or land. Second, personal possessions could serve as security for business loans and capital. To the creditors' way of thinking, no barrier existed between business and familial assets. All the properties of a bankrupt, regardless of their use, formed part of a single mass, from which their legally recognized, financial demands should be settled. This was more than a legal formality; it was a business reality. The *cessio bonorum*, a central feature of bankruptcy proceedings throughout late medieval and early modern Europe, signaled as much, as did the fluidity of personal property and business capital. For their part, the bankrupts attempted to uphold a strict separation of business and family properties, protecting the latter from claims against the former. In terms of resilience, this makes sense. Unless some capital remained in the hands of the Höchstetter family, their eventual reemergence from bankruptcy – the entire point of resilience – became far less likely. Ambrosius II's explanation of his wife's financial arrangement with Philipp I Gassner – to say nothing of the testimony of the wives, their servants, the firm's employees and the bankrupts' associates – demonstrates quite clearly, however, that any such separation was largely fictional.

* * *

By mid-century, "Ambrosius and Hans, the Brothers Höchstetter and Associates" had long since ceased business, and all of the partners had died or disappeared. Their immediate families lived as wards of the city, receiving an annual allowance from the *Stadtvogt* and living in houses or on estates they no longer controlled. Civil authorities administered all their real and moveable properties to settle old debts.[101] Ernst Kern summarized the situation accordingly:

> The heyday of the house of Höchstetter ended irrevocably with collapse; a rebirth of the famous old firm was out of the question. Only in a few centers of European economic life did a few branches of the family flourish, but completely independent of one another. In Tyrol, in the glass manufactory of Hall under the leadership of Sebastien Höchstetter, a nephew of old Ambrosius, the family name reappeared in a position of leadership. Another branch of the family became active in a remarkable manner in English

> mining under the son of old Ambrosius, the oft-mentioned Joachim and his son Daniel. In comparison to the earlier splendor of the Augsburg house, however, these renewed swells of economic vitality can at this point only be described as after-effects.[102]

Other scholars concurred in the finality of the collapse. Ehrenberg concluded that "[t]he family never recovered from this blow in Augsburg", but noted that the son and grandson of Ambrosius I, Joachim I and Daniel, founded a "new branch of the family that continued to flourish for some time in England".[103] Strieder cites Kern without further comment.[104] The verdict of history seems unanimous.

Family firms are understood to be particularly susceptible to failure, particularly lacking in resilience. When the interests of family and firm no longer align, whether in matters of business leadership, management or capitalization, the firm goes into decline and collapses. The Höchstetters under Ambrosius I provide evidence of all three problems: The generation of Ambrosius's sons and nephews were profligate and self-indulgent; the partners did not communicate with one another or keep and review accounts regularly; they borrowed on a massive scale, leveraging their firm at a critical juncture. It has also been argued that their status as parvenus may have left them less able to call upon social capital as a means to escape insolvency and bankruptcy. Such weaknesses prevented the Höchstetter firm from responding effectively to the wave of crises that swept over them all at once: Failed monopoly, plundered caravans, seized cargoes, inadequate liquidity, dubious trust.

Yet the theory of resilience applies most aptly to modern organizations, especially the modern corporation. This chapter has sought to demonstrate how family firms, especially in the late medieval and early modern periods might demonstrate resilience differently. Survival depended less on *a priori* policies or planned strategies than on ruthless actions and an iron determination to survive. These actions extended to – that determination was shared by – not only the immediate leadership and management of the firm but by a community of employees and servants, colleagues and officials, friends and neighbors, shopkeepers and peddlers, all of whom willingly supported, whether out of solidarity or opportunity, the family firm's measures to raise and preserve capital. Many of those measures – the ones that most concerned the creditors – can be described in terms of "financialization", a sophisticated turn to money and financial markets to move capital from form to form, place to place, and hand to hand, liquidating real and moveable property through a variety of intermediaries, leveraging the company through borrowing and discounting and transferring capital among members of the firm and branches of the family. Such activities make clear that the "family" of the firm could and did extend well beyond the nuclear unit of modern imagination to include distant kin and cadet branches. By the same token, the "firm" might carry a family name, but leadership could pass to persons more distantly related. The economic, social and familial environments of the firm may work in ways more complex than the simple, dichotomous cause-and-effect that seems to characterize so much of the current discussion of resilience: structure and function; plan and action; crisis and response. The fall of the house of Höchstetter suggests that this is so and that the outcomes are not always predictable.

The creditors may have thought the movement of people and capital resembled a vast shell game. They wondered where the Höchstetters had hidden their wealth, whether in a hole in the garden, a chest in some neighbor's house or transferred through fictive sale to the nominal ownership of someone else. Both family and firm provided rich possibilities for concealing capital, a fact that scholars tend to overlook by virtue of the modern assumptions that the family includes only parents and children and that the family firm is somehow identical with this nuclear family and its line of descent. Families often supported multiple firms through cadet branches, however, which might allow them to shift financial, social and symbolic capital away from those that were threatened by internal or external problems.

Beginning with the generation of Ambrosius I's father, Ulrich II, the family's structure separates into multiple lines with multiple enterprises. Though scholarship refers to "Ambrosius and Hans, the Brothers Höchstetter and Associates" as *the* family firm, rather than *a* family firm, the family pursued different enterprises and had different businesses both over time and at the same time. Ambrosius began his career as a junior partner to his father and rose to become senior partner with his brother Georg I, with Georg's sons and his brother Hans and, finally, twice with his brother Hans and his sons. In his lifetime, his immediate family possessed seriatim no fewer than five family firms. His brothers, Jacob I and Hieronymus I, had no connection to the family firm; each pursued his own economic interests. Add the enterprises of Georg's three sons after they ceased partnership with Ambrosius, and it can be said that heirs of Ulrich II operated no fewer than ten family firms, five of them simultaneously.

Early modern, long-distance commercial and financial companies usually operated for limited periods of time, from three to eight years, after which point they ceased operations, distributed profits and losses and, if conditions were advantageous, created new charters, often with new partners and new capital, intent on continuing old business and entering new markets. Any discussion of resilience needs to set the effects of crisis and change in this context of limited-term operation. Under the circumstances, resilience has to include the possibility of ceasing, reorganizing and renewing business. And, in families with multiple firms, such as the Höchstetters, it has to extend to the possibility that a reorganization, a response to crisis and change, might pass capital – and the baton, so to speak – to a cadet branch of the family. There is some evidence that this occurred in the course of the Höchstetter bankruptcy, large transfers of capital that escaped the claims – but not the attention – of the creditors and eventually found their way back to the family.

★ ★ ★

The further career of Joachim I Höchstetter demonstrates the point. Diplomatic dispatches, sent to King Christian II of Denmark by Johan, Archbishop of Lund, who represented the king in the matter of a debt of 30,000 fl at the Höchstetter bankruptcy proceedings, indicate that Joachim, who claimed that he was no longer a partner in the company, wished to negotiate an individual settlement for himself.[105] After a meeting, Johan brought Joachim to the Netherlands as part of his diplomatic entourage, beyond the grasp of the other creditors. Though a settlement was negotiated, it remains unclear whether the debt with Denmark was ever paid. It is clear, by contrast, that the creditors accused him of absconding with approximately 30,000 fl in capital that belonged properly to his firm and, by virtue of the bankruptcy and Ambrosius I's *cessio bonorum*, to them. No sources indicate what became of the money, but it seems possible that Joachim or his descendants used these assets, not only capital, but also patronage, to help reestablish themselves in business.

These new beginnings had deeper roots, however. Joachim, as noted, had become his firm's factor in Antwerp in 1524.[106] There he established his initial contact with Christian II, at that time a refugee.[107] He provided financial services and rose to become a close advisor to the king. Royal influence may have helped him become involved in a project to develop mining in Scotland. He appears to have been engaged with other English merchants in prospecting there by 1526.[108] A year later, perhaps as a result of his own growing contact with and interest in England, Joachim was able to offer assistance to English merchants held captive in the Low Countries, including Richard Gresham. He and his brother John, who would become Lord Mayor of London and a member of the Royal household, recommended him in turn to Cardinal Thomas Wolsey, Lord Chancellor of England, the result of which was a ten-year trading privilege for "Ambrosius and Hans, the Brothers Höchstetter and Associates" to import commercial wares, especially grain from Eastern Europe, and to export English wool. When Dutch authorities seized a small flotilla of Höchstetter cargo ships and the first rumors of his firm's insolvency began to circulate in 1528, Joachim traveled personally to London where he accused the Greshams of slander. So impressed was Henry VIII that he granted Joachim the grandiose title of "principal surveyor and master of all mines in England" with the responsibility to reform English mining and the unlimited right to dig for copper, lead, gold and silver in all of England and Scotland for 43 years. Those plans came to naught, according to Blendinger, because Joachim I suddenly left England when a Hungarian at court offered him the contract for the Fugger copper works in Neusohl.[109] This relationship paid dividends, as noted, when "Ambrosius and Hans, the Brothers Höchstetter and Associates" went bankrupt in 1529.[110] Having escaped his creditors with the help of the king's representative, Joachim accompanied Christian II on his invasion of Denmark in 1531 that ended in the king's capture and imprisonment. Joachim managed to escape this fate by changing sides at the last moment, a move that his chronicler and critic, Clemens Sender, might have recognized with grim satisfaction. The reward for this ability to judge the tide of events and ingratiate himself with the powerful led him to be named Master of Mines (*Bergmeister*) in Denmark 1532 by Christian's captor, King Frederick I. His star appeared to be on rising again, but he died in 1535, having escaped prison, hatched plans, but achieved little. His descendants managed to ascend a bit further.

Joachim's wife, Anna Langenmantel, remained in Augsburg with their four children. The eldest, Joachim II, eventually established himself in the "second or third rank of merchants" there, according to Hammersley.[111] Yet, he served as named partner in a series of companies: "Abraham Rem, Joachim Höchstetter and Associates", 1570; "Joachim Höchstetter, Philipp König and Associates", 1572–1580; and "Joachim Höchstetter and Friedrich Rentz", which ended in bankruptcy in 1586. In 1575, he paid a tax of 68 fl 30 kr, placing him approximately in the top 10 percent of the city's taxpayers.[112] His sole surviving male heir, Philipp, studied medicine at the University of Basel, served Augsburg as *Stadtmedikus* and died of the plague in 1632. He made no mention of his grandfather's and his father's bankruptcies or, for that matter, of his father's death in his *Familienbuch*, noting ambiguously: "After my mother's pious end, Fortune played wondrously with us and my father and behaved badly toward him. God considered us children with His Grace, however, and gave to each of us according to His mercy, as much as each needed".[113] His descendants continue to conduct business in Augsburg and elsewhere in southern Germany to the present day.

Joachim's second son, Daniel I, was ten years old when his father died. His relatives placed him with a branch of his grandmother's Wieland family in the Rauris Valley, south of Salzburg, where he eventually learned mining technique.[114] A document sealed by Queen Elizabeth I, dated 1563, offers the first documentation of his presence in England. It authorized him to explore England for exploitable mineral deposits. A year later, he concluded a contract with the Augsburg firm "Haug, Langnauer and Company" to finance a smelting operation in Keswick that he would manage. By 1568, he had been named "Managing director" of the "Company of Mines Royal".[115] In 1580, unwilling to expand its investment, the company leased the Keswick smeltery to Daniel and a partner, Thomas Smith.[116] After Daniel's death in 1581, his sons Emanuel and David II succeeded him as managers of the Keswick works and with extensive mining interests elsewhere in England. This line of descendants of Ambrosius I and Joachim I also survives to the present.

Joachim was not the only partner of the bankrupt firm, suspected of sequestering capital and making a new start. The creditors asked repeatedly how Wolfgang Vittel, the Höchstetter factor in Tyrol, acquired the funds to engage in ambitious new building and commercial projects in the town of Hall (Map 6.1). All wondered how a person who had inherited no money and claimed to have no partners could manage to begin a wide-ranging business and construct a fine house.[117] Had he, in fact, misappropriated 20,000 fl from the Höchstetters?[118] Vittel and Ambrosius I answered coyly that whatever he had undertaken, he had done on his own. They denied neither the disappearance of capital nor the appearance of a new enterprise.

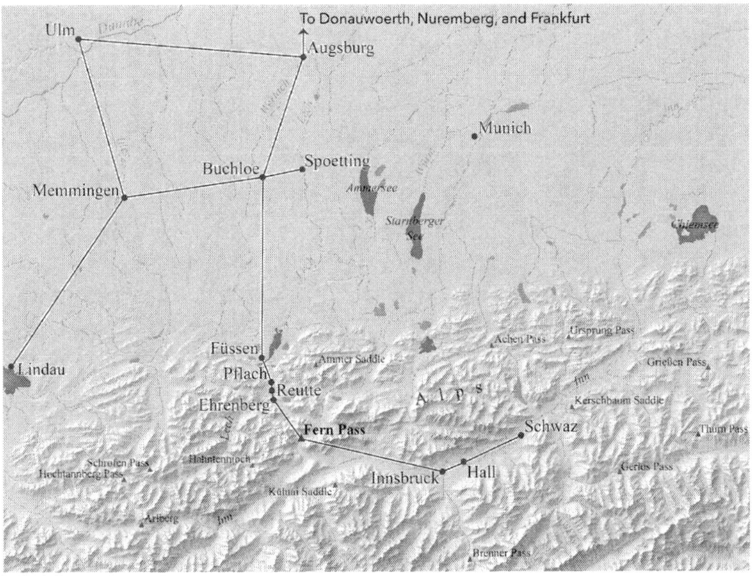

Map 6.1 Detail of Tyrol, showing Hall and Reutte

In 1533, as his former employers began the last phases of their imprisonment, Vittel began to traffic in various chemical and mineral commodities in Tyrol.[119] He petitioned for and received authorization to mine and process alum (aluminum sulphate), vitriol (sulphuric acid) and sulphur in the Voldertal, a valley that opens to the south of the town of Volders, itself just to the east of Hall in the Inn Valley of Tyrol.[120] It is not entirely clear to what purpose he sought these minerals; perhaps they formed one of several enterprises. The following year, in 1534, he received permission to construct and operate a glass manufactory in Hall, Tyrol.[121] He intended "to sow and harvest there the essential plants for making glass".[122] Ferdinand I gave him permission to do so and to buy and sell ash duty-free everywhere in his realm for five years. It appears to have been a profitable enterprise: Vittel petitioned the regional government regularly to harvest lumber in increasing quantities to fire the ovens and render into potash for his glassworks.[123] He was soon supplying glass for representative buildings from Hall to Innsbruck.[124] Vittel died in 1540, and his widow, pressed by the claims of various creditors upon her late husband's estate, was forced to sell the glassworks.[125] Emperor Ferdinand I, who had promoted Höchstetter interests before and during the bankruptcy, ordered the glassworks sold to Sebastian Höchstetter, the son of Jakob and nephew of Vittel's old employer, for a token price of 253 fl, a fraction of its original value.[126] The question, as intriguing as it is unanswerable, is whether an eventual transfer to the Höchstetter had been the plan all along.

Sebastian did not follow in his father's footsteps as a textile retailer, but spent his early years learning mining techniques in Tyrol. Earliest accounts place him in Schwaz, Tyrol, engaged in the foundry there, which he operated on his own account in 1534 at the age of 23.[127] He purchased the glassworks in Hall in 1542, and his fortunes appear to have risen steadily. He maintained certain contacts to Augsburg and its still powerful merchant community. An official document of 1548 lists him as a factor of the Herwart family firm, engaged in the purchase of mining shares, while he operated his glassworks.[128] His enterprise continued to expand, as demonstrated by petitions to increase timber harvests, ash purchases and glass exports. Sebastian raised it among the premier manufactories of the Archduchy of Austria, making glass that competed with that of Murano to the south. The House of Habsburg continued the patronage it had first granted his Augsburg ancestors. It restricted the importation of foreign potash and glass into the Archduchy of Austria and the County of Tyrol. It encouraged the movement of skilled labor from competing centers, especially Venice, to the Höchstetter works at Hall. It granted freedom from customs and tolls to glass produced there. And, it purchased glass from Hall for its own use. At some point, Sebastian became a member of the merchant association (*Stubengesellschaft*) of Hall. Its book of crests (*Wappenbuch*) lists "Sebastian Hoechstetter von und zu Scheibenegg", a title for which he received an official diploma in 1551.[129] In 1552, he became a member of the Imperial household with an annual honorarium of 200 fl.[130] In 1559, he received the title of Imperial counselor.[131] When Sebastian died in 1569, the glassworks that had become the foundation for a new, prominent line of Höchstetters passed to his sons Walter and Johann Chrisostomus, who continued to lead the new family firm successfully into the seventeenth century.

It is impossible to answer Kern's dismissive observation that these latter-day offshoots (*Nachblüte*) failed to achieve anything like the stature of the Höchstetter family and firm under "old Ambrosius". Surviving documents do not permit a reconstruction much less a comparison of their various companies. What can be said is that the family and its family firms did not disappear. The crisis that overwhelmed it in 1529 forced it to adapt. Cadet branches migrated to new locations and established new enterprises, some of which flourished at a very high level. Whether by design or by chance, substantial capital earned and preserved by "Ambrosius and Hans, the Brothers Höchstetter and Associates" underwrote these new beginnings. Those descendants of Ulrich II and Ambrosius I who remained in Augsburg continued to enjoy elite status in urban society, marry into elite merchant and patrician families, hold offices in urban government, participate in substantial business enterprises and enjoy a degree of prosperity, even as the economy of South Germany began to contract. As old Ambrosius lay neglected and dying, chained to stone wall, as the wives of the family struggled to make ends meet, his heirs crafted new beginnings based on his ambitions and his resources. The Höchstetter family firms demonstrated resilience in a minor key.

Notes

1 Clemens Sender, *Die Chronik von Clemens Sender von den ältesten Zeiten der Stadt bis zum Jahre 1536. Die Chroniken der schwäbischen Städte. Augsburg*, Vol. IV (Leipzig 1894), 236.
2 Ibid.
3 Ibid., fn 1.
4 Hellmann, *Das Konkursrecht der Reichsstadt Augsburg* (Breslau 1905), 97.
5 Sender, *Die Chronik*, 236.
6 Ibid.
7 Ibid.
8 Ibid., 237.
9 "Wolf" DWB = *Deutsches Wörterbuch von Jacob und Wilhelm Grimm*. 16 Bde. in 32 Teilbänden. Leipzig 1854–1961. Quellenverzeichnis Leipzig 1971.
10 Recent study of resilience has prompted a rapidly growing volume of publications, especially with regard social and ecological applications of the term. Interest has grown to such an extent that dedicated research centers and working groups have emerged, notable among which are the Stockholm Resilience Center at Stockholm University and the *DFG-Forschergruppe 2539, "Resilienz – Gesellschaftliche Umbruchphasen im Dialog zwischen Mediävistik und Soziologie"*, at the University of Trier.
11 "resilience, n.," OED Online, June 2018. Oxford University Press. Available at: www.oed.com/viewdictionaryentry/Entry/163619?print (accessed 3 August 2018).
12 Ian P. McCarthy, Mark Collard, Michael Johnson, "Adaptive Organizational Resilience: An Evolutionary Perspective," *Current Opinion in Environmental Sustainability* 28 (2017): 33–40. https://doi.org/10.1016/j.cosust.2017.07.005.
13 Donald Sull, *The Upside of Turbulence: Seizing Opportunity in an Uncertain World* (New York 2009).
14 Gary Hamel and Liisa Välikangis, "The Quest for Resilience," *Harvard Business Review* (September 2003). Available at: hbr.org/2003/09/the-quest-for-resilience; K. M. Sutcliffe and T. J. Vogus, "Organizing for Resilience," in: K. S. Cameron, J. E. Dutton and R. E. Quinn (eds.), *Positive Organizational Scholarship: Foundations of a New Discipline* (San Francisco 2003), 94–110; Yossi Sheffi, *The Resilient Enterprise: Overcoming Vulnerability for Competitive Enterprise* (Cambridge, MA 2005); Louise K. Comfort, Arjen Boin and Chris C. Demchak, *Designing Resilience: Preparing for Extreme Events* (Pittsburgh 2010).
15 Randy Starr, et al., "Enterprise Resilience: Managing Risk in the Networked Economy," *Srategy and Business* 30 (2003): 56–69.
16 Richard Segal notes that the adage may have its roots in an older, English saying, "There's nobbut three generations between a clog and clog", but has, in fact, parallels in most European languages. See Richard M. Segal, "Shirt Sleeves to Shirt Sleeves in Three Generations," *Corp!* (1 July 2008). Available at: www.corpmagazine.com/special-interests/family-business/shirt-sleeves-to-shirt-sleeves-in-three-generations/.
17 StAA, Literaliensammlung, Höchstetter-Selekt I, Dok. 24, Erste Hochstetters Fragstuck.
18 "*Zufragen, das dieselb Hochstetterische Anntwurt nicht ansechlich noch der Warhait gleich sech. Das Hochstetter sein Verderben, weder im 27 noch 28 Jar nit gewisst, noch das er sein Uberschlag dannzumal biss in hundert tausennt Gulden Uberschuss zuhaben, gemach hab, dessen Ursach dieweil in seiner aignen Exception Shrifft gegen Hannsen Marschallck gerichtlich eingepracht befunden, das er zur selben Zeit Marschallckhs gemachte Shuldt sein Hochstetters Verderben gewisst hab, gipt die Exception Shrifft Zeugkhnus, dessgleichen der Argkwon unnd Verdacht seiner aigen Schuldtbucher im 27 und 28 Jar, derhalben er die Warhait zubekennen angeredt werden soll*". StAA, Literaliensammlung, Höchstetter-Selekt I, Dok. 25, Contra altem Hochstetter anndere und newe Fragstuckh auch weiter Anfrag auf die Allten zu ferrer Erleuterung derselben.
19 "*Den vierdten Articul soll man dem Hochstetter sagen unnd im den wider vorlessen, mit den ernsthafften Wortten, es sey ain gemain Geschray davon in der gannzen Statt, darumb soll er die Warhait bekennen, oder man werde verursacht gegen jm zuhanndlen wie die Notturfft ervordert*

[. . .] Uff den newntten Articul soll man allten Hochstetter lautter fragen unnd seinen schlechten Wortten nit also glauben, dann ob schon sein Hausfraw des alles gehanndellt, so hat sy jme nit verhallten sonnder er hat aller Sachen gut Wissen getragen [. . .] Uff den aillfften ist nit zuglauben, sonnder soll hocher gefragt werden, was er Hochstetter nach seinem Glupt Bargellt unnd an Schulden ampfanngen unnd wa ers hinthan hab oder jemanndts von seinenntwegen". Ibid.

20 "*Hochstetter clare lautere Anntwurtt unnd Anzaigen geben*". Ibid.

21 "*laut des Articul hab auch danzumal nicht gewisst, das sein Sach so ubel gestanden seie, hab auch vom Niderland und dem selben Leger kein Wissen gehapt, sondern erst biss er auf das Rathaus kommen, habe er denselbenn Bericht empfangen*". StAA, Literaliensammlung, Höchstetter-Selekt I, Dok. 26, Actum auf 26 Tag Septembris Anno 31, jn praesentibus Herrn Hofmann, Sighart, Paler, Schollenberger, Ambrosi Hochstetter der Elter sagt an gutlichen Frag wie hernachfolgt.

22 "*Zum 12. Articul wisse nichts darvon zu sagenn, dann alles das da gewesenn seie verkaufft unnd den Shuldnern bezalt worden,*". StAA, Literaliensammlung, Höchstetter-Selekt I, Dok. 26, Actum auf 26 Tag Septembris Anno 31, jn praesentibus Herrn Hofmann, Sighart, Paler, Schollenberger, Ambrosi Hochstetter der Elter sagt an gutlichen Frag wie hernachfolgt.

23 "*haben die Weiber etwas austragen, wiss er bey dem hochste in Warhait nit anzuzaigen*". Ibid.

24 This despite the fact that Burgwalden served as security for the dowry of Ambrosius's wife, Anne Rehlinger. "*vor seiner Aufstand ein gwiss Zeit hab er zu Rettung seins Glaubens und Aufstand versetzt Burckwalden mit aller Zugehorung dem Anthoni Fugger jnn alls umb 10000 Gulden haupt ye 100 mit 5 Gulden zu verzinzen sint zwai Zile onbezalt belibenn bringt 1000 Gulden so er auch auf Burckwalden hat thet jn Summa Hauptguet und verfallen Zins 11000 Gulden. Wol aber uff Burckwalden verhanden ist mein Hausfraw daruf verwisen unnd verschenkt die Versatzung ist gescheen jn 29 Jar uf Liechtmess*". Ibid.

25 Ibid.

26 "*Uff 19. Articul sagt, er hab 20 Vassel zwischen hie und Venedig mit Messing gehapt, darvon 7 Vasst mit Messing und ain Vessel mit Drat so lang Zeit zum Newemmarckt gelegen, verschaft mit eine Sendbrief Cunrath Rechlinger bei Hansen Nollen zu Trient, das er dieselben Vessel soll antworten Cunrath Rechlinger oder wen er schicke, so ferer sie mech da synnt, wo sie aber ferner auf wem das gesant werenn, so soll er Rechlingers Gesanten Schrift geben an sein diener in Venedig Joachim Krauss genannt das er dem Rechlingers oder Endres Grander Factor wie man sie dann jn Venedig nennt soll gebenn, die 8 Fesslenn darbei Hochstetter die Sachenn also gelassen*". Ibid.

27 The court secretary clearly wrote Prien, located on the Chiemsee in Bavaria. It seems an unlikely location to store large quantities of brass, however. Another possibility would be Rinn, north of Innsbruck in Tyrol.

28 Ibid.

29 "*Nachdem er Hochstetter in seinem Jnventari anzaigt, was fur Quecksilber und Zinober Ressten auf allen Ortten, und wer sy Pfandtsweyss jnnhat auch vertrewlich Kauffbriefe daruber [. . .] aigentlich und fleyssig zuerkhundigen, das Werttlin uff vertrawen und vertrewlich Khauffbriefe, was das Wort 'Vertrawen' bedeut oder vermug. Obs ain Sheinkhauff sey, oder ain Versatzung ains Sheins, ob nicht pillich ain Ubershatz und Uberthewrung verhannden sey*". StAA, Literaliensammlung, Höchstetter-Selekt I, Dok. 25, Contra altem Hochstetter anndere und newe Fragstuckh auch weiter Anfrag auf die Allten zu ferrer Erleuterung derselben.

30 "*der Maynung Hochstetter solt jnen vertrawen, so er die wider losen oder umb das bestimbt Kaufgellt wider von jnene losenn das sie jme das zustellen wolten*". Ibid.

31 Ibid.

32 "*das alles hab er jme kauflich auf guet Vertrawen zugestellt, er hab auch vil Leit auf den Fugger die zu bezallen von 28 biss jn das 29 Jar von dem Glibt und Gewet verwisen die Fugger angenommen unnd zufriden gestellt wer oder wievil deren gewesen seie jme nit Wissen*". StAA, Literaliensammlung, Höchstetter-Selekt I, Doc. 27, Actum den 9 Tag Octobris Anno 31 Ambrosi Hochstetter der Elter sagt uf die gestreckten Articul wie hernachfolgt.

33 "*Hochstetter in seinen Shadenregistern deren zwai mit No. 9 und des dritt jm schwarzen Segklin mit J. verzaichnet gibt fur, under anndern Ursachenn die jme zu Verderben gebracht,*

das er vonn dem aufgenomen Zinsgelt 5 % pro Jnteresse gebenn muessen". StAA, Literaliensammlung, Höchstetter-Selekt I, Dok. 21, Allten Hochstetters unvershambt Lugina, die man greiffen mag.

34 Modern historical studies of family firms often seem to suggest that survival or resilience over generations relies on luck or genetics. See Harold James, *Family Capitalism: Wendels, Haniels, Falcks, and the Continental European Model* (Cambridge, MA 2006); David Landes, *Dynasties: Fortunes and Misfortunes of the World's Great Family Businesses* (New York 2006); Niall Ferguson, *The House of Rothschild*, 2 vols. (New York 1998).

35 "*auss jnen zu bringen mit peinlicher strenger frag gegen jnen gehanndlet wurde*". StAA, Literaliensammlung, Höchstetter-Selekt I, Dok. 11, Verhoersprotokolle, 1531/32.

36 "*Wolches man jnen nit wollt gaunen, dann sie durch zerreissung jrer glider nit allein den gesundthait jres leibs (der uber alle Reichtumb wer) sonnder auch jre leib unnd gut verliern mochten, jnen jn ewig jr lebenlanng unnd jrn kindern unnd freunden zu nachred kommen unnd auffheben lassen musse, welches jme niemants hett zuergetzen*". Ibid.

37 Rehlinger is clearly not the eponymous patrician, Conrad III Rehlinger, with whose family the Höchstetters had multiple, close relations. Quite apart from the questions and the manner in which they were posed, all available evidence suggests that this Rehlinger was a minor figure in society and business. Erasmus Villsecker served Ambrosius II as a personal secretary and may have had no formal connection to his master's firm. Noll was probably the son of long-term employee, Simon Noll, while Nusshart may be Anton II Nusshart, son of a prominent, Ausburg merchant, Anton I Nusshart.

38 "*Sagt, er hab jn craft ains usgerichts Pacts ain aigen freyen Handl gen Nurnberg und ander halben gehapt, vor etlichen Jaren sei jm dan durch den selben Handl umb sein Dienst etwas zugestanden, darumb bedanck er sich Got*". StAA, Literaliensammlung, Höchstetter-Selekt I, Dok. 15, Urgichten 1531/32, 31 Oktober 1531.

39 StAA, Literaliensammlung, Höchstetter-Selekt I, Dok. 11, Verhoersprotokolle, 1531/32.

40 "*Sagt zum ersten, wiss nit anderst dann wie die jn der Schreibstuben ligen.*" StAA, Literaliensammlung, Höchstetter-Selekt I, Dok. 15, Urgichten 1531/32, 23 Oktober 1531.

41 Ibid.

42 "*Uff den andern, sagt wievor, hab der Hochstetter halb jn Bayrn nichts gehandlt, und was er und sein Son der End gehandlt, sei sein aigen Sach gewest*". StAA, Literaliensammlung, Höchstetter-Selekt I, Dok. 15, Urgichten 1531/32, 20 November 1531.

43 Ibid.

44 "*Jtem dieweil er von seinen Elltern nicht ererbt, wovon er bissher ain solhen Pracht gefuert und wo er das Gellt genommen das er zu Hall so ain treffennlichen Paw gethon unnd noch nit vollenndt unnd dannocht daneben so ain grossen ainsehenlichen Hanndl von allerlai Waren unnd Gueter gefuert*". StAA, Literaliensammlung, Höchstetter-Selekt I, Dok. 11, Verhoersprotokolle, 1531/32.

45 "*ob es not sein werd, welle er wie sich geburt antwurt geben so es darzu kompt*". StAA, Literaliensammlung, Höchstetter-Selekt I, Dok. 15, Urgichten 1531/32, 23 Oktober 1531.

46 StAA, Literaliensammlung, Höchstetter-Selekt I, Dok. 15, Urgichten 1531/32, 24 Oktober 1531.

47 It is impossible to determine whether the Leonhard Beck in question was the painter, associated with the atelier of Hans Holbein the Elder, remembered for his frescoes and altarpieces, as well as his wood-cut engravings on commission from Maximilian I, or the merchant who was a member of the "Patrons of Society" (*Mehrer der Gesellschaft*) and husband of Katharina Wolf. The latter seems more likely due to his social position and his financial activities.

48 "*Die obgemelten drey Personen haben jn Pfister gebeten, jnen das Gelt zu den Hochstettern zupringen, und er Pfister sy gar nichts seidther bemelter Zeit biss uff hewtigen Tag hab er den Hochstetter seins Achtens weder wenig noch vil als benantlich 5 % zugestelt, wol habe er jnen den Hochstettern nach dem allem wie obstet gehandlt mit Geselschafter und ain hiesigen Kauf Lewten Wexel gemacht, die den Hochstettern vertrawt habe, benantlich uber 47000 Gulden Reinisch und*

Ducaten 6900 mer 2850 Mark Silber". StAA, Literaliensammlung, Höchstetter-Selekt I, Dok. 15, Urgichten 1531/32, 27 Oktober 1531.

49 Friedrich Blendinger, *Zwei Augsburger Unterkaufbücher aus den Jahren 1551 bis 1558. Älteste Aufzeichnungen zur Vor- und Frühgeschichte der Augsburger Börse* (Stuttgart 1994), 15.

50 StAA, Literaliensammlung, Höchstetter-Selekt I, Dok. 15, Urgichten 1531/32, 27 Oktober 1531. "Zettel. Zu merckhen was jch Othmair Fugger verkauft hab von den Guter, die ich von Philip Gasner seligen empfangen hab, nemlich wie hernach stet – 1530 28 Mai.

51 Oscar Gelderblom, *Cities of Commerce: The Institutional Foundations of International Trade in the Low Countries, 1250–1650* (Princeton 2013), 16.

52 They gained European fame for craftsmanship in the seventeenth and eighteenth centuries, completing large commissions for private and princely houses across the continent, and setting a standard for luxury that remains a benchmark to this day. Less attention has been paid to their role in finance, however. See Sylvia Rathke-Köhl, *Geschichte des Augsburger Goldschmiedegewerbes vom Ende des 17. bis zum Ende des 18. Jahrhunderts* (Augsburg 1964); Helmut Seling, *Die Kunst der Augsburger Goldschmiede 1529–1868* (Munich 1980); Helmut Seling, "Silberhandel und Goldschmiedekunst in Augsburg im 16. Jahrhundert," in: *Welt im Umbruch*, vol. III (Augsburg 1981), 162–70; Anton Werner, *Augsburger Goldschmiede: Verzeichnis der Augsburger Goldschmiede, Silberarbeiter, Juweliere und Steinschneider von 1346–1803* (Augsburg 1913).

53 Goldsmiths have long been viewed as one of the early sources for banking in Italy and England. They issued receipts for deposits of gold and silver that eventually circulated from hand to hand, a development viewed by some as a forerunner of paper money. The deposited metal provided these artisans with an opportunity to function also as lenders. In seventeenth-century England, goldsmiths evolved into bankers in the formal sense, though whether they were the first has been openly debated. See Raymond de Roover, *The Rise and Fall of the Medici Bank, 1397–1494* (New York 1966); Richard Ehrenberg, *Capital and Finance in the Age of the Renaissance: A Study of the Fugger* (New York 1928); Charles P. Kindelberger, *A Financial History of Western Europe*, 2nd ed. (Oxford 1993); R. H. Tawney (ed.), "Introduction," in: Thomas Wilson (ed.), *A Discourse on Usury* (1572 [London 1925]); D. J. van Dillen, *History of the Principal Public Banks* (The Hague 1934).

54 StAA, Literaliensammlung, Höchstetter-Selekt I, Dok. 15, Urgichten 1531/32, 29 Oktober 1531.

55 DWB = *Deutsches Wörterbuch von Jacob und Wilhelm Grimm*. 16 Bde. in 32 Teilbänden. Leipzig 1854–1961. Quellenverzeichnis Leipzig 1971, käufler bis käuflin (Bd. 11, Sp. 335 bis 336). Available at: http://woerterbuchnetz.de/cgi-bin/WBNetz/wbgui_py?sigle=DWB&mode=Vernetzung&lemid=GK02743#XGK02743 (accessed 10 December 2018).

56 "*Gemain Verkaufferin wolcher Namen den Stattknecht wol bewisst*". StAA, Literaliensammlung, Höchstetter-Selekt I, Dok. 11, Verhoersprotokolle, 1531/32.

57 It is also interesting to note that some of these "peddlers" lived or worked in close proximity to the businesses of prominent wholesale merchants.

58 StAA, Literaliensammlung, Höchstetter-Selekt I, Dok. 15, Urgichten 1531/32, 4 November 1531.

59 Anna Zimmermann seems to have specialised in an elevated clientel. Ibid.

60 Bech appears to have worked with local artisans, especially a goldsmith named Fugger. Ibid.

61 Ibid.

62 Artzt was an established member of the *Kaufleuteschaft*; Ratold would join its ranks in 1538.

63 " *es seye etliche vier der funff Mal by nechtlicher weis zu seiner Gelegenhait, ye zu zehen, ye zu aylff, ye zu zwolff Urn fur des alten Ambrosy Hochstetters Haus anhaym gangen und gesehen zum Thor, darauff der Schreibstub stet, ain Zeichkarlin hinus furn, was als darob gewesen, wiss er nit, wer es aber herauss zogen oder wo dz hinkommen, trage er auch kain Wissen, dann er sich*

des nicht geachtet". StAA, Literaliensammlung, Höchstetter-Selekt I, Dok. 15, Urgichten 1531/32, 29 October 1531.

64 "*Er habe auch vergangner Zeit, wolhs jars wiss er nit aigentlich, gesehen, dz Joseph Hochstetters junger Knecht an ainem abent ungevar umb die funften Stund hab ain Raistruchen mit zwayen Marckschlosen uff ainem Ziechkarlin zu dem Jacoberthor hinus gefurt und gezogen, ob aber die Truch uff die Floss oder sonst anderst wo hinkommen, und was darjnn gewesen sei, wiss er nit, die Zeit aigentlich anzuzaigen, wiss er nit anderst, dann dz es geschehen sei zu der Zeit als die Hochstetter jn Verwarung gewesen seyen*". Ibid.

65 StAA, Literaliensammlung, Höchstetter-Selekt I, Dok. 11, Verhoersprotokolle, 1531/32.

66 StAA, Literaliensammlung, Höchstetter-Selekt I, Dok. 15, Urgichten 1531/32, 31 October 1531.

67 Ibid.

68 Ibid.

69 Ibid.

70 Ibid.

71 Ibid.

72 Ibid.

73 "*sy hab auch von jrer Frawen gehort, der Joachim hab sein und jr Silbergeshir erschmelten und hinweg gefurt, dann er ein Schmelzoffen jm Hauss gehapt, ferner hab sy von der magt gehoert, Magdalena hab ain Man zu Aratzried, als Joachim hinweg gezogen, hab er sein Wames voller Gulden eingenaeht, weiter sei jr nichts wissen*". Ibid.

74 StAA, Literaliensammlung, Höchstetter-Selekt I, Dok. 15, Urgichten 1531/32, 13 November 1531.

75 The list included 54 questions to which each of the wives had to respond. StAA, Literaliensammlung, Höchstetter-Selekt I, Dok. 11, Verhoersprotokolle, 1531/32.

76 Ibid., 22 December 1531.

77 "*dan sy jetz jm driten Jar auss dem Schreibstuben nichts empfangen*". StAA, Literaliensammlung, Höchstetter-Selekt I, Dok. 15, Urgichten 1531/32, 22 December 1531.

78 "*hab sy Hans Hochstetterin dz jhenigen, dz jr zugehorig und verschriben sei, mit Brief und Sigl zu jrer Gelegenhait usgeflohnet, der Maynung, als man gesagt, man wird jr zu Haus geen, hab sy Fursorg gehapt, jr mocht ain dem jren zu Nachteil gehandlt worden sein, darumb sy verursacht, dz jr und sonst nichts dan dz jr zugehorig gewesen ab und weg zuthon*". Ibid.

79 Ibid.

80 StAA, Literaliensammlung, Höchstetter-Selekt I, Dok. 11, Verhoersprotokolle, 1531/32.

81 Anna Rehlinger, for example, dismissed the notion as absurd: "She knows nothing of any trench" (*Wiss von kain Grub nichts*). See StAA, Literaliensammlung, Höchstetter-Selekt I, Dok. 15, Urgichten 1531/32, 22 December 1531.

82 Ibid.

83 "*Alles, dz von jrm Vater an sy kommen, sei jrm man undterthanig gemacht und jr weder Haller noch Pfennig darvon worden*". Ibid.

84 Ibid.

85 "*Das Gelts halben, so sy jn der Geselschaft haben solt, wiss sy nichts zesagen, anderst dann jr Heyratgut 4000 Gulden hab jr man vom Jorg Wielandt empfangen und, jrs Achtens, jr man jn Geselschaft gelegt, wie er jr vorgesagt*". Ibid.

86 Hellmann, *Das Konkursrecht der Reichsstadt Augsburg*, 106.

87 StAA, Literaliensammlung, Höchstetter-Selekt I, Dok. 17, "Uff welhe Posten die Hochstetter mit Ernst anzusprechen sein".

88 StAA, Literaliensammlung, Höchstetter-Selekt I, Dok. 20, Actum auf 13. Tag Aprilis Anno 32, jn praesentibus Herrn Wilhalm Rechlinger, Miller, Paler, alt Ambrosi Hochstetter zaigt an guetlicher Frag an.

89 StAA, Literaliensammlung, Höchstetter-Selekt I, Dok. 18, Actum 13. Aprilis Anno 32, jn praesentibus Herrn Wilhalm Rechlinger, Miller, Paler, Ambrosi der junger Hochsteter sagt an guetlicher Frag.

90 "*Wol hab Ungelter etwas darjnn gehapt was aber wiss er nit*". StAA, Literaliensammlung, Höchstetter-Selekt I, Dok. 19, Jn praesentibus Herrn Wilhalm Rechlinger, Miller, Paler, Actum 13 April Anno 32, Joseph Hochstetter sagt.

91 "*der jung Ambrosi hab es gehandlt*". StAA, Literaliensammlung, Höchstetter-Selekt I, Dok. 20, Actum auf 13. Tag Aprilis Anno 32, jn praesentibus Herrn Wilhalm Rechlinger, Miller, Paler, alt Ambrosi Hochstetter zaigt an guetlicher Frag an. Charles V had granted the right to collect and retain these duties to Count Palatine Ludwig, and Ludwig had discounted it to the Höchstetter for 5,000 fl at the Frankfurt fair.

92 StAA, Literaliensammlung, Höchstetter-Selekt I, Dok. 18, Actum 13. Aprilis Anno 32, jn praesentibus Herrn Wilhalm Rechlinger, Miller, Paler, Ambrosi der junger Hochsteter sagt an guetlicher Frag.

93 Ibid.

94 Otmar Fugger's testimony revealed sales in excess of 900 fl. See n. 50.

95 The creditors suspected Philipp I Gassner had a stake in the Höchstetter firm, that he was a silent partner and, therefore, liable with the other bankrupts for all of its debts. During the transfer in Linz, two individuals, Niclas Schindberger and Hans von Lamberg, whom Gassner identified as officials of Ferdinand I, but who might have been acting on their own or the creditors' behalf, seized two bales of clothe valued at 650 fl. They claimed to have acted on information that Gassner was "a partner in the Höchstetter company" (*Mitverwandter in der Hochstetter Gesellschaft*). Gassner denied the allegation, claiming that he had a letter of discharge from the Höchstetters and no further interest in their firm. The creditors appear to have entertained doubts about Gassner's relationship to the firm and hopes that they might recover damages from him. Though Gassner died in 1530, at the height of the bankruptcy proceedings, claims might still be made against his estate. This is the reason why they questioned his son, Joachim I Gassner, then a merchant-apprentice with the Höchstetters. He knew nothing. Nor did other *Geheimdiener*. See StAA, Kaufmannschaft und Handel, Fazc. IV, 24/16, Höchstetter Handel 1529; StAA, Literaliensammlung, Höchstetter-Selekt I, Dok. 2, Wievil Hoechstetter in Zeit seines Verderbens Gellt auffgenommen unnd von wem; StAA, Literaliensammlung, Höchstetter-Selekt I, Dok. 15, Urgichten 1531/32, 23 October 1531.

96 "*dann der seie so jrrig gewesen, das man nit wol darauss moge kommen.*" StAA, Literaliensammlung, Höchstetter-Selekt I, Dok. 18, Actum 13. Aprilis Anno 32, jn praesentibus Herrn Wilhalm Rechlinger, Miller, Paler, Ambrosi der junger Hochsteter sagt an guetlicher Frag.

97 StAA, Literaliensammlung, Höchstetter-Selekt I, Dok. 19, Jn praesentibus Herrn Wilhalm Rechlinger, Miller, Paler, Actum 13 April Anno 32, Joseph Hochstetter sagt.

98 "*Dieweil jnn der letzten Gesellshaft Verschreibung unnder anndern Articuln ausstruckhenlich bedingt wurdt, das die Gesellschaffter unnd Diener etlich Hanndlungen und Anshleg bei guten Trewen jnn gehaim zuhallten, was dieselben Anshleg oder Hanndlungen gewesen, darumb er sy des Gehaims halben so hoch gegen jme verstrickht*". StAA, Literaliensammlung, Höchstetter-Selekt I, Dok. 17, Uff welhe Posten die Hochstetter mit Ernst anzusprechen sein.

99 "*wiss nit anders dan gehaim zu halten jnn Handlungen*". StAA, Literaliensammlung, Höchstetter-Selekt I, Dok. 18, Actum 13. Aprilis Anno 32, jn praesentibus Herrn Wilhalm Rechlinger, Miller, Paler, Ambrosi der junger Hochsteter sagt an guetlicher Frag.

100 "*seie bei allenn Gesellschaften der Brauch jm Handlung verschwigen zu haltenn damit sie jnn Kaufen und Verkauffen nit gehindert werden, wiss sonst von keinem sondern Geheim*". StAA, Literaliensammlung, Höchstetter-Selekt I, Dok. 20, Actum auf 13. Tag Aprilis Anno 32, jn praesentibus Herrn Wilhalm Rechlinger, Miller, Paler, alt Ambrosi Hochstetter zaigt an guetlicher Frag an.

101 These narrowed circumstances did not sit well. Anna Rehlinger, Katharina Ehinger and Katharina Neumann had to petition the *Stadtvogt* for payment of their stipends, a mere 300 fl, 100 fl and 200 fl per annum, respectively, a dramatic reduction from

the affluence they and their families had recently enjoyed. The authorities hesitated to make these payments, because the wives continued to resist the settlements reached in the city court, which involved the final sale of their property, especially the family estate of Burgwalden to settle creditor demands. Rather, they appealed repeatedly to the *Reichskammergericht* and were ultimately successful. See StAA, Literaliensammlung, Höchstetter-Selekt I, Dok 50, Herr D. Helens Ratschlag die alt Fraw Hochstetterin belangendt, s.d., s.a; BHStA, Reichskammergerichtsakten, 6771, 6772, 6773, 6774.

102 Kern, *Studien zur Geschichte des Augsburger Kaufmannshauses der Höchstetter*, 34–5.

103 Ehrenberg, *Das Zeitalter der Fugger*, 217.

104 Strieder, *Das Reiche Augsburg*, 101.

105 Christian C. A. Lange, et al. (eds.), *Diplomatarium Norvegicum*, vol. 8, 21 vols. (Christiana 1847-[Oslo 1995]), 630–3, Nos. 546–7. See also Staatsarchiv Schleswig-Holstein, Bergwerksrechte in Schweden 10, Urkunde aus dem Jahre 1532 betr. Bestellung Joachim Hoechstetters I. zum Bergmeister: 250r–255r: "Privilegia der Beckwerck aus Schonn / Joachim Hoechsteder gegeben / Anno etc. 1532 as cited in Höchstetter, *Stammtafel*, 4–5.

106 For a brief sketch of the Höchstetters in England, see George Hammersley (ed.), *Daniel Hechstetter the Younger: Memorabilia and Letters, 1600–1639* (Stuttgart 1988), 28–50.

107 Christian II had a tumultuous career. Under the Kalmar Union, he reigned as King of Denmark and Norway from 1513 until 1523 and of Sweden from 1520 until 1521. Denmark was an elective monarchy, in which the nobility chose the king and shared power with him. Frederick came into conflict with the Danish nobility when he was forced to sign a charter to share his authority to ensure his election. Through domestic reforms he later sought to evade these restrictions. His attempt to preserve his authority by maintaining the Kalmar Union also involved him in war with Sweden from 1518 to 1523. Though he captured the country in 1520, his rule did not last. His slaughter of leading Swedish noble families, which became known as the Stockholm Bloodbath and earned him the title in Sweden of Christian the Tyrant, led to his being overthrown in a rebellion led by Gustav Vasa. His reign in Denmark and Norway ended in 1523 when his uncle seized the thrones as Frederick I. He was exiled to the Netherlands, ruled by his brother-in-law, Charles V. An unsuccessful attempt to reclaim the thrones in 1531 ended in his arrest. He spent the rest of his life in captivity.

108 Friedrich Blendinger, "Hoechstetter, Joachim," *Neue Deutsche Biographie* 9 (1972), S. 304 f. [Online-Version]. Available at: www.deutsche-biographie.de/pnd131595237.html#ndbcontent.

109 Ibid.

110 For a detailed account of Joachim I's dealings with Denmark, see Otto Nübel, "Das Augsburger Kaufherrengeschlecht Hoechstetter und die Restitution König Christian II. von Dänemark," *Zeitschrift des Historischen Vereins für Schwaben* 73 (1979): 126–247.

111 Hammersley, *Daniel Hechstetter the Younger*, 28.

112 StAA, Notariatsarchiv Spreng, IV, Nr. 14; Stadtgerichtsakten, Nr. 42. Cited in Reinhard, Augsburger Eliten des 16. Jahrhunderts, 310; Steuerbücher, 1575.

113 "*Nach meiner Muetter seligem Endt, Hatt das glückh wunderbarlich mit uns und unserm Vatter gespielt. Und übel sich mit Ihm verhalten. Doch hatt uns Kind Gott widerumb mit seinre gnad angesehen; Und einen Jeden nach seiner ggnad mit getheilt, als vil es vonn nöthen gehabt*". StAA, Höchstettersammlung, Tagebuch des Dr. Philipp Hoechstetter, 1578–1635, pp. 8–9. See also Josef Herz, "Das Tagebuch des Augsburger Arztes und Stadtphysikus Dr. Philipp Höchstetter," *Zeitschrift des historischen Vereins für Schwaben* 70 (1976): 180–224.

114 Hammersley, *Daniel Hechstetter the Younger*, 28.

115 Höchstetter, Stammtafel, 63.

116 Hammersley, *Daniel Hechstetter the Younger*, 30–1.

117 "*Jtem dieweil er von seinen Elltern nicht ererbt, wovon er bissher ain solhen Pracht gefuert und wo er das Gellt genommen das er zu Hall so ain treffennlichen Paw gethon unnd noch nit vollenndt*

unnd dannocht daneben so ain grossen ainsehenlichen Hanndl von allerlai Waren unnd Gueter gefuert". StAA, Literaliensammlung, Höchstetter-Selekt I, Dok. 11, Verhoersprotokolle, 1531/32.

118 TLA, Gemeine Missiven 1531, fol. 79v, 14 March 1531.

119 For a history of the glassworks in Hall and its relationship to the Höchstetter family, see Heinrich Heimer, *Die Glashütte zu Hall in Tirol und die Augsburger Kaufmannsfamilie der Höchstetter* (Munich 1959).

120 TLA, Bekennen 1533, fol. 73–5; Geschäfte vom Hof, 24 November 1533, fol. 291–2.

121 TLA, An die Kgl. Majestät, 1534, fol. 419r–19v, 21 March 1534; Geschäfte vom Hof, 1534, fol. 78r–79v, 26 March 1534; Bekennen 1534, fol. 79–81. For a complete history of the glass manufactory at Hall in Tyrol, see Heinrich Heimer, *Die Glashütte in Hall in Tirol und die Augsburger Kaufmannsfamilie der Hoechstetter* (Munich 1959); Hans Zedinek, *Die Glashütte in Hall zu Tirol* (Vienna 1927).

122 The "essential plants" in this case would most likely have been broadleaf plants, such as beech trees or ferns, which were burned to render potash, potassium carbonate, used in the manufacturing of class since ancient times. "*will er Pflanzen zu Verbrennen anbauen*". TLA, Abteilung IV b, KS III 46, Pos. I, fol. 42v, 3 August 1536.

123 TLA, Embieten und Befelch 1534, fol. 312, 377–8; Geschäfte vom Hof 1536, Nrs. 2006, 2014

124 TLA, Geschäfte vom Hof 1538, Nrs. 2102, fol. 164; Raitbuch, Nr. 2157, fol. 310–11; Gemeine Missiven, Nr. 2141, fol. 101–2.

125 TLA, An die Kgl. Majestät, KS 2197, 1540, fol. 227r; 1541, fol. 316r–21r; 1542, fol. 467v.

126 TLA, Gemeine Missiven, 1531, fol. 79v, 14 March 1531.

127 Hoechstetter, *Stammtafel der Hoechstetter*, 59–60.

128 TLA, Gemeine Missiven 1548, fol. 445v, 28 June 1548.

129 Hoechstetter, *Stammtafel der Hoechstetter*, 59.

130 TLA, Bekennen 1552/1553, fol. 156r–56v, 26 July 1552; HofkammerbuchTirol 1552/1553, fol. 54r–54v, 27 July 1552.

131 Hoechstetter, *Stammtafel der Hoechstetter*, 59. See also Geschäft vom Hof 1557, fol. 175v, 21 September 1557.

Conclusion

"Ambrosius and Hans the Brothers Höchstetter and Associates" ceased business in 1529. By 1531, the partners had fled or been imprisoned. The testimony gathered in that year documented clearly to what extent and by what means the Höchstetters had violated their oath to cede all their property and to transact no business. The conclusion was swift and final: The elder Höchstetter and his partners had violated their oath; they had borrowed money with no intention to repay it.[1] The court's declaration ran to four pages and 17 points. There would be no compromise settlement. In 1534, Ambrosius I died in chains. The junior partners would remain in prison for another decade.

Yet, though the Höchstetter bankruptcy had formally concluded, the Höchstetter bankrupts continued to attract the attention of the authorities. Ambrosius II and Joseph never ceased protesting their innocence and petitioning for their freedom. They campaigned relentlessly to restore their *Trauen und Glauben* and escape imprisonment. In doing so, they unwittingly delivered a concluding statement on the organization of family firms, the nature of capitalistic practices, the management of information, the lability of institutions, the vagaries of networks and the limits of resilience in a capitalistic age.

* * *

In June 1541, all previous appeals having proven futile, they petitioned Emperor Charles V, summarizing their view of the injustice done to them. They had been held in prison for 12 years as partners of Ambrosius I and, therefore, liable for his and the firm's accumulated debts. They insisted, however, that they should not be required to make restitution, because they were under the authority of their seniors at the time of the bankruptcy, were not responsible for the actions of Ambrosius I and had no interest in his remaining estate.[2] "As sons of the family under paternal authority, we lived and worked obediently according to his [Ambrosius I's, tms] commands, as became proper sons according to God and the law" (*wie wir dann damals Filii Families under vatterlicher Gewaltsam gewest, gehorsamblich jrm Bevelch gemessen gelebt und gehandlet, wie sollichs von Got unnd dem Rechten frumen Sunen gezimbt*).

According to them, the notion of "brotherhood" had given no shape to relationships among the Höchstetter partners. Quite the contrary, Ambrosius II and Joseph portrayed "Ambrosius and Hans, the Brothers Höchstetter and Associates" as a closely managed, vertically organized firm under the undisputed leadership and sole responsibility of Ambrosius I. They had never been in a position to conduct their own business, make independent decisions and, as a result, assume liability for the firm's failure. Here was the reverse of the medal: Their testimony signals that family ownership and control applied not to the family as a whole but to a *pater familias*, whose commands all obeyed, but whose deeds and misdeeds should have no impact on anyone else, much less his son and nephew.

The emperor responded promptly. A mandate, issued in his name on 11 July 1541 ordered the immediate release of the Höchstetters, against appropriate surety, "by avoidance of our and the Empires severe disgrace and punishment".[3] In November 1541, the city authorities received a mandate from Ferdinand, King of the Romans, who repeated the threat.[4]

In appealing to the long-term patrons of their family and firm, the House of Habsburg, Ambrosius II and Joseph utilized a standard capitalistic practice. Patronage had long served the Höchstetters well. As capitalists, the protection of princes in the form of legal agreements had guaranteed them access to resources at fixed, stable prices, lowered transaction costs across the entire process of production, transportation and sale, provided competitive advantage that assured a degree of success and, finally, freed them from interference by others It continued to do so.

Their representation of an unjust confinement was, of course, instrumental testimony, designed to win their freedom, not to review the facts. Sufficient evidence existed to prove that Ambrosius II and Joseph were neither entirely innocent nor unjustly treated. The claim of legal incapacity, coming as it did from signatories to the firm's 1524 charter, who were also married heads of households, would have struck the authorities and creditors as improbable. Quite apart from the accusations of reckless gambling and conspicuous consumption that pursued them, Ambrosius II and Joseph conducted business in their own right as well as on behalf of their principals as partners and factors of a family firm in early modern Augsburg. After the declaration of bankruptcy, for example, Joseph had traveled to Antwerp to raise 13,000 fl.[5] There a consortium of Augsburg merchant-bankers, including the Fuggers, Welsers, Herwarts, Manlichs and Bimmels, extended him the credit.[6] Most of them could not recall details of the transaction, but one, Anton Fugger, quoted the promissory note in his keeping to prove that Joseph had borrowed on his own behalf, not as a partner. Regardless, his transaction violated both his oath to cede property and his pledge to repay his debts.

Fugger's revelation confirms that the market for information was surprisingly dense in the late medieval and early modern economy. In an age before probability statistics and risk calculation, it served an arguably more important function than it does in the modern economy. It traveled slowly, but was exact, and its management took on added significance. Documentation circulated as well. Yet, information is not knowledge, as Hayek and others have argued, raising questions about the rationality of the Höchstetters' campaign for release from prison. It existed not in abstract terms of cost versus benefit, but in the specific situation. Ambrosius II and Joseph thought they had nothing to lose.

They did not reckon with the civic authorities, however. Despite Imperial and royal pressure, Augsburg resisted the campaign of the bankrupts and their supporters. The authorities believed the bankrupts had called into question the city's jurisdiction and sovereignty. In reply to the Emperor, they insisted that "an honorable council had dealt with them [the Höchstetters, tms] in no other manner than is proper according to law, propriety and equity" (*ein erber Rath mit jnen nichts annderst dann sich dem Rechten der Gebur und Billichait nach gezimbt hatt, gehanndlet*).[7] The City Council was willing to release the bankrupts under political duress, but it imposed an *Urfehde*, a legal acknowledgement by the Höchstetters that the Council had acted according to the letter of the law and that they would never take retaliatory action of any sort against the city or its leadership.[8] It demanded as well payment of a surety to guarantee compliance.

Council and court acted to defend Augsburg's right as a free Imperial city not only to exercise its own jurisdiction but to do so according to its own laws. This customary law and usage had arisen over centuries, constantly created and recreated by the very economic agents, whose activities it supposedly governed. It was not imposed from the top down by higher authority, as Northian institutions are too often assumed to be, but generated from the bottom up by the economic behaviors of debtors and creditors. Its formalization into law, which occurred only hesitantly in Augsburg, occurred in reaction to the opportunism of these same behaviors. That helps to explain the inadequacies of customary law and usage, against which the bankrupts and their creditors so often protested, through which the bankruptcy remained unresolved. Small wonder then that civic authoritiess refused to release Ambrosius II and Joseph on any but its own terms

The efforts of the bankrupts to win their freedom drew support from a community of relatives, friends and associates, some of whom were also creditors. They petitioned on their own, stating that "in twelve years of legal proceedings at difficult, unbearable cost [we] had reached such agreement with the imprisoned Höchstetters that we not only will tolerate their release, but wish it".[9] Twenty-one signatures appear on the supplication, the majority of which belonged to members of the Ehinger and Rehlinger families, relatives of Höchstetter wives and widows, a fact that was not lost on the authorities.[10] Yet, a further 29 creditors, most of whom were landed aristocrats or imperial functionaries with no other apparent connection to the Höchstetters also signaled their support.[11] And the Höchstetters needed that support. Stripped of all property and banned from all business, Ambrosius II and Joseph alone could never meet the city's demand. Nor could those supporters who initially agreed to pay it for them. Georg Besser, the Bürgermeister of Ulm, Hans Walter and

Wilhelm Ehinger, and Mang Kraffter, all Bürger of Ulm, protested: "We find the form of your document so sharp even burdensome and unusual that for us to thus oblige, involve and commit ourselves is not acceptable, tolerable or bearable".[12]

The willingness of these people to lend material or moral support to Ambrosius II and Joseph reminds us that family firms extended well beyond the nuclear family. They involved cadet branches and married relatives. The interests that bound were not merely financial but also social and emotional. It reminds us as well of the inadequacies of network theory and research to explain these ties. Family firms reached beyond themselves for financial, social and political capital, not only to networks of equals, but to communities of associations high and low, official and unofficial, intimate and distant. The assumptions of network theory fail to capture the diachronic dynamism of individual relationships, the varying degrees of intensity and intimacy that can change suddenly and inexplicably, so far as the historian is concerned, in light of which any network remains a post hoc artefact.

Ambrosius II and Joseph emerged from prison in 1544. They admitted that they had "themselves through a too severe approach hindered the process".[13] They insisted that they had been "held and treated in a Christian, paternal and sympathetic manner with all goodness, appropriate legality, imparted justice, protection and care". They promised "to conduct and show ourselves in all ways as befits submissive, obedient burgher". To describe them as broken men would not be far from the truth. Ambrosius II never reentered business, whether of his own volition or through his peers' exclusion cannot be determined, but rather retired to his heavily mortgaged estate of Burgwalden, where he died in 1550, less than three weeks after the death of his wife, Catharina Neumann. Of their eight children, two eventually married, but died without issue.[14] The eldest son, Carl, received Imperial confirmation of his right of high justice at the family's castle and estate of Burgwalden from Ferdinand I in 1559 only to sell the property and associated rights to Georg von Stetten a decade later in 1569.[15] Joseph reentered business in a modest fashion, but only at far remove from the place of his disgrace. He earned a living as a commission agent in Venice for various German merchants until his death in 1565.[16] Though married twice, first to Benigna Adler just before the bankruptcy in 1528 and then to a member of the Rem family just after his release from prison, he had no heirs. His line of the family died with him, as that of Ambrosius II appears to have done in the following generation. The survival of the Höchstetters, to say nothing of the resilience of their business, depended on others.

* * *

Bankruptcy, whether one understands it as a phenomenon or an epiphenomenon of business life, reveals much about the workings of an economy. In the present, as in the past, failure was by no means uncommon. The very existence of a "Buddenbrooks Syndrome" speaks to the common assumption of a commonplace event.

Though each individual case displays its own characteristics, making comparison in all but the crudest, most general form impossible, bankruptcy records provide a unique window onto the economic life of the past. Frequently, they preserve the only surviving documentation of economic agents and their companies. In their efforts to excavate the causes of failure, creditors and authorities also exposed the grounds for success. Moreover, their compilation and review of economic accounts and correspondence, claims and counterclaims, arguments and appeals provide a critical perspective, one that reveals the institutions and organizations, communities and relationships that shaped the activities of individual merchants and their firms.

Those firms were usually organized around family groups, depending on their resources and leadership, in the late medieval and early modern economy. The study of a single firm's failure, like that of the Höchstetters, reveals degrees of vitality and flexibility that do not correspond to these common assumptions. Though they relied on family capital, they could make creative use of financial markets to attract foreign depositors and investors to the point that family ownership was in name only. The same applies to management: They could draw on external expertise as changing circumstances and new enterprises required. These qualities enabled family firms past and present to adapt and survive over generations, displaying a resilience that suits them well for the exigencies of business.

Discussions of capitalism usually assume that those exigencies were fundamentally different in the past. Whether because of inadequate institutional development or incomplete market integration, economic life in the past is understood to be less developed, less efficient, less stable, less profitable. Financial markets, for example, are assumed to have been under-developed, because they lacked impersonal organizations and institutions and relied instead on personal relationships of trust. This assumption ignores the officials and individuals who exercised legal functions that stabilized financial transactions in the absence of fixed organizations and institutions. Modernity is the measure, as reflected by the common habit of predicating the term "capitalism" with a modifier, such as feudal, commercial or early, to name a few. The study of bankruptcies like that of the Höchstetters reveals, by contrast, the common qualities. It may be said at a minimum that capitalism in all ages involves private ownership of the means of production, creation of goods and services for profit in a market and, to a varying degree, governmental support in the form of appropriate legal institutions. Yet bankruptcy emphasizes the dynamism that is characteristic of capitalistic organizations and practices in all periods of time: Firms alter capitalization and management, structure and function, in pursuit of profits; they adopt practices pragmatically and idiosyncratically, not according to abstract reason or prescript, in an attempt to reduce uncertainty and manage costs; they seek information and control its flow, both internal and external to the firm, adapting business life to its speed and accuracy; they shape institutions, ignoring or obeying them as business circumstance dictates; they rely on trust and the social relations that may underwrite it, but also create such organizational and institutional structures as strengthen the predictability of outcomes and do not hesitate to act opportunistically; and, finally, they have unique qualities of resilience, determined by the social and economic environments in which they operate. Attempts to arrive at theoretical definitions for and discussion of capitalism, distract from those qualities that make it timeless. They also obscure those qualities that make it utterly unique, a human story of economic success and failure.

Notes

1 StAA, Literaliensammlung, Höchstetter-Selekt I, Dok. 23, Des allten Hochstetter und seiner Mitverwanndten betruglichen Hanndlung, s.d., s.a.

2 "*das wir jnen den Hochstetterishen Glaubigern nichtzit shuldig noch verpunden, unnd ob wir gleich als Mitgeselshaffter obligiert (das doch on Grund), so weren wir doch zu restituiren, dann wir minores Jung und hetten an unnsers Vatters und Vetter Hanndlung und Verderben gar khain Shuld unnd mit jme weder Tail noch Gemain, begerten auch seiner verlassen Hab unnd Gutter weder zu geniessen noch zu entgelten, unnd demnach wie billich unnser unvershuldten Gefenckhnus gemuessigt unnd ledig zewerden*". StAA, Literaliensammlung, Höchstetter-Selekt I, Dok. 48, Sup. Ambrosien unnd Joseph die Hochstetteran den Kay. Mt., 11 Junii Anno 41.

3 StAA, Literaliensammlung, Höchstetter-Selekt I, Dok. 55, 1541 Kay. Mandat die gefanngen Hochstetter zuledigen, 11 July 1541.

4 StAA, Literaliensammlung, Höchstetter-Selekt I, Dok. 32, Mandat den ersamen unnsern unnd des Reichs lieben getrewen N. Burgermayster unnd Rath der Statt Augspurg, s.d., s.a.

5 "*Jtem als Joseph Hochstetter nach der Beshrayung gen Antorff geritten alda von den Geselshaffte 13000 fl. auffgebracht. Ob er sich nit als ain Geselshaffter neben den anndern Hochstettern unnd jrn Mitverwanndten (dern Namen sonnders austruckhs sollenn angezaigt werden) umb Bezalung vershriben*". StAA, Literaliensammlung, Höchstetter-Selekt I, Dok. 11, Verhoersprotokolle, 1531/32.

6 "*Uff den dritten, die Fugker 2000, Bartholme Welser 2000, Jacob Welser 1000, Cristoff Herwart 1000, Jorg Herwart 1000, Hans Herwart 1000, Lisabeth von Munichen 1000, Erasmen Schetz jn Antdorff 1000, Matheus Manlich 1000, Laserus Tucher 1000, mer haben [die] Bymel fur 1000 Gulden versprochen, darfur die Fugker Burg worden sein, und die Brief ligen, seines Achtens, hinder den Fugker oder Bartholme Welser jn Antdorff*". Ibid.

7 StAA, Literaliensammlung, Höchstetter-Selekt I, Dok. 49, Urphede, s.d., s.a.

8 StAA, Literaliensammlung, Höchstetter-Selekt I, Dok. 48, Sup. An die Ro. Kay. Mt. der Statt Augspurg Bericht der Hochstetter belangend, s.d., s.a.

9 "*nun die Glaubiger vil unnd mancherlai Rechtverttigungen gegen genannten altem Ambrosi Hochstetter seinem gefanngnem Son und Vettern jetzunder jn das zwelfft Jar mit grossem schwerem unleidenlichen Costen geiebt, unnd zu lezt unns zu baiden Tailen dermassen vergleicht und verainigt, das wir jr der ermelten gefanngen Hochsteter Erledigung auss billichem Mitleiden jrer lanngwerunden halten Gefenckhnus und erbermlicher Naigung nit allain vol leiden mugen unnd darvon hiemit verwilligen, sonnder auch neben und mit jnen Eur. Ro. Kay. Mt. jn aller unnderthenigister Gehorsame umb sollich jr Erledigung bittend, das umb E. Kay. Mt. sambt dem solichs ein gotlich unnd milt Werckh der Barmherzigkhait ist, wir alle samentlich und sonnderlich zuverdienen jn aller Unnderthenigkhait unnd Gehorsam zum hochsten geflissen sien Wollen*". StAA, Literaliensammlung, Höchstetter-Selekt I, Dok. 44, Supplication Hochstetterischer Glaubiger., s.d., s.a.

10 StAA, Literaliensammlung, Höchstetter-Selekt I, Dok. 43.

11 Ibid., Dok. 56, Hochstetterische Glaubiger so jr Entledigung leiden mogen unnd jm Gewalt Doctor Christoff Lanngen geben haben, s.d., s.a.

12 "*Wir befinden doch aber die Gestelt E. F. Vershreibung ettwas so sharpf gar beshwerlich unnd ungewonlich verszigt, das unns derselben gemess zu obligieren, verstricken unnd verpflichten nit annemblich erleidenlich noch treglich sein will*". StAA, Literaliensammlung, Höchstetter-Selekt I, Dok. 54, Sup. an den edlen voessten fursichtigen ersamen unnd weisen Herrn Burgermaister unnd Rathgeben der Statt Augspurg unnsern lieben Herren unnd Freunden, 20 February 1544.

13 StAA, Literaliensammlung, Höchstetter-Selekt I, Dok. 34, Supplication der gefangen Hochstetter, s.a., d.s.

14 Reinhard lists seven children, but Höchstetter adds an eighth, a daughter Catharina, who was born at Burgwalden in 1542 and died in infancy. The date suggests that the imprisonment of Ambrosius II did not involve strict separation from his wife. In fact, according to Höchstetter, all of the children of Ambrosius II appear to have been conceived during the bankruptcy, when he was confined. Cf. Hoechstetter, *Stammtafel der Hoechstter*, 5; Reinhard, *Augsburger Eliten des 16. Jahrhundert*, 303–4.

15 FA, 172/3 Confirmation von 17 July 1559, 172/1 Verkaufsbrief von 19 December 1569.

16 Hoechstetter, Stammtafel der Hoechstter, 4.

Appendix 1

Rising Höchstetter Fortunes[1]

Appendix 1

Appendix 1 Rising Hochstetter Fortunes as Reflected in Their Tax Assessments[1]

Year	*Seyfrid/ Sigfird*	*Ulrich I*	*Ulrich II*	*Georg I, son of Ulrich II*	*Ambrosius I, son of Ulrich II*	*Jacob,son of Ulrich II*	*Hans, son of Ulrich II*	*Hieronymus, son of Ulrich II*	*Georg II, son of Georg I*	*Wilhelm, son of Georg I*	*Sigmund, son of Georg I*	*Ambrosius II, son of Ambrosius I*	*Joachim, son of Ambrosius I*	*Joseph, son of Hans*	*Anton, son of Hieronymus*
1/1/1403	1.5														
1/1/1408	2	2													
1/1/1413	3	3													
1/1/1418	4	5													
1/1/1422		7													
1/1/1428		7.5													
1/1/1434		15													
1/1/1441		17													
1/1/1448		15	15												
1/1/1455			10.5												
1/1/1462			52												
1/1/1466			80												
1/1/1471			36												
1/1/1475			95												
1/1/1480			72												
1/1/1486			109	40											
1/1/1489			145.4	53.4											
1/1/1494			120	61.8	36			18							
1/1/1498				81.75	51.75	11.75		11							
1/1/1501				81.75	51.75	11.75	31	11							
1/1/1504				259.75	170.75	23.75	85	23							
1/1/1509				101.33	85.33	32	42.5	17	23.5						
1/1/1512				265	167.5	36	62		36						9
1/1/1516				171.75	202.5	47	76.6		73	46.25	35				11

(*Continued*)

(Continued)

Year	*Seyfrid/ Sigfird*	*Ulrich I*	*Ulrich II*	*Georg I, son of Ulrich II*	*Ambrosius I, son of Ulrich II*	*Jacob,son of Ulrich II*	*Hans, son of Ulrich II*	*Hieronymus, son of Ulrich II*	*Georg II, son of Georg I*	*Wilhelm, son of Georg I*	*Sigmund, son of Georg I*	*Ambrosius II, son of Ambrosius I*	*Joachim, son of Ambrosius I*	*Joseph, son of Hans*	*Anton, son of Hieronymus*
1/1/1522					275	50	93		68.75	56.2	60				12
1/1/1528					0	16			70		80	0	0	0	
1/1/1534						16.67									
1/1/1540						14					47				

[1] *StAA Steuerbücher. See also Strieder, Zur Genesis des modernen Kapitalismus: Forschungen zur Entstehung der großen bürgerlichen Kapitalvermögen am Ausgange des Mittelalters und zu Beginn der Neuzeit, zunachst in Augsburg* ([Munich 1935] New York 1968), 160–61.

Appendix 2

Höchstetter Creditors

Appendix 2a

Name	*Place of Birth*	*Gender*	*Corporation*	*Occupation*	*Debt I*	*Debt II*	*Relationship to the Höchstetters*
Hans Ott von Achterdingen		M		Royal Hauszeugmeister			
Philipp Adler	Augsburg	M	Salzfertigerzunft	Merchant	26,000	8,100	father-in-law to Joseph
Jörg Aichelberger	Salzburg	M			800		
Almosenamt	Augsburg	NA			400		
Moritz von Altmannshofen		M	Knight of Wangen	Bailiff of the County ofKempten	2,000		
Sebastian Antinger		M			400		
Barbara von Argon	Augsburg	F	Kaufleutezunft		315		
Anna Arzt	Augsburg	F					
Hans Arztin	Augsburg	M		Artisan	1,900		
Hans Erhart von Au		M	Knight of Felldorf	Superior bailiff of Tübingen	1,260		
Jörg von Auersberg		M		Kärntner nobleman	4,700		
Simprecht Bair	Augsburg	M	Artisan	Master goldsmith	1,400		
Nicholas Baum		M			600		
Michael Baumann	Augsburg	M	Artisan	Master furrier	500		
Jacob Baurnstoffel	Augsburg	M		Servant of Hans Ungelters	300		
Blasius Behaim	Pressburg	M			2,000		
Bettelsack	Augsburg				1,200		
Benedict Berfelder von Greiffenberg	Greiffenberg	M	Bavarian noble		2,000		
Eitel Sigmund von Berg	Opfingen	M	Swabian noble		1,000		
Burchard von Bernhausen		M			2,000		

Barbara Bestler	Augsburg	F			1,500	
Anna Bihler	Augsburg	F			1,300	1,200
Anton Bimmel	Augsburg	M	Weberzunft	Merchant	3,078	
Hans Bimmel	Augsburg	M	Kaufleutezunft	Merchant		
Bischof von Chur (Paul Ziegler)		M		Bishop of Chur	11,000	12,600
Bischof von Freising		M		Bishop of Freising	706	
Bernhard Brack	Augsburg	M		Servant of Ulrich Rehlinger	50	50
Catharina Braun	Mainz	F			1,500	
Jörg Braun	Augsburg	M			1,500	300
Conrad von Buhel		M	Swabian noble		1,000	
Eustachius Brunnenmair	Augsburg	M			1,500	
Gebhart von Castelmur	Graubünden	M		Ministerial of the Bishop of Chur	1,500	1,300
Conrad		M		Augsburger canon	300	
Cäcilie Dorfwirtin	Mühldorf am Inn	F			1,000	1,000
Heimbrand Edelmann	Augsburg	M		Augsburger Stadtsyndicus	1,650	2,050
Magdalena Eder		F			700	
Balthasar Eggenberger	Augsburg	M		Merchant	1,200	
Sebastian Emart	Württemberg	M				
Peter Enckenhauser	Salzburg	M			400	
Georg Fraidings Erben	Günzburg				491	
Ursula Franck	Augsburg	F			300	
Marquart Freer	Augsburg	M		Physician	600	2,200
Eberhard von Freyberg		M	Swabian noble		1,000	7,000

(Continued)

(Continued)

Name	*Place of Birth*	*Gender*	*Corporation*	*Occupation*	*Debt I*	*Debt II*	*Relationship to the Höchstetters*
Werner Volkhart von Freyberg		M	Swabian noble				
Wolf von Freyberg			Swabian noble	Captain of the Augsburg city guard		6,000	
Dorothea von Fronhofen		F	Swabian noble		2,000		
Jacob Fuerer	Salzburg	M		Artisan		640	
Conrad Gerung	Augsburg	M			1,000		
Jörg Gervel	Speyer	M		Bürgermeister of Speyer	600		
Sebastian Ginzburger	Augsburg	M	Salzfertigerzunft	Merchant		1,000	
Andreas Grander	Augsburg	M	Salzfertigerzunft	Merchant	2,000	2,100	
Onofrius Gremp	Vaihingen	M		Chamber master of the Austiran government in Württemberg	1,020		
Gabriel Gutrater	Laufen bei Salzburg	M			1,000		Factor of the Höchstetter in Nuremberg
Conrad Hagenbachs Geschäft					200		
Agnes Haller	Tübingen	F			4,000	4,200	
Thomas Haugs Kinder	Augsburg		Kaufleutezunft	Merchant	1,000		
Hans Hausner	Salzburg	M			2,000		
Jacpb Haustetter Pfleger	Augsburg			Merchant	3,000		
Veit Herriszeller	Schrobenhausen	M			1,000	2,000	
Ulrich Hermann	Augsburg	M		Servant	150		Servant of Ambrosius I Höchstetter

Anton Herwarts Witwe	Augsburg	F			2,700		
Erasmus Herwart	Augsburg	M	Herrentrinkstube	Merchant	1,100		
Barbara Höchstetter	Augsburg	F			1,260		Daughter of Jacob Höchstetter
Sigmund Höchstetter	Augsburg	M	Mehrer der Gesellschaft	Merchant	5,800		Son of Georg I Höchstetter
Lienhart Hofer	Innsbruck	M			2,000		
Blasius Hötzls Erben	Innsbburck	M		Secretary to Maximilian I	2,000	3,000	Idrian mine operator
Anna Hosser	Augsburg	F			400		
Hans Höβln	Augsburg	M		Housekeeper of the Bürgermeister Ulrich Rehlinger	100		
Martin Iphofer	Innsbruck	M					
Ambrosius Jung	Augsburg	M	Noble	Physician	1,000		Brother of the personal physician of Karl V. and Ferdinand I.
Hans Kalbsor	Salzburg	M			300		
Ursula Kaufmann		F			1,000		
Wendel Kirchaimer	Vienna	M			700		
Ulrich von Knöringen	bei Burgau	M	Swabian noble		6,000		
Wolfgang Kolers Erben	Augsburg				4,000		
Magdalena Kon		F			130		
Regina Königsberger	Augsburg	F			5,000		
Lienhart Kramer	Salzburg	M			600		

(*Continued*)

(Continued)

Name	*Place of Birth*	*Gender*	*Corporation*	*Occupation*	*Debt I*	*Debt II*	*Relationship to the Höchstetters*
Erhart Kreller	Landberg	M		Bürgermeister of Landsberg	2,000		
Jacob Kreel	Speyer	F		Jurist at the Reichskammergericht	1,700		
Hans Küffner	Rattenberg am Inn	M		Physician			
Sigmund Kunderskofer	Augsburg	M		Merchant	1,400		Factor of the Höchstetter
Jacob Hans von Landau	Landau bei Riedlingen, Donau	M	Swabian noble	Son of the territorial bailiff in Schwaben of Maximilian I.	4,000	5,000	
Dorothea Lang	Augsburg	F			1,500	3,300	
Andreas Langs Witwe	Augsburg	F			500		
Joachim Langenmantel	Augsburg	M	Herrentrinkstube		3,000		
Marx Langenmantel	Augsburg	M		Captain of the Augsburg city guard	3,000		
Appolonia Lauginger	Augsburg	F			600		
Hans Lauginger	Augsburg	M	Kaufleutezunft	Merchant	1,200		
Hans Lauterer	Täfering	M			1,000		
Georg von Liechtenstein		M	Tyrolean noble		1,700		
Barbara Mader	Donauwörth	F		Wife of the city secretary	400		
N. Manlich	Augsburg		Kaufleutezunft		3,400		
Hans Marschalck von Ehingen		M	Swabian noble		2,000	3,800	
Hans Mayr	Augsburg	M			2,400		
Hans Mayr	Augsburg	M		City Werkmeister	2,000		

Hans Mayr	Steinkirchen	M			2,000	1,000	
Sebastian Metzger	Ulm	M			500		
Michael N.	Augsburg	M		Servant of Sigmund Höchstetter	300		Servant of Sigmund Höchstetter
Georg von Montfort		M	Vorarlsberg noble		11,486	9,000	
Ambrosius Murauer	Rattenberg am Inn	M		Royal foundry overseer	2,000		
Anna Neglin	Vienna	F			1,000		
Jörg Nestlin	Augsburg	M	Schuhmacherzunft	Artisan	40		
Wilhelm Neumann	Villach	M		Idrian mine operator; merchant	8,520		father-in-law of Ambrosius II Höchsteetter
Wildhans von Neuneck		M	Swabian noble	Bailiff of Altenstaig	900		
Appolonia Nördlinger	Augsburg	F			1,000		
Hans Oswaldt	Augsburg	M	Salzfertigerzunft	Merchant	3,000	3,250	
Andreas Ott		M			1,100		
Pankraz von Palau		M			3,400		
BalthasarPaumgartner					2,000		
Hans Paumgartner	Augsburg	M	Kaufleutezunft	Merchant	23,000		
Hans Franz Paumgartner	Augsburg	M	Kaufleutezunft	Merchant	2,000		husband of Ottilie; partner in firm
Martin Paumgartner	Kufstein	M		Mine operator in Tyrol			
Claus Paur	Lauingen	M			600		
Hans Pfisters Witwe	Augsburg	F		Artisan	3,000		

(Continued)

(Continued)

Name	*Place of Birth*	*Gender*	*Corporation*	*Occupation*	*Debt I*	*Debt II*	*Relationship to the Höchstetters*
Pfleger von St. Jacob	Augsburg				1,600		1528/1529 Konrad Herwart, Hans Manlich and Melchior Funck
Hans Pflügls Erben	Salzburg			Merchant	8,600		Widow is the sister of Wilhelm Neumann of Villach
Johann Pimman		M			200		
Jörg Praim		M			3,300		
Hans von Praitenstain		M	Noble		1,200		
Hans Prantmair	Augsburg	M	Kürschnerzunft	Artisan	3,000		
Georg Prawr		M			300		
Lorenz Rait		M			4,000		
Ambrosius Reitmayr		M			4,000		
Wilhelm Rauschs Frau	Augsburg	F			1,000	1,050	
Leonhard Ravenspurger	Augsburg	F	Herrentrinkstube		2,000		husband of Anna Peutinger, aunt of Ambrosius Höchstetter
Anna Rehlinger	Augsburg	F	Herrentrinkstube		4,000		
Anton Rehlinger	Augsburg	M	Herrentrinkstube		6,000		
Bernhard Rehlinger	Augsburg	M	Herrentrinkstube	Jurist	1,000	800	

Conrad Rehlinger	Augsburg	M	Herrentrinkstube	Merchant	700		Question of identification: Who is this guy?
Jacob Rehlinger	Augsburg	M	Herrentrinkstube	Merchant	1,200		
Johann Rehlinger	Augsburg	M	Herrentrinkstube	Stadtsyndikus	5,000	7,000	
Ulrich Rehlinger	Augsburg	M	Herrentrinkstube	Merchant	250	1,690	
Ulrich II Rehlinger	Augsburg	M	Herrentrinkstube	Merchant	1,000	3,000	
Wolfgang Rehlinger	Augsburg	M	Herrentrinkstube	Merchant	3,966	2,666	
Wilhelm von Reichenbach		M	Noble		7,200	4,000	
Florian Reiff	Innsburck	M		Jurist	1,000	1,900	
Hans Reitmair	Munich	M			4,000		
Andreas Rem	Augsburg	M	Kaufleutezunft	Merchant	7,184		
Lucas Rem	Augsburg	M	Kaufleutezunft	Merchant	7,184		
Nicolaus Ribeisen	Salzburg	M		Jurist	1,332	2,000	
Hans Ridler and mother	Munich	M			6,000		
Marquart Rideler	Augsburg	M		Merchant	600		
Leonhard I Riederer	Augsburg			Merchant	3,600		Factor of the Höchstetter
Conrad von Riedheim	Riedheim bei Günzburg	M	Swabian noble		5,000		
Melchior Riemer	Salem	M		Artisan	2,000		
Wolfgang Rumlers Erben	Augsburg				3,000		His wife is the sister of Paul Ziegler, Bishop of Chur
Hans Rupp	Hall in Tyrol	M			4,200	4,300	
Ruprecht Rupp	Hall in Tyrol	M			4,200	4,300	
Lienhart Rupp		M			2,000		

(*Continued*)

(Continued)

Name	*Place of Birth*	*Gender*	*Corporation*	*Occupation*	*Debt I*	*Debt II*	*Relationship to the Höchstetters*
Lucas Schellenberger	Augsburg	M		Apotheker	1,200	1,000	
Sebastian Schermair	Augsburg	M			600		
Nicolaus Schindtberger		M			600		
Conrad Schmuckers Erben	Augsburg	M			1,600		
Magdalena Schmucker	Augsburg	F			700	1,700	
Wilhelm Schurpf	Rattenberg am Inn	M	Knight	Trustee of Ambras and Rattenberg in Tyrol			
Hans Schweitzers Erben	Augsburg			Member of city guard	1,100		
Arnold von Siegen	Cologne	M		Bürgermeister of Cologne	1,800		
Gotthard von Siegen	Cologne	M			1,026		
Melchior Sendt	Vienna	M			2,000		
Gordian Seuter	Kempten	M		Bürgermeister of Kempten; Pfennigmeister of the Swabian League	1,000		
Philipp Sigwein	Frankfurt am Main	M		Jurist or physician?	600		
Andreas Stainbacher		M			800		
Albrecht von Stams	Stams bei Innsbruck	M	Tyrolian noble		4,000		
Martin Stöcklin	Augsburg	M			2,000		
Anton Stoβ	Innsbruck	M		Secretary to Maximilian I and Ferdinand I	1,000	3,700	

Georg Strölin	Loppenhausen bei Mindelheim	M		Captain of soldiers	1,400	5,050	
Jörg Stubman	Augsburg	M		Barber	84		
Philipp Stumpf	Tyrol	M		Captain of the Swabian League	1,680	3,800	
Hartmann Sulzer	Augsburg	M		Merchant	400		
Johann Thenn	Salzburg	M		Münzmeister	5,000	8,000	
Anna Thurzo	Augsburg	F			16,000		
Ulrich Varnbichler	Lindau	M		Jurist	2,000	4,000	
Conrad Vegels Geschäft	Augsburg				1,000		
Matthäus Vesser	Dinkelsbühl	M		Bürgermeister of Dinkelsbühl	1,000		
Hans Vessler		M			220		
Karl Villinger	Augsburg	M	Kaufleutezunft	Merchant	11,598		Philipp Adler is the father-in-law of Jacob V., father of Karl.
Jörg I Vittel	Augsburg	M			300		Father of Jörg II Vittel, Factor of the Fuggers
Wolfgang Vittel	Augsburg	M		Merchant	3,000		Factor of the Höchstetters; brother of Jörg II Vittel, Factor of the Fuggers
Georg Vogel	Augsburg	M		Personal physician to Maximilian I	2,000	1,000	
Barbara Wallderstain	Augsburg	F			500		
Bernhard Walther	Augsburg	M	Kaufleutezungt	Merchant	1,500	2,500	
Lucas Walther	Augsburg	M	Kaufleutezungt	Merchant	2,000		

(*Continued*)

(Continued)

Name	*Place of Birth*	*Gender*	*Corporation*	*Occupation*	*Debt I*	*Debt II*	*Relationship to the Höchstetters*
Ulrich II Walther	Augsburg	M	Mehrer der Gesellschaft	Merchant	3,400		
Ulrich Walthers Frau	Augsburg	F			1,000	1,400	
Magdalena Weg	Nördlingen	F			600		
Anna Weinmann	Augsburg	F			1,500		
Anastasia von Welden			Swabian noble		3,000	2,000	
Hans Welling	Württemberg	M			1,500		
Lucas Welser	Augsburg	M	Herrentrinkstube	Merchant	2,000		
Ulrich Welser	Augsburg	M	Herrentrinkstube	Merchant	600		
Christoph Melchior von Weyenburg		M					
Sebastian Widenmann	Ulm	M			800		
Georg Wielandt	Augsburg	M	Kaufleutezunft	Merchant	2,000	7,000	Sister is the mother-in-law of Joachim Höchstetter
Sebastian Wiener	Krummau in Bohemia	M			5,000		
Hans Wolf	Augsburg	M		Servant of Kardinal Matthäus Lang, Bishop of Augsburg	1,000		

Appendix 2b

Corporate Creditors[1]

Name	*Amount*	*Paid*
King of the Romans	40,075	Y
Steinfelden mines	15,353	Y
Steinfelden foundry	12,800	Y
Idrian mines	12,800	Y
Hungarian and Austrian obligation	1,800	Y
Venetian goods and notes	21,113	Y
Lyon obligation	13,314	Y
Unnamed obligations	1,816	Y
Linz obligation	10,003	Y
Lisbon obligation	40,962	Y
Frankfurt obligation	2,980	Y
Milan obligation	4,320	Y
Schwaz mines	31,473	Y
Hall obligation	1,392	Y
Damask obligation	1,050	Y
Tauffer copper obligation	10,000	Y
Count of Montfort	6,000	N
Mine operators at Idria	75,000	Y

[1] StAA, Literaliensammlung, Hochstetter-Selekt I, II.

Bibliography

Unpublished Sources

Bayerisches Hauptstaatsarchiv München

Reichskammergericht

Reichsstadt Augsburg Literalien

Fürstlich und Gräflich Fuggersches Familien- und Stiftungsarchiv Dillingen

Gemeiner Handel und Auslösung, 2.2.1 ½

Handel 2, 2, 1

Tyroler Handel, 40.1

Österreichisches Staatsarchiv Wien

Allgemeines Verwaltungsarchiv, Adelsarchiv, Reichsadelsakten

Finanz- und Hofkammerarchiv, Gedenkbuch Nr. 13. Augsburg

Finanz- und Hofkammerarchiv, Innerösterreichischen Miszellen und Briefe, 134/1-3

Haus-, Hof- und Staatsarchiv, R. F. Ferdinand I

Haus-, Hof- und Staatsarchiv, Reichsarchiv, Reichshofrat, Judicialia

Stadtarchiv Augsburg, Kommunales Archivgut, Altbestände (Reichsstadt bis 1806)

Nachlässe, Höchstetter-Sammlung

Rats- und Ämterwesen, Baumeisteramtsbücher, Baurechnungen, 1531

Rats- und Ämterwesen, Evangelisches Wesensarchiv

Rats- und Ämterwesen, Katholisches Wesensarchiv

Rats- und Ämterwesen, Literaliensammlung, Höchstetter-Selekt I, II

Rats- und Ämterwesen, Ordnungen und Statuten

Rats- und Ämterwesen, Ratsprotokolle

Rats- und Ämterwesen, Steueramt, Steuerbücher

Selekte und MIschbestände, Kaufmannschaft und Handel

Selekte und MIschbestände, Notariatsarchiv Spreng

Selekte und MIschbestände, Schätze

Stadtgericht, Schuld-, Klag- und Appellationsakten, Teil 2

Stadtgericht, Stadtgerichtsakten, Klag- und Appellationssachen

Zucht- und Strafamt, Stadtgerichtsbuch, 1531

Stadtarchiv Nürnberg

B 14/II, Libri conservatorii des Stadt-, Bauern- und Untergerichts

Ratsprotokolle S I

Stadtarchiv Ulm
Urkundenregesten A

Tiroler Landesarchiv, Innsbruck
Zentralbehörden vor 1868, Buch Geschäft von Hof (Hofresolutionen)
Zentralbehörden vor 1868, Buch Gutachten an Hof
Zentralbehörden vor 1868, Buch Entbieten und Befelch
Zentralbehörden vor 1868, Buch Gemeine Missiven
Zentralbehörden vor 1868, Buch Bekennen
Zentralbehörden vor 1868, Raitbücher
Tiroler Landschaft und Landtag, Urkunden

Published Sources and Literature

Abulafia, David. *Commerce and Conquest in the Mediterranean, 1100–1500* (Aldershot 1993).
Agee, James, and Walker Evans. *Let Us Now Praise Famous Men* (New York 1941).
Agricola, Georgius. *De re metallica*, translated by Herbert Clark Hoover and Lou Henry Hoover (New York 1950).
Allende, Fermín. "Poor Thomas Buddenbrook! Family Business in Literature," *Business and Economic History On-Line* 7 (2009). Available at: www.thebhc.org/publications/BEHonline/2009/allende.pdf.
Althoff, Gerd. *Verwandte, Freunde und Getreue. Zum politischen Stellenwert der Gruppenbindungen im früheren Mittelalter* (Darmstadt 1990).
Althoff, Gerd. *Spielregeln der Politik im Mittelalter. Kommunikation in Frieden und Fehde* (Darmstadt 1997).
Amussen, Susan. *An Ordered Society: Gender and Class in Early Modern England* (London 1988).
Anderson, Michael. *Approaches to the History of the Western Family, 1500–1914* (London 1980).
Angiolini, Franco, and Daniel Roche (eds.). *Cultures et formations négociantes dans l'Europe moderne* (Paris 1995).
Apellániz, Franscisco. "Venetian Trading Networks in the Medieval Mediterranean," *Journal of Interdisciplinary History* 44 (2013): 157–79.
Arbel, Benjamin. *Trading Nations: Jews and Venetians in the Early Modern Eastern Mediterranean* (Leiden 1995).
Archer, Margaret S. *Making Our Way Through the World: Human Reflexivity and Social Mobility* (Cambridge, UK 2008).
Aristotle. "Politica," in: Richard McKeon (ed.), *The Basic Works of Aristotle* (New York 1970), 1127–325.
Arlinghaus, Franz-Josef. "Bookkeeping, Double-Entry Bookkeeping," in: Christopher Kleinhenz (ed.), *Medieval Italy: An Encyclopedia* (New York 2004), 147–50.
Aston, Trevor, and C. H. E. Philpin. *The Brenner Debate: Agrarian Class Structure and Economic Development in Pre-Industrial Europe* (Cambridge, UK 1985).
Baer, Wolfram, et al. (eds.). *Augsburger Stadtlexikon. Geschichte, Gesellschaft, Kultur, Recht, Wirtschaft* (Augsburg 1985).
Baptist, Edward E. *The Half Has Never Been Told: Slavery and the Making of American Capitalism* (New York 2014).
Barbour, Violet. *Capitalism in Amsterdam in the Seventeenth Century* (Ann Arbor 1950).
Barro, Robert. "Are Government Bonds Net Wealth?" *Journal of Political Economy* 82 (1974): 1095–117.

Baskin, Jonathan Barron. "The Development of Corporate Financial Markets in Britain and the United States, 1600–1914: Overcoming Asymmetric Information," *Business History Review* 62 (1988): 199–237.

Batori, Ingrid. "Das Patriziat der deutschen Stadt. Zu den Forschungsergebnissen über das Patriziat besonders der süddeutschen Städte," *Zeitschrift für Stadtgeschichte, Stadtsoziologie und Denkmalspflege* 2 (1975).

Bauer, Clemens. *Unternehmung und Unternehmungsformen im Spätmittelalter und in der beginnenden Neuzeit* ([Jena 1936], Aalen 1982).

Bayerische Akademie der Wissenschaft (ed.). *Die Chroniken der deutschen Städte vom 14. bis ins 16. Jahrhundert*, vols. 23, 25, 29, 32–34 (Gottingen 1965–7).

Becker, Gary. *A Treatise on the Family* (Cambridge, MA 1991).

Beckert, Sven. *Empire of Cotton: A Global History* (New York 2014).

Beerbühl, Margrit Schulte, et al. (eds.). *Spinning the Commercial Web: International Trade, Merchants, and Commercial Cities, c. 1640–1939* (Frankfurt Main 2004).

Behringer, Wolfgang. *Im Zeichen des Merkur: Reichspost und Kommunikationsrevolution in der Frühen Neuzeit* (Göttingen 2003).

Beito, David T. *From Mutual Aid to the Welfare State: Fraternal Societies and Social Services, 1890–1967* (Chapel Hill 2000).

Bellavitis, Anna. *Identité, marriage, mobilité sociale: Citoyennes et citoyes à Venisa au XVIe siècle* (Rome 2001).

Bergstrom, Theodore C. "On the Evolution of Altruistic Ethical Rules for Siblings," *American Economic Review* 85 (1995): 58–81.

Berkner, Lutz. "The Stem Family and Developmental Cycle of the Household: An Eighteenth- Century Austrian Example," *American Historical Review* 76 (1972): 398–418.

Birnbaum, Sabina. *Konkursrecht der frühen Augsburger Neuzeit mit seinen gemeinrechtlichen Einflüssen* (Münster 2014).

Black's Law Dictionary. Available at: https://thelawdictionary.org/.

Blair, Ann M. *Too Much to Know: Managing Scholarly Information before the Modern Age* (New Haven 2010).

Blanc, Louis. *Organisation du travail* (Paris 1850).

Blanchard, Ian, Anthony Goodman, and Jennifer Newman (eds.). *Industry and Finance in Early Modern History: Essays Presented to George Hammersley on the Occasion of His 74th Birthday* (Stuttgart 1972).

Blanchard, Ian, Anthony Goodman, and Jennifer Newman. *Mining, Metallurgy and Minting in the Middle Ages*, 3 vols. (Stuttgart 2001/2005).

Blank, Heinrich. "Der Villacher Bürger Wilhelm Neumann als Kaufmann und Gewerke in Idria," in: Gotbert Moro (ed.), *700 Jahre Stadt Villach* (Villach 1940), 116–37.

Blendinger, Friedrich. "Die wirtschaftlichen Führungsschichten in Augsburg 1430–1740," in: Herbert Helbig (ed.), *Führungskräfte der Wirtschaft in Mittelalter und Neuzeit, 1350- 1850*, vol. I, 2 vols. (Limburg an der Lahn 1973), 51–86.

Blendinger, Friedrich. "Zur Geschichte der Messinghütte am Steinenberg bei Pflach bzw. Reutte," in: F. Huber and G. Zwanowek (eds.), *Erzeugung, Verkehr und Handel in der Geschichte der Alpenländer. Festschrift für Herbert Hassinger* (Innsbruck 1977).

Blendinger, Friedrich. *Zwei Augsburger Unterkaufbücher aus den Jahren 1551 bis 1558. Älteste Aufzeichnungen zur Vor- und Frühgeschichte der Augsburger Börse* (Stuttgart 1994).

Boettke, Peter J. "Information and Knowledge: Austrian Economics in Search of Its Uniqueness," *The Review of Austrian Economics* 15 (2002): 263–74.

Bog, Ingomar. "Wachstumsprobleme der oberdeutschen Wirtschaft, 1540–1618," *Jahrbücher für Nationalökonomie und Statistik* 179 (1966): 493–537.

Bonoldi, Andrea, and Markus A. Denzel (eds.). *Bozen im Messenetz Europas (17. – 19. Jahrhundert)/Bolzano nel sistema fieristico europeo (secc. XVII – XIX)* (Bolzano 2007).

Bosher, John F. *The Canada Merchants, 1713–1763* (Oxford 1987).

Bourdieu, Pierre. *Distinction: A Social Critique of the Judgment of Taste* (Cambridge, MA 1984).

Bourdieu, Pierre. *Outline of a Theory of Practice* (Cambridge, UK 1977).

Bourdieu, Pierre. "The Forms of Capital," in: John G. Richardson (ed.), *Handbook for Theory and Research for the Sociology of Education* (Westport, CT 1986), 241–58.

Bourdieu, Pierre. *The Logic of Practice* (Stanford 1992).

Bourdieu, Pierre, and Jean-Claude Passeron. "Cultural Reproduction and Social Reproduction," in: Richard K. Brown (ed.), *Knowledge, Education and Cultural Change* (London 1977).

Boyajian, James C. *Portuguese Trade in Asia under the Habsburgs, 1580–1640* (Baltimore 1993).

Braudel, Fernand. *La Méditerranée et le monde Méditerranéen a l'époque de Philippe II*, 2 vols. (Paris 1966).

Braudel, Fernand. *Civilisation matérielle, économie et capitalisme, XVe-XVIIIe siècle*, 3 vols. (Paris 1979/1993).

Braun, Lilly. *Die Frauenfrage: Ihre geschichtliche Entwicklung und wirtschaftliche Seite* (Leipzig 1901).

Brenner, Robert. "Agrarian Class Structure and Economic Development in Pre-Industrial Europe," *Past & Present* 70 (1976): 30–75.

Britnell, Richard H. *The Commercialization of English Society, 1000–1500* (Cambridge, UK 1993).

Brown, Richard C. A. *A History of Accounting and Accountants* (Edinburgh 1905).

Bruchhäuser, Hanns-Peter. *Kaufmannsbildung im Mittelalter. Determinanten des Curriculums deutscher Kaufleute im Spiegel der Formalisierung von Qualifizierungsprozessen* (Cologne 1989).

Brunner, Otto. "Das 'ganze Haus' und alteuropäische 'Oekonomik'," in: Otto Brunner (ed.), *Neue Wege der Verfassungs- und Sozialgeschichte*, 2nd ed. (Göttingen 1968).

Bücher, Karl. *Die Frauenfrage im Mittelalter*, 2nd ed. (Tubingen 1910).

Bull, Ida. "Merchant Households and Their Networks in Eighteenth-Century Trondheim," *Continuity & Change* 17 (2002): 213–31.

Burkhardt, Johannes (ed.). *Augsburger Handelshäuser im Wandel des historischen Urteils* (Berlin 1996).

Carande, Ramón. *Carlos V. y sus banqueros*, 3 vols. (Madrid 1942/47).

Carocci, Sandro (ed.). *La mobilità sociale nel medioevo* (Rome 2010).

Carocci, Sandro. "Social Mobility and the Middle Ages," *Continuity and Change* 26 (2011): 367–404.

Casson, Mark. "The Economics of the Family Firm: An Analysis of the Dynastic Motive," University of Reading Discussion Papers in Economics and Management 1998.

Casson, Mark. "The Economics of the Family Firm," *Scandinavian Economic History Review* 47 (1999): 10–23.

Cavaciocchi, Simonetta (ed.). *La famiglia nell'economia europea. Secoli XIII 2 XVIII/The Economic Role of the Family in the European Economy from the 13th to the 18th Centuries: atti della "Quarantesima settimana di studi", 6–10 aprile 2008* (Florence 2009).

Chami, Ralph. "What Is Different About Family Businesses?" (May 2001), IMF Working Paper, 01/70. SSRN. Available at: https://ssrn.com/abstract=879571.

Chandler, Jr., Alfred D. *The Visible Hand: The Managerial Revolution in American Business* (Cambridge, MA 1977).

Chandler, Jr., Alfred D. *Scale and Scope* (Cambridge, MA 1990).

Chaudhuri, Kirti N. *Trade and Civilisation in the Indian Ocean: An Economic History from the Rise of Islam to 1750* (Cambridge, UK 1985).

Chaunu, Pierre. *Séville et l'Atlantique (1504–1650)*, 12 vols. (Paris 1955–1960).

Chaunu, Pierre. *Séville et l'Amérique aux XVIe et XVIIe siècles* (Paris 1977).

Cipolla, Carlo. *Before the Industrial Revolution: European Society and Economy, 1000–1700* (New York 1976).

Cipolla, Carlo. *The Emergence of Industrial Societies, Pt. 1: The Fontana Economic History of Europe*, vol. 4 (Hassocks 1976).

Cipolla, Carlo. *The Sixteenth and Seventeenth Centuries: The Fontana Economic History of Europe*, vol. 2 (London 1978).

Cipolla, Carlo. *Money in Sixteenth-Century Florence* (Berkeley 1989).

Cipolla, Carlo. *Clocks and Culture, 1300–1700* (New York 2003).

Ciriachy-Wantrup, Katharina von. *Familien- und erbrechtliche Gestaltungen von Unternehmen der Renaissance. Eine Untersuchung der Augsburger Handelsgesellschaften zur frühen Neuzeit* (Münster 2007).

Clark, Alice. *Working Life of Women in the Seventeenth Century* (London 1919).

Clasen, Claus-Peter. *Die Augsburger Steuerbücher um 1600* (Augsburg 1976).

Clasen, Claus-Peter. *Die Augsburger Weber: Leistungen und Krisen des Textilgewerbes um 1600* (Augsburg 1981).

Clow, Archibald, and Nan L. Clow. *The Chemical Revolution: A Contribution to Social Technology* (London 1952).

Coing, Helmut. *Die Frankfurter Reformation von 1578 und das gemeines Recht ihrer Zeit* (Weimar 1935).

Colli, Andrea. *The History of Family Business, 1850–2000* (Cambridge, UK 2003).

Colli, Andrea, Mary Rose, and Carole Howorth. "Long-Term Perspectives on Family Business," *Business History* 55 (2013): 841–54.

Comfort, Louise K., Arjen Boin, and Chris C. Demchak. *Designing Resilience: Preparing for Extreme Events* (Pittsburgh 2010).

Constable, Olivia Remie. *Trade and Traders in Muslim Spain: The Commercial Realignment of the Iberian Peninsula, 900–1500* (Cambridge, UK 1994).

Coquery, Natacha, et al. (eds.). *Ecrire, compter, mesurer. Vers une histoire des rationalités pratiques* (Paris 2006).

Dahl, Gunnar. *Trade, Trust, and Networks: Commercial Culture in Late Medieval Italy* (Lund 1998).

Dattel, Gene. *Cotton and Race in the Making of America: The Human Costs of Economic Power* (Chicago 2009).

Davies, Simon F., and Puck Fletcher (eds.). *News in Early Modern Europe: Currents and Connections* (Leiden 2014).

Davis, Ralph H. C. *The Rise of the Atlantic Economies* (Ithaca, NY 1973).

de Roover, Raymond. "Aux d'une technique intellectuelle: la formation et l'expansion de la comptabilité à partie double," *Annales d'histoire économique et sociale* 9 (1937): 171–93, 270–97.

de Roover, Raymond. "The Development of Accounting Prior to Luca Pacioli According to the Account Books of Medieval Merchants," in: Ananais C. Littleton and B. S. Yamey (eds.), *Studies in the History of Accounting* (Homewood, IL 1956), 114–74.

de Roover, Raymond. *The Rise and Decline of the Medici Bank, 1397–1494* (Cambridge, MA 1963).

de Roover, Raymond. "The Development of Accounting Prior to Luca Pacioli According to the Accounts Books of Medieval Merchants," in: Julius Kirshner (ed.), *Business, Banking, and Economic Thought in Late Medieval and Early Modern Europe* (Chicago 1974), 119–80.

De Vries, Jan. *The Economy of Europe in an Age of Crisis, 1600–1750* (Cambridge, UK 1976).

De Vries, Jan, and Ad van der Woude. *The First Modern Economy: Success, Failure, and Perseverance of the Dutch Economy, 1500–1850* (Cambridge, UK 1997).

Deininger, Heinz Friedrich (ed.). *Das Reiche Augsburg. Ausgewählte Aufsätze Jakob Strieders zur Augsburger und süddeutschen Wirtschaftsgeschichte des 15. Und 16. Jahrhunderts* (Munich 1938).

Denzel, Markus. "Professionalisierung und sozialer Aufstieg bei oberdeutschen Kaufleuten und Faktoren im 16. Jahrhundert," in: Günther Schulz (ed.), *Sozialer Aufstieg: Funktionseliten im Spätmittelalter und in der frühen Neuzeit* (Munich 2002), 413–42.

Denzel, Markus. *Das System des bargeldlosen Zahlungsverkehrs europäischer Prägung vom Mittelalter bis 1914* (Stuttgart 2008).

Dickson, P. G. M. *The Financial Revolution in England: A Study of the Development of Public Credit, 1688–1756* (New York 1967).

Dirr, Pius. "Kaufleutezunft und Kaufleutestube in Augsburg zur Zeit des Zunftregiments (1368–1548)," *Zeitschrift des Historischen Vereins für Schwaben* 35 (1909): 132–51.

Dirr, Pius. "Zur Geschichte der Augsburger Zunftverfassung 1368–1548," *Zeitschrift des Historischen Vereins für Schwaben und Neuburg* 39 (1913): 144–243.

Dobb, Maurice. *Studies in the Development of Capitalism* (New York 1946).

Doehaerd, Renée. *Etudes anversoises. Documents sur le commerce international à Anvers, 1488–1514*, 3 vols. (Paris 1962–3).

Doogan, Kevin. *New Capitalism? The Transformation of Work* (Cambridge, UK 2009).

Dooley, Brendan (ed.). *The Dissemination of News and the Emergence of Contemporaneity in Early Modern Europe* (Farnham 2010).

Dooley, Brendan, and Sabrina Baron (eds.). *The Politics of Information in Early Modern Europe* (London 2001).

Du Boulay, Francis R. H. *An Age of Ambition: English Society in the Late Middle Ages* (London 1970).

Duffy, Jan P. H. "English Bankrupts, 1571–1861," *American Journal of Legal History* 24 (1980): 283–305.

DuPâquier, Jacques, et al. (eds.). *Marriage and Remarriage in Populations of the Past* (New York 1981).

Duplessis, Robert. *Transitions to Capitalism in Early Modern Europe* (Cambridge, UK 1997).

Dyer, Christopher. *An Age of Transition? Economy and Society in England in the Later Middle Ages* (Oxford 2005).

Ehrenberg, Richard. *Das Zeitalter der Fugger: Geldkapital und Kreditverkehr im 16. Jahrhundert*, 2 vols. ([Jena 1896] New York 1990).

Elsas, M. I. *Umriß einer Geschichte der Preise und Löhne in Deutschland vom ausgehenden Mittelalter bis zu Beginn des neunzehnten Jahrhunderts*, 2 vols. (Leiden 1949).

Eltis, David. *The Rise of African Slavery in the Americas* (Cambridge, UK 2000).

Eltis, David. *Slavery in the Development of the Americas* (Cambridge, UK 2004).

Emmendörffer, Christoph, and Helmut Zäh. *Bürgermacht und Bücherpracht: Augsburger Ehren- und Familienbücher der Renaissance* (Lucerne 2011).

Endemann, Wilhelm. *Studien in der romansich-kanonistischen Wirtschafts- und Rechtslehre bis gegen Ende des 17. Jahrhunderts*, vol. I (Berlin 1874).

Ennen, Edith. "Die Frau in der mittelalterlichen Stadtgesellschaft Mitteleuropas," *Hansische Geschichtsblätter* 98 (1980): 1–22.

Ennen, Edith. *Frauen im Mittelalter* (Munich 1984).

Epstein, Steven A. *Genoa and the Genoese, 928–1528* (Chapel Hill 1993).

Favier, Jean. *Gold and Spices: The Rise of Commerce in the Middle Ages* (New York 1998).

Ferguson, Nial. *The Ascent of Money: A Financial History of the World* (New York 2008).

Fiedler, Martin. "Vertrauen ist gut, Kontrolle ist teuer: Vertrauen als Schlüsselkategorie wirtschaftlichen Handelns," *Geschichte und Gesellschaft* 27 (2001): 576–92.

Flandrin, Jean-Louis. *Families in Former Times: Kinship, Household and Sexuality* (Cambridge, UK 1979).

Flessner, Axel. "Philosophies of Business Bankruptcy Law: An International Overview," in: Jacob S. Ziegel (ed.), *Current Developments in International and Corporate Insolvency Law* (Oxford 1994), 19–28.

Fontaine, Laurence. *Le Marché. Histoire et usages d'une conquête sociale* (Paris 2014).

Frevert, Ute (ed.), *Vertrauen: Historische Annäherungen* (Göttingen 2003).

Fuhrmann, Bernd. *Mit barer Münze. Handel im Mittelalter* (Darmstadt 2010).

Fusaro, Maria. *Political Economies of Empire in the Early Modern Mediterranean: The Decline of Venice and the Rise of England 1450–1700* (Cambridge, UK 2015).

Fusaro, Maria. *Reti commerciali e traffic globali in età moderna* (Rome 2008).

Geffcken, Fritz Peter. "Soziale Schichtung in Augsburg 1396–1521: Beitrag zu einer Strukturanalyse Augsburgs im Spätmittelalter" (unpublished dissertation, University of Munich 1983).

Geffcken, Fritz Peter. "Kaufleutestube," in: *Augsburger Stadtlexikon Online* (Augsburg 2010). Available at: www.wissner.com/stadtlexikon-augsburg/artikel/stadtlexikon/kaufleutestube/4359.

Gelderblom, Oscar. *Cities of Commerce: The Institutional Foundations of International Trade in the Low Countries, 1250–1650* (Princeton 2013).

Gersick, Kelin E., et al. *Generation to Generation: Lifecycles of the Family Business* (Cambridge, MA 1997).

Glamann, Kristof. "The Changing Patterns of Trade," in: E. E. Rich and C. H. Wilson (eds.), *Cambridge Economic History of Europe, vol. 5: The Economic Organization of Early Modern Europe* (Cambridge, UK 2008), 208–10, 283–6.

Godinho, Vitorino Malgahâes. *Os descobrimentos e a economia mundial* (Lisbon 1982–84).

Goldberg, Jessica. *Trade and Institutions in the Medieval Mediterranean: The Geniza Merchants and Their Business World* (Cambridge, UK 2012).

Goldthwaite, Richard. *Private Wealth in Renaissance Florence* (Princeton 1968).

Goldthwaite, Richard. *Banks, Palaces and Entrepreneurs in Renaissance Florence* (Aldershot 1995).

Goldthwaite, Richard. *The Economy of Renaissance Florence* (Baltimore 2009).

Gottlieb, Gunther, et al. (eds.). *Geschichte der Stadt Augsburg: 2000 Jahre von der Römerzeit bis zur Gegenwart* (Stuttgart 1985).

Goubert, Pierre. "Family and Province: A Contribution to the Knowledge of Family Structure in Early Modern France," *Journal of Family History* 2 (1977): 179–95.

Granovetter, Mark, and Richard Swedburg (eds.). *The Sociology of Economic Life*, 2nd ed. (Boulder, CO 2001).

Greif, Avner. *Institutions and the Path to the Modern Economy: Lessons from Medieval Trade* (Cambridge, UK 2010).

Greiff, Benedict. *Tagebuch des Lucas Rem aus den Jahren 1494–1541. Ein Beitrag zur Handelsgeschichte der Stadt Augsburg* (Augsburg 1861).

Grieco, Sara F. Mathews. "Breastfeeding, Wet Nursing and Infant Mortality in Europe (1400-1800)," in: Sara F. Matthews Grieco and Carlo A. Corsini (eds.), *Historical Perspectives on Breastfeeding* (Florence 1991), 15–62.

Grimm, Wilhelm. *Deutsches Wörterbuch von Jacob und Wilhelm Grimm*, 16 vols. (Leipzig 1854–1961, 1971).

Groebner, Valentin. *Gefährliche Geschenke. Ritual, Politik und die Sprache der Korruption in der Eidgenossenschaft im späten Mittelalter und am Beginn der Neuzeit* (Constance 2000).

Groesen, Michiel van, and Helmer Helmers (eds.). "Managing the News in Early Modern Europe. 1550–1800," *Media History* 22, 3–4 (2016).

Großhaupt, Walter. "Die Welser als Bankiers der spanischen Krone," *Scripta mercaturae* 21 (1987): 158–88.

Großhaupt, Walter. "Commercial Relations Between Portugal and the Merchants of Augsburg and Nuremberg," in: Jean Aubin (ed.), *La Découverte, le Portugal et l'Europe. Actes du Colloque Paris, les 26, 27 et 28 mai 1988* (Paris 1990).

Häberlein, Mark. *Brüder, Freunde und Betrüger. Soiale Beziehungen, Normen und Konflikte in der Augsburger Kaufmannschaft um die Mitte des 16. Jahrhunderts* (Berlin 1998).

Häberlein, Mark. *The Fuggers of Augsburg: Pursuing Wealth and Honor in Renaissance Germany* (Charlottesville 2012).

Häberlein, Mark. "Der Kopf in der Schlinge: Praktike deutschen Kaufleute im Handel zwischen Sevilla und Antwerpen um 1540," in: Häberlein and Jeggle (eds.), *Praktiken des Handels: Geschäfte und soziale Beziehungen europäischer Kaufleute im Mittelalter und früher Neuzeit* (Constance 2010), 335–54.

Häberlein, Mark, and Christoph Jeggle (eds.). *Praktiken des Handels: Geschäfte und soziale Beziehungen europäischer Kaufleute im Mittelalter und früher Neuzeit* (Constance 2010).

Häbler, Konrad. *Die Geschichte der Fugger'schen Handlung in Spanien* (Weimar 1897).

Häbler, Konrad. *Die überseeischen Unternehmungen der Welser und ihrer Gesellschafter* (Leipzig 1903).

Hamel, Gary, and Liisa Välikangis. "The Quest for Resilience," *Harvard Business Review* 81 (September 2003): 52–63. Available at: hbr.org/2003/09/the-quest-for-resilience.

Hamilton, Roberta. *The Liberation of Women: A Study of Patriarchy and Capitalism* (London 1978).

Hämmerle, Albert. *Die Canoniker der Chorherrenstifte St. Moritz, St. Peter und St. Gertrud in Augsburg bis zur Säkularisation* (Privatdruck 1938).

Hämmerle, Albert (ed.). *Deren von Stetten Geschlechterbuch MDXXXXVIII* (Munich 1955).

Hancock, David. *Citizens of the World: London Merchants and the Integration of the British Atlantic Community, 1735–1785* (Cambridge, UK 1995).

Handwörterbuch zur deutschen Rechtsgeschichte, edited by Adalbert Erler and Ekkehard Kaufmann (Berlin 1971).

Hanley, Sarah. "Engendering the State: Family Formation and State Building in Early Modern France," *French Historical Studies* 16 (1989): 4–27.

Harreld, Donald J. *High Germans in the Low Countries: German Merchants and Commerce in Golden Age Antwerp* (Leiden 2004).

Hartmann, Heide. "The Family as the Locus of Gender, Class and Political Struggle: The Example of Housework," *Signs* 6 (1981): 366–94.

Hartwell, R. M., and Stanley L. Engerman. "Capitalism," in: *The Oxford Encyclopedia of Economic History* (Oxford 2003). Available at: http://proxy.library.upenn.edu:2400/view/10.1093/acref/9780195105070.001.0001/acref-9780195105070-e-0104.

Hatcher, John, and Mark Bailey. *Modelling the Middle Ages: The History and Theory of England's Economic Development* (Oxford 2001).

Hayek, F. A. "Economics and Knowledge," *Economica*, New Series 4 (1937): 33–54.

Hayek, F. A. "The Use of Knowledge in Society," *The American Economic Review* 35 (1945): 519–30.

Heers, Jacques. *Family Clans in the Middle Ages* (Amsterdam 1977).

Heichelcheim, Fritz E. *An Ancient Economic History*, 2 vols. (Leiden 1965).

Heimer, Heinrich. "Die Glasshutte zu Hall in Tirol und die Augsburger Kaufmannsfamilie der Höchstetter" (unpublished dissertation, University of Munich 1959).

Helczmanovski, Heimo (ed.). *Beiträge zur Bevölkerungs- und Sozialgeschichte* (Vienna 1973).

Hellmann, Friedrich. *Das Konkursrecht der Reichsstadt Augsburg* (Breslau 1905).

Herlihy, David. "Three Patterns of Social Mobility in Medieval Society," *Journal of Interdisciplinary History* 3 (1973): 623–47.

Herlihy, David, and Christiane Klapisch-Zuber. *Les Toscans et leurs familles. Une étude du catasto Florentin de 1427* (Paris 1978).

Hertner, Peter. "Bankrott," in: *Handwörterbuch zur deutschen Rechtsgeschichte*, vol. I (Berlin 1971), 429–32.

Hetzer, Gerhard, and Wolfgang Zorn. "Augsburger Börse," in: *Augsburger Stadtlexikon Online* (Augsburg 2010). Available at: www.wissner.com/stadtlexikon-augsburg/artikel/stadtlexikon/boerse/3374.

Hildebrandt, Reinhard. "The Effects of Empire: Changes in the European Economy After Charles V," in: Ian Blanchard, Anthony Goodman and Jennifer Newman (eds.), *Industry and Finance in Early Modern History: Essays Presented to George Hammersley on the Occasion of His 74th Birthday* (Stuttgart 1972), 58–76.

Hildebrandt, Reinhard. "Zum Verhältnis von Wirtschaftsrecht und Wirtschaftsprazis im 16. Jahrhundert: Die Fallitenordnungen des Augsburger Rates 1564–1580," in: Anita Mächler, et al. (eds.), *Historische Studien zu Politik, Verfassung und Gesellschaft: Festschrift für Richard Dietrich zum 65. Geburtstag* (Frankfurt Main 1976).

Hildebrandt, Reinhard. "Augsburger und Nürnberger Kupferhandel, 1570–1580: Produktion, Marktanteile und Finanzierung im Vergleich zweier Städte und ihrer wirtschaftlichen Führungsschicht," in: Hermann Kellenbenz (ed.), *Schwerpunkte der Kupferproduktion und des Kupferhandels in Europa, 1500–1650* (Cologne 1977), 190–224.

Hildebrandt, Reinhard. "Diener und Herren: Zur Anatomie großer Unternehmen im Zeitlater der Fugger," in: Johannes Burkhardt (ed.), *Augsburger Handelshäuser im Wandel des historischen Urteils* (Berlin 1996), 149–74.

Hilton, Rodney H. *Class Conflict and the Crisis of Feudalism: Essays in Medieval Social History* (London 1985).

Hirschman, Albert O. *The Passions and the Interests: Political Arguments for Capitalism Before Its Triumph* (Princeton 1977).

Hochstetter, Wilhelm, and Walter Hochstetter. *Stammtafel der Hochstetter. Hochstetter von Burgwalden, Hochstetter von und zu Scheibenegg* (Munich 1976).

Höffner, Josef. *Wirtschaftsethik und Monopole im 15. und 16. Jahrhundert* (Darmstadt 1969).

Horrox, Rosemary, and W. Mark Ormrod (eds.). *A Social History of England, 1200–1500* (Cambridge, UK 2006).

Howell, Martha C. *Commerce Before Capitalism in Europe, 1300–1600* (Cambridge, UK 2010).

Howell, Martha C. *The Marriage Exchange. Property, Social Place, and Gender in Cities of the Low Countries, 1300–1500* (Chicago 1988).

Hunt, Istvan, and Michael Ignatieff (eds.). *Wealth and Virtue: The Shaping of Political Economy in the Scottish Enlightenment* (Cambridge, MA 1983).

Inikori, J. E., and Stanley L. Engerman. *The Atlantic Slave Trade: Effects on Economies, Societies, and Peoples in Africa, the Americas, and Europe* (Durham 1992).

James, Harold. *Family Capitalism: Wendels, Haniels, Falcks, and the Continental European Model* (Cambridge, MA 2006).

Jansen, Max. *Jakob Fugger der Reiche: Studien und Quellen*, vol. I (Leipzig 1910).

Jensen, Michael C. "Self-Interest, Altruism, Incentives and Agency," in: *Foundations of Organizational Strategy* (Cambridge, MA 1998).

Jensen, Michael C., and William H. Meckling, "Theory of the Firm: Managerial Behavior, Agency Costs and Ownership Structure," *Journal of Financial Economics* 3 (1976): 305–60.

Jones, Geoffrey, and Mary B. Rose. "Family Capitalism," *Business History* 35 (1993): 1–16.

Kaiser, Wolfgang, and Biagio Salvemini (eds.). "Informazione e scelte economiche," *Quaderni storici* 42 (2007).

Kamen, Henry. *The Iron Century* (London 1971).
Kamen, Henry. *Who's Who in Europe, 1450–1750* (London 2002).
Kammerer, Klaus. *Das Unternehmensrecht süddeutscher Handelsgesellschaften in der Montanindustrie des 15, und 16. Jahrhunderts* (Stuttgart 1977).
Kellenbenz, Hermann (ed.). *Fremde Kaufleute auf der iberischen Halbinsel* (Cologne 1970).
Kellenbenz, Hermann (ed.). *Schwerpunkte der Kupferproduktion und des Kupferhandels in Europa, 1500–1650* (Cologne 1977).
Kellenbenz, Hermann. "Gewerbe und Handel, 1500–1648," in: Hermann Aubin and Wolfgang Zorn (eds.), *Handbuch der deutschen Wirtschafts- und Sozialgeschichte*, vol. I (Stuttgart 1971).
Kellenbenz, Hermann. "Handelsgesellschaft," in: *Handwörterbuch zur deutschen Rechtsgeschichte*, vol. I (Berlin 1971), 1936–42.
Kellenbenz, Hermann. "Die frühen Bankgeschaäfte der Fuggerschen Faktorei in Sevilla," *Revue international d'Histoire de la Banque* 8 (1974): 200–15.
Kellenbenz, Hermann. *Handelsbräuche des 16. Jahrhunderts. Das Meder'sche Handelsbuch und die Welser'schen Nachträge* (Wiesbaden 1974), 6–8.
Kellenbenz, Hermann. *The Rise of the European Economy: An Economic History of Continental Europe from the Fifteenth to the Eighteenth Century* (New York 1976).
Kellenbenz, Hermann. *Deutsche Wirtschaftsgeschichte*, 2 vols. (Munich 1977).
Kellenbenz, Hermann. "The Organization of Industrial Production," in: *The Cambridge Economic History of Europe*, vol.V (Cambridge, UK 1977), 462–548.
Kellenbenz, Hermann. "Augsburger Wirtschaft, 1530 bis 1620," in: *Welt im Umbruch: Augsburg zwischen Renaissance und Barock*, vol. I (Augsburg 1980).
Kellenbenz, Hermann. "Europäische Wirtschafts- und Sozialgeschichte vom ausgehenden Mittelalter bis zur Mitte des 17. Jahrhunderts," Bd. 3, in: *Handbuch der europäischen Wirtschafts- und Sozialgeschichte* (Stuttgart 1986).
Kellenbenz, Hermann. *Die Fugger in Spanien und Portugal bis 1560*, 2 vols. (Munich 1990).
Kern, Ernst. *Studien zur Geschichte des Augsburger Kaufmannshauses der Höchstetter* (Berlin 1935).
Keutgen, Friedrich. "Der Großhandel im Mittelalter," *Hansische Geschichtsblätter* 34 (1901): 67–138.
Kießling, Rolf. *Bürgerliche Gesellschaft und Kirche in Augsburg im Spätmittelalter. Ein Beitrag zur Strukturanalyse der oberdeutschen Reichsstadt* (Augsburg 1971).
Kindelberger, Charles P. *A Financial History of Western Europe*, 2nd ed. (Oxford 1993).
Kirschner, Julius, and Anthony Molho. "The Dowry Fund and the Marriage Market in Early Quattrocento Florence," *Journal of Modern History* 50 (1978): 403–38.
Kirzner, Israel. *Competition and Entrepreneurship* (Chicago 1973).
Klapisch-Zuber, Christiane. *Women, Family and Ritual in Renaissance Italy* (Chicago 1985).
Klein, Herbert S. *The Atlantic Slave Trade* (Cambridge, UK 1999).
Klier, Richard. "Der Konkurrenzkampf zwischen dem böhmischen und dem idrianischen Quecksilber in der ersten Hälfte des 16. Jahrhunderts," *Bohemia: Jahrbuch des Collegium Carolinum* 8 (1067): 82–110.
Klinkert, Ulrich. "Die Augsburger Handelsgesellschaft der Höchstetter. Zusammenbruch 1529, Gläubiger und soziale Verflechtung" (unpublished Hausarbeit, University of Augsburg 1983).
Kocka, Jurgen (ed.). *Theorien in der Praxis des Historikers* (Göttingen 1977).
Kocka, Jurgen. *Geschichte des Kapitalismus* (Munich 2013).
Koenigsberger, Helmut G., and George L. Mosse. *Europe in the Sixteenth Century* (New York 1968).
Kreidte, Peter. *Peasants, Landlords and Merchant Capitalists* (Cambridge, MA 1983).

Kuehn, Thomas. *Law, Family and Women: Toward a Legal Anthropology of Renaissance Italy* (Chicago 1991).

Kulischer, Josef. *Allgemeine Wirtschaftsgeschichte des Mittelalters un der Neuzeit* (Munich 1958).

Kunkel, Wolfgang, Hans Thieme, and Franz Beyerle (eds.). *Quellen zur neueren Privatrechtsgeschichte Deutschlands* (Weimar 1936).

Kuske, Bruno. "Die Frau im mittelalterlichen Wirtschaftsleben," *Zeitschrift für handelwissenschaftliche Forschung* 11 (1959): 554–77.

Lachmann, Ludwig. *Capital, Expectations and the Market Process* (Kansas City, MO 1977).

Ladurner, P. Justinian. "Veste und Herrschaft Ernberg," *Neue Zeitschrift des Ferdinandeums für Tyrol und Vorarlberg* 15 (1870): 6–208.

Lanaro, Paola (ed.). *La pratica dello scambio. Sistemi di fiere, mercanti e città* (Venice 2003).

Landes, David. *The Unbound Prometheus: Technological Change and Industrial Development in Western Europe from 1750 to the Present* (Cambridge, UK 1969).

Landes, David. *The Rise of Capitalism* (New York 1972).

Landes, David. *The Wealth and Poverty of Nations: Why Some Are so Rich and Some Are so Poor* (New York 1998).

Landes, David. *Revolution in Time: Clocks and the Making of the Modern World* (Cambridge, MA 2000).

Landes, David. *Dynasties: Fortunes and Misfortunes of the World's Great Family Businesses* (New York 2006).

Landes, David, Joel Mokyr, and William J. Baumol (eds.). *The Invention of Enterprise: Entrepreneurship from Ancient Mesopotamia to Modern Times* (Princeton 2010).

Lange, Christian C. A., C. R. Unger, H. J. Huitfeldt-Kaas, Gustav Storm, Alexander Bugge, Christopher Brinchmann, and Oluf Kolsrud (eds.). *Diplomatarium Norvegicum*, 21 vols. (Christiana [Oslo] 1847–[1995]).

Laslett, Peter. *The World We Have Lost: England Before the Industrial Revolution*, 2nd ed. (New York 1971).

Laslett, Peter, and Richard Wall (eds.). *Household and Family in Past Time* (Cambridge, UK 1972).

Lavoie, Donald. *Rivalry and Central Planning: A Re-Examination of the Debate over Economic Calculation under Socialism* (New York 1985).

Le Goff, Jacques. *Marchands et Banquiers du Moyen Age* (Paris 1956).

Le Goff, Jacques. *La bourse et la vie: économie et religion au Moyen Age* (Paris 1986).

Le Play, Frédéric. *Les ouvriers européens. Études sur les travaux, la vie domestique et la condition morale des populations ouvrières de l'Europe*, 6 vols. (Paris 1855–78).

Lee, W. R. "Past Legacies and Future Prospects: Recent Research on the History of the Family in Germany," *Journal of Family History* 6 (1981): 156–76.

Leiser, W. *Die Bedeutung des Augsburger Stadtrechts: Festvortrag anlässlich der Ausstellung des Stadtarchivs Augsburg "700 Jahre Augsburger Stadtrecht 1276–1976"* (Augsburg 1976).

Leitherer, Eugen. *Geschiche der handels- und absatzwirtschaftlichen Literatur* (Cologne 1961).

Lenk, Leonhard. *Augsburger Bürgertum im Späthumanismus und Frühbarock (1580–1700)* (Augburg 1968).

Lesger, Clé. *The Rise of the Amsterdam Market and Information Exchange: Merchants, Commercial Expansion and Change in the Spatial Economy of the Low Countries, c. 1550–1630* (Aldershot 2006).

Levine, David. *Family Formation in an Age of Nascent Capitalism* (London 1977).

Levine, David, and Keith Wrightson. *The Making of an Industrial Society: Whickham, 1560–1765* (Oxford 1991).

Levinson, Harry. "Conflicts that Plague Family Business," *Harvard Business Review* 49 (1971): 90–8.

Liedl, Eugen. *Gerichtsverfassung und Zivilprozeß der freien Reichsstadt Augsburg* (Augsburg 1958).
Lopez, Robert S. *The Commercial Revolution of the Middle Ages, 950–1350* (Cambridge, UK 1976).
Lorandini, Cinzia. "Looking Beyond the Buddenbrooks Syndrome: The Salvadori Firm of Trento, 1660s – 1880s," *Business History* 57 (2015): 1005–19.
Lütge, Friedrich. *Studien zur Sozial- und Wirtschaftsgeschichte. Gesammelte Abhandlungen* (Stuttgart 1963).
Lutz, Elmar. *Die rechtliche Struktur süddeutschen Handelsgesellschaften in der Zeit der Fugger*, 2 Bde. (Tübingen 1976).
Macfarlane, Alan. *The Origins of English Individualism: The Family, Property and Social Transition* (Oxford 1978).
Machlup, Fritz. *Knowledge: Its Creation, Distribution, and Economic Significance*, vol. 1 (Princeton 1980).
Maddern, Philippa C. "Social Mobility," in: Rosemary Horrox and W. Mark Ormrod (eds.), *A Social History of England, 1200–1500* (Cambridge, UK 2006), 113–33.
Mair, Paul Hektor. "Chroniken des Augsburger Ratsdieners Paul Hektor Mair," in: Bayerische Akademie der Wissenschaft (ed.), *Die Chroniken der deutschen Städte vom 14. bis ins 16. Jahrhundert*, vol. 23 (Gottingen 1965–7).
Mann, Thomas. *Buddenbrooks. Verfall einer Familie* (Berlin 1901).
Margolis, Howard. *Selfishness, Altruism and Rationality* (Cambridge, UK 1982).
Marriner, Sheila. "English Bankruptcy Records and Statistics Before 1850," *The Economic History Review* 33, 3 (1980): 351–66.
Marx, Karl. *Capital: A Critique of Political Economy*, 3 vols. (New York 1992/1993).
Mayer, Valentin. *Die "Fürlegung" in den Handelsgesellschaften des Mittelalters und desFrühkapitalismus* (Munich 1925).
Mayr, Anton. *Die großen Augsburger Vermögen in der Zeit von 1618 bis 1717* (Augsburg 1931).
McCarthy, Ian P., Mark Collard, and Michael Johnson. "Adaptive Organizational Resilience: An Evolutionary Perspective, " *Current Opinion in Environmental Sustainability* 28 (2017). Available at: https://doi.org/10.1016/j.cosust.2017.07.005.
McCusker, John J. "Introduction," in: John J. McCusker, and Cora Gravesteijn (eds.), *The Beginnings of Commercial and Financial Journalism: The Commodity Price Currents, Exchange Rate Currents, and Money Currents of Early Modern Europe* (Amsterdam 1991), 21–41.
McCusker, John J. *The Economy of British America, 1607–1789* (Chapel Hill 1991).
McCusker, John J. *Essays in the Economic History of the Atlantic World* (London 2005).
McCusker, John J., and Cora Gravesteijn. *The Beginnings of Commercial and Financial Journalism: The Commodity Price Currents, Exchange Rate Currents, and Money Currents of Early Modern Europe* (Amsterdam 1991).
Meder, Lorenz. *Handel Buch. Darin angezeigt wird/welcher gestalt inn den fürnmbsten Hendelstetten Europe/allerley Wahren anfencklich kaufft/diselbig wider mit nutz verkaufft/Wie die Wechsel gemacht/Pfund/Ellen/unnd Müntz uberal verglichen/und zu welcher zeit die Merckten gewönlich gehalten werden. Sampt anderen mehr nutzungen darzu gehörig. Allen Hanchieren/und Jungen Kauffleuten/gantz nützlich und dienstlich* (Nuremberg 1558).
Medick, Hans. "The Proto-Industrial Family Economy: The Structural Function of the Household and Family During the Transition from Peasant Society to Industrial Capitalism," *Social History* 1 (1976): 291–315.
Meillassoux, Claude. *Femmes, greniers et capitaux* (Paris 1975).
Menger, Carl. *Grundsätze der Volkswirtschaftslehre* ([Vienna 1881] Aalen 1968).
Menger, Carl. *Untersuchungen über die Methode der Sozialwissenschaften und der politischen Ökonomie insbesondere*, edited by F. A. Hayek ([Vienna 1883] Tubingen 1969).

Mertens, Bernd. *Im Kampf gegen die Monopole: Reichstagsverhandlungen und Monopolprozesse im frühen 16. Jahrhundert* (Tubingen 1996).

Miskimin, Harry A. *The Economy of Early Renaissance Europe, 1300–1460* (Cambridge, MA 1975).

Miskimin, Harry A. *The Economy of Late Renaissance Europe, 1460–1600* (Cambridge, MA 1977).

Miskimin, Harry A. *Money and Power in Fifteenth-Century France* (New Haven 1984).

Miskimin, Harry A. *Cash, Credit and Crisis in Europe, 1300–1600* (London 1989).

Mitterauer, Michael. "Zur Familienstruktur in ländlichen Gebieten Österreichs im 17. Jahrhundert," in: Heimo Helczmanovski (ed.), *Beiträge zur Bevölkerungs- und Sozialgeschichte* (Vienna 1973), 167–222.

Mitterauer, Michael. "Probleme der Stratifikation in mittelalterlichen Gesellschaftssystemen," *Sozialwissenschaftliche Informationen für Unterricht und Studium* 5 (1976): 67–73.

Mitterauer, Michael, and Reinhard Sieder. *The European Family: Patriarchy to Partnership from the Middle Ages to the Present* (Oxford 1989).

Mokyr, Joel. *The Gifts of Athena* (Princeton 2002).

Molho, Ian. *The Economics of Information: Lying and Cheating in Markets and Organizations* (Oxford 1997).

Mollat, Michel. *Jacques Cœur, ou, l'esprit d'entreprise au XVe siècle* (Paris 1988).

Mörke, Olaf, and Katharina Sieh. "Gesellschaftliche Führungsgruppen," in: Günther Gottlieb, et al. (eds.), *Geschichte der Stadt Augsburg: 2000 Jahre von der Römerzeit bis zur Gegenwart* (Stuttgart 1984), 301–12.

Mueller, Reinhold C. *The Venetian Money Market: Banks, Panics, and the Public Debt, 1200-1500* (Baltimore 1997).

Muldrew, Craig. *The Economy of Obligation: The Culture of Credit and Social Relations in Early Modern England* (London 2001).

Müller, Johannes. "Der Anteil der Familien Ehinger-Güttingen von Konstanz und der Oesterreicher-Ehinger von Ulm an den überseeischen Unternehmungen der Welser," *Vierteljahrschrift für Sozial- und Wirtschaftsgeschichte* 22 (1929): 373–87.

Murphy, Raymond. *Social Closure: The Theory of Monopolization and Exclusion* (Oxford 1988).

Murray, James. "Of Nodes and Networks: Bruges and the Infrastructure of Trade in the Fourteenth Century," in: Peter Stabel, Bruno Blondé and Anke Greve (eds.), *International Trade in the Low Countries (14th-16th Centuries)* (Leuven 2000).

Mutschlechner, Georg, and Rudolf Palme. *Das Messingwerk in Pflach bei Reutte: Ein bedeutsames Industrieunternehmen zu Begin der Neuzeit* (Innsbruck 1976).

Neal, Larry. *The Rise of Financial Capitalism: International Capital Markets in the Age of Reason* (New York 1990).

Nenadic, Stana. "The Small Family Firm in Victorian Britain," *Business History* 35 (1993): 86–114.

Neuschütz, Eduard. *Die Nürnberger Reformation und das Recht der Reichsstädte Dinkelsbühl und Rothenburg ob der Tauber* (Leipzig 1936).

Newfield, Christopher. "Reviewed Work: Richard Sennett, *The Culture of the New Capitalism*," *Enterprise & Society* 7 (2006): 816–18.

Nicholas, David. *The Domestic Life of a Medieval City: Women, Children and the Family in Fourteenth-Century Ghent* (Lincoln, NE 1985).

North, Douglass C. *Institutions, Institutional Change and Economic Performance* (Cambridge, UK 1990).

North, Douglass C. *Understanding the Process of Economic Change* (Princeton 2005).

North, Douglass C. *Violence and Social Orders: A Conceptual Framework for Interpreting Recorded Human History* (New York 2009).

North, Douglass C., and Lance E. Davis. *Institutional Change and American Economic Growth* (Cambridge, UK 1971).

North, Michael. *Kommunikation, Handel, Geld und Banken in der frühen Neuzeit* (Oldenbourg 2014).

Nußer, Horst G.W. *Frühe deutsche Entdecker: Asien in Berichten unbekannter deutscher Augenzeugen: 1502–1506* (Munich 1980).

Obenchain, Roman. "Roman Law of Bankruptcy," *Notre Dame Law Review* 3 (1928): 169–200.

Occhi, Katia. *Boschi e mercanti. Traffici di legname tra la contea di Tirolo e la Repubblica di Venezia (secoli XVI-XVII)* (Bologna 2006).

Oexle, Otto Gerhard. "Deutungsschemata der sozialen Wirklichkeit im frühen und hohen Mittelalter. Ein Beitrag zur Geschichte des Wissens," in: Frantisek Graus (ed.), *Mentalitäten im Mittelalter. Methodische und inhaltliche Probleme* (Sigmaringen 1987), 65–117.

Oexle, Otto Gerhard. "Die funktionale Dreiteilung als Deutungschema der sozialen Wirklichkeit in der ständischen Gesellschaft des Mittelalters," in: Winfried Schulze (ed.), *Ständische Gesellschaft und soziale Mobilität* (München 1988), 19–51.

Oexle, Otto Gerhard. "Gruppen in der Gesellschaft. Das wissenschaftliche Oeuvre von Karl Schmid," *Frühmittelalterliche Studien* 28 (1994): 410–23.

Ogger, Günter. *Kauf dir einen Kaiser: Die Geschichte der Fugger* (Munich 1980).

Ogilvie, Sheilagh. *Institutions and European Trade: Merchant Guilds, 1000–1800* (Cambridge, UK 2011).

Origo, Iris. *The Merchant of Prato: Francesco di Marco Datini, 1335–1410* (New York 1957).

Ormrod, David. *The Rise of Commercial Empires: England and the Netherlands in the Age of Mercantilism, 1650–1770* (Cambridge, UK 2003).

The Oxford Encyclopedia of Economic History, edited by Joel Mokyr (Oxford 2003).

Payling, Simon J. "Social Mobility, Demographic Change, and Landed Society in Late Medieval England," *Economic History Review* 45 (1992): 51–73.

Pettegree, Andrew. *The Invention of News: How the World Came to Know about Itself* (New Haven 2014).

Phelps, Edmund S. (ed.). *Altruism, Morality and Economic Theory* (New York 1975).

Piketty, Thomas. *Capital in the Twenty-first Century*, translated by Arthur Goldhammer (Cambridge, MA 2017).

Pirenne, Henri. *Mohammed and Charlemagne* (London 1939).

Pirenne, Henri. *Histoire économique de l'occident medieval*, edited by Emile Coornaert (Bruges 1951).

Pirenne, Henri. *Medieval Cities* (Princeton 1952).

Pocock, J. G. A. *Virtue, Commerce, and History: Essays on Political Thought and History, Chiefly in the Eighteenth Century* (Cambridge, MA 1985).

Polanyi, Karl. *The Great Transformation: The Political and Economic Origins of Our Time* (Boston 1944).

Pölnitz, Götz, Freiherr von. *Jakob Fugger: Kaiser, Kirche und Kapital in der oberdeutschen Renaissance* (Tubingen 1949).

Pölnitz, Götz, Freiherr von. "Augsburger Kaufleute und Bankherren der Renaissance," in: Hermann Rinn, et al. (eds.), *Augusta 955–1955: Forschungen und Studien zur Kultur- und Wirtschaftsgeschichte Augsburgs* (Munich 1955), 187–218.

Pölnitz, Götz, Freiherr von. *Anton Fugger*, 4 vols. (Tubingen 1958–86).

Postan, M. M., et al. (eds.). *The Cambridge Economic History of Europe, vol. III, Economic Organization and Policies in the Middle Ages* (Cambridge, UK 1965).

Postan, M. M., et al. (eds.). *The Cambridge Economic History of Europe, vol. II, Trade and Industry in the Middle Ages* (Cambridge, UK 1987).

Powell, Walter W. "Neither Market nor Hierarchy: Network Forms of Organization," *Research in Organizational Behavior* 12 (1990): 295–336.

Power, Eileen. *Medieval Women* (Cambridge, UK 1975).

Prak, Marten Roy (ed.). *Early Modern Capitalism: Economic and Social Change in Europe, 1400-1800* (London 2000).

Prakash, Om. *European Commercial Enterprise in Pre-Colonial India, vol. II, 5: The New Cambridge History of India* (Cambridge, UK 1998).

Price, Jacob M. *Perry of London: A Family and a Firm on the Seaborne Frontier, 1615–1753* (Cambridge, MA 1992).

Proudhon, Pierre-Joseph. *Système des contradictions économiques ou philosophie de la misère* (Paris 1846).

Puchner, Karl, and Gustav Wulz. *Die Urkunden der Stadt Nördlingen* (Augsburg 1952).

Rathke-Köhl, Sylvia. *Geschichte des Augsburger Goldschmiedegewerbes vom Ende des 17. bis zum Ende des 18. Jahrhunderts* (Augsburg 1964).

Raymond, Joad (ed.). *News Networks in Seventeenth-century Britain and Europe* (Abingdon 2006).

Rehm, Wilhelm. "Chronica newer geschichte," in: Bayerische Akademie der Wissenschaft (ed.), *Die Chroniken der deutschen Städte vom 14. bis ins 16. Jahrhundert*, vols. 23 (Gottingen 1965–7).

Reinhard, Wolfgang. *Freunde und Kreaturen. "Verflechtung" als Konzept zur Erforschung historischer Führungsgruppen. Römische Oligarchie um 1600* (Munich 1979).

Reinhard, Wolfgang. *Geschichte der europäischen Expansion. Die alte Welt bis 1818*, 4 vols. (Stuttgart 1983).

Reinhard, Wolfgang, et al. (eds.). *Augsburger Eliten des 16. Jahrhunderts: Prosopographie wirtschaftlicher und politischer Führungsgruppen 1500–1620* (Berlin 1996).

Ricardo, David. *On the Principles of Political Economy, and Taxation* (London 1816).

Riebartsch, Joachim. *Augsburger Handelsgeschichte des 15. und 16. Jahrhunderts* (Bergisch Gladbach 1987).

Riehl, Wilhelm. *Die Naturgeschichte des Volkes als Grundlage einer deutschen Sozial-Politik*, 3rd ed., 3 vols. (Stuttgart 1855).

Riello, Giorgio. *Cotton: The Fabric That Made the Modern World* (Cambridge, UK 2013).

Robisheaux, Thomas W. *Rural Society and the Search for Order in Early Modern Germany* (Cambridge, UK 1989).

Rockman, Seth. *Scraping By: Wage Labor, Slavery and Survival in Early Baltimore* (Baltimore 2009).

Roeck, Bernd. *Eine Stadt in Krieg und Frieden: Studien zur Geschichte der Reichsstadt Augsburg zwischen Kalenderstreit und Parität*, 2 vols. (Göttingen 1989).

Rogge, Jörg. *Für den gemeinen Nutzen. Politisches Handeln und Politikverständnis von Rat und Bürgerschaft in Augsburg im Spätmittelalter* (Tubingen 1996).

Roper, Lyndal. *The Holy Household: Women and Morals in Reformation Augsburg* (Oxford 1989).

Rössner, Philipp Robinson. *Deflation – Devaluation – Rebellion: Geld Im Zeitalter der Reformation* (Stuttgart 2012).

Rotberg, Robert I. (ed.). *Social Mobility and Modernization* (Cambridge, MA 2000).

Rothbard, Murray. *Man, Economy and State*, 2 vols. (Princeton 1962).

Runciman, Walter Garrison. *A Treatise on Social Theory*, 3 vols. (Cambridge, UK 1983–1997).

Sabean, David Warren. *Property, Production and Family in Neckarhausen, 1700–1870* (Cambridge, UK 1990).

Safley, Thomas Max. *Let No Man Put Asunder: The Control of Marriage in the German Southwest, a Comparative Study, 1550–1610* (Kirksville, MO 1984).

Safley, Thomas Max. "Production, Transaction and Proletarianization: The Textile Industry of Upper Swabia, 1580–1660," in: Thomas Max Safley and Leonard N. Rosenband (eds.), *The Workplace Before the Factory: Artisans and Proletarians, 1500–1800* (Ithaca 1993), 118–45.

Safley, Thomas Max. *Charity and Economy in the Orphanages of Early Modern Augsburg* (Leiden 1996).

Safley, Thomas Max. "Die Fuggerfaktoren Hörmann von und zu Gutenberg: Werte und Normen einer kaufmännischen Familie im Übergang zum Landadel," in: Johannes Burkhardt (ed.), *Augsburger Handelshäuser im Wandel des historischen Urteils* (Tübingen 1996), 118–29.

Safley, Thomas Max. *Matheus Miller's Memoir: A Merchant's Life in the Seventeenth Century* (London 1999).

Safley, Thomas Max. "Bankruptcy: Family and Finance in Early Modern Augsburg," *Journal of European Economic History* 29 (2000): 53–75.

Safley, Thomas Max. "Der 'Bürger' im Spiegel des Augsburger Intelligenzzettels," in: Sabine Doering-Manteuffel, et al. (eds.), *Pressewesen der Aufklärung: Periodische Schriften im Alten Reich* (Berlin 2002), 381–90.

Safley, Thomas Max. "Die Frage einer frühneuzeitlichen Standardisierung des Rechtsprozesses in Bankrottsfällen am Beispiel des Höchstetter Konkurs 1529," in: Thomas M. J. Möllers (ed.), *Vielfalt und Einheit. Wirtschaftliche und rechtiche Rahmenbedingungen von Standardisierung* (Baden-Baden 2008), 107–26.

Safley, Thomas Max. "Business Failure and Civil Scandal in Early Modern Europe," *Business History Review* 8 (2009): 35–60.

Safley, Thomas Max. "The Question of Early Modern Business Culture: Methodological Reflections on the Firm, 'Ambrosius and Hans, the Brothers Höchstetter and Company' 1524–1529," *Wiener Zeitschrift zur Geschichte der Neuzeit* 8 (2009): 7–23.

Safley, Thomas Max. "Staatsmacht und geschäftliches Scheitern. Der Bankrott der Handelsgesellschaft 'Ambrosius und Hans, Gebrüder Höchstetter, und Mitverwandte' im Jahr 1529," *Österreichische Zeitschrift für Geschichtswissenschaften* 19 (2009): 36–55.

Safley, Thomas Max (ed.). *The History of Bankruptcy: Economic, Social and Cultural Implications in Early Modern Europe* (London 2013).

Safley, Thomas Max. "Institutions and Their Discontents," *Tijdschrift voor Sociale en Economische Geschiedenis* 11 (2014): 61–73.

Safley, Thomas Max, and Leonard N. Rosenband (eds.). *The Workplace Before the Factory: Artisans and Proletarians, 1500–1800* (Ithaca 1993).

Sallaberger, Johann. *Kardinal Matthäus Lang von Wellenburg (1468–1540): Staatsmann und Kirchenfürst im Zeitalter von Renaissance, Reformation und Bauernkriegen* (Munich 1997).

Schiele, Hartmut, and Manfred Ricker. *Betreibswirtschaftliche Aufschlüsse aus der Fuggerzeit* (Berlin 1967).

Schmidt, Carl F. *Geschichte Augsburgs* (Handelsgesellschaften in den deutschen Stadtrechtsquellen des Mittelalters: Untersuchungen zur deutschen Staats- und Rechtsgeschichte, 15) (Breslau 1883).

Schmidt, Gertrud. *Die Berufstätigkeit der Frau in der Reichsstadt Nürnberg bis zum Ende des 16. Jahrhunderts* (Erlangen 1950).

Schmidt, Rolf. "Zum Augsburger Stadtbuch von 1276," *Zeitschrift des historischen Vereins von Schwaben* 70 (1976): 80–179.

Schmied, Robert. *Kapitalbeschaffungsformen des Frühkapitalismus. Die Formen der Kapitalbeschaffung und der Vergrösserung des Eigenkapitals der frühkapitalistischen Kaufleute und Handelsgesellschaften des 15. und 16. Jahrhunderts* (Berlin 1936).

Schmoller, Gustav von. *Grundriss der allgemeinen Volkswirtschaftslehre*, 2 vols. (Leipzig 1900–1904).

Schnurmann, Claudia. *Atlantische Welten. Engländer und Niederländer im amerikanischen-atlantischen Raum, 1648–1713* (Cologne 1998).

Schöningh, Franz Josef. *Die Rehlinger von Augsburg* (Paderborn 1927).

Schremmer, Eckart. "Die Wirtschaftsmetropole Augsburg," in: Max Spindler (ed.), *Handbuch der bayrischen Geschichte*, vol. III (Munich 1971), 1080–96.

Schulze, William S., Michael H. Lubatkin, Richard N. Dino, and Ann K. Buchholtz. "Agency Relationships in Family Firms: Theory and Evidence," *Organizational Science* 12 (2001): 99–116.

Schumpeter, Joseph A. *The Theory of Economic Development* (Cambridge, MA 1934).

Schumpeter, Joseph A. *Business Cycles: A Theoretical, Historical and Statistical Analysis of the Capitalist Process*, 2 vols. (New York 1939).

Schumpeter, Joseph A. *Capitalism, Socialism and Democracy* (New York 1942).

Schumpeter, Joseph A. *History of Economic Analysis* (New York 1954).

Schumpeter, Joseph A. *Essays on Entrepreneurship, Innovation, Business Cycles, and the Evolution of Capitalism* (London 2000).

Seater, John J. "Ricardian Equivalence," *Journal of Economic Literature* 31 (1993): 142–90.

Sée, Henri. *Modern Capitalism: Its Origins and Evolution* (New York 1968).

Segal, Richard M. "Shirt Sleeves to Shirt Sleeves in Three Generations," *Corp!* (1 July 2008). Available at: www.corpmagazine.com/special-interests/family-business/shirt-sleeves-to-shirt-sleeves-in-three-generations/.

Seibold, Gerhard. *Die Manlich: Geschichte einer Augsburger Kaufmannsfamilie* (Sigmaringen 1995).

Seling, Helmut. *Die Kunst der Augsburger Goldschmiede 1529–1868*, 2 vols. (Munich 1980).

Seling, Helmut. *Die Augsburger Gold- und Silberschmiede 1529–1868* (Munich 2007).

Sender, Clemens. *Die Chronik von Clemens Sender von den ältesten Zeiten der Stadt bis zum Jahre 1536. Die Chroniken der schwäbischen Städte. Augsburg*, vol. IV (Leipzig 1894).

Sennett, Richard. "The New Capitalism," *Social Research* 64 (1997): 161–80.

Sennett, Richard. *The Culture of the New Capitalism* (New Haven 2006).

Shanker, Melissa Carey, and Joseph H. Astrachan. "Myths and Realities: Family Businesses' Contribution to the US Economy – A Framework for Assessing Family Business Statistics," *Family Business Review* (1996): 107–23.

Sharma, Pramodita, James J. Chrisman, and Jesse H. Chua (eds.). *A Review and Annotated Bibliography of Family Business Studies* (Boston 1996).

Sharma, Pramodita, and Carlo Salvato. "Family Firm Longevity: A Balancing Act Between Continuity and Change," in: Paloma Fernández Pérez and Andrea Colli (eds.), *The Endurance of Family Businesses: A Global Overview* (Cambridge, UK 2013), 34–56.

Sheffi, Yossi. *The Resilient Enterprise: Overcoming Vulnerability for Competitive Enterprise* (Cambridge, MA 2005).

Shraga, Biran F. *Opportunism: How to Change the World – One Idea at a Time* (New York 2011).

Sieh-Burens, Katherina. *Oligarchie, Konfession und Politik im 16. Jahrhundert: Zur sozialen Verflechtung der Augsburger Bürgermeister und Stadtpfleger* (Munich 1986).

Simnacher, Georg. *Die Fuggertestamente des 16. Jahrhunderts*, 2 vols. (Tubingen 1960, Weissenhorn 1992).

Simonsfeld, Henry. *Der Fondaco dei Tedeschi in Venedig und die deutsch-venetianischen Handelsbezeihungen. Quellen und Forschungen* (Stuttgart 1887).

Smelser, Neil, and Richard Swedburg (eds.). *The Handbook of Economic Sociology* (New York 1994).

Smith, Adam. *An Inquiry into the Nature and Causes of the Wealth of Nations*, edited with an introduction and notes by Edward Cannan ([London 1776] New York 1994).

Smith, George David, and Richard Sylla. *The Transformation of Financial Capitalism: An Essay on the History of American Capital Markets* (Cambridge, MA 1993).

Smith, Woodruff D. "The Function of Commercial Centers in the Modernization of European Capitalism: Amsterdam as an Information Exchange in the Seventeenth Century," *Journal of Economic History* 44 (1984): 985–1005.

Söhnchen, Markus. *Die historische Entwicklung der rechtlichen Gründungsvoraussetzungen von Handels- und Aktiengesellschaften* (Berlin 2005).

Soll, Jacob. *The Reckoning: Financial Accountability and the Rise and Fall of Nations* (New York 2014).

Sombart, Werner. *Der modern Kapitalismus*, 2 vols. (Berlin 1902).

Sombart, Werner. *Der moderne Kapitalismus. Historisch-systematische Darstellung des gesamteuropäischen Wirtschaftslebens von seinen Anfängen bis zur Gegenwart*, 2nd ed. (Munich 1916).

Sombart, Werner. "Capitalism," in: *Encyclopedia of the Social Sciences*, vol. III (New York 1930), 195–208.

Sorokin, Pitirim. *Social Mobility* (New York 1927).

Sperling, J. "The International Payments Mechanism in the Seventeenth and Eighteenth Centuries," *Economic History Review* 14 (1961): 446–68.

Stark, Oded. "Altruism and the Quality of Life," *American Economic Review* 79 (1982): 86–90.

Starr, Randy, et al. "Enterprise Resilience: Managing Risk in the Networked Economy," *Strategy and Business* 30 (2003): 56–69.

Steichele, Anton. *Das Bisthum Augsburg, historisch und statistisch beschrieben* (Augsburg 1872).

Stinchcombe, Arthur. *Economic Sociology* (New York 1983).

Stone, Lawrence. *The Family, Sex and Marriage in England, 1500–1800* (New York 1977).

Strieder, Jakob (ed.). *Die Inventur der Firma Fugger aus dem Jahre 1527* (Tübingen 1905).

Strieder, Jakob. *Zwei Handelsverträge aus dem 15. und 16. Jahrhundert: Ihre Geschichte und ihr Recht* (Leipzig 1908).

Strieder, Jakob. "Die sogenannte Fürlegung, eine Institution des deutschen Gesellschaftsrechts im Zeitalter des Frühkapitalismus," *Vierteljahrschrift für Sozial- und Wirtschaftsgeschichte* 10 (1912): 521–7.

Strieder, Jakob. *Studien zur Geschichte kapitalistischer Organisationsformen. Monopole, Kartelle und Aktiengesellschaften im Mittelalter und zu Beginn der Neuzeit* (Munich 1925).

Strieder, Jakob. *Jacob Fugger the Rich, Merchant and Banker of Augsburg, 1459–1525* (New York 1931).

Strieder, Jakob. *Zur Genesis des modernen Kapitalismus. Forschungen zur Entstehung der großen bürgerlichen Kapitalvermögen am Ausgange des Mittelalters und zu Beginn der Neuzeit, zunächst in Augsburg* (Leipzig 1935).

Stromer, Wolfgang von. "Das Schriftwesen der Nürnberger Wirtschaft vom 14. bis 16. Jahrhundert," *Beiträge zur Wirtschaftsgeschichte Nürnbergs* 2 (1967): 751–99.

Stuart Mill, John. *The Principles of Political Economy: With Some of Their Applications to Social Philosophy* (London 1848).

Subrahmanyam, Sanjay. *The Political Economy of Commerce: Southern India, 1500–1650* (Cambridge, UK 1990).

Sull, Donald. *The Upside of Turbulence: Seizing Opportunity in an Uncertain World* (New York 2009).

Supple, Barry. "The Nature of Enterprise," in: E. E. Rich and C. H. Wilson (eds.), *The Cambridge Economic History of Europe: Vol. 5. The Economic Organization of Early Modern Europe* (Cambridge, UK 1977), 394–461.

Sutcliffe, K. M., and T. J. Vogus. (2003). "Organizing for Resilience," in: K. S. Cameron, J. E. Dutton and R. E. Quinn (eds.), *Positive Organizational Scholarship: Foundations of a New Discipline* (San Francisco 2003), 94–110.

Swedburg, Richard. "Economic Sociology: Past and Present," *Current Sociology* 35 (1987): 1–22.

Swedburg, Richard. "Major Traditions in Economic Sociology," *Annual Review of Sociology* 17 (1991): 251–76.

Swedburg, Richard. "New Economic Sociology: What Has Been Accomplished? What Is Ahead?" *Acta Sociologica* 40 (1997): 161–82.

Sweezy, Paul, et al. *The Transition from Feudalism to Capitalism* (London 1978).

Tawney, Richard H. (ed.). "Introduction," in: Thomas Wilson, *A Discourse on Usury*, ([London 1572] London 1925).

Tawney, Richard H. *Religion and the Rise of Capitalism: A Historical Study* (London 1926).

Thackeray, William Makepeace. *The Newcomes: Memoirs of a Most Respectable Family* (London 1854).

Thaler, Richard H., and Hersh M. Shefrin. "An Economic Theory of Self-Control," *Journal of Political Economy* 89 (1981): 392–406.

Theophilus. *An Essay upon Various Arts in Three Books*, translated by Robert Henrie (London 1847).

Thomas, Hugh. *The Slave Trade: The Story of the Atlantic Slave Trade: 1440–1870* (New York 1999).

Thompson, Edward P. *The Making of the English Working Class* (New York 1966).

Thrupp, Sylvia. *A Short History of the Worshipful Company of Bakers* (London 1933).

Thrupp, Sylvia. *The Merchant Class of Medieval London, 1300–1500* (Chicago 1948).

Tilly, Louise A., and Joan Scott. *Women, Work and Family* (New York 1978).

Tracy, James D. *The Rise of Merchant Empires: Long Distance Trade in the Early Modern World 1350 – 1750* (Cambridge, UK 1990).

Tracy, James D. *The Political Economy of Merchant Empires* (Cambridge, UK 1991).

Trivellato, Francesca. *The Familiarity of Strangers: The Sephardic Diaspora, Livorno, and Cross-Cultural Trade in the Early Modern Period* (New Haven 2009).

Unger, Eike Eberhard. *Die Fugger in Hall in Tirol* (Tübingen 1967).

Unger, Richard W. "Thresholds for Market Integration in the Low Countries and England in the Fifteenth Century," in: Lawrin Armstrong, et al. (eds.), *Money, Markets and Trade in Late Medieval Europe: Essays in Honour of John H.A. Munro* (Boston 2007), 349–80.

Valentinitsch, Helfried. *Das landesfürstliche Quecksilberbergwerk Idria, 1575–1659. Produktion – Technik – rechtliche und soziale Verhältnisse – Betriebsbedarf – Quecksilberhandel* (Graz 1981).

Van der Wee, Herman. *The Growth of the Antwerp Market and the European Economy* (The Hague 1963).

Van der Wee, Herman. *The Low Countries in Early Modern Times* (London 1994).

Van der Wee, Herman, Raymond Bogaert, and G. Kurgan-van Hentenryk. *A History of European Banking* (Antwerp 2000).

Van Dillen, D. J. *History of the Principal Public Banks* (The Hague 1934).

Vanja, Christina. "Frauen im Dorf. Ihre Stellung unter besonderer Berücksichtigung landgräflich-hessischer Quellen des späten Mittelalters," *Zeitschrift für Agrargeschichte und Agrarsoziologie* 34 (1987): 147–51.

Vann, Richard. "Toward a New Lifestyle: Women in Preindustrial Capitalism," in: Renate Bridenthal and Claudia Koonz (eds.), *Becoming Visible: Women in European History* (Boston 1977).

Veblen, Thorsten. *The Theory of the Leisure Class* (New York 1899).

Vogelsang, Thilo. *Die Frau als Herrscherin im hohen Mittelalter* (Göttingen 1954).

Volckart, Oliver. "Social Mobility, Institutional Choice and Economic Performance: Germany from the Fourteenth to the Eighteenth Centuries," VIII Annual Conference (2004), International Society for New Institutional Economics. Available at: www.isnie.org/ISNIE04/Papers/volckart.pdf.

Wachendorf, Helmut. *Die wirtschaftliche Stellung der Frau in den deutschen Städten des späteren Mittelalters* (Quakenbrück 1934).

Wallerstein, Immanuel. *The Modern World System*, 3 vols. (New York: Academic Press 1974).

Warnemünde, Christel. "Augsburger Handel in den letzten Jahrzehnten des 16. Jahrhunderts und dem beginnenden 17. Jahrhundert" (Unpublished dissertation, University of Freiburg 1956).

Weber, Matthias. *Die Reichspolizeiordnungen von 1530, 1548 und 1577: Historische Einführung und Edition* (Frankfurt Main 2002).

Weber, Max. *Die protestantische Ethik und der "Geist" des Kapitalismus*, reprint 1904/05 ed. (Weinheim 1996).

Welt im Umbruch: Augsburg zwischen Renaissance und Barock, 2 vols. (Augsburg 1980).

Wensky, Margret. *Die Stellung der Frau in der stadtkölnischen Wirtschaft im Spätmittelalter* (Cologne 1980).

Werner, Anton. *Augsburger Goldschmiede: Verzeichnis der Augsburger Goldschmiede, Silberarbeiter, Juweliere und Steinschneider von 1346–1803* (Augsburg 1913).

Westermann, Ekkehard. "The Brass-Works of the Höchstetter at Pflach near Reute in the Tirol, 1509–1529," in: Ian Blanchard, et al. (eds.), *Industry and Finance in Early Modern History: Essays Presented to George Hammersley on the Occasion of His 74th Birthday* (Stuttgart 1992), 161–85.

Westermann, Ekkehard, and Marcus A. Denzel. *Das Kaufmannsnotizbuch des Matthäus Schwarz aus Augsburg von 1548* (Stuttgart 2011).

White, Harrison. "Where Do Markets Come from," *American Journal of Sociology* 87 (1981): 517–47.

White, Harrison. *Identity and Control: A Structural Theory of Action* (Princeton 1992).

Wiesner, Merry. *Working Women in Renaissance Germany* (New Brunswick, NJ 1986).

Williams, Eric. *Capitalism and Slavery* (Chapel Hill, NC 1944).

Williamson, Oliver. *The Economic Institutions of Capitalism* (Boston 1985).

Wilson, Charles. *Anglo-Dutch Commerce and Finance in the Eighteenth Century* (Cambridge, UK 1966).

Wrigley, E. A., and R. S. Schofield. *The Population History of England, 1541–1871: A Reconstruction* (London 1981).

Yamey, Basil Selig. "Accounting and the Rise of Capitalism: Further Notes on a Theme by Sombart," *Journal of Accounting Research* 2 (1964): 117–36.

Yamey, Basil Selig. "Notes on Double-Entry Bookkeeping and Economic Progress," *Journal of European Economic History* 4 (1975): 717–23.

Young, Arthur. *Travels, During the Years 1787, 1788, and 1789: Undertaken More Particularly with a View of Ascertaining the Cultivation, Wealth, Resources, and National Prosperity, of the Kingdom of France* (London 1792).

Zamagni, Stefano (ed.). *The Economics of Altruism* (Aldershot 1995).

Zedler, Johann Heinrich. *Grosses vollständiges Universal-Lexicon aller Wissenschafften und Künste*, 64 vols. (Leipzig 1731–54).

Zeller, J. "Das Augsburger Burggrafenamt," *Archiv für die Geschichte des Hochstifts Augsburg* 5 (1916/19): 321–410.

Zellweger, Thomas Markus, Richard S. Nason, and Mattias Nordqvist. "From Longevity of Firms to Transgenerational Entrepreneurship of Families: Introducing Family Entrepreneurial Orientation," *Family Business Review* 25 (2012): 136–55.

Zorn, Wolfgang. *Augsburg: Geschichte einer deutschen Stadt* (Augsburg 1972).

Zorn, Wolfgang. *Augsburg: Geschichte einer europäischen Stadt* (Augsburg 2001).

Zorn, Wolfgang, and Leonhard Hillenbrand (eds.). *Sechs Jahrhunderte Schwäbische Wirtschaft. Beiträge zur Geschichte der Wirtschaft im bayerischen Regierungsbezirk Schwaben* (Augsburg 1969).

Index

Page numbers in italics indicate figures; page numbers in bold indicate tables; page numbers that include n indicate notes.